CUBAN STUDIES 34

ADVISORY BOARD

Ruth Behar (2000–2004)
Alejandro de la Fuente (2000–2003)
Sergio Díaz-Briquets (2000–2004)
Jorge I. Domínguez (2000–2004)
Jorge Duany (2000–2003)
Susan Eckstein (2000–2003)
Ada Ferrer (2000–2004)
Roberto González-Echevarría (2000–2003)
Aline Helg (2000–2004)
William Luis (2000–2003)
Sheryl L. Lutjens (2000–2003)
Carmelo Mesa-Lago (2000–2004)
Nivia Montenegro (2000–2003)
Eusebio Mujal-León (2000–2003)
Louis A. Pérez, Jr. (2000–2004)
Gustavo Pérez-Firmat (2000–2003)
Jorge Pérez Lopez (2000–2004)
Marifeli Pérez-Stable (2000–2003)
Archibald R. M. Ritter (2000–2003)
Enrico Mario Santí (2000–2004)
K. Lynn Stoner (2000–2003)
María de los Angeles Torres (2000–2004)
Alan West (2000–2004)

CUBAN STUDIES 34

LISANDRO PÉREZ, *Editor*
UVA DE ARAGÓN, *Associate Editor*

UNIVERSITY OF PITTSBURGH PRESS

CUBAN STUDIES

LISANDRO PÉREZ, Editor
UVA DE ARAGÓN, Associate Editor

Manuscripts in English and Spanish may be submitted to the Editor, *Cuban Studies*, Cuban Research Institute, DM 364, Florida International University, University Park, Miami, Fla. 33199, U.S.A. Maximum length is forty pages, double-spaced, *including tables and notes*. Please submit two copies, with an abstract of no more than two hundred words. Either MLA or APA reference style is acceptable. *Cuban Studies* takes no responsibility for views or information presented in signed articles. Please submit review copies of books to the Book Review Editor at the same address as above. For additional inquiries, contact us by telephone at (305) 348-1991; by fax at (305) 348-3593; by email at *crinst@fiu.edu*; or visit us on the World Wide Web at *http://lacc.fiu.edu/cri*

Back issues of volumes 1–15 of *Cuban Studies,* when available, may be obtained from the Center for Latin American Studies, 4E04 Forbes Quadrangle, University of Pittsburgh, Pittsburgh, PA 15260, U.S.A.

Articles appearing in this volume are abstracted and indexed in *Historical Abstracts* and *America: History and Life.*

Published by the University of Pittsburgh Press, Pittsburgh, Pa.
Copyright © 2003, University of Pittsburgh Press
All rights reserved
Manufactured in the United States of America
Printed on acid-free paper

Library of Congress Card Number
ISBN 0-8229-4244-5
US ISSN 0361-*n*4441
10 9 8 7 6 5 4 3 2 1

Contents

Preface ix

Trespassing Historic Gender Boundaries
Sherry Johnson and K. Lynn Stoner, guest editors
Introduction: *Señoras no ordinarias* 1
Sherry Johnson
"*Señoras en sus clases no ordinarias*":
Enemy Collaborators or Courageous Defenders of the Family? 11
Sherry Johnson
La División de La Habana: Territorial Conflict and Cultural Hegemony
in the Followers of Oyo Lukumí Religion, 1850s–1920s 38
Miguel Ramos
Militant Heroines and the Consecration of the Patriarchal State:
The Glorification of Loyalty, Combat, and National Suicide in
the Making of Cuban National Identity 71
K. Lynn Stoner
Murder in San Isidro: Crime and Culture during the
Second Cuban Republic 97
Mayra Beers
The Radical Muse: Women and Anarchism in
Early-Twentieth-Century Cuba 130
Kirwin Shaffer
"Toward the Gates of Eternity": Celia Sánchez Manduley and
the Creation of Cuba's New Woman 154
Tiffany A. Thomas-Woodard
Conclusion: Enshrined on a Pedestal 181
K. Lynn Stoner

Archives

Cuba-Related Archival Holdings in Miami 187
Marisa Montes

**Comment and Reply: Operation Northwoods and the
Covert War against Cuba, 1961–1963**

Comment 194
James G. Hershberg

Reply   198
Anna Kasten Nelson

Reviews

Sherry Johnson and Damián Fernández, editors

Alfredo A. Fernández. *Adrift: The Cuban Raft People.* Houston: Arte Público Press, 2000. 263 pp. Reviewed by Holly Ackerman.   201

Gustavo Pérez Firmat. *My Own Private Cuba: Essays on Cuban Literature and Culture.* Boulder, Colo.: Society of Spanish and Spanish-American Studies, 1999. 251 pp. Reviewed by Madeline Cámara.   202

Alexander von Humboldt. *The Island of Cuba: A Political Essay.* Kingston, R.I.: Ian Randle Publishers, 2001. 280 pp. Reviewed by John Clune.   204

Jorge Ibarra. *Prologue to Revolution: Cuba, 1898–1958.* Translated by Marjorie Moore. Boulder, Colo.: Lynne Rienner Publishers, 1998. 229 pp. Reviewed by John Dumoulin.   205

Charley Gerard. *Music from Cuba: Mongo Santamaría, Chocolate Armenteros, and Cuban Musicians in the United States.* Westport, Conn.: Praeger, 2001. 155 pp. Reviewed by Raul Fernandez.   207

Alberto F. Alvarez García and Gerardo González Nuñez. *¿Intelectuales vs. revolución?: El caso del Centro de Estudios sobre América, CEA.* Montreal: Ediciones Arte D.T., 2001. 212 pp. Reviewed by Peter T. Johnson.   208

Carlos Lechuga. *Cuba and the Missile Crisis.* Translated by Mary Todd. Melbourne, Australia: Ocean Press, 2001. 174 pp.; and Robert M. Levine. *Secret Missions to Cuba: Fidel Castro, Bernardo Benes, and Cuban Miami.* New York: Palgrave, 2001. 323 pp. Reviewed by Juan J. López.   209

Antoni Kapcia. *Cuba: Island of Dreams.* New York: Berg, 2000. 295 pp. Reviewed by Anthony P. Maingot.   212

Jaime Suchlicki. *Historical Dictionary of Cuba*, 2d ed. Lanham, Md.: Scarecrow Press, 2001. 880 pp. Reviewed by Luis Martínez-Fernández.   214

Madeline Cámara. *Vocación de Casandra: Poesía femenina cubana subversiva en María Elena Cruz Varela.* New York: Peter Lang, 2001.131 pp. Reviewed by Adriana Méndez-Rodenas.   215

Pedro Pérez Sarduy and Jean Stubbs, eds. *Afro-Cuban Voices: On Race and Identity in Contemporary Cuba.* Gainesville: University Press of Florida, 2000. 200 pp. Reviewed by Robin Moore.   217

María de los Reyes Castillo Bueno. *Reyita: The Life of a Black Cuban Woman in the Twentieth Century.* With a new introduction by Elizabeth Dore. Edited by Daisy Rubiera Castillo. Translated by Anne McLean. Durham, N.C.: Duke University Press, 2000. 182 pp. Reviewed by Kym Morrison.   219

Katherine J. Hagedorn. *Divine Utterances: The Performance of Afro-Cuban Santería.* Washington, DC: Smithsonian Institute Press, 2001. 296 pp. Reviewed by Terry Rey.   221

Marta Bizcarrondo and Antonio Elorza. *Cuba/España: El dilema autonomista, 1878–1898.* Madrid: Editorial Colibrí, 2001. 452 pp. Reviewed by Joaquín Roy. 222

Sherry Johnson. *The Social Transformation of Eighteenth-Century Cuba.* Gainesville: University Press of Florida, 2001. 267 pp. Reviewed by Christopher Schmidt-Nowara. 224

Efrén Córdova. *El trabajo forzoso en Cuba: Un recorrido amargo de la historia.* Miami: Ediciones Universal, 2001. 262 pp. Reviewed by Kirwin Shaffer. 225

Recent Work in Cuban Studies   229
Marian Goslinga, compiler

Contributors   287

Preface

In this volume we continue a venerable tradition in *Cuban Studies:* articles organized around a theme, with a guest editor, or, in this case, two guest editors. The historians Sherry Johnson and K. Lynn Stoner have brought to the readers of *CS* a collection of essays they have fashioned and edited around the theme, "Trespassing Gender Boundaries." Thematic issues with guest editors play an important role in multidisciplinary journals such as *CS,* for they borrow the talents of colleagues in different fields in order to bring readers articles that might otherwise not have appeared in the journal through the efforts of the general editors.

In her introduction to the essays in this issue, Johnson explains the unifying themes of the assembled pieces. We would add here only one additional explanation of what made these essays attractive to us as editors: the six authors presented here have done some trespassing of their own—across the boundaries of traditional scholarly research on Cuba. All six pieces represent innovative approaches to "fresh" topics. Even the most seasoned scholars of Cuba are likely to learn something new from each of the essays in this volume.

Rounding out the issue is a guide to the research collections found in various libraries in Miami, and, as a reminder that *CS* is read and can spark controversy, the issue also contains a comment on a research note that appeared in *CS 32,* along with a reply from the original author of that note.

In this, the fifth issue under our editorship, we admit to a temporary failure. In the previous four issues (30–34), we have kept our pledge to include articles written by colleagues in Cuba and also to publish some contributions in Spanish. But each issue is a reflection of the flow of manuscripts across our desks, and, alas, despite our best efforts, we received no publishable manuscripts either from Cuban authors or in Spanish in our editorial inbox this year. Readers should know that this is merely an accident of circumstances and not an intentional change from our original commitment.

As we have with all issues since *CS 30,* we gratefully acknowledge the administrative work of Susie Penley in attending to the many details that make it possible for us to produce this journal.

Lisandro Pérez, Editor
Uva de Aragón, Associate Editor

CUBAN STUDIES 34

SHERRY JOHNSON

Introduction: Señoras . . . no ordinarias

High atop the Castillo de la Real Fuerza in old Havana a bronze wind vane crafted in the figure of a woman sways in the breeze as she surveys the horizon that stretches to her north. Official guidebooks and architectural histories of the city relate that the statue symbolizing victory was inspired by a similar figure, La Giraldilla, that watches over the city of Seville, Spain.[1] Local Cuban lore tells a different story, however, as Cubans claim the woman atop La Fuerza as one of their own: Doña Isabel de Bobadilla, the widow of Hernán de Soto, who came to Cuba in 1538 to organize and equip his ill-fated expedition to conquer La Florida.[2] Isabel remained in Cuba while her husband sailed on his fateful voyage in May 1539. According to Cuban legend, when the news of de Soto's death reached Havana, Doña Isabel died of a broken heart.[3] The figure atop La Fuerza, then, symbolizes the faithful wife, who scans the Straits of Florida for eternity, always turning toward the wind that will bring her missing husband home.[4]

Beginning with the life history of Isabel de Bobadilla, it is Cuban women, nurtured in a tradition of gender relations particular to the island, who have lent their life experiences to the inspiration and conceptual framework for the essays in this issue. The essays provide an interdisciplinary analysis of women's contributions to political, social, and economic processes on the island that reads across the grain of patriarchal history. They emphasize the female experience, at various times and within various groups in Cuban society, as a means of exploring the tumultuous road to national identity. Building upon established concepts that inform women's studies, this collection identifies unique themes that recur throughout Cuban history and contributed to women's lives: the malleability of Cuban identity, militarization and militancy, and disorder and uncertainty in politics, the economy, and society. Individually and collectively, these factors have often allowed—indeed, *demanded*—that Cuban women trespass traditional gender boundaries. In this, the unique circumstances of the island differentiates Cuban women's experiences from those of women in other regions. Beginning with the earliest years of settlement and continuing into the twenty-first century, the degree to which Cuban women have participated in extraordinary activities has became increasingly more frequent, so that, in turn, their ability to trespass grew to be the norm, an expectation that presented the island's people with openings for the evolution of a unique identity. The expectation that they would cross gender boundaries represents a constant in Cuban women's lives, whether applied to Isabel de Bobadilla in the sixteenth century, to the *mambisas* of the independence struggles from 1868 to 1898, or to women such as Celia Sánchez who made the Cuban Revolution a reality.

Setting the Historic Precedent

Many books have been written about the conquerors of the Americas but virtually nothing is known about their women, among them Isabel de Bobadilla, a remarkable woman by modern standards, who was even more remarkable for her day. Born into the highest nobility in Spain, Doña Isabel led a colorful and exciting life. Her family associations linked her with the Hapsburg Court and also with many of the men who were at the vanguard of exploration, conquest, and settlement of the Americas.[5] She was most certainly related to Francisco de Bobadilla, the *visitador* who was sent to Hispaniola in 1499 to bring Christopher Columbus's recalcitrant colony under control, and who ultimately arrested the Admiral and returned him to Spain in chains.[6] Her uncle, the Count of Gómera, served as the governor of that island in the Canary Islands that was the stopover point for ships sailing to the New World.[7] Isabel's first husband, Pedro d'Arias (Pedrarias), was one of the conquerors of Central America, who was subsequently rewarded with the governorship of Nicaragua. In compliance with the decrees that dictated that married men must bring their wives with them to the Indies, Isabel accompanied d'Arias to Central America in 1514.[8] After Arias's death in 1531, Isabel returned to Spain, where she married Hernán de Soto. Later, in similar fashion, she would accompany her new husband to his post in Cuba, from whence he would launch his expedition to conquer Florida.[9]

The sixteenth century was a dangerous time in the Spanish Empire. One could never be certain who was friend and who was foe, either on a personal or a political basis. The conquerors of the Americas were an unruly bunch who would casually discard any loyalty to their comrades in order to serve their own interests.[10] Compounding matters, Spain's American possessions were under attack from her European rivals, and beginning in 1504, French "raiders, traders and invaders" led the assault against Spanish settlements in the Caribbean.[11] Under such circumstances, de Soto's decision to name Isabel de Bobadilla as acting governor of Cuba in his absence was an extraordinary (and telling) act.[12]

Hernán de Soto's unusual decision not only broke with tradition within sixteenth-century patriarchal society, but it also spoke volumes as to his opinion of her capacity to govern. In the cutthroat atmosphere of the early colonies, Isabel de Bobadilla would have been granted no concessions for her gender; thus, she must have possessed the toughness, shrewdness, and good judgment required to negotiate the political minefield of Spanish Court politics.[13] Significantly, de Soto trusted her above his male counterparts, so he certainly was convinced of her competence and loyalty to the union formed by their marriage. A wealth of surviving documents demonstrate that she was not merely the de jure governor of the island, but the de facto governor as well. During her tenure (1539–1543), she dealt with many of the mundane issues that confronted all New World governors, such as the treatment of the Cuban Indians, but at the same time she was able to neutralize the bitter partisan rivalries among the European settlers.[14] Simultaneously, she advanced the work, begun by her husband, on Havana's first fortress—the predecessor of La Fuerza, which would bear her image—so that the city would be able to withstand the enemy attacks that daily were becoming more frequent.[15] More important, correspondence addressed directly to Isabel from the king of Spain acknowledged her status as governor, thereby setting the precedent for legitimate trespass for the generations of women to come.

The conditions that shaped Isabel de Bobadilla's life became the circumstances under which the women of Cuba would live their lives for the following five centuries. French freebooters led by Jacques Sores sacked Havana and burned Doña Isabel's fortress in 1555. Over the next two centuries attacks on and invasions of Cuba were frequent; only Havana, with its immense fortifications and military presence, was immune to the daily threat. Even that changed in 1762 when the city fell to a siege and bombardment mounted by a British naval squadron. As a consequence, the province of Florida was ceded to Britain in 1763 and the Florida community evacuated to Havana. From the moment they set foot on Cuban soil, the women from Florida petitioned the Spanish monarch for an acknowledgment of their sacrifices, for a recognition of their status, and for financial redress. In 1772 Charles III (1759–1788) agreed to the women's demands, writing: "These are not ordinary women [*señoras . . . no ordinarias*] . . . and so they shall be recognized."[16] In so doing, he reinforced and legitimized the singular range of behavior allowed to Cuban women.

Concepts and Themes

This collection of articles addresses a long-neglected area of Cuban studies, the role of women in shaping the island's identity. Over the past several decades, the study of women's issues in Latin America has evolved to a relatively high level of sophistication, but scholarship on Cuba lags behind.[17] With some notable exceptions, the use of gender as a conceptual category has been underutilized for the island.[18] The study of gender becomes more complicated when the concept of national identity (*cubanía, cubanidad, lo cubano*) is factored in to the analysis. Just what and who are Cuban are contested concepts. And while a long scholarly tradition has developed which seeks to define the complex development of national identity, and many authors who contribute to the tradition find various ways of describing the enigma, few offer explanations of how and/or why identity is so elusive.[19] Moreover, a gendered dimension is rarely included. By viewing identity formation from the inside out—that is, from a subjective perspective—we hope to begin to understand this problem.

We begin with the historical circumstances that guided Isabel de Bobadilla and the lives of the women who followed in her footsteps. To be sure, the established caveats of Latin American women's studies in general—family, paternalism, religion, race, honor, shame, status, and subordination—must play a strong conceptual role in any gendered study. The fundamental concepts of women's studies combine with recurrent and pervasive themes particular to Cuba that run throughout this collection of essays. The first of these themes is the malleability of Cuban identity. Perhaps more than in any other region, Cuba was shaped by its immigrants. Clearly, Isabel de Bobadilla was a *peninsular*; she lived in Cuba but six years. Yet she has been adopted in Cuban popular culture as one of the fundamental symbols of how immigrant women—European noblewomen, Canary Island commoners, Floridana exiles, African priestesses, and French prostitutes—were transformed into the mothers of subsequent generations of *creole* Cubans. Perhaps as in no other region, the island was most successful in incorporating its waves of immigrants, providing them with a feeling of Cubanness.[20] A second, closely related conceptual category is that of racial identification, race mixture, and/or the social consequences of race mixture among European, African, indigenous, and Asian peoples. All these races added to the ethnic mix in Cuba that has come to be termed *ajiaco,* a type of stew.[21] Like national identity, ethnic identity is also malleable, depending upon time and place. Combined with a militant Cuban nationalism that emerged in the nineteenth century, this ethnic component of identity has developed into a complex and ever-changing aspect of modern Cuban identity.

Among the more important factors in creating a national identity are national myths.[22] Although romantic myths contribute to the concept of national identity (often at the expense of historical accuracy), for Cuban women, these myths universally involve the ideal of sacrifice. The creation of the myth of Isabel de Bobadilla began as early as 1605; by 1634, when the original bronze statue of the conqueror's wife was placed atop La Fuerza, her transformation into a national icon had already begun.[23] According to the myth, Isabel represented the original, ultimate sacrifice, through the loss of her husband, which led, in turn, to the loss of her own life from the grief of a broken heart. It would be nearly three hundred years before the "unpoetic documents [that] prove[d] that she lived many years longer in Spain" would be discovered, thanks to the dogged scholarship of another woman, Irene A. Wright, whose work has left a lasting imprint on studies of the island.[24]

Mythmaking was also a powerful component in reinforcing Cuba's loyalty to Spain. In the eighteenth century, the "Damas de la Havana" were once again called upon to sacrifice for Cuba. This time, they were asked to give up their jewels so as to finance the French fleet that was ready to sail to Yorktown to engage the British in their war with the American colonies. Ultimately, it was said, this sacrifice had led to the independence of the former British colonies in America. Two centuries would pass before the historian James A. Lewis would establish that the actual source of funds for this operation was the *situado* (subsidy), a fund that originated in Mexico that was usually earmarked to pay the salaries of soldiers, but was used instead to subsidize the French fleet.[25]

The most enduring example of the power of mythmaking is in the legend that has grown up around Mariana Grajales, mother of the Maceo brothers and the quintessential example of sacrifice, since nine of her children lost their lives in the wars of independence. By the mid–twentieth century, the myth of Mariana had assumed such proportions that she was designated the "official mother of Cuba."[26] This contrasts with other Latin American nations who often have difficulty in reconciling their myths about heroic female protagonists.[27] Such is not the case in Cuba, however, where even into the present, the unequivocal measure of womanhood in Cuba remains her duty to sacrifice for the good of the nation.

The malleability of Cuban identity, the racial component of identity in Cuba, and mythmaking are all conceptual categories that contribute to understanding Cuban women's experiences in general, but certain themes influence this collection of essays in particular. The first is the pervasive influence of militarization that, over a period of five centuries, became ingrained in the collective Cuban mentality.[28] From its earliest days, Cuba was forced to dedicate enormous resources to its own defense. By the nineteenth century, the danger of invasion had abated, but the military then became preoccupied with struggles from within, which took the shape of slave rebellion, protests against Spanish rule, and uprisings against elected governments in the Republic. Because their men were often absent and life was precarious, Cuban women became accustomed to being in charge and assumed tasks that were not generally performed by women. Moreover, living in a militarized society led to a unparalleled degree of militancy on the part of Cuban women.

The permanent state of political instability also created an internal climate predicated upon disorder and uncertainty.[29] Political instability goes hand-in-hand with economic insolvency. As Cuba moved toward a monoculture economy based upon sugar production, its economic foundations became increasingly less stable and its internal economy increasingly more precarious. Uncertainty even extended to the environment. The island was continually at risk for hurricanes alternating with drought, and the effects of climate and disaster became more severe as the island's population increased. In addition, until the early twentieth century, the multitude of fevers and epidemics made life both miserable and vulnerable for the island's residents. As a consequence, Cubans continually lived on the brink of disaster, in a paradoxical state of both apprehension and constant readiness. Women were expected to be able to take charge of their families on a moment's notice, and thus, the women of Cuba became accustomed to a blurring of gender roles between proper and improper female behavior, lines of demarcation that were inviolable elsewhere.

The essays presented here share one or more of the themes outlined above, and all point to a repeated phenomenon: the traversing of gender boundaries and the exalting of women who traversed such boundaries to defy invaders and uphold the government, be it monarchy or nation, democracy or socialist revolution. From colonial Hispanic society, Cuba inherited a patriarchal society. Yet, circumstances propelled the women of Cuba, willingly and unwillingly, to invade masculine territory over and over again. Still, the fact that women assumed men's tasks or were identified as symbols of leadership or images of the nation did not imply a defiance of the incumbent patriarchy. Quite the contrary: it meant executing extreme bravery for the island and for the men who governed it.

Our studies of how Cuban women traversed gender boundaries have led us to new understandings — of the origins of patriotic loyalty, of the idea of female honor and fidelity to a nation, of feminine purity applied to politics, of the promotion of commercialized sex as a means for men to ascend to political power, and of female acquisition of power through the practice of Afro-Cuban religion. In short, because Cuba experienced rapid and disorienting change, women were consistently challenged to behave exceptionally in the male domain without toppling the myth of the patriarchy. The essays here also contribute to Cuban historiography by associating the constant threat the island has faced since the Spanish conquest with the expectation that women will assume extraordinary responsibilities. Such expectations have had an effect on Cuba's national image and on the gendering of its national culture. Over time, social norms were so often violated that the definitions of the norms themselves became blurred. The trespassing of boundaries led to new understandings, bridges to new social relations in keeping with social desires. It also resulted in the absence of defining qualities, a lack of clear direction, and a constant state of "becoming" that never crystallized into a shared sense of self. Gender relations and divisions are, of course, foundational norms that have governed families, neighborhoods, and communities from colonial times to the present. If these distinctions are blurred, then the larger institutions of politics and society are also unclear, uncertain, and potentially contested.[30]

The Contributions

The selection of contributors balances the work of established scholars with that of relative newcomers to the field, and the theoretical and methodological approaches are deliberately multidisciplinary. The collection begins with an essay by Sherry Johnson that challenges one of the most enduring myths about female behavior during the British occupation of Havana in 1762. Set within the theoretical framework of recent scholarship on honor, Johnson argues that because of the exigencies of the conflict, rather than engaging in traitorous activities, white women, free women of color, and slave wives assumed responsibilities normally reserved for men. The author speculates that the experiences of Cuba's eighteenth-century women, forged in the crucible of continual warfare, provided the roots for the *mambisa* tradition in the following century. Miguel W. Ramos's essay establishes the consequences of a personal feud among three female priestesses of the African religion Regla de Ocha, which led to the cult's dispersion to Matanzas in the late 1880s. Ramos's work combines historical evidence, folklore, and oral history in the tradition of Fernando Ortiz and Lydia Cabrera. It offers, perhaps, the most salient example of the multiplicity of issues that are raised in this collection of essays. K. Lynn Stoner's contribution follows the evolution of the woman warrior as a cultural symbol from the Ten Years War through the Revolution. Stoner's analysis demonstrates how individual heroines sacrificed themselves and their families in challenging colonialism, imperialism, and dictatorship, and how each heroic warrior was appropriated by the regime in power to create national myths to sustain its authority. Drawing upon method and theory in recent scholarship on prostitution, Mayra Beers examines the demimonde of Havana in 1908 and establishes the power of mythmaking in a society searching for an independent identity. Her work explores Cuba's nascent nationalism through a biography of one of its most enigmatic figures, Alberto Yarini y Ponce de León — descended from an aristocratic family, but renowned as the most famous pimp in Cuban history. Yarini's wide appeal to many sectors of Havana society makes him the quintessential example of an individual whose identity crossed race, class, and gender boundaries. In his piece, Kirwin (Kirk) Shaffer demonstrates how anarchists used gender issues to critique the unsatisfying reality that faced the Cuban nation after 1902. Through an analysis of anarchists' political tracts and popular culture, Shaffer demonstrates how the victimization of women was both a reality and a powerful tool used by radicals to enlist new recruits to their cause. Tiffany Thomas-Woodard reveals mythmaking in action in her profile of one of the most important women in recent Cuban history, Celia Sánchez Manduley. Sánchez was Fidel Castro's constant companion beginning with their guerrilla activities against Fulgencio Batista's dictatorship in the 1950s and continuing until her death in January 1980. She was one of the most influential personalities of revolutionary Cuba and her life story has given rise to some of the most enduring and pervasive gender images and behavioral norms of modern Cuba. K. Lynn Stoner's conclusion recapitulates how Cuban scholarship has recorded the female experience throughout the twentieth century. She finds that the story of women's lives has rarely been told by women themselves, that their experiences have been appropriated to project national values, and that traversing gender lines has not challenged the patriarchy but instead has bolstered it.

NOTES

1. Joaquín E. Weiss, *La architectura colonial cubana,* vol. 1 (Havana: Editorial Letras Cubanas, 1979), 36.
2. Nicolás Quintana, personal communication, 22 May 2001.
3. Irene A. Wright, *The Early History of Cuba* (1916; reprint, New York: Octagon Books, 1970), 170–72.
4. Quintana, personal communication.
5. Queen of Spain to Isabel de Bobadilla, 14 January 1532, in *Colección de documentos inéditos relativos al descubrimiento, conquista, y organización de las antiguas posesiones españolas de américa y oceanía* (Madrid: Imprenta de Manuel G. Hernández, 1864–84), 41:493–94 (hereafter cited as *Colección de documentos inéditos*).
6. Carl Ortwin Sauer, *The Early Spanish Main* (Berkeley and Los Angeles: University of California Press, 1966), 102–7. The familial relationship between Doña Isabel and Francisco de Bobadilla remains a mystery, complicated because as least two accounts incorrectly identify her as the daughter of Pedro d'Arias; see El Inca Garcilaso (de la Vega), *La Florida del Inca*, introducción y notas por Carmen de Mora (1605; reprint, Madrid: Alianza Universal, 1988), 138; and Wright, *Early History of Cuba*, 167. Documentary evidence demonstrates that she was d'Arias's wife (see note 8, below).
7. Wright, *Early History of Cuba*, 167.
8. King of Spain to Pedrarias Dávila, 1514, *Colección de documentos inéditos*, 39:325–29; Escritura de Doña Isabel de Bobadilla viuda de Pedrarias de Avila, 10 May 1532, *Colección de documentos inéditos*, 41:497–503.
9. License granted to Isabel de Bobadilla, Seville, 16 February 1538, legajo 1962, Indiferente General, Archivo General de Indias (hereafter AGI), Seville, Spain.
10. Sauer, *Early Spanish Main* (248) describes the conquest as being marked by "naked greed and cold cruelty."
11. Paul E. Hoffman, *The Spanish Crown and the Defense of the Caribbean, 1535–1585: Precedent, Patrimonialism, and Royal Parsimony* (Baton Rouge: Louisiana State University Press, 1980), 39–62, 112.
12. Wright, *Early History of Cuba*, 170–71.
13. Representative examples of the labyrinthine morass of court politics are the suits filed by Isabel Ponce de Leon against Hernán Ponce de León, her late husband's partner. These include Isabel de Bobadilla vs. Hernán Ponce de León, 28 January 1550, 3 November 1550, Valladolid, número 2, ramo 143, legajo 280, Patronato Real 280, AGI; Hernán Ponce de León vs. Isabel de Bobadilla, 12 May 1552, Madrid, número 2, ramo 108 & 109, legajo 281, Patronato Real, AGI; and Hernán Ponce de León vs. Isabel de Bobadilla, 12 March 1554, legajo 750A and legajo 750B, Justicia, AGI.
14. "Averiguación sobre indios," 9 May 1545, Seville, legajo 1963, Indiferente General, AGI.
15. Real Cédula to Doña Isabel de Bobadilla, 7 October 1540, legajo 1121, Audiencia de Santo Domingo, AGI.
16. Royal Order, 14 August 1772, Madrid, legajo 1154, Papeles Procedentes de Cuba, AGI. The passage reads: "Es el animo del Rey que las familias floridanas se las distinga y mire segun sus

piadosas intenciones; estas sras en sus clases no ordinarias, que con su modo de pensar lo acreditan merecer que assi se las trate."

17. Sueanne Caulfield, "The History of Gender in the Historiography of Latin America," *Hispanic American Historical Review* 81 (August–November 2001): 449–90, provides a recent look at how the field has grown. Other important works are Asunción Lavrin, "In Search of the Colonial Woman in Mexico: The Seventeenth and Eighteenth Centuries," in *Latin American Women: Historical Perspectives,* ed. Asunción Lavrin (Westport, Ct.: Greenwood Press, 1978), 23–61; Asunción Lavrin, "Women in Spanish American Colonial Society," *The Cambridge History of Latin America,* vol. 2., *Colonial Latin America,* ed. Leslie Bethell (Cambridge: Cambridge University Press, 1984), 321–55; K. Lynn Stoner, "Directions in Latin American Women's History, 1977–1985," *Latin American Research Review* 22 (January 1987): 101–34; and Susan Midgen Socolow, *The Women of Colonial Latin America* (Cambridge: Cambridge University Press, 2000). In addition, although the essays here are primarily about women, any study of gender, by definition, must consider relationships between men and women. Also, recent trends in gay and lesbian studies are important but are beyond the scope of our volume (see Ian Lumsden, *Machos, Maricones, and Gays: Cuba and Homosexuality* [Philadelphia: Temple University Press, 1996]).

18. The list of scholars who have written about Cuban women and their works includes: Verena Martínez-Alier, *Marriage, Class, and Colour in Nineteenth-Century Cuba: A Study of Racial Attitudes and Sexual Values in a Slave Society* (1974; reprint, Ann Arbor: University of Michigan Press, 1992); Carmen Diana Deere, "Rural Women and Agrarian Reform in Peru, Chile, and Cuba," in *Women and Change in Latin America,* ed. June Nash and Helen Safa (South Hadley, Mass.: Bergin and Garvey, 1986), 189–207; Helen Safa, ed., *The Myth of the Male Breadwinner: Women and Industrialization in the Caribbean* (Boulder, Colo.: Westview Press, 1995); Raquel Vinat de la Mata, "El Trabajo de la Aguja," unpublished manuscript in possession of the editors, 1999; Catherine Davies, *A Place in the Sun? Women Writers in Twentieth-Century Cuba* (London: Zed Books, 1997); Jean Stubbs, "Gender Constructs of Labor in Prerevolutionary Tobacco," *Social and Economic Studies* 37 (March–June 1988): 241–69; Jean Stubbs, "Social and Political Motherhood in Cuba: Mariana Grajales Cuello," in *Engendering History: Caribbean Women in Historical Perspective,* ed. Verene Shepherd, Bridget Brereton, and Barbara Bailey (New York: St. Martin's Press, 1995), 296–317; Lois M. Smith and Alfred Padula, eds., *Sex and Revolution: Women in Socialist Cuba* (Oxford: Oxford University Press, 1996); Vera Kutzinski, *Sugar's Secrets: Race and the Erotics of Cuban Nationalism* (Charlottesville: University of Virginia Press, 1995); K. Lynn Stoner, ed. and comp., with Luís Hipólito Serrano Pérez, *Cuban and Cuban American Women: An Annotated Bibliography* (Wilmington, Del.: Scholarly Resources, 2000); and K. Lynn Stoner, *From the House to the Streets: The Cuban Woman's Movement for Legal Reform, 1898–1940* (Durham, N.C.: Duke University Press, 1991). An important recent study published in Cuba is Instituto de Literatura y Lingüística, *Con el lente oblicuo: Aproximaciones cubanas a los estudios de genero* (Havana: Editorial de la Mujer, 1999); coordinated by Susana Montero Sanchez and Zaida Capote Cruz, this volume contains essays by many important writers on gender in present-day Cuba, including Zaida Capote, "La doncella y el minotauro," 38–44; Susan Montero, "Apostillas a la generacion del 98: Una mirada desde la ginocritica," 111–19; Nara Araújo, "Aceptar y escapar: Viajeras mexicanas en el siglo XIX: Una cuestion de genero," 92–110; and Luisa Campuzano, "Últimos textos de una dama: Crónicas y memorias de Dulce María Loynaz," 77–89.

19. The list of works analyzing Cuban identity is endless. We cite here only the most recent or most significant: Damián J. Fernández and Madelín Cámara, eds., *Cuba, The Elusive Nation: Interpretations of National Identity* (Gainesville: University Press of Florida, 2000); Jorge Duany, *From the Cuban Ajiaco to the Cuban-American Hyphen: Changing Discourses of National Identity on the Island and in the Diaspora* (Miami: Cuban Studies Association, 1997); Gustavo Pérez

Firmat, *Life on the Hyphen: The Cuban-American Way* (Austin: University of Texas Press, 1994); Uva de Aragón Clavijo, *El caimán ante el espejo: Un ensayo de interpretación de lo cubano* (Miami: Ediciones Universal, 1993); Fernando Ortiz, *Entre cubanos: Psicología tropical* (La Habana: Editorial de Ciencias Sociales, 1987); Jorge Mañach, *Indagación del choteo* (Havana: Revista del Avance, 1928).

20. Fernando Ortiz's famous term *transculturation* is appropriate here (see Ortiz, *Cuban Counterpoint: Tobacco and Sugar,* trans. Harriet de Onis [Durham, N.C.: Duke University Press 1995], 97–103).

21. Fernando Ortiz, "Los factores humanos de la cubanidad," *Revista Bimestre Cubana,* no. 45 (1940), 165–69. The editors thank Leonardo Falcón for providing the correct citation for this well-known phrase.

22. Doris Sommer, *Foundational Fictions: The National Romances of Latin America* (Berkeley: University of California Press, 1991).

23. Garcilaso (de la Vega), *La Florida del Inca,* 125, 138; Weiss, *La architectura colonial cubana,* 1:36, 177.

24. Wright, *Early History of Cuba,* 172.

25. James E. Lewis, "Las Damas de la Havana, el Precursor, and Francisco de Saavedra: A Note on Spanish Participation in the Battle of Yorktown," *The Americas* 37 (July 1980): 83–99.

26. Stubbs, "Social and Political Motherhood," 296–317; Adys Cupull, *Mariana: Raíz del alma cubana* (Havana: Editora Política, 1998).

27. Sandra Messinger Cypess, *La Malinche in Mexican Literature from History to Myth* (Austin: University of Texas Press, 1991).

28. For the negative effects of militarization and the development of *caudillismo* in Cuba, see de Aragón Clavijo, *El caimán ante el espejo.*

29. Anyone familiar with Cuban history can recite the list of internal and external conflicts: the Haitian Revolution from 1791 to 1804; the Infante Conspiracy of 1810; the Aponte Conspiracy of 1812; the Soles y Rayos de Bolivar in 1823; the Lorenzo Conspiracy in 1837; the Conspiracy of La Escalera in 1843–44; the Narciso López expeditions from 1849 to 1851; the Ten Years War, 1868–78; the Guerra Chiquita in 1879; and the War of Independence, 1895–98. The twentieth century was little better, with various rebellions against the constitutional government in 1906, 1912 and 1917; the U.S. interventions in 1906 and 1921; the Revolution of 1933; the coup d'état in 1952; and the Revolution of 1959. These "official" conflicts do not include the various conspiracies, insurgencies, and skirmishes that led up to the wars. And if we take into account the plague of piracy from 1816 to 1830 and a similar plague of banditry from the 1880s through 1898, the degree of uncertainty in daily life cannot be underestimated.

30. Many thanks to my co-editor, K. Lynn Stoner, for contributing the majority of the preceeding passage.

SHERRY JOHNSON

"Señoras en sus clases no ordinarias": *Enemy Collaborators or Courageous Defenders of the Family?*

ABSTRACT

This article examines female behavior in the late eighteenth century in light of the myth of disloyalty that arose in the following century. Set within a recent historiographical trend that examines the significance of female honor in Spanish society, this study argues that Cuban women, regardless of status and/or ethnicity, faced challenges unique to the island. It begins by establishing the reality of the pervasive influence of militarization, a consequence of the defensive function of the island. Even from the earliest years of settlement, questions of honor and loyalty in Cuba were, quite literally, matters of life and death. During and after the most traumatic event in the island's history, the fall of Havana to the British in 1762, Cuban women not only behaved in an honorable manner, they also supported their men and maintained the family in the face of foreign occupation and constant danger. This was due in no small measure to their ability to acquire and maintain family property during their husbands' absences. Significantly, the Cuban women's honorable behavior was not limited to free, white women. Equally loyal and competent, Cuba's free women of color and female slaves faced danger and deprivation in much the same way as their white counterparts. Slave women were doubly affected by militarization, as uniquely Cuban circumstances provided a vehicle through which they and their families could gain their freedom. Their legacy provided a tangible example for their female descendants, the *mambisas* of the nineteenth century.

RESUMEN

Este artículo examina el comportamiento femenino en la última parte del siglo dieciocho a la luz del mito de la deslealtad que surgió en el siglo siguiente. Situado en una tendencia historiográfica reciente que examina el significado del honor de la mujer en la sociedad española, este estudio arguye que las mujeres cubanas, independientemente de su estatus u origen étnico, confrontaron desafíos particulares de la isla. Comienza por establecer la realidad de la penetrante influencia de la militarización, consecuencia de la función defensiva de la isla. Incluso desde los primeros asentamientos, las cuestiones de honor y lealtad eran en Cuba asuntos, literalmente, de vida o muerte. Durante y después del evento más traumático en la historia de la isla, la toma de la Habana por los ingleses en 1762, las mujeres cubanas no sólo se comportaban de forma honorable. También apoyaban a sus hombres y mantenían a la familia en medio de la ocupación extranjera y el peligro constante. Esto se debió, en gran medida, a la habilidad que mostraron para adquirir y mantener las propiedades de la familia durante la ausencia de sus maridos. Es significativo que este comportamiento honorable no era exclusivo de mujeres blancas y libres. Igualmente competentes y leales, las mujeres libres de color y las esclavas enfrentaron peligros y privaciones de maneras muy similares a sus contrapartes blancas. Las esclavas fueron doblemente afectadas por la militarización, ya que circunstancias que se dieron únicamente en Cuba les ofrecieron un vehículo para que ellas y sus familias pudieran ganar la libertad. El legado de estas mujeres brindó un ejemplo tangible a sus descendientes femeninos, las mambisas del siglo diecinueve.

> Las muchachas de la Habana
> no tienen temor de Dios
> pues se van con los ingleses
> en los bocoyes de arroz.

Sometime after the fall of Havana to the British siege in 1762, a short but telling *décima* (verse) circulated in Cuba. Scathingly critical of several young ladies who fraternized with the enemy during the hostilities, the rhyme chastised their actions in the worst way possible: "They do not fear even God himself since they will go with the English among barrels of rice." Just when the verse entered Cuban popular culture is difficult to determine, but by the late nineteenth century it had become sufficiently entrenched in the national mythology to be enshrined in print.[1] Like most foundational fictions, it had a didactic purpose: to set standards and to establish behavioral norms for Cuban women.[2] It railed against traitorous women who sold or gave away their sexual favors to the enemy, but like most legends, the reality of the situation was far removed from the moral of the poem. The behavior of Havana's women in the face of foreign occupation was less a matter of fact than a product of the imagination of nineteenth-century mythmakers, but myths have an insidious way of infiltrating themselves into a nation's historiography and being perpetuated for generations to come.

This essay challenges the negative portrayal of female behavior, as it explores how militarization affected women's lives in the late eighteenth century. It examines the conduct of Cuba's women — wives, widows, mothers, daughters, orphans — and their families who were influenced by the presence of military forces in Cuba by evaluating the intersection of militarization, community attitudes, and women's lives. The dominant paradigm for historical studies of gender in Cuba is predicated in the literature of the nineteenth century that posits gender relations within the context of sexual liaisons and race relations.[3] This simplistic framework continues to govern most studies in Cuban social history. It rarely seeks — and therefore, does not find — any degree of agency for Cuban women. White women are consigned to suffer in silence while their husbands dally with slave women in the plantation slave quarters and/or with *mulatta* mistresses in town. Women of color, both free and enslaved, are relegated to the demeaning position of seeking sexual liaisons with white men to further their economic aspirations, regardless of personal cost. The notion that white women could enjoy the love and trust of their husbands, fathers, and sons, or that free women of color were cherished and supported by their menfolk, or that slave women were valued and encouraged to live in a stable family relationship has been rejected—even ridiculed—by a historiography established on the basis of antiquarian writings.

This article breaks with tradition and argues that for the majority of Cuba's women the reality of their lives was sharply at variance with the impression portrayed both in recent historiography and national mythology. It draws its inspiration from a current trend in historiography that focuses upon relationships among gender, power, honor, and shame.[4] Most studies accept implicitly that gendered relations of power were rooted in patriarchy and that "social circumstances distributed virtue."[5] Honor and virtue accrued to women of the higher ranks, whereas plebeian women, because of their status and ethnicity, were susceptible to temptations that led to dishonor and disloyalty. This study does not challenge the basic tenets of gender relations for Spanish America in a generalized sense. It does, however, demonstrate that Cuban gender relations were formed within a different context than those elsewhere in the Caribbean, in Spanish America, and even in Spain. Social relations on the island were predicated on the defense function of Cuba in general that demanded an overwhelming military presence; this, in turn, made the life experiences of Cuban women unique. For Cuban women, honor and loyalty within the family context had the same intrinsic meaning as they had for women elsewhere in the empire, but in the face of war and foreign invasion, the concepts of dishonor and betrayal expanded to encompass society as a whole. For all Cubans the consequence of dishonor was (quite literally) death. Through their honorable behavior, the women of eighteenth-century Cuba, regardless of status and ethnicity, established behavioral norms for their female descendants in the subsequent century. The *mambisas* of Cuba's nineteenth-century wars of independence could trace their cultural heritage to the experiences of their grandmothers and great-grandmothers, whose lives contradict the impression portrayed in the verses of their time.

Life at the Turn of the Century

One of the keys to understanding Cuban female behavior is recognizing the importance of militarization to the island's life. Cuba's heritage of militarization is as long as the island's recorded history. As the key to the defense of the Spanish Caribbean, Havana, in particular, was characterized by a military presence that was many times greater than in other areas of the Spanish empire. In addition, Havana differed from Lima and Mexico City in that it was the maritime hub between Spanish America and Spain; thus, the city and its inhabitants were far more cosmopolitan than those of other Spanish American cities. Life was transient by nature. Combined with these historical realities were changes brought by the fall of Havana and the subsequent reforms enacted by Field Marshall Alejandro O'Reilly in 1763. These reforms are well studied, as discreet events and from a political and economic perspective.[6] Elsewhere, I have established the social dimension of reform and the arrival of significant numbers of peninsular men, but some salient points bear repeating, particularly in establishing how widespread and inclusive these policies were to Cuba's population.[7] As the military staging ground for Caribbean operations, Cuba garrisoned regular army troops and naval personnel whose numbers were greater than or equal to the number of adult civilian men in the island. Civilian men, both white and free men of color, did their part by serving in local militias, so that at any given location on the island, between 33 and 66 percent of an area's civilian males aged 15 to 45 might be under arms. These local male conscripts became inculcated with an esprit de corps for military life. They also benefited from privileges associated with the military and militia service and came under the jurisdiction of military law.[8] Many adult males in the militia were heads of households, and the privileges and responsibilities associated with military service were extended to their wives, children, and household dependents. Furthermore, a number of families benefited indirectly by being suppliers of goods and services to garrison and naval installations.[9] Studies of militarized societies show that if 20 to 25 percent of a population is under arms, the society is considered to be fully mobilized.[10] Given that in Cuba between 30 and 66 percent of civilian men were under arms, in addition to the regular military forces, one can surmise that the extent of military influence on the island's society must have been truly staggering. Women within this society could not help but be affected by such military influence.

Regardless where a woman might live in Spanish America, her behavior was constrained by custom, Catholicism, and civil law. A woman's life was framed within the context of her family, and she was expected to be an obedient daughter, a submissive wife, and a devoted mother; ideal female traits were chastity, modesty, piety, and obedience to the will of God, her father or other male guardian, and her husband.[11] A proper Spanish maiden remained under her father's or guardian's protection until she reached adulthood at age twenty-five. Her highest goal would have been to marry within her own status and according to her parents' wishes. If she married prior to reaching adulthood, she would come under the legal protection of her husband, where she would remain until one of the two of them died. A second alternative open to young girls everywhere in Spanish America was to enter a convent, but marriageable daughters rarely were allowed to squander their potential by cloistering themselves within the Church. Rather, they were intended to be used strategically to increase a family's social standing in the community.[12]

Marriage and the establishment of her own family was one of the milestones in a woman's life, but family formation took on a different dimension in Cuba than in the rest of Spanish America. The existence of large numbers of peninsular soldiers on the island, coupled with incentives from the Spanish Crown that encouraged them to remain in Cuba when their terms of service were over, promoted a situation in which many former military men married Cuban women and raised their children as Cubans. The population distribution of the island was always characterized by more men than women, so the military presence skewed the figures for marriage even further. It also contributed to a population in which Europeans—both men and women—predominated over people of color. For their part, Cuban families reaped the benefits of a marriage market in which there was no shortage of grooms or "protectors" for their daughters. The privilege of marrying one's daughter to a peninsular soldier came with a price, however. After 1764 strict regulations were enacted governing military marriages; Creole families were now required to prove their worthiness before permission to marry would be granted by royal officials. A second major shift in colonial legislation occurred in 1776, when the strict rules governing marriage were extended to the civilian population. The fact that Crown officials permitted and even encouraged peninsular/Creole intermarriage in Cuba was in sharp contrast to the disparaging attitude held by most *peninsulares* concerning the populations of Mexico City or Peru. In allowing such marriages, the Crown bound the island closer to the metropolis and demonstrated that its inhabitants enjoyed a unique and privileged position in the wider imperial context.[13]

Assuring the Present: The Fuero Militar

One of the most tangible enticements of military service was the *fuero militar*, privileges granted to both regular military and militia units in Cuba in 1771. In general, *fueros* granted privileges and benefits to specific corporate groups in Spanish society and were not available to the general population. For example, under the *fuero criminal,* members of the military and their families who were accused of crimes were tried by special military tribunals under military law, or in case of arrest, they were held in their barracks or in their homes rather than in ordinary prisons. In addition, officers and some enlisted men enjoyed certain exemptions from civic obligations, and their personal property could not be attached for the payment of debts. In Cuba, *fuero* privileges were extended to all military members and their families, both those in the regular army and navy but also those in the civilian militias as well.[14]

The significance of such privileges to Cuban women on a daily basis can best be understood when compared to other areas of Spanish America and the Caribbean. To begin, from 1763 through the 1780s Havana experienced a prosperous economy. But military families enjoyed an even better financial position than the average Cuban *jornalero* (day worker). Officers and their families received *raciones de la mesa* (meal allowances), and military families also had access to their own bakery and commissary close to the Castillo de la Fuerza.[15] Members of the military also received medical treatment courtesy of the Crown.[16] Upon their retirement from the military, former soldiers and sailors, especially lower-echelon officers, often found employment in various departments of the bureaucracy, and in rural areas ordinary soldiers often received grants of land, slaves, and money for the purchase of seeds or cuttings of fruit-bearing trees and plants such as *plátanos*. They also received implements such as hoes.[17] On occasion, retired military families were even provided with housing free of charge.[18]

Protection under the *fuero militar* bordered on the sacred, and the issue of whether and to what extent the families of military members were covered was tested shortly after the extension of privileges to the island. In November 1772 the local *capitán del partido* (constable) of Guanabacoa, Antonio Laso de la Vega, arbitrarily arrested the wife of one Captain Gabriel de Zubieta. The response of the captain-general, the Marqués de la Torre, to this unlawful arrest was swift and unequivocal. De la Torre scathingly reprimanded the local constable for violating the woman's rights under the *fuero militar* and for holding her in an ordinary jail rather than putting her under house arrest. Moreover, de la Torre accused Laso de la Vega of acting in a disingenuous manner by pretending that he was not aware that *fuero* privileges extended to military family members. De la Torre ordered Laso de la Vega to release the woman immediately, and to make sure that his order was carried out, he sent a copy of his letter mandating that the woman be freed to the second-in-command in the village, a Lieutenant Rafael Rivero.[19] Neither did *fuero* privileges end with a military man's death. One Manuela de Cárdenas was apparently outraged that some soldiers did not treat her with the respect she felt she deserved as the widow of the highest-ranking naval officer in the Spanish Caribbean fleet, Juan de Colina. She complained to the commander of the troops that "when she passed by the guardhouse, the men did not give her the respect that she merited." In response, de la Torre instructed the commander to order his soldiers to extend her the honor and respect that her gender and status demanded.[20]

Twenty years later, during the administration of Luis de las Casas (1790–96), the privileges enjoyed by Cuban women under the *fuero militar* were challenged on an institutional level, when Las Casas and his lieutenant governor, José de Ilincheta, led an all-out assault on the military privileges enjoyed by the majority of the Cuban people. Michaela and Candelaria Álvarez were caught up in this struggle in February 1794 when they witnessed an argument between the constable of Guanabacoa, Agustín Fleitas, and the civilian, Cristóval Aguila. Constable Fleitas summoned the women to appear before him to testify to what they had seen and heard. Citing the immunity granted to daughters of a military man by the *fuero militar,* the two women refused, asserting that "they were not the ones to be inconvenienced." Angered at their refusal, the captain general ordered the women to appear.[21] But, fortunately for the two women, in an unrelated case the Ministry of War upheld the application of the *fuero* to all of Cuba's military families.[22] The decision was a victory for the island, and as a consequence, it appears that the women were never forced to testify.[23]

Assuring One's Future: Dowries

Dowries represented important financial security for the families of both the bride and groom. For civilian families, the minimum dowry was 1,000 pesos fuertes. For a maiden, her ability to bring a dowry to her union meant the difference between an advantaged marriage and spinsterhood, which brought perpetual disgrace and made her a liability to her family. Worse still, without some form of financial security, many women faced destitution. For both church and state, dowries represented a measure of security that a woman would not become a public liability if her husband or father died. Royal officials were concerned with keeping women off the public charity rolls as early as 1669. In that year, Governor Martín Calvo de Arreta left 102,000 pesos to provide dowry support for five orphaned or impoverished girls; the annual interest from the fund generated 5,000 pesos to be used for that purpose. Certain restrictions applied: recipients had to be from Havana or from some other Spanish possession; they had to be virtuous and of recognized *limpieza de sangre* (purity of blood); and no member of their family could have been cited by the Inquisition. In addition, surviving family members could not have 3,000 pesos of combined wealth, which would imply that the family was not destitute. The dowry recipients were chosen by lottery, and the money was disbursed when the girls chose either to marry or to enter a convent[24]

At the other end of the spectrum were the enormous dowries provided to the maidens from Cuba's wealthy families. Feliciana de Herrera, the daughter of the Marqués de Villalta, brought a dowry to her marriage to Diego Calvo de la Puerta valued at over 41,000 pesos, including 6,000 pesos in silver, numerous slaves, and some rural land, upon which her husband founded an *ingenio,* San Nicolás.[25] When María Dolores de Lisundia, the daughter of Domingo de Lisundia, the Marqués de Real Agrado, married Matias de Armona, control of the family's property and money remained with her father, but upon Lisundia's death, the couple inherited several diversified agricultural enterprises and Armona received his father-in-law's title of nobility.[26] María

Thomasa de Florencia brought so much land to her marriage to Manuel García Barrera that it made him eligible to petition the Council of the Indies for permission to establish a settlement that he hoped to name Río Blanco.[27] His request was denied, in part because the lands were part of the dowry belonging to María Tomasa and García Barreras could not alienate the property. Instead, he was obliged to divide the holdings among the couple's twelve children.[28]

Because of the predominance of military influence in almost every aspect of Cuban life, military unions held extraordinary importance. To be able to marry into the officer corps (and enjoy the significant benefits of the *fuero militar*), families were required to post a dowry bond (*fianza*) of no less than 2,500 pesos, which was increased to 3,000 pesos in 1789.[29] Wealthy families could afford a substantial cash outlay, but for less affluent families the requirement represented a considerable financial investment. To raise the necessary collateral, most families capitalized on their interests in real property, for example, their ownership of houses in town or farms and ranches in the surrounding countryside. For families with few resources, provisions were enacted to allow the family to retain control of the land if they obligated themselves to the royal treasury with a mortgage against the value of the property.[30] María del Pilar García Barrera y Florencia was one of twelve children who received the dower lands of María Thomasa de Florencia; she, in turn, mortgaged six of the ninety-six *caballerías* of land she inherited from her parents.[31] Her brother, Manuel García Barrera y Florencia, utilized a portion of his inheritance to help Nicolás Antonio de Quiñones, a lawyer with the Audiencia in Havana, provide the necessary funds so his daughter, María de la Luz, could marry Lieutenant Francisco Xavier de la Madrid.[32] Likewise, Antonio Betancourt pledged his interest in an *estancia* in Jesús del Monte, appraised at 5,000 pesos, for his daughter's dowry bond.[33]

Marriage to a military man was so desirable that families were willing to utilize the resources not just of immediate relatives but also of grandparents, aunts, cousins, in-laws, and stepfathers to accumulate the requisite 3,000 pesos. Colonel Antonio Fernández pledged one of his houses on Calle Havana to provide for his niece María Blanco; his wife's dowry collateral in St. Augustine was mortgaged for the marriage of their daughter Rafaela.[34] Master masons and master carpenters were called in to certify that the house that Josefa Rodríguez, offered as security for her niece Jacinta Fiallo's marriage, was indeed valued at over 9,400 pesos.[35] In a complex arrangement, María Dolores Guerra pledged the value of a *sitio de labor* in Arroyo Naranjo for her niece Rita Gonzáles Guerra's marriage to Lieutenant Francisco Clos in 1783.[36]

Dowry obligations were not static, and as long as collateral was equal to or greater than the requisite 3,000 pesos, agreements could be modified at any time. Domingo Pérez de Molina modified the dowry collateral for his daughter Angela by adding a new house he had purchased in Puerto Príncipe.[37] In 1796

Rafael Catalá requested that the Treasury substitute a house that he inherited on the Plaza de los Mercaderes, valued at over 40,000 pesos, for the cash sum on deposit for the dowry of his wife Rosalía de Arango.[38] Similarly, dowry mortgages could be nullified if something interfered with the matrimonial bond or with the consummation of the marriage. Francisco Clos was widowed prior to his retirement, so the 3,000 peso security obligation pledged by his late wife's aunt against her farm was discharged.[39] Similarly, Carlos Barreyro successfully petitioned that the mortgage on a house received from his mother for his daughter's marriage be lifted.[40] One poignant entry in Havana's notarial records is the deathbed testament of Rosalía Morejón, affianced to Lieutenant Dionisio Valdésnoche. On the night of her death, as one of her last conscious acts, Morejón enumerated the 1,100 pesos from her aunt and uncle and the four slaves from her father so that the collateral would be returned to her family.[41]

Royal policies in Cuba contrasted with those for Brazil, where the use of dowries diminished over the colonial period.[42] In Cuba there was a move toward more widespread use of dowries; moreover, the trend toward more stringent regulation in the 1770s also stands in sharp contrast to regulations of alliances formed on the island prior to 1769. Prior to the reforms, royal officials did not enforce the requirements for military marriages, and the posting of a dowry bond was often waived, even when marriages involved officers of the highest rank. In the 1750s Isabel Fernández married Juan Bautista Valliant, who eventually rose to the position of Brigadier General and Governor of Santiago de Cuba, but the military regulations that required her family to establish her dowry were not enforced.[43] In the union of Sergeant-Major Hilario Remírez de Esteñóz and Nicolasa Mancebo Betancourt in the early 1760s (discussed in greater detail below), her dower money totaled a mere 235 pesos.[44] Margarita Castrillón from Trinidad married sergeant Juan Villanó with but 118 pesos in dower money, and he brought to the marriage just the clothes he wore and a few trinkets.[45]

Sacrifice and Reward: The Crown's Pension System

The trend toward more stringent enforcement of dowry requirements is directly attributable to the fact that Cuban women enjoyed privileges far beyond those of other women in the Spanish empire. Perhaps the greatest reward for Cuba's military wives was financial, in the form of pensions and *limosnas* (alms, i.e., charity payments) for surviving mothers, widows, and orphans of military men.[46] The royal pension system operated throughout Spanish America, but outside of Cuba it was applicable to only a very small percentage of the female population.[47] In Cuba, however, three separate welfare measures for military and bureaucrats' families were in operation: (1) the general *monte pío* (pension system), which provided for families of bureaucrats and treasury officials; (2)

the *monte pío militar* for military families; and (3) the specialized *limosna de florida*, created in 1731 specifically for surviving mothers, widows, and orphans of military personnel of the Florida *presidios*.[48] In 1763 Florida had been ceded to Great Britain, and families there had lost everything when they were forced to evacuate to Cuba.[49] Because of the territorial cession, being a *floridana* became synonymous with duty, loyalty to Spain, and, above all, sacrifice.[50] To assure that their sacrifices did not go unrewarded, the widows, wives, and female children of Florida's military men besieged royal officials, demanding the pensions that had been promised to them. In one pitiful example, the four daughters of a deceased lieutenant colonel of the grenadiers, Juan Leandro de Landa, pleaded that they "were reduced to the most desperate of circumstances."[51] In 1772 a royal order arrived that expressed the king's sentiments: "It is the desire of the monarch that the *floridana* families be distinguished and be seen according to their pious purposes. Because of their way of life, those extraordinary women merit distinction, and so shall they be treated." Thus, the militant Florida women won their personal battle, but more importantly, the recognition and financial concessions they were granted would later be extended to all military women on the island.[52]

Beginning in 1772, women who had dedicated their lives to men in military service could expect to receive compensation for their sacrifices. Pension and *limosna* awards were based upon the military member's rank, and however small, the concession provided a measure of financial security equivalent to the normal daily wages of an average civilian family.[53] María de la Concepción Núñez, the widow of soldier Nicolás Gutiérrez, was one of the recipients of the minimum award of two reales per day.[54] María Carrillo y Munive also received this minimum amount, although her husband had advanced from the ranks of ordinary soldiers into the officer corps.[55] The award for a lieutenant's widow and orphans was slightly higher. Agustina Ferrara y Ramírez, as the widow of Gines Pomares, was granted 124 pesos annually, and Manuela Josepha de la Parra, the widow of Juan Fio de Velasco, received 169 pesos.[56] If a soldier had achieved the rank of captain, his surviving family members could receive a pension nearly double that for the family of a common soldier. Manuela Burguete, the widow of Antonio Rechani, who had been captain of the Regiment of Lombardy, and Thomasa and María Josepha de Castilla, the orphaned children of Captain Juan de Castilla, each received 188 pesos per year.[57]

At the other end of the spectrum were the payments granted to the widows and orphans of the highest ranking military officers. Josefa de Justíz, daughter of the Marqués de Justíz and widow of the Conde de Buena Vista, Field Marshall Francisco de Calvo, was granted 625 pesos per year for herself and her daughter María Francisca.[58] When Matias de Armona died in 1796, his widow María Dolores de Lizundia was awarded a pension of 500 pesos per year; the official bequest came with the stipulation that she remain unmarried and that she care for and educate the couple's six minor children.[59] Wives and children were not the only beneficiaries of Charles III's generosity toward Cuban families. Francisca Mendoza de Sotomayor, as mother of *comisario de guerra,* Juan José de Loyola, was also eligible for a *limosna.*[60]

Carrying On, Alone

Pensions and *limosnas* acknowledged the monarch's obligation to reward the men who had served him well by guaranteeing that their families would be cared for upon their death. Such men literally pledged their lives to royal service. Cuba's notarial records abound with examples in which a military man would write about his immediate and unavoidable departure and how he was duty bound to follow his flag.[61] Military men and their women recognized that families took a subordinate position to obligations to the state, and all who chose to ally themselves with officers or soldiers accepted the responsibilities of military life.

A large body of scholarship establishes that a Spanish woman's role was to help and support her husband, manage the home, bear and raise children, and remain loyal, honorable, and pure in spirit.[62] All of these desirable qualities held true for Cuban women, but unlike families who lived in more secure areas of the empire, the women of Havana were charged with obligations over and above normal female responsibilities. Cuba's military community was always in a state of readiness; thus, women needed to be prepared to single-handedly manage their households and care for family members at a moment's notice. In case of emergency, women were expected to act as "deputy husbands" and take over the family's affairs.[63] It mattered little whether such responsibility was to be for a short period or for the remainder of their lives: male family members recognized that their wives were equal to the task.

Even under normal peacetime circumstances, Havana's women could still expect to manage the family's affairs on their own at some time during their married life. Havana was the administrative hub of the Spanish Caribbean, and men whose primary residence was in the capital were routinely assigned to remote duty in posts such as New Orleans, Pensacola, Puerto Príncipe, St. Augustine, or Santiago de Cuba. Havana was also the maritime hub between Spanish America and Spain, and the women of naval families, of providers of the royal mail system, and of Cuba's merchants also learned to manage on their own. Frequent and prolonged absences demanded that men take the necessary measures to provide for their families. Prior to leaving on a campaign, soldiers would appear before the Intendant to authorize an allotment to be paid to their wives and families in their absence.[64] In addition, men drafted powers-of-attorney in favor of their wives or mothers.[65] This allowed women to carry on the daily business of managing the family and providing for its needs. It also allowed women to cope with minor emergencies and to buy and sell family property, particularly slaves, should the need arise. The importance of leaving proper documentation was not lost on one Caribbean merchant, who, when drafting a power-of-attorney in favor of his wife, specified that she could "act in all matters in [his] stead."[66] Powers-of-attorney were especially important to military families, as the men could never be sure how long they would be gone. In 1779, with Spain at war with Great Britain, Vicente Folch left a power-of-attorney with his wife María de las Mercedes Rodríguez del Junco.[67] More than a decade later, one Captain Gines de Oliva followed the same procedure prior to leaving for a campaign in Santo Domingo.[68] There always existed the very real possibility that a husband might not return, and in this contingency, a man would often name his wife as the primary executor of his estate. Sebastián Piñero, a lieutenant in the American Dragoons, empowered his wife of sixteen years, María Leonora Mungrey, to collect the debts owed to him, to pay his creditors, to care for their three children, and to care for his property, which stretched from Havana to Florida to Spain.[69]

Military men did not hesitate to leave their wives and mothers in charge of family matters, for Havana's women had proven their merit under the most difficult of circumstances — the British occupation of Havana. In 1762, when British forces had entered the city, the Spanish garrison had been forced to evacuate, leaving their families at the mercy of the enemy. Instead of an unrestrained orgy of capitalistic consumption, however, the occupation was characterized by shortages and misery for the city's inhabitants.[70] Far from engaging in traitorous behavior or in flirtations and sexual escapades with British soldiers, women from military families, along with civilians, suffered through shortages, sickness, and uncertainty alone. Rosa Llanes Perdomo headed one family while her husband, Lieutenant Colonel Tomás de Cotilla, and her sons, Rafael, Juan Tomás, and José, were prevented from returning to the city.[71] Another military household, that of Sergeant-Major Antonio Remírez de Esteñóz, was headed by his wife, Luisa de Sotolongo. Remírez de Esteñóz had over forty years of service and was one of the most senior officers in the city.[72] He and his son Hilario, along with countless other members of the military, had been duty bound to follow their flag and leave the city on the first transport ship that had sailed for Spain. Meanwhile, his wife Luisa de Sotolongo served as a role model for her children, for her daughter-in-law Nicolasa Mancebo Betancourt, and for the countless other women from military families in occupied Havana.[73]

The occupation of Havana underscored that separation and danger were always very near for Cuban women. Similar circumstances could at any time once again force them to take over many of the administrative tasks that were not normally women's tasks. Women lived with the possibility of widowhood being suddenly thrust upon them, so, in a way, their behavior was a rehearsal for the inevitable. While there was a tangible difference, both legally and emotionally, between being a wife and a widow, in actual practice, both conditions demanded strength and spirit. Time and again, Havana's women, such as Sotolongo, Mancebo Betancourt, and Llanes Perdomo, proved themselves equal to the task. Such experience allowed Hilario Remírez de Esteñóz to place his confidence in the women of his family. Prior to departing on campaign, he left a power-of-attorney in favor of his wife Mancebo Betancourt, in which she and her mother-in-law, Luisa de Sotolongo, were designated as co-executors of his estate.[74] The bachelor José de Cotilla left a general power-of-attorney to his mother, Llanes Perdomo, before he sailed on the Pensacola expedition, under which his sister Teresa manumitted one of her brother's slaves.[75] During the war with Great Britain (1779–83), Victorina Guillén, Angela Huet, and Maria de Berrio Campo y Cos all were legally charged with managing their families' affairs, although their husbands could have chosen male relatives to do so.[76] The degree of love and trust that existed between husbands and wives is touchingly evident in the testament of Adjutant Major Tomás García. Before he left on the disastrous campaign in Santo Domingo in 1794, García drafted his will, in which he expressed his "profound love" for his wife and his gratitude "for the good union that she has maintained in our marriage." García died suddenly during the campaign; the will that he wrote prior to his departure was discovered among his personal belongings in the cramped, dirty quarters of the barracks at San Rafael. His widow in Havana was left with the task of mourning the death of a man who clearly adored her and dividing his estate among herself and their children.[77]

Women and Property

In many instances, financial solvency was linked to the control and management of real property, and Cuban women were keenly aware of their range of possibilities. Prior to his death, Juan Esquivel had built a house for his family's recreation in the Cano district outside the city of Havana. The residence was placed in jeopardy when in 1795 Luis de las Casas attempted to expropriate it for use as a barracks for the mounted cavalry. Esquivel's widow, Tomasa Muxica, fought tooth and nail to prevent the seizure of her home.[78] Tomasa Basabe was equally perseverant in demanding compensation when the houses belonging to the estate of her deceased husband, Martín Estéban de Aróstegui, were demolished to make way for a fortification atop the hill bearing the family's name.[79] When Florencia de Linares sold an *estancia* in Guatao, she did so with a power-of-attorney from her husband, Jacinto Rodríguez Pimienta.[80] His permission was merely a formality, however, for when she described the property, which covered a *caballería* of land, she specified: "I am the owner."[81] Likewise, Josefa Benedict Horruytiner, wife of Benito Ximénez de Guzmán, sold an *estancia* in Jubajay without her husband's signature.[82]

The depth and breadth of women's financial acumen in handling real property is exemplified in the actions of Bárbara Rodríguez Ortega y Sigler, a member of one of the wealthiest families in Havana. The family's financial network rested on their extensive landholdings, accumulated during the half-century prior to 1762. In 1766 Rodríguez Ortega dedicated the income from a cattle ranch that had been owned by her family since 1738, along with income from two urban lots, to create an endowment for the nunnery of Nuestra Señora de Monserrat. Although there were many men in her family, Doña Bárbara vested the administration of the endowment with her niece, Rosalía Gallegos. When and if Rosalía could no longer serve, Bárbara specified, the administration would pass to her sister's remaining children, "with a preference for the girls rather than the boys."[83]

A recent trend in feminist historiography has shown that widowhood conferred certain freedom upon married women that they were otherwise prohibited from attaining. In general, and in the context of the eighteenth century, female behavior in Cuba conforms to this finding, but the range of possibilities for Cuban women who were not yet widowed goes far beyond what was permissible for women elsewhere. Perhaps the precariousness of life in the Caribbean and the constant threat of warfare allowed single and married women to act independently above and beyond behavioral norms. On several occasions María Luisa de Herrera approached military officials on behalf of her husband Blas du Bouchet, hoping to gain a promotion for him or to have his salary increased.[84] Rafaela Fernández, the daughter of the commander of the Cabaña fortress, went over the head of her husband's superior officer, Juan José de Estrada, and demanded that the governor of Florida intervene to stop the unfair treatment of her husband, Manuel de Castilla.[85] In 1783, once the fate of the Floridas had been assured, Magdalena Piña y Muñoz petitioned the captain general, demanding that her husband, artilleryman Manuel de Nova, be returned to Havana from his post in Pensacola. The couple had exchanged their mutual promise to marry, and then he had been shipped out suddenly on the expedition that conquered the city in 1781. They had been married by proxy, and now that the campaign was over, the woman demanded that her husband be returned to her. Magdalena reminded the captain general that regulations established that soldiers should be rotated every six months. Artillery commander Vicente Risel replied that the problem was complicated because there was no other artillery soldier of equal rank in Pensacola, and he admonished the woman that "every military bride must understand that marriage entails suffering in silence." But Risel closed his response with an acknowledgment that her request was justified, and he promised that he would do everything he could to rotate her husband back to the island, including sending a request to Santiago de Cuba to find a replacement soldier of the same rank as her husband.[86]

Militarization and Women of Color

Militarization also extended an unprecedented degree of status and autonomy to Cuba's free women of color, who made up approximately 25 percent of the total female population in the western end of the island in the late eighteenth century.[87] The centuries-long defensive position of Havana had led the Crown to approve the formation of militia battalions made up of free *pardos* and free *morenos*, a situation unique to Cuba.[88] Men who were prohibited from service in the regular army served with distinction in these specially created militia companies alongside white civilians and regular troops. As in the white community, militia service invariably led to elevated status. And intermarriage among militia families led to the creation of interconnected kin and *compadrazco* networks that evolved into the equivalent of a free colored elite. The surnames of militiamen from such families as Oquendo, de Flores, Alvarez, Sánchez, Pérez, Arenciba, and Díaz resonated throughout the eighteenth century as the most prestigious free-colored members of Havana's military community.[89]

Free women of color who were members of these families carried on their lives in much the same fashion as white women of similar status. Gabriela Pérez was the wife of the free-colored militia captain Francisco Xavier Carques, who served in the *pardo* militia company in the first half of the eighteenth century. Their legitimate, and literate, son, Cristóval Carques, followed in his father's footsteps as a member of Havana's *pardo* militia company from 1744 to 1794.[90] Through Cristóval's successive marriages to María Josepha de Flores and the sisters María Rosa Alvarez and María Isabel Alvarez, the Carques–Pérez families became linked to other free-colored militia families. In addition, by the time of the younger man's death in 1794, the family enjoyed a financial status that was enviable by any standards. Cristóval's widow, María Isabel Alvarez, inherited the family dwelling at Calle Obrapía #151; a two-story house on Calle Compostela; another on Calle Jesús María; and a fourth house on Calle Paula, in addition to other personal property and six slaves.[91]

The wartime experiences of the free women of color mirror those of their counterparts within the white female ranks. Josefa de Flores and the Alvarez sisters were each required, in their own turn, to take responsibility for the family when Cristóval Carques left on campaigns. They each suffered from his absence, as when he participated in the naval battle against British Admiral Vernon in 1748, or in the defense of the Cojímar bridge during the siege and subsequent occupation of Havana, or in the Pensacola campaign. Like his white counterparts in the regular forces, Carques drafted powers-of-attorney in favor of his wives before leaving, and he could do so with confidence because his second wife, María Rosario de los Angeles Alvarez, was unquestionably literate, which suggests that her sister, María Isabel Alvarez, was literate also.[92] María Isabel celebrated when her husband was awarded a silver medal in recognition of his service to the Crown, and the reward was doubly sweet when her brother Francisco Antonio Alvarez of the *pardo* battalion received a similar honor in 1792.[93] Three of Carques's and Alvarez's comrades-in-arms in the *pardo* battalion, and seven men in the *moreno* battalion, perished in the Pensacola campaign, and royal officials dealt with their deaths in exactly the same manner as they did for the deaths of regular troops and white militia units. Josefa Joaquina Sanabría, widow of Antonio Castellanos of the *moreno* battalion, was left alone with five minor children to raise; like other widows, she received half of her husband's monthly salary for the remainder of her life, as long as she remained a widow. More mothers (five of them) than wives (four) were apparently eligible for survivor's benefits from the Pensacola campaign. These included Manuel de Prados's mother, Gabriela Josefa Oquendo, and Eliseo Pedroso's elderly widowed mother, María Dionisia Rosario. All of the mothers received half of their son's military salary.[94] Soldiers who served in the battalions of free *pardos* and free *morenos* retired with full *fuero* privileges, and their widows and orphans enjoyed similar privileges as white women and children. María Loreto Escovedo, the widow of *pardo* militiaman José Ricardo Escovedo, was one such recipient, as was Margarita Sánchez of Guanabacoa.[95] In October 1793, as María Teresa de Silva, wife of Joachim Hernández, a sergeant in the *pardo* battalion, lay on her deathbed, her testament was recorded by the same notary who had taken the deathbed testimonies of white officers and soldiers and their wives.[96]

Even more than for their counterparts in the white community, property ownership provided a powerful vehicle through which free women of color advanced or maintained their family's status. Hard work and determination allowed the free *morena* Rosalía Garro to accumulate 132 pesos in cash (which represented nearly two years' worth of wages for an ordinary male laborer) so as to purchase an urban lot on Calle San Telmo.[97] For European families, military and militia service provided status and financial security; for families of color, status and wealth were equally important, but there was always the added possibility of gaining one's freedom. An example of this process is the kinship or fictive kinship group that was created around Juan de Dios Arenciba and Juan Bautista Arenciba.[98] Juan de Dios Arenciba, a member of the free black militia, had been married to Ana Josepha Marroto for twenty-five years. Upon his death, she was entitled to his *fuero* privileges. She also inherited their farm, consisting of 1.5 *caballerías* of land along with three slaves in Santiago de las Vegas. But the greatest beneficiary of Juan de Dios's death was the youngest of his and Ana Josepha's slaves: the young child Josefa Rafaela was formally granted her freedom under the terms of Juan de Dios's will.[99] María Antonia Díaz and Juan Bautista Arenciba (both from Guinea) married in the 1740s while they were still enslaved. Over the next fifteen years, they earned their freedom and managed to acquire considerable property, including a house in Havana, four slaves, a gold chain, and a gold and emerald rosary. Once emancipated, Juan Bautista joined the *moreno* militia, and upon his death Maria Antonia inherited their property and his *fuero* privileges.[100] Their son, militiaman Antonio José Díaz (born while the couple was still enslaved and also emancipated), retired from the *moreno* battalion with the rank of captain, so he was probably literate, since literacy was a fundamental requirement for entry into the officer corps. Antonio Jose's wife, Catalina Serafina Díaz, would later inherit the family's primary residence, which her husband had purchased "with [their] own money." Like all military widows, Catalina also came under the privileges of her dead husband's *fuero militar*.[101] Their daughter, María Soledad Díaz, extended the family's financial network even further when she purchased a wattle-and-daub house, located on a lot owned by the Cabildo de Negros Carabali, from the free *morena* María Rosario Oquendo.[102]

An extraordinary example of the ways in which militarization could benefit Cuban families of color was a royal proclamation in 1769 that created an artillery company of one hundred slave men. The men chosen for this select force performed the heavy lifting and carrying associated with the artillery brigades. Though enslaved, they were considered to be the property of the monarch, as was the case for another group of slave men who worked alongside condemned criminals on Havana's fortifications. Nonetheless, the men in the artillery brigade were acknowledged to be a slave "elite," and they enjoyed significant privileges, which extended to their wives and families. To begin, a chaplain was assigned to minister to the group, and all members of the artillerymen's families had unrestricted access to Catholic sacraments. Marriage was encouraged, and the sanctity of the family was paramount. The slaves' wives found employment in such useful, wage-earning enterprises as making uniforms for the garrison or washing laundry for the hospitals.[103] From 1767 to 1772, treasury officials paid out to the slave wives over 3,370 pesos for the uniforms they sewed in their homes on a piecework basis.[104] A slave woman was even allowed to work outside her home, if she secured the permission of their husband. At the end of the workday, however, her employer was required to escort the woman back to her housing unit. If he could not do so, that obligation would fall to her husband or to the lieutenant in charge of their housing complex.[105]

Housing for artillerymen and their families was constructed in the southern part of the city.[106] The families occupied individual units that closely resembled modern-day efficiency apartments, in spite of being termed *quarteles* (barracks). The individual household was sacrosanct. "Every matrimony was considered a separate family," and no family was forced to share their housing with another. Personal foodways were to be preserved, and the women were encouraged to prepare their meals in their homes in the style to which the family was most accustomed. At the military commissary, wives would receive the family's daily ration based upon the number of occupants in their household. The diet provided to the artillerymen consisted of 10 ounces of protein (beef, dried beef, pork), 10 ounces of beans, an equivalent amount of an appropriate starch (usually rice or yuca) and vegetables (*viandas*) when available. Wives and children each received half of the artilleryman's ration.[107] The menus were rotated on a daily basis and were available 270 days a year, excepting Sundays and feast days, when the family was encouraged to partake of their meals outside the home. The family's medical needs were also provided for by the Crown. Artillerymen received medical treatment in the royal hospital, and female dependents were usually cared for at home by the royal doctor or surgeon. Their medicines, if necessary, came from the military pharmacy. Importantly, the privileges for housing and medical care were extended for life. The family's children were educated in a useful trade or occupation, and boys were to be given preference to follow in their father's footsteps when openings occurred within the company ranks. If a man and woman produced twelve children, the couple would be emancipated. In addition, if an artilleryman performed with exceptional valor in time of war, his family members could freed, depending upon the recommendation of his commanding officers.[108]

The fact that the Crown created an elite artillery battalion of slaves is, perhaps, not surprising. After all, the island was an armed camp. What *is* surprising is the extensive provisions concerning family life. Cynics might argue that the existence of humanitarian provisions does not necessarily guarantee that such regulations were acknowledged, much less enforced.[109] But that would deny the personal account of how one family of once-enslaved Africans, the Conga Rosalía Sabiona and her legal husband Antonio Abad del Rey from Guinea, came to be not just free but also affluent. Their designations *conga* and *de Guinea* make it virtually certain that each of them was enslaved upon their arrival on the island. The surname chosen for Antonio, "del Rey," verifies that he was a king's slave. While it is possible that Antonio worked in the ranks of ordinary slave laborers, his later membership in the *moreno* battalion suggests that he had gained some kind of valuable military experience before his enlistment in the militia. During his time in militia service, Antonio's full *fuero* privileges were extended to Rosalía, and upon his death in 1796, his pension benefits continued to flow to his wife.[110]

But Antonio Abad del Rey and Rosalía Sabiona were not simply emancipated slaves; even by the standards of their day, they were affluent. During the course of their lives, the couple acquired a house on Calle San Juan de Dios across the street from the *pardo* militia barracks. The house was a substantial structure, made of *tapía* (mortar) rather than the wattle-and-daub that was more typical of the homes of militiamen in the more marginal ranks. In addition, the house was located in the northern portion of Havana, not in the marginal southern half of the city or outside the city walls. Although they themselves had once been enslaved, the couple owned their own black female slave and a mulatto youth. They were even sufficiently acculturated into European culture and sufficiently wealthy that upon Abad del Rey's death in 1796, he could afford to leave a bequest of two reales to every forced laborer in the city, a provision rarely included except in the testaments of the richest residents. The pair was also sufficiently acculturated so that Antonio chose to be buried in the habit of San Francisco, as happened with many of his white counterparts.[111]

How did this exceptional couple gain their freedom and take their place among Havana's most prestigious free-colored families? Documentary evidence for successful freed families of color is frustratingly elusive. At present, it is impossible to determine what was Antonio's occupation or when he and his wife were emancipated. Most likely, Antonio earned his and Rosalía's freedom under a provision that rewarded meritorious military service with emancipation. There were numerous occasions between 1769, when the corps was created, and 1788, when Abad's original will was written, when he could have performed with courage under fire. The couple had no children, so it is not possible that they earned their freedom in that manner. The unusual amount of property they owned strongly suggests that Rosalía worked outside the home; perhaps she was among the slave women who sewed troop uniforms in the 1770s. What is clear, however, is that this couple lived in a remarkable and stable union that benefited themselves and the community as a whole. Their life histories contradict studies that conclude that royal regulations regarding slave treatment were ignored, while at the same time, their story fuels speculation about the number of other families who might have shared the same fortune created by military necessity.

Militarization also influenced the life history of free *parda* Juana Pastor. Juana's father, Ignacio Pastor, was a second lieutenant in the *pardo* militia in 1765, serving in the unit's color guard.[112] Sometime between 1765 and his death in 1794, Pastor rose through the ranks, retiring from military service with the rank of captain. Obviously literate, he then opened a school for children of members of the city's lower ranks, which he located outside the city walls in the barrio Jesús María. His daughter Juana assisted her father in his duties and also shared in the family's status and privileges under the *fuero militar*. At the time of Pastor's death in 1794, father and daughter were educating forty-six boys and thirteen girls at their school. When the captain general ordered the local constable to investigate and report on the status of the school, the official reported that Juana was "quite capable" (*de mucha habilidad*) of continuing her father's work.[113] Juana Pastor was recognized as a pillar of her community;

as late as 1835, she continued to offer classes in her school in barrio Jesús María. In that year, her achievements were once again recognized by the authorities, when the education inspector of the Real Sociedad Económica de Amigos del País certified her "aptitude" to teach.[114] For nearly half a century this remarkable woman, a direct beneficiary of militarization, educated—inculcated—generations of Cuban children.

Conclusion

The military influence in Cuban society in the late eighteenth century was pervasive, and it had an impact on the lives of all Cuban women, regardless of status or race. Militarization, and the need for constant readiness, demanded initiative and responsibility. For Cuba, a state of emergency was a state of normalcy, and in responding positively, Cuban women earned respect, honor, and autonomy. In certain instances, Cuba's women probably were not atypical of other Spanish American women in their range of permissible behavior. The difference lies in the circumstances of their existence, constantly under threat of invasion, continually ready and capable of maintaining the family while their men were away and in the event they did not return. Notarial records are literally full of examples of situations in which Havana's women acted independently, particularly in financial matters. The perception of the women's competence was shared by their men, from individual male family members to the Spanish monarch himself. Equally important, the Cuban female experience was not limited by race. White, free, colored, and even enslaved women were called upon to sacrifice for Cuba, and in turn, they and their families were rewarded with privileges, status, and financial compensation.

Empirical research, then, challenges the mythology of female behavior that has been perpetuated in the *décima*. To be sure, trading sexual favors for economic gain is not unusual in a society based upon a military presence, and this work does not argue that such behavior did not exist. Instead, my research demonstrates that such a portrayal of Havana's women is simplistic at best and exaggerated at worst. Cuban women's lives were far more nuanced than the stanza implies, but challenging one of Cuba's foundational fictions calls into question what has become the standard interpretation of gender relations. If the fundamental myth of Cuban female behavior is proven false, then subsequent interpretations are, and should be, subject to reevaluation. And well they should be, for courage, not treason, governed women's lives in eighteenth-century Cuba. This is evident in the bravery of Cuban women: from the *mambisas* during the wars of independence, to the members of the resistance movements in the twentieth century, the courage of the colonial women of Cuba would be passed down to the many *señoras no ordinarias* for generations to come.

NOTES

Funding for the research that contributed to this article was provided, in part, by the John D. and Catherine MacArthur Foundation; a National Endowment for the Humanities Extending the Reach Research Grant; The Ford Foundation; a Lydia Cabrera Award for Cuban Historical Studies from the Conference on Latin American History; a Library Travel Grant to Collections from the Center for Latin American Studies, University of Florida; a U.S. Department of Education Title VI Award; and an Andrew P. Mellon Foundation Fellowship in Latin American Studies; and from continuing support from the Jay I. Kislak Foundation, the Florida International University Foundation/Provost's Office, the Latin American and Caribbean Center, the Cuban Research Institute, and the College of Arts and Sciences, Florida International University.

1. Antonio Bachiller y Morales, *Cuba: Monografía histórica* (Havana: M. de Villa, 1883), 137, reprinted in Amalia A. Rodríguez, ed., *Cinco diarios del sitio de la Habana* (Havana: Archivo Nacional de Cuba, 1963), 19.

2. Doris Sommer, *Foundational Fictions: The National Romances of Latin America* (Berkeley: University of California Press, 1991).

3. Cirilo Villaverde, *Cecilia Valdés, o la loma del Angel (Novela de costumbres cubanas)* (Havana: Biblioteca Básica de Cultura, 1977); Verena Martínez-Alier, *Marriage, Class, and Colour in Nineteenth-Century Cuba: Attitudes and Sexual Values in a Slave Society* (1974; reprint, Ann Arbor: University of Michigan Press, 1992); Vera Kutzinski, *Sugar's Secrets: Race and the Erotics of Cuban Nationalism* (Charlottesville: University Press of Virginia, 1993).

4. Steve J. Stern, *The Secret History of Gender: Women, Men, and Power in Late Colonial Mexico* (Chapel Hill: University of North Carolina Press, 1995), 11–20; Ann Twinam, *Public Lives, Private Secrets: Gender, Honor, Sexuality, and Illegitimacy in Colonial Spanish America* (Stanford, Calif.: Stanford University Press, 1999); Susan Midgen Socolow, *The Women of Colonial Latin America* (Cambridge: Cambridge University Press, 2000); Sueanne Caulfield, "The History of Gender in the Historiography of Latin America," *Hispanic American Historical Review* 81 (August–November 2001): 477–81; Martinez-Alier, *Marriage, Class, and Colour in Nineteenth-Century Cuba*.

5. Stern, *The Secret History of Gender*, 15.

6. Lyle N. McAlister, *The "Fuero Militar" in New Spain, 1764–1800* (Gainesville: University Press of Florida, 1957); Mark A. Burkholder and David S. Chandler, *From Impotence to Authority: The Spanish Crown and the American Audiencias, 1687–1810* (Columbia: University of Missouri Press, 1977); Nancy M. Farriss, *Crown and Clergy in Colonial Mexico, 1759–1821* (London: University of London, Athelone Press, 1968). John Lynch, *The Spanish American Revolutions, 1808–1826* (New York: W. W. Norton, 1973), 8, describes the reforms measures of the Spanish crown as nothing less than a "second conquest." Works particular to Cuba include Allan J. Kuethe, *Cuba, 1753–1815: Crown, Military, and Society* (Knoxville: University of Tennessee Press, 1986); Jorge I. Domínguez, *Insurrection or Loyalty: The Breakdown of the Spanish Empire* (Cambridge, Mass.: Harvard University Press, 1980); and John Robert McNeill, *Atlantic Empires of France and Spain: Louisbourg and Havana, 1700–1763* (Chapel Hill: University of North Carolina Press, 1985).

7. Sherry Johnson, *The Social Transformation of Eighteenth-Century Cuba* (Gainesville: University Press of Florida, 2001).

8. In the city of Havana and its immediate suburbs, among eligible civilian adult males ages 15 to 50, approximately 30 percent of whites and 66 percent of free colored males were militiamen. Similar figures exist for population centers throughout the island, e.g., Cuatro Villas (16 percent), Puerto Príncipe (30 percent); Santiago/Bayamo (whites, 28 percent; pardos and morenos, 40 percent); and Matanzas (51 percent). These calculations are based upon the number of troops in 1776 (see Revista de la Tropa, 9 May 1776, legajo 2: 11, Asuntos Políticos, Archivo Nacional de Cuba,

Havana, Cuba [hereafter cited as ANC]. Troop numbers are compared to population figures for the census of 1778 in Diego José de Navarro, "Padrón General de la Isla de Cuba formado a consequencia de Real Orden de 1ro de noviembre de 1776," 1778, legajo 1527, Indiferente General [hereafter cited as IG], Archivo General de Indias, Seville, Spain [hereafter cited as AGI], photocopies of which are available in the Levi Marrero Collection, Special Collections, Florida International University, Miami, and in *Revista de la Biblioteca Nacional José Martí* 29 (September–December 1987), 25.

9. Johnson, *Social Transformation,* 64–96; Kuethe, *Cuba,* 46–48; McAlister, *"Fuero Militar,"* 6–11, 45–51; Juan Marchena Fernández, *Oficiales y soldados en el ejército de América* (Seville: Escuela de Estudios Hispanoamericanos, 1983).

10. Stanilas Andreski, *Military Organization and Society* (Berkeley: University of California Press), 33–74.

11. Asunción Lavrin, "In Search of the Colonial Woman in Mexico: The Seventeenth and Eighteenth Centuries," in *Latin American Women: Historical Perspectives,* ed. Asunción Lavrin (Westport, Ct.: Greenwood Press, 1978), 24–34; Silvia Marina Arrom, *The Women of Mexico City, 1790–1857* (Stanford, Calif.: Stanford University Press, 1985), 19–31.

12. Lavrin, "In Search of the Colonial Woman," 30; Martínez-Alier, *Marriage, Class, and Colour*; Patricia Seed, *To Love, Honor, and Obey in Colonial Mexico: Conflicts over Marriage Choice, 1574–1821* (Stanford, Calif.: Stanford University Press, 1986); Susan M. Socolow, "Acceptable Partners: Marriage Choice in Colonial Argentina, 1778–1810," in *Sexuality and Marriage in Colonial Latin America,* ed. Asunción Lavrin (Lincoln: University of Nebraska Press, 1989), 209–47; Mark D. Szuchman, "A Challenge to the Patriarchs: Love among the Youth in Nineteenth-Century Argentina," in *The Middle Period in Latin America: Values and Attitudes in the Seventeenth–Nineteenth Centuries,* ed. Mark D. Szuchman (Boulder, Colo.: Lynne Rienner, 1989), 141–64; Daisy Ripodas Ardanáz, *El matrimonio en indias: Realidad social y regulación jurídica* (Buenos Aires: Conicet, 1977); Elizabeth Anne Kuznesof, "The Construction of Gender in Colonial Latin America," *Colonial Latin American Research Review* 1 (1992): 253–70. For Cuba, see Johnson, *Social Transformation,* 97–120; "Marriage and Community Construction in St. Augustine, 1784–1804," in *Florida's Heritage of Diversity: Essays in Honor of Samuel Proctor,* ed. Mark D. Greenberg, William Warren Rogers, and Canter Brown Jr. (Tallahassee: Sentry Press, 1997), 1–13.

13. Marriage statistics reflect the phenomenon of peninsular/creole intermarriage. From 1758 through 1800 the number of marriages between European men and Cuban women was never less that 30 percent of all marriages in Havana, and during most years the number of peninsular/creole marriages stayed steady at a ratio of 1:1. During the artificial situation created by the aftermath of war (1781–84), the number of Spanish men who married Cuban women skyrocketed to more than 80 percent of marriages in the city (see Johnson, *Social Transformation,* 97–120).

14. McAlister, *"Fuero Militar,"* 6–11, 45–51; Kuethe, *Cuba,* 46–48, 142; Marchena Fernández, *Oficiales y soldados,* 33, 81–82.

15. Correspondence of the Cuban Captain(s) General, 18 December 1770, legajo 1071, Papeles de Cuba [hereafter cited as PC], AGI; Antonio José Valdés, *História de la isla de Cuba y en especial de la Habana* (Havana: Oficina de la Cena, 1813; facisimile ed., Havana: Comisión Nacional Cubana de UNESCO, 1964), 208.

16. Correspondence of the Cuban Captain(s) General, 15 October 1791, legajo 1472, PC, AGI. See also Manuel Pérez Beato, *Habana antigua: Apuntes históricos* (Havana: Seoane, Fernández, y Compañía, Impresores, 1936), 1:229; Levi Marrero, *Cuba: Economía y sociedad* (Madrid: Playor, 1972–88) 8:81; Bibiano Torres Ramírez, "Alejandro O'Reilly en Cuba," *Anuario de estudios americanos* 24 (1967): 1379.

17. Johnson, *Social Transformation,* 39–70.

18. "Expediente sobre establecer reglas seguras para el arendamiento y cobro y entero en la

"Señoras en sus clases no ordinarias" : 33

Tesoría del producto de los Barracones . . . ," 1793, legajo 73: 33, Realengos, Extramuros, ANC. See also Marchena Fernández, *Oficiales y soldados,* 335–36.

19. Correspondence of the Cuban Captain(s) General, 19 November 1772, legajo 1166, PC, AGI.

20. Correspondence of the Cuban Captain(s) General, 3 January 1773, legajo 1165, PC, AGI. She complained: "Quando passa por las guardias no la hassen los honores que la corresponden."

21. Correspondence of the Cuban Captain(s) General, 22 February 1794, legajo 1470, PC, AGI.

22. Kuethe, *Cuba,* 163; Johnson, *Social Transformation,* 147–50.

23. Correspondence of the Cuban Captain(s) General, 22 February 1794, legajo 1470, PC, AGI.

24. *Papel Periódico de la Havana,* 4 February 1792, Colección Cubana, Biblioteca Nacional José Martí, Havana, Cuba. The dowry fund, distributed on 26 March 1794, bequeathed 1,000 pesos to each of six maidens and a 500-peso award to another.

25. Diego Calvo de la Puerta, Testament, 15 October 1777, Escribanía de Gobierno, ANC.

26. Matias de Armona, Testament, 6 June 1797, Escribanía de Guerra, ANC.

27. Manuel García Barreras, Petition to the Council of the Indies, 30 April 1767, legajo 1461, Audiencia de Santo Domingo [hereafter cited as SD], AGI.

28. Manuel García Barreras, Petition to the Council of the Indies, 12 July 1768, legajo 1461, SD, AGI.

29. Domingo Cabello to Vicente de Zéspedes, 6 October, 8 October, 1789, reel 1, bundle 13, East Florida Papers [hereafter cited as EFP], Manuscript Division, Library of Congress, microfilm copies in P. K. Yonge Library of Florida History, University of Florida, Gainesville. Cabello was quoting the regulation of 30 June 1788, which established a 3,000-peso dowry, increasing the required sum from the 2,500 pesos previously demanded.

30. Pedro Castillo, Mortgage on several city lots, 22 May 1777, for 3,250 pesos; Ursula de Avero, Mortgage on a house in Havana, valued at 3,640 pesos 12 December 1782; Antonio Betancourt, mortgage on 1 2/3 caballerías of land valued at 5,000 pesos, 14 June 1783, all Escribanía de Guerra, ANC. These were termed *obligación hipotecaria* and were specifically intended for a bride's dowry, and so shall be termed Mortgage/Dowry Bond hereafter.

31. María del Pilar García Barrera y Florencia, Mortgage/Dowry Bond, 18 October 1788, Escribanía de Guerra, ANC.

32. Nicolás Antonio de Quiñones, Permission to Marry, 9 May 1780, Mortgage/Dowry Bond, 20 May 1780, Escribanía de Guerra, ANC.

33. Antonio Betancourt, Mortgage/Dowry Bond, Escribanía de Guerra, 14 June 1783, ANC.

34. Antonio Fernández, Mortgage/Dowry Bond, 25 June 1782, Escribanía de Guerra, ANC; Victorina Guillén, Mortgage/Dowry Bond, 6 July 1794, reel 170, bundle 369, Escrituras, EFP.

35. Josefa Rodríguez, Mortgage/Dowry Bond, 14 December 1796, Escribanía de Guerra, ANC.

36. María Dolores Guerra, Mortgage/Dowry Bond, 31 May 1783, Escribanía de Guerra, ANC.

37. Correspondence of the Cuban Captain(s) General, 3 March 1773, legajo 1169, PC, AGI.

38. Rafael Catalá, Mortgage/Dowry Bond, 14 December 1796, Escribanía de Guerra, ANC.

39. Francisco Clos, Satisfaction of Dowry Bond, 26 March 1795, Escribanía de Guerra, ANC.

40. Carlos Barreyro, Satisfaction of Mortgage, 29 May 1788, Escribanía de Guerra, ANC.

41. Rosalía Morejón, Dowry Bond (revoked), 23 March 1781, Escribanía de Guerra, ANC.

42. Muriel Nazarri, *The Disappearance of the Dowry: Women, Family, and Change in São Paulo, Brazil, 1600–1900* (Stanford, Calif.: Stanford University Press, 1991). Asunción Lavrin's and Edith Couturier's seminal examination of Mexico, "Dowries and Wills: A View of Women's Socioeconomic Role in Colonial Guadalajara and Puebla, 1640–1790," *Hispanic American His-*

torical Review 59 (February 1979): 280–304, relies upon a sample and uses its evidence for a different purpose.

43. Isabel Fernández Barea, Testament, [month and day illegible] 1786, Escribanía de Guerra, ANC.

44. Hilario Remírez de Esteñóz, Testament, [day illegible] August 1785, Escribanía de Guerra, ANC; Correspondencia del Capitán General, legajo 7: 176, 1755; Secretaría de Guerra Moderna [hereafter cited as Guerra], Archivo General de Simancas, Simancas, Spain [hereafter cited as AGS], legajo 7223, expediente 44, 4 February 1789.

45. Margarita Castrillón, Testament, 21 December 1791, Escribanía de Guerra, ANC.

46. Kuethe, *Cuba,* 46–48; McAlister, *"Fuero Militar,"* 6–11, 45–51.

47. The general *monte pio* system for military members and bureaucrats was not instituted until 1761 (see D. S. Chandler, *Social Assistance and Bureaucratic Politics: The Montepíos of Colonial Mexico, 1767–1821* [Albuquerque: University of New Mexico Press, 1991]. See also Susan M. Socolow, *The Bureaucrats of Buenos Aires, 1769–1810: Amor al Real Servicio* (Durham, N.C.: Duke University Press, 1987) 185–91; and Archer, *The Army in Bourbon Mexico*, 206–9.

48. For the *limosna de Florida,* see "Relación de las floridanas," 30 October 1789, legajo 14: 93, Fondo de las Floridas, ANC.

49. Report of Juan Eligio de la Puente, 8 May 1770, legajo 2585, SD, AGI. I am grateful to Eugene Lyon and Jane Landers for sharing a copy of this document with me. Several additional *limosnera* lists detail the amounts of money provided to Floridanas: "Relación de las floridanas," 30 October 1789, legajo 14: 93, Fondo de las Floridas, ANC; and "Certificación de las Familias de Florida," Correspondence of the Cuban Captain(s) General, 1 September 1795, legajo 412-A, PC, AGI. These lists do not include the innumerable individual requests from widows, orphans, and mothers for royal assistance, which are scattered throughout Cuban, Spanish, and Florida archives. See also Sherry Johnson, "Casualties of Peace: Tracing the Historic Roots of the Florida–Cuban Diaspora, 1763–1804," *Colonial Latin American Historical Review* (Winter 2002): 91–125; and Duvon C. Corbitt, "Spanish Relief Policy and the East Florida Refugees of 1763," *Florida Historical Quarterly* 27 (July 1948): 70, 75–76.

50. From time immemorial, serving in Florida had been a sacrifice. The Crown specifically recognized how dangerous Florida duty was for men, and by extension, granted special privileges to Florida women (see "Relación de las floridanas," 30 October 1789, legajo 14: 93, Fondo de las Floridas, ANC, which reiterates the concessions granted to Florida women since 1731).

51. María de los Angeles de Landa to the Cuban Captain(s) General, 22 August 1772, 2 March 1774, legajo 1154, PC, AGI.

52. Cuban Captain(s) General to Francisco López de Toledo [representing the Florida families], 14 August 1772, 31 October 1774, legajo 1154, PC, AGI. The passage reads: "Es el animo del Rey que las Familias Floridanas se las distinga y mire segun sus piadosas inctenciones; estas ssras en sus clases no ordinarias que con su modo de pensar lo acreditan merecer que assi se las trate . . ."

53. It was never less than the minimum two reales earned by an ordinary day laborer.

54. Cuban Captain(s) General to María de la Concepción Nuñez, 18 November 1773, legajo 1154, PC, AGI.

55. Cuban Captain(s) General to María Carrillo y Munive, legajo 1155, 25 April 1775, PC, AGI.

56. Cuban Captain(s) General to Agustina Ferrara y Ramírez, 25 April 1776, legajo 1153; Cuban Captain(s) General to Manuela Josepha de la Parra, 26 June 1776, legajo 1153, PC, AGI.

57. Cuban Captain(s) General to Manuela Burguete, 21 May 1776, legajo 1153; Cuban Captain(s) General to Thomasa and María Josepha de Castilla, 5 February 1776, legajo 1153, PC, AGI.

"Señoras en sus clases no ordinarias" : 35

58. Josepha de Justíz, Pension Request, 4 January 1797, legajo 7230, expediente 46, Guerra, AGS.
59. María Dolores de Lizundia, Pension Request, 18 August 1798, legajo 7231, expediente 71, Guerra, AGS.
60. Cuban Captain(s) General to Francisca Mendoza de Sotomayor, 25 February 1774, legajo 1154, PC, AGI.
61. Pedro Moncada, Power-of-attorney, 30 December 1779; Joseph López de Soto, Power-of-attorney, 27 March 1782; Jacinto Sánchez, Power-of-attorney, 20 February 1783; Francisco Martínez, Power-of-attorney, 26 July 1784, Escribanía de Guerra, ANC.
62. Lavrin, "In Search of the Colonial Woman," 24–34; Arrom, *Women of Mexico City,* 26.
63. Laurel Thatcher Ulrich, *Good Wives: Image and Reality in the Lives of Women in Northern New England, 1650–1750* (New York: Oxford University Press, 1982), 35–50.
64. Juan Ignacio de Urriza to José de Gálvez, 13 May 1780, legajo 2082, SD, AGI.
65. Antonio Alonzo, Power-of-attorney (to his sister), [day illegible] January 1793; Alonzo García Cáceres, Power-of-attorney (to his wife), 19 August 1793, Escribanía de Guerra, ANC.
66. Bernardo Seguí, Power-of-attorney, 7 October 1786, reel 148, bundle 323A, Escrituras, EFP.
67. Vicente Folch, Power-of-attorney, 1 March 1783, Escribanía de Guerra, ANC.
68. Gines de Oliva, Power-of-attorney, 17 February 1792, Escribanía de Guerra, ANC.
69. Sebastián Piñero, Power-of-attorney, 9 March 1795, Escribanía de Guerra, ANC.
70. Celia María Parcero Torre, *La pérdida de La Habana y las reformas Borbónicas en Cuba (1760–1773)* (Madrid: Consejo de Castilla y León, 1998).
71. For Tomás Cotilla: Tomás Cotilla, Méritos, 20 February 1738, folio 10, legajo 148, Indiferente General, AGI, and Inspection Report, Fixed Infantry Regiment of Havana, 31 December 1765, expediente 16, legajo 7259, Guerra, AGS. For Rafael Cotilla: Governor of Santiago de Cuba to Council of the Indies, 21 February 1761, legajo 1134, SD, AGI, and Inspection Report, Fixed Infantry Regiment of Havana, 30 June 1769, expediente 15, legajo 7259, Guerra, AGS. For José Cotilla: José Cotilla, Power-of-attorney, 13 February 1767, Escribanía de Gobierno, ANC, and Inspection Report, Fixed Infantry Regiment of Havana, 30 June 1769, expediente 15, legajo 7259, Guerra, AGS. For Juan Tomás de Cotilla: Juan Tomás de Cotilla, Fianza, 11 March 1767, Escribanía de Gobierno, ANC. For Rosa Llanes Perdomo: Rosa Llanes Perdomo to the Captain General of Cuba, 3 July 1775, legajo 1154, PC, AGI, and Captain General of Cuba to Rosa Llanes Perdomo, 6 December 1775, legajo 1154, PC, AGI.
72. Inspection Report, Fixed Regiment of Havana, 30 June 1769, expediente 15, legajo 7257, Guerra, AGS; Antonio Remírez de Esteñóz, Permission to return to Havana, 29 August 1765, legajo 5508, number 1, Contratación, AGI.
73. Nicolasa Mancebo Betancort, Pension Request, 4 February 1789, expediente 44, legajo 7223, Guerra, AGS; Antonio Remírez de Esteñóz to Captain General of Cuba, 1755, legajo 7: 176, Correspondencia del Capitán General, ANC; Hilario Remírez de Esteñóz, Testament, [date illegible] August 1785, Escribanía de Guerra, ANC.
74. Hilario Remírez de Esteñóz, Power-of-attorney, 8 May 1778, Escribanía de Gobierno, ANC; Hilario Remírez de Esteñóz, Testament, Escribanía de Guerra, [date illegible] August 1785, ANC.
75. José de Cotilla, Power-of-attorney, [date illegible] September 1779; Teresa de Cotilla, Slave Sale, 20 October 1779, Escribanía de Guerra, ANC.
76. Antonio Fernández, Power-of-attorney (to Victorina Guillén), 9 October 1780; Mariano de la Roque, Power-of-attorney (to Angela Huet), 7 October 1782; Pedro Moncada, Power-of-attorney (to Maria de Berrio Campo y Cos), 30 December 1779, all Escribanía de Guerra, ANC.
77. Tomas García, Testament and Proceedings, 3 July 1794, Escribanía de Guerra, ANC.

78. Tomasa Muxica to the Cuban Captain(s) General, 19 July 1795, legajo 1470, PC, AGI.
79. Tomasa Basabe to the Cuban Captain(s) General, 15 July 1776, legajo 1153, PC, AGI.
80. Jacinto Rodríguez Pimienta, Power-of-Attorney, 19 September 1766, Escribanía de Gobierno, ANC.
81. Florencia de Linares, Land Sale, 21 September 1766, Escribanía de Gobierno, ANC. The description reads: "de que soy la dueña" (of which I am the owner).
82. Josefa Benedict Horruytiner, Land Sale, 6 May 1766, Escribanía de Gobierno, ANC.
83. Bárbara Rodríguez Sigler y Ortega, Renunciation, 28 October, 29 October 1766, Escribanía de Gobierno, ANC.
84. María Luisa de Herrera, Petition, 27 November 1792, legajo 7222, expediente 15, Guerra, AGS.
85. Rafaela Fernández to the Governor of Florida, 17 April 1809, reel 90, bundle 198C16, Papers on Various Subjects, EFP.
86. Magdalena Piña y Muñoz to the Cuban Captain(s) General, 28 January 1783, legajo 1344, PC, AGI.
87. Diego José Navarro, "Padrón General," 1778, legajo 1527, IG, AGI. During the eighteenth century, the island was divided into but two provinces: Havana in the west and Oriente in the east.
88. Herbert S. Klein, *Slavery in the Americas: A Comparative Study of Virginia and Cuba* (1967; reprint, Chicago: Ivan R. Dee, Inc., 1989), 193–227.
89. Johnson, *Social Transformation*, 66–68; Klein, *Slavery,* 211–20; Pedro Deschamps Chapeaux, *El negro en la economía habanera del siglo XIX* (Havana: Insitituto Cubano del Libro, 1971) 59–102.
90. Cristóval Carques, Power-of-attorney, 6 March 1780, Escribanía de Guerra, ANC; Inspector of the Troops to the Cuban Captain(s) General, 26 September 1783, legajo 1357, PC, AGI.
91. Cristóval Carques, Testament, 29 November 1794, Escribanía de Guerra, ANC.
92. Cristóval Carques, Power-of-attorney, 6 March 1780, Escribanía de Guerra, ANC.
93. *Papel Periódico de la Havana,* 15 November 1792, Colección Cubana, Biblioteca Nacional José Martí, Havana, Cuba.
94. "Relación que manifiesta los individuos de los cuerpos que se hallan de Guarnición en esta Plaza, y fallecieron en la conquista de Panzacola, con expreción de las Familias que dexan," 2 November 1781; "Relación de los Individuos que fallecieron en la conquista de Panzacola, a cuias viudas, padres, y madres respectivamente . . . ," 6 February 1782, legajo 6913, expediente 9, Guerra, AGS. The other recipients were María Quiros, mother of Juan Machado; María Josefa del Espíritu Santo, mother of Jacinto Navarro; Gregoria Martínez, mother of Francisco del Castillo; Agustina Bayona, wife of Basilio Pérez; María Pastora de Leon, wife of Pedro Arriasola; and María Soledad Marrero, wife of Vicente Marrero. Marcos Martínez's elderly father, Juan Antonio Martínez, also was awarded his son's benefits. Ironically, since militia members only received a salary when they were activated, the pension privileges granted to survivors may have been greater than their regular civilian wages.
95. "Certificación de las Familias de Florida," Correspondence of the Cuban Captain(s) General, 1 September 1795, legajo 412-A, PC, AGI.
96. María Teresa de Silva, Testament, 2 October 1793, Escribanía de Guerra, ANC.
97. Nicolás Sigler de Espinosa, Land Sale, 24 August 1766, Escribanía de Gobierno, ANC.
98. Whether there was a familial relationship between the two men is unclear. Juan de Dios Arenciba and Juan Bautista Arenciba may have been related, but it is more likely that they earned their freedom around mid-century from an owner named Arenciba. This is further suggested by their given names, Juan de Dios and Juan Bautista, and by the second couple's decision to give their children the surname Díaz rather than Arenciba (Juan de Dios Arenciba, Testament, 29 August 1766, Escribanía de Gobierno, ANC; Juan Bautista Arenciba and María Antonia Díaz, Testament,

"Señoras en sus clases no ordinarias" : 37

18 August 1756, Escribanía de Gobierno, ANC; Antonio José Diaz, Testament, 11 December 1795, Escribanía de Guerra, ANC).

99. Juan de Dios Arenciba, Testament, 29 August 1766, Escribanía de Gobierno, ANC.

100. Juan Bautista Arenciba and María Antonia Díaz, Testament, 18 August 1756, Escribanía de Gobierno, ANC; José Antonio Díaz, Testament, 11 December 1795, Escribanía de Guerra, ANC.

101. Antonio José Díaz, Testament, 11 December 1795, Escribanía de Guerra, ANC. The phrase reads "mi dinero."

102. María Rosario Oquendo, Land Sale, 30 March 1767, Escribanía de Gobierno, ANC.

103. *Reglamento para el govierno militar político y económico de la compañía de artillería compuesta de negros de SM y sus familias* (Havana: Imprenta de D. Blas de Olivos, 1768), in part II, box 1, folder 20, José Escoto Archive, Houghton Library, Harvard University, Cambridge, Mass. [hereafter cited as Escoto Archive].

104. Intendant of Havana to the Cuban Captain(s) General, 18 May 1773, legajo 1153, PC, AGI.

105. *Reglamento . . . de la compañía de artillería,* part II, box 1, folder 20, Escoto Archive.

106. *División de la ciudad de la Havana en quarteles . . . ,* n.d., part II, box 1, folder 20, Escoto Archive.

107. Ironically, this official provision from two centuries in the past is greater than the average allotment at present.

108. *Reglamento . . . de la compañía de artillería,* part II, box 1, folder 20, Escoto Archive.

109. A frequent, almost hallowed, theme that runs throughout Cuban historiography is the ability of Cuban planters to evade or ignore ameliorative legislation that was intended to govern the lives of slaves.

110. Antonio Abad del Rey, Testament, written 15 July 1788, probated late October 1796, Escribanía de Guerra, ANC.

111. Antonio Abad del Rey, Testament, written 15 July 1788, probated late October 1796, Escribanía de Guerra, ANC.

112. Inspection Report, Battalion of Free Mulatos, 18 February 1765, legajo 1212, SD, AGI.

113. Constable (Capitán del Partido) of Jesús María to the Cuban Captain(s) General, 3 December 1794, legajo 1471, PC, AGI.

114. Deschamps Chapeaux, *El negro,* 127–29.

MIGUEL W. RAMOS

La división de la Habana:
Territorial Conflict and Cultural Hegemony in the Followers of Oyo Lukumí Religion, 1850s–1920s

ABSTRACT

The Yoruba presence in the Americas, particularly in Brazil and Cuba, has been the topic of much research in past years. The role of the individuals who molded and guided the new directions taken by these cultural manifestations, however, continues to be virgin terrain. In particular and without doubt, women were the most important contributors to these acculturative processes. The present article examines the influence of three African women and their contribution to the evolution and survival of Lukumí religion in Cuba. In so doing, it brings to the fore other important issues that cast light on the lives of Afro-Cuban women in nineteenth-century Cuba forced to live in a Eurocentric society in which they occupied the lowest rung of the ladder. These issues highlight the hardships and impediments that in many ways all Afro-Cubans had to overcome in their struggle for power and respect—even among members of their own ethnic groups. Eventually, this struggle played an important role in the contributions made by these groups to Cuban culture and society.

RESUMEN

La presencia Yoruba en las Américas, especialmente en Brasil y Cuba, ha sido objeto de muchas investigaciones en los últimos años. El papel de los individuos que moldearon y guiaron las nuevas direcciones tomadas por estas manifestaciones culturales, continúa siendo, sin embargo, un terreno virgen. En particular, y sin lugar a dudas, las mujeres fueron las que más contribuyeron a estos procesos de aculturación. Este artículo examina la influencia de tres mujeres africanas y su contribución a la evolución y supervivencia de la religión Lukumí en Cuba. El estudio saca a la palestra otros temas de importancia que arrojan luz sobre la vida de las mujeres afrocubanas en la Cuba del siglo XIX, forzadas a vivir en una sociedad eurocéntrica en la que ocupaban el peldaño más bajo de la escalera. Estos temas enfatizan las dificultades y los impedimentos que las afrocubanas tuvieron que enfrentar en su lucha para adquirir poder y ganarse el respeto, incluso de los miembros de sus propios grupos étnicos. A la larga, esta lucha jugó un papel importante en las contribuciones de este grupo a la cultura y la sociedad cubana.

La División de la Habana : 39

In the latter half of the nineteenth century, Cuban society faced controversies that threatened to undermine the considerable economic expansion the island had recently experienced. Two important issues divided society and subverted its foundations: the barbaric institution of slavery and the illegal slave trade that brought so many human beings to the island. In the mid–nineteenth century, after the triumph of the revolution on the island of St. Domingue and the establishment of the Haitian Republic in 1803, Cuba had blossomed into Spain's most prized possession in the Caribbean. With the destruction of Haiti's sugar industry, Cuba became the world's leading sugar producer. This sudden economic expansion depended heavily on manual labor provided by African slaves. In a little over one hundred years, Cuba also had become Spanish America's largest importer of African slaves in the four-century history of the slave trade.[1] Scholarship that recognizes the contributions of Cubans of African descent in areas such as art, music, dance, religion, folklore, and herbal medicine is a fundamental part of Cuban studies.[2] On an individual level, however, it is Afro-Cuban men who claim the spotlight, while, with a few notable exceptions, Afro-Cuban women are virtually invisible.[3]

Methodological Approach

Drawing upon methodologies in history, anthropology, mythology, folklore, and on more than fifty oral testimonies collected in Cuba and outside the island, this article reconstructs the life histories of three important African priestesses of the religion Regla de Osha in the nineteenth century. It will elaborate on the existing literature in order to broaden and add depth to our understanding of the Yoruba/Lukumí culture, which represents one of the most important African groups in the New World. The anthropologist William Bascom accentuated the importance of this ethnic group when he noted that "no group has had greater influence on New World culture than the Yoruba."[4] With respect to the lives of the three women presented here, much oral history survives, recounted by their descendants, both in Cuba and throughout the Cuban Diaspora. Individuals are, perhaps, the best repositories for their own histories. Miguel Barnet's *Biography of a Runaway Slave* and Daisy Rubiera Castillo's story of her mother, *Reyita, sencillamente,* illustrate the value of oral sources and the importance — indeed, the urgency — of documenting and preserving the chronicles and accounts of the people who themselves were part of this history.[5] In the insightful words of Reyita:

Some of the things they [writers] say upset me; I don't know, I think that they do not delve deeply enough, they don't interview the elderly, after all we were the ones who suffered all those situations. I believe that as we [the elderly] die off, writers will be further distanced from the truth. Because it is not only what is said in those papers [primary documents]: those [papers], according to the proverb " 'sustain all that is placed on them.' " Another thing is how these [documents] are interpreted by each person that uses them. I recognize the effort and the determination that they put into it; but in the end, the books that result do not properly reflect the reality.[6]

Because of their gender, race, and enslaved status, the task of reconstructing the life histories of the three priestesses presented here was a challenge. Nonetheless, research reveals that these three women, and others, were important conduits of African religious beliefs. They were not simply responsible for the preservation of their beliefs, but through their personal and professional rivalry, they became the reason why the religion spread out from Havana to Matanzas. More important, their rivalry reveals more than enmity. By looking at the causes of the dispute, we have been able to establish that each of the priestesses was fighting for the supremacy of African traditions in certain of the religious ceremonies she had brought with her to Cuba. One faction fought for the supremacy of "court traditions," while another favored the less elaborate use of "regional traditions." Eventually, the more ritualistic "court traditions" became predominant in Havana, but the conflict between the two traditions demonstrates the vitality of African cultural and political survival in Cuba.

The accounts that follow are for the most part based on oral histories collected by a Lukumí priest whose insight lends an insider's perspective to this work.[7] They tell the history of a disenfranchised, mostly illiterate people. These are chronicles that the more "enlightened" sectors of Cuban society had no desire to document and/or save. Like most oral histories, Lukumí renditions can disagree over specific details, and the narrator's perspective and/or emphases can affect many aspects of the story. While it is undeniable that there are weaknesses in these accounts, especially in the various and varying versions that exist in Cuba and in the Lukumí Diaspora, there is an almost universal consensus concerning the important elements of the story, which accentuates their veracity. The oral traditions that survive in the Lukumí community are so strong that we can rely upon this consensus to confirm the validity of historic events. Ironically, this is also the story of a people whose ancestors were formidable oral historians. What more fitting tribute than to gather and recount their histories through the same medium they employed?[8]

African Antecedents

From the late eighteenth century onward, while Cuba was being transformed into a plantation society, events were unfolding on the African continent that would also have significant repercussions across the Atlantic. The Oyo Empire, a powerful political entity in West Africa for at least three centuries, had begun to buckle under pressure from various sources: internal political strife and power struggles; the revolt of the Dahomey and their ensuing slave raids into Yoruba territories that had earlier been under the protection of the Oyo; the slave trade itself; and, finally, a *jihad* conducted against the Oyo by their northern neighbors, the Fulani. The Oyo's ascendancy probably began early in the seventeenth century.[9] Like many other West African kingdoms during that time, Oyo had not become a politically unified empire until the early seventeenth century. Greatly aided by its geographic location—in an area of vast savannas—as well as by the introduction and adoption of the horse as one of its principal military resources, by the late eighteenth century the Oyo exercised considerable control in West Africa and also had become an important supplier of human cargo for the slave trade. The strategic location of the Oyo along the trans-Saharan trade routes that traversed the continent contributed to the development of the empire as well. The Oyo gained a considerable income from the sale of northern war captives and other unfortunates, who were purchased from the traders for whom Oyo was an important stop on their southward journey.[10]

The earliest evidence of Oyo involvement in the slave trade is found in the work of a Dutch writer, Olfert Dapper, published in 1668, and it clearly illustrates Oyo's active participation in the trade since at least the seventeenth century. Dating its existence to the 1640s, Dapper described "a large kingdom in the interior, north-east of Allada, called 'Ulkami' [Oyo] which sent large numbers of slaves for sale through Allada and imported salt, which was extracted locally from sea water, in exchange."[11] Later authors also spoke of trade between the Allada area and the kingdom of "Lucamee," which was reputed to be a source of cloth and slaves.[12] Still, at this early stage of the slave trade, Oyo's participation was not as considerable as it would become in the late eighteenth century.

Before the 1770s, little evidence exists to identify Oyo either as a slave-raiding state or as a major source of slaves.[13] Oyo's interest in direct participation in the slave trade probably began around 1774 during the reign of Alafin [king] Abiodun, after he overthrew the tyrant Gaha, who had headed the Alafin's governing council, the Oyo Mesi. At the time that Abiodun ascended to the throne, Gaha had been the ruling Bashorun—a sort of Prime Minister whose power often surpassed that of the king.[14] Gaha's heavy-handed domination of Oyo and its subordinated kings began in 1754 and lasted until Abiodun's ascent in 1774.[15] In 1776 the French travelers De Chenevert and Abbé Bullet reported that the Oyo were furnishing slaves at Badagry, Porto Novo, and Whydah. They described Oyo as a "free fair where the different nations resort to trade; it is the Ayaux [Oyo] who currently hold the key to trade, and through whose hands pass the greater part of the slaves who are sold on this coast."[16] Abiodun was believed to have been active in this trade before his accession to the throne, by which time Oyo had attained its greatest imperial expansion.[17]

The number of slaves supplied by Oyo for export, primarily Hausas purchased from northern trade caravans, reached its peak in the 1780s.[18] But Gaha's tyranny and his ruthless disregard of the empire's laws had set an ugly precedent that would culminate in the revolt of Oyo's subject states and the empire's demise, something Abiodun was unable to prevent.[19] By the mid 1830s, Oyo was no more.

It was during this period — of instability in Africa and the intensification of sugar production in Cuba — that the Yoruba people, then known as Lukumí, made their appearance in the Americas in considerable numbers.[20] Although some Yorubas had been present on slave plantations in the New World since at least the seventeenth century, they were not a considerable presence until the nineteenth century.[21] Thereafter, the Lukumí presence in Cuba grew at an impressive rate. In one study, for the years 1760–69, the Lukumí made up 8.22 percent of the total number of slaves in Cuba (354 slaves based on a sample population of 4,307 slaves); and even between 1800 and 1820, their numbers remained relatively unchanged, at 8.38 percent of the sample population (453 of 5,245). Fifty years later, the increase was significant. By 1850, less than twenty years after the Oyo Empire's demise, the Lukumí made up a demonstrable plurality in Cuba: almost 35 percent of the total slave population of the island.[22] This large Yoruba presence in the Americas, particularly in Brazil and Cuba, would be the most important progenitor of the Orisha religions that evolved in the Diaspora: Candomblé in Brazil and Regla de Osha in Cuba.[23]

The Priestesses

Women have always played a pivotal role in Lukumí religion.[24] According to Lukumí oral tradition, fundamental to the preservation of the Lukumí religion in Cuba were three priestesses (*iyalorishas*[25]): Ma Monserrate "Apóto" González (Obá Tero), and Ñá Rosalía Abreú (Efunshé Warikondó),[26] both believed to be from the Egbado region of Yorubaland; and Timotea Albear (Ajayí Lewú but better known as Latuán), believed to have been an Oyo native. Within the Lukumí Orisha community,[27] these three women were highly esteemed and respected for their position within the religious hierarchy and the knowledge they possessed. Of the three, only Latuán has identifiable living blood descendants. Nevertheless, all three are well remembered by their religious descendants in Cuba and abroad, who vividly keep alive many aspects of their history in the preservation of specific religious rites or traditions that are observed according to religious lineage. One of the traditional stories most present for today's practitioners of Orisha is the conflict over territory known to many as *La división de la Habana*, which resulted in the dividing up of religious jurisdiction for the island between Obá Tero and Latuán. Unintended yet important consequences of this clash were the spread of the Havana-centric Oyo-Lukumí ordination ceremony to Matanzas and the reconciliation of the Arará and the Lukumí, two related West African peoples whose already strained relationship had further deteriorated as a direct result of the slave trade.

Obá Tero (Ma Monserrate "Apoto" González)

Of the three *olorishas*,[28] the legends that surround the life and activities of Obá Tero in Matanzas represent the richest source of information. In all probability, Obá Tero was the oldest of the three, although it is impossible to know exactly when she was born. Many accounts speculate that she was well over one hundred years old when she died in 1907, from what most agree were natural causes and old age.[29] It is highly probable that Obá Tero was from the Egbado region of ancient Yorubaland and was brought to Cuba as a slave. Descendants agree that her Yoruba birth name was Apóto, and that Obá Tero — "the king has great calm" — was the name she was given when she was ordained in her native Egbado to Shangó, the *orisha* of thunder, patron deity of Oyo, and possibly one of the empire's earliest kings.

According to oral tradition, Obá Tero arrived in Cuba around the middle of the nineteenth century, possibly in the 1840s or 1850s. Because of Britain's attempts to stamp out the transatlantic slave trade, she may have been smuggled into the island on one of the many clandestine slave ships that illegally transported African slaves at that time.[30] If so, her experience would have been similar to that of Soledad Crespo, a Lukumí Obatalá priestess who probably traveled to Cuba via Sierra Leone and was smuggled into the island hidden inside a barrel.[31] Nothing is known about Obá Tero's initial years on the island. Most informants emphasized that she had been a slave on an unnamed sugar plantation, possibly in Havana province, though one source insisted that Obá Tero had been brought directly to Matanzas and not Havana.[32] The harshness of plantation life may have been one reason she was reluctant to discuss the early part of her life in Cuba with her descendants. Or, if she did discuss it, it may not have been considered relevant by her descendants, for any details that might have been known have been long forgotten.

Though the details of Obá Tero's life under slavery may have lapsed from the consciousness of her religious descendants, the pride they take in her place of origin remains extremely strong. It is universally agreed upon that Obá Tero originated in Egbado. In Matanzas, where her legacy retains much of its original purity, the lineage and its traditions were carried on by Obá Tero's immediate religious heiress Fermina Gómez (Oshabí) until 1950, and since then by Oshabí's descendants.[33] Even today, when members of the lineage discuss issues relating to religious authenticity and the group's links to Africa, which continue to be the source of many heated debates, they emphasize that they are

Lukumí Egbado and that Obá Tero was born in Egguadó (Egbado).[34] This contention is supported by the existence, within Obá Tero's *ilé osha*,[35] of *orishas* that are considered to be of Egbado origin.[36] Although Yemojá is the *orisha* that is most closely linked to the Egbado, the two *orishas* that in Cuba are most commonly associated with Egbado are Oduduwá, the eponymous progenitor of the Yoruba people, and Olokún, the Yoruba *orisha* of the ocean. While these deities are known in many areas of Yorubaland and not exclusively among the Egbado, most *olorishas* on the island consider them to be of Egbado origin, possibly because they were introduced by the Egbado. Undoubtedly, these *orishas* were of great importance in nineteenth-century Egbado. In his review of primary documents written by Europeans living in Yorubaland in the nineteenth century, Peter McKenzie stated that in 1846 "all of Ado's [an Awori-Egbado town] citizens were seen as being dedicated to one or other of these *orisá* [Oduá, Obatalá, or Yewá]."[37] So strong is the association between the two deities and this religious lineage that Obá Tero, the best-known among only a handful of Cuban *iyalorishas* with these *orishas*,[38] is the one who is credited with having introduced the worship of Oduduwá and Olokún to the island. And until around 1950, through her descendants, Obá Tero's lineage continued to be the most important source for the worship and dissemination of Olokún on the island.

There are many cultural artifacts in Oshabí's home on Salamanca Street in Matanzas, which were entrusted to her by Obá Tero upon her death in 1907, that serve as further evidence to support Obá Tero's Egbado origins. Among these are Obá Tero's drums, the only known set of "Egbado" drums that still exist in Cuba.[39] These drums were in all probability made for Obá Tero in Havana by the famous *onilú* (drum maker) Ño Filomeno García (Atandá), who is also believed to have sculpted the first set of orthodox *batá* drums in Cuba.[40] In many ways, it is ironic that elements of Obá Tero's life can be reconstructed through musical instruments that women were forbidden to play. Obá Tero probably had these drums built while she lived in Guanabacoa, a suburb of Havana, and the neighboring town of Regla, the Lukumí "cradle." Regla was an important Lukumí enclave in nineteenth- and early-twentieth-century Cuba. Many Lukumí traditions that survived in Cuba came to the island through Regla's port. During the early nineteenth century, Egbado influence appears to have been strong there. Fernando Ortiz reports that a celebration for Olokún took place in Regla on the sixth of January annually, alongside the Catholic celebration of Three King's day. Egbado drums, according to Ortiz, were played by *egguado* musicians who "knew the beats and rhythms." Eventually, Ortiz says, as these musicians died, there was no one around to replace them who knew how to play the Egbado drums. As time passed, Oyo traditions eclipsed those of the Egbado and the Oyo *batá* drums became the dominant musical instrument.[41]

Obá Tero probably acquired her freedom sometime in the late 1860s, after which she came to Havana, leaving behind the plantation and the memories of its dehumanizing system of labor. The city offered ex-slaves many possibilities in terms of employment and survival. Ortiz dates Obá Tero's presence in Havana to the early 1870s, when she and her husband Ño Julio directed a *cabildo* in Guanabacoa.[42] Around this time, Ño Julio commissioned a set of *batá* drums for the *cabildo* from the famous Havana drummakers Ño Juan "El Cojo" (Añabí) and Ño Filomeno García (Atandá).[43] Ortiz has clearly shown that Ño Julio and his wife directed the *cabildo*.[44] Although Ño Julio was important in the association, the principal *olorisha* in the *cabildo* was his wife, which oral tradition says was Ma Monserrate González—Obá Tero.

By the final quarter of the nineteenth century, Obá Tero was living on Dahoiz Street in the barrio of Alturas de Simpson, in the city of Matanzas, a place that many *olorishas* considered Matanzas's heart of Africa.[45] When Julio and Monserrate closed their *cabildo* in Guanabacoa and left for Matanzas, they took with them both the Egbado drums and the set of *batá* drums that Añabí and Atandá had constructed. Mystery surrounds the journey of the drums, and one account maintains that after Julio's death, the set of *batá* drums disappeared without a trace.[46] The mystery is complicated by the testimony of Obá Tero's religious descendants, who do not seem to know what became of them. Some even dispute or negate her role in bringing the *batá* drums to Matanzas.[47]

But, indisputably, *batá* drums did appear in Matanzas. Documentary evidence establishes the earliest usage of *batá* drums at a celebration that took place at the Cabildo Santa Bárbara on 4 December 1873:

An inspector from the town of San Francisco informed the Civil Governor of the city of Matanzas about a significant incident in the Lucumí Cabildo Santa Bárbara, situated on Manzaneda Street, on the corner of Velarde, where Ño Remigio Herrera Addéchina [Adeshina] played three strange drums he called *batá*, in the celebrations of December 3.[48]

The drummer and *babalawo*[49] Adeshina was probably the link through which Obá Tero came to reside in Matanzas. Oyo native Ño Remigio Herrera, better known by his Lukumí name Adeshina, was possibly one of the earliest *babalawos* brought to Cuba.[50] Adeshina entered Cuba through Matanzas, probably in the late 1820s, and was put to work as a slave in a sugar mill in that province. Tradition has it that soon after he came to the mill, he was recognized as an important priest by a group of fellow Lukumís who had acquired their freedom prior to his arrival. Adeshina's compatriots pooled their resources and raised enough money to purchase his freedom. Like most liberated Africans, Adeshina sought out the city, in this case Matanzas, and specifically the Simpson barrio.[51] Soon after acquiring his liberty, Adeshina established the Cabildo Lucumí Santa Bárbara at 175 Dahoiz Street, on the corner of Manzaneda Street, where he began to practice as a *babalawo*.

Adeshina had obvious ties to Matanzas since it was his point of entry to the island, but he probably moved from that city (or was at least in the process of doing so) to Havana sometime around 1866, the same year that he established the Cabildo Yemayá in Regla, which is confirmed by the commissioning of the drums for this *cabildo* in 1866.[52] According to the archival documents, by 1872, Adeshina was established in Regla in a house at 23 San Ciprián Street. The house was valued at 1,800 Spanish pesetas.[53] He was still in Regla in 1881, although by then he had moved to 31 San Ciprián Street, where he lived with his wife Francisca Buzlet, his twenty-one-year-old stepdaughter Eugenia Lausevio, his daughter Norma Josefa, better known as "Pepa," then seventeen, and his son Teodoro, fifteen.[54]

Why, then, do we find Adeshina back in Matanzas playing *batá* drums in 1873, when by that time he had already established his residence in Regla? Though it is possible that he lived in both towns and traveled back and forth, this seems unlikely, considering his advancing age and the historical period in question.[55] More likely, Adeshina, already well known in Simpson, made a trip to Matanzas to accompany Obá Tero and the drums that would be used in her *cabildo* there, as well as to introduce the priestess and the *batá* drums to the Orisha community. Ortiz has established that the use of *batá* drums in Cuba originated in Havana, in the town of Regla, where the drums were made. And according to archival records from Matanzas, until 1873 such drums were not known in that city.[56] Moreover, the oral tradition of the *batá* drummers themselves maintains that it was Adeshina who trained the first generations of *batá* drummers in that city.[57]

Adeshina, then, was most likely the connection through which Obá Tero came to reside in Matanzas. By the time of Obá Tero's move to Matanzas, the two had established a close and trusting relationship. According to all sources, they were inseparable allies. So much did Adeshina trust Obá Tero that he allowed her to ordain his daughter Pepa (Eshubí) as a priestess of Elegbá, the Orisha of destiny and the crossroads.[58] Most probably it was Adeshina who helped Obá Tero establish contact with the Lukumí of Matanzas. The *cabildo* that Obá Tero directed in Simpson was the very same Cabildo Lucumí Santa Bárbara that Adeshina had originally established there after his emancipation. The rapid growth of Obá Tero's reputation as a priestess was greatly aided by Adeshina's affirmation of her status. Many in Simpson also continued to associate the *cabildo* with Adeshina and considered it his residence in Matanzas.[59]

Obá Tero's move to Matanzas may have been propelled by a series of competitive scuffles among Havana's Lukumí *olorishas* in the latter half of the nineteenth century. In what is referred to as *La división de la Habana*, it is said that some friction developed in Havana between Obá Tero and an Oyo priestess from another Havana *ilé osha*, the distinguished Latuán. During this period, the few Lukumí *cabildos* that existed in Havana were primarily headed by emancipated *iyalorishas*, possibly of Egbado origin, who represented the earliest Yorubas brought to Cuba during the late eighteenth and early nineteenth centuries. In Africa, women had played a pivotal role in Lukumí/Yoruba religious ritual; in the Oyo palace, for example, eight *iyalorishas*, titled ladies, had tended to the Alafín's religious duties and needs.[60] By the 1860s, these *iyalorishas*, who had been transported as slaves to Cuba, wielded much power in the Lukumí community and made no effort to hide it. The Lukumí Regla de Osha that took hold on the island is indebted to the persistence, rigidity, and sturdiness of these women.[61]

Latuán (Timotea Albear)

Latuán, an Oyo priestess of Shangó, arrived in Cuba in 1863.[62] Her descendants claim that she entered the island through Matanzas, and based on the date, she probably entered clandestinely. It is not clear if Latuán worked on any of the plantations in Matanzas province for any period of time. It is known, however, that eventually she and her husband Evaristo Albear, a Congo,[63] wound up as domestic slaves in the home of Colonel Francisco Albear y Lara, a military engineer who is famous for having built a new aqueduct to supply water to Havana's then growing population, a project that lasted from 1858 to 1893.[64] It is believed that Latuán and Evaristo met on the slave ship that brought them to the New World, as her descendants insist that they met and married in Africa.[65] Since they share the Albear surname, it is highly probable that at some point they were the colonel's "property" and not just his employees. Still, her grandchildren claim that Latuán was not a slave but an *emancipada*, and insist that legislation forced Colonel Albear to teach her to read and write and to pay her a salary for her work. They say that under the series of laws that led to the gradual abolition of slavery, she had to work as an *emancipada* for a period of ten years, after which she would have been given her freedom.[66]

Latuán apparently was a favored slave in Albear's home, something suggested by her literacy, since the fact that a law existed that required masters to instruct their slaves did not necessarily mean that everyone obeyed it. Being literate afforded Latuán a strong degree of respect among her contemporaries, which further buttressed her religious hierarchy.[67] Oral sources emphasize that Latuán was an avid reader; after her emancipation, relatives say, she would not budge from her house until she had read the day's newspaper. She was very proud of this achievement and boasted about being "una negra lukumí pero yo sé las cuatro reglas. Yo sé leer y escribir!" (a black Lukumí woman but I know the four rules [of literacy]. I know how to read and write!).[68]

Latuán and Evaristo had six children: Rosa, Isabel, Dominga, Martin, Eligio, and Herminio Severino. Their grandson Martin Zurria Albear, Dominga's son and the oldest of the surviving relatives, remembers that Latuán would gather all her children and grandchildren around her on the floor so she could tell them stories of Africa and of the *orishas*. In the religious realm, Lukumís from as far away as Santiago de Cuba would travel to Havana to request her services as a priestess and Obá Oriaté — master of ceremonies[69] — especially for ordination rituals. She was well known for her profound knowledge of divination, prayers, and chants to the *orishas*, and she shared much of this knowledge with her religious descendants and followers.[70] Despite her unyielding nature in religious matters, she was described as a very gentle, soft-spoken, and well-mannered woman who treated everyone with the utmost respect.

Sometime during the 1870s Latuán became affiliated with a *cabildo* in Havana, where she eventually exercised considerable influence in her capacity as Obá Oriaté. The *cabildo* was known only by its address, San José 80, which was in the Atarés section of Havana. It was considered an authoritative Lukumí cult house, and many powerful priestesses of the era were associated with it. In the nineteenth and twentieth centuries, Atarés was an African enclave within the city of Havana. The Cabildo San José 80 had probably been founded by the first wave of Lukumís who came to reside in the city in the latter eighteenth century. Many of the Cabildo's founders are remembered in the prayers or salutations that are recited at the onset of most rituals. It was also presumably at the Cabildo San José 80 that Latuán met Efunshé, the other important priestess who would be involved in the subsequent struggle for power and territory.[71]

Efunshé (Ña Rosalía Abreú)

Like Latuán, Efunshé was a highly respected and revered Lukumí *olorisha* in Havana. She was an Egbado, like Obá Tero, and possibly of royal origin. Some of her religious descendants insist that Efunshé was a princess in Africa. They emphasize that her disciples never allowed her to walk in the city; instead, they transported her around Havana in a sedan chair.[72] This emphasis on Efunshé's royal roots possibly is justification for the fact that she occupied the role of "queen" of the Cabildo San José 80. Efunshé's importance was unquestionable. At times, her personal presence there even overshadowed the important role of the *cabildo* as an institution. In the 1950s, for example, the researcher Lydia Cabrera confused Efunshé's name with that of the *cabildo* she directed, writing that "Efuché [was] the name of a late-nineteenth-century *cabildo* in Havana."[73] How Efunshé arrived in Cuba is somewhat of a mystery, since most sources stress that she did not come to the island as a slave. Efunshé may have been one of those few fortunate Africans who, having been smuggled into the island prior to the emancipation decrees, nevertheless gained their freedom immediately after arrival. Another possibility is that Efuché may have purchased her liberty elsewhere in the Caribbean and then traveled to Cuba in search of work.

The facts surrounding Efunshé's arrival are not the only enigmas, as various other unanswered questions surround her. Efunshé seems to have left no trace whatsoever of her life before arriving in Havana. To start, there is some confusion about her Spanish surname: Abreú, Agramosa, Gramosa, Rosalía, and Rosarena have all been mentioned as possible surnames for the Lukumí princess. Most *olorishas* refer to her as Ña Rosalía, or by her Lukumí name, Efunshé, but they seldom mention a Spanish surname. Present thinking is that Abreú was most probably her name.[74] Two sources say that she was originally brought to a sugar mill in Havana province, the Ingenio Agramosa (or Gramosa), which belonged to a family of the same name, but thus far, no records of this sugar mill have been found.[75] Roque Duarte, the oldest Obá Oriaté in the United States, in a work in progress on Lukumí religion, uses Rosalía as her surname, referring to Efunshé as Ña Victoriana Rosalía.[76] Rosarena, another name that has appeared, may have been derived from Rosalía.

Additionally, Efunshé has no living blood descendants. Only one daughter has been identified with any degree of confidence: Calixta Morales (Odé Deí). In apparent compliance with societal norms, Africans gave their children Spanish names, but many Cuban Lukumí also gave them extra-official African names.[77] Odé Deí, therefore, is also known by her Lukumí name, Atikeké ("small gift"), a name that was usually given in recognition of a deity's intervention in the person's birth. Odé Deí's Lukumí birth name suggests that Efunshé may have had problems conceiving the child and that she was considered as a gift from the deities.[78] The oral record also mentions two other relatives, either daughters or nieces, depending on the variant of the story. These two women are only known to us by their Lukumí names, Ashijú and Ashijú'rolá. One other possible relation was Kaindé, a *babalawo* associated with the Cabildo San José 80 who many say was married to Efunshé.[79] There is even some contradiction regarding Efunshé's *orisha*.[80] While most informants agree that she was ordained to Oshosi, some believe she was a priestess of Yewá, and at least one source has connected her with Obatalá. The link with Obatalá may derive from her name, which some believe alludes to *efún*, a white chalk used for Obatalá's worship.[81]

What is certain is that by the 1870s Efunshé and Latuán had joined forces and had established a strong reputation in Havana. Latuán acted as Obá Oriaté for all of her godchildren (*omó orisha*, literally, "child in *orisha*"), including Odé Deí, who was ordained by Efunshé's first godchild in Cuba, Luis Suarez (Oshún Miwá). In the late 1800s, Efunshé inherited the direction of San José 80, and she ordained various *olorishas* in Havana in the last quarter of the nineteenth century.[82] Until her death in the late 1920s, she and Latuán continued to work side by side, and Latuán was the Obá Oriaté for many of the ordinations conducted by Efunshé.[83] It is highly probable that Latuán either performed or directed Efunshé's funerary rituals.[84] Efunshé's influence was so strong that even today most practitioners of Lukumí religion in Havana claim to be descended directly from her, and not from the Cabildo San José 80.[85] For the most part, oral historians agree that when Latuán and Efunshé directed San José 80, the two priestesses were very close and expressed a mutual admiration for one another.

Efunshé's role in *La división de la Habana* is not clear. Obviously, she was a participant, since she was directing the Cabildo when the struggle took place. It is quite possible that she was the main protagonist in the contest, although she may have chosen to remain behind the scenes. One variant of the story of *La división de la Habana* insists that the real rivalry was not between Latuán and Obá Tero, but between Efunshé and Latuán, and that Latuán's move to Buena Vista in Marianao occurred as a result of friction with Efunshé.[86] There is little evidence to support this account; indeed, there is strong evidence to the contrary. What we can surmise is that there was a great deal of cooperation or, at the very least, some level of compromise between Latuán and Efunshé, for the rituals of their two lineages, unlike those of Obá Tero's, vary little, if at all, to this day. At the very least, we can conclude that Efunshé supported Latuán throughout *La división*, allowing the process to play itself out, which eventually brought a result that benefited everyone involved.

Origin of the Dispute

Both Latuán and Obá Tero are revered today, and few Lukumís recall the territorial clash that resulted in Obá Tero's decision to leave Guanabacoa and move to Simpson. Of those who do remember, still fewer can say what led Obá Tero to move to the second most important city of the western end of the island. In the growing Lukumí community, which was expanding to include non-Lukumís as well, power and prestige were inseparable allies that everyone sought to attain and to maintain. Within their own "territories" in Havana, the Lukumí set their own rules. Anything or anyone that would counter any aspect of these rules was considered a threat. In a society where Africans and their descendants occupied the lowest rungs of the social ladder, the Lukumí fought tenaciously to retain their hard-won status, even if this meant resorting to *ogú* (spiritual power) and slander. The friction between Obá Tero and Latuán became much more than a contest for popularity, escalating to become a subtle, although by no means discreet, war that lasted for several years. Within the established rules of the combat, both *iyalorishas* used every resource at their command, including negative propaganda, intimidation, and spiritual power.

The propaganda became so vitriolic that Obá Tero's *cabildo* became known disparagingly as the Cabildo Alakisá — the House of Rags.[87] Eventually, after numerous encounters and scuffles, the two factions reached an understanding. Obá Tero moved to Matanzas, and Latuán, whom most say was the victor, stayed in Havana. From that day forward, neither priestess would set foot in the other's "kingdom."[88]

Beyond personal animosity and professional rivalry, however, several other factors contributed to *La división de la Habana*. West African antecedents probably fostered some bitterness between the Egbado and the Oyo. The Egbado in Yorubaland had been "very loyal subjects of the Alafin [king of Oyo]" since at least the mid–seventeenth century. But that did not necessarily mean that they were on the best of terms with the Oyo people, whose numerous incursions into Egbado territory in the latter half of the 1700s subjected the Egbados to Oyo rule.[89] Those Egbado who had suffered as a result of the Oyo's incursions, those who possibly lost relatives, or whose offspring or siblings had been captured as war bounty and sold as slaves, would not have held the Oyo in high esteem.

In Cuba, there were clear signs of unresolved tensions between the two groups. Many Egbados had been brought to Cuba in the late 1700s when the port town of Regla, which would soon become an important Lukumí enclave, was in its infancy. The number of Oyo slaves in Cuba would grow considerably after the 1780s, which signaled the onset of friction in West Africa that eventually escalated and led to the empire's downfall in the 1800s. But the Egbados definitely preceded the Oyos in Cuba. In the early nineteenth century, the Kingdom of Dahomey had rebelled against Oyo, extending its slave raids into southern Yoruba territories, including Egbado, that had formerly enjoyed Oyo's protection. As a consequence, the Dahomey enslaved many Egbado citizens and shipped them to the New World, especially to Cuba. At the time, the Oyo were too preoccupied with their own troubles to reprimand Dahomey for its defiance, and the empire stood silently by while its territories were invaded.[90] Accordingly, in Cuba, Egbado traditions originally dominated Lukumí religious practices, particularly in Regla. It was not until about 1825, then, that Oyo practices became paramount.[91]

As the Oyo grew in numbers and importance in Havana, they sought to expand their political and cultural hegemony by establishing their patterns of ordination and worship as the official patterns for Lukumí religion in Cuba. In the environs of Havana, until the Oyos' arrival in large numbers, the Lukumí religion had been conducted in a manner similar to the more personal, family-oriented worship that was commonly practiced in Yoruba compounds in Africa. In that system, the *orisha* was consecrated for the entire compound or household. Through possession or consulting the oracles, a representative from the family was selected to attend to the deity's worship, and certain ceremonies were performed to grant this individual the right to do so. This person, although considered an *olorisha* because he or she attended to the deity, was not duly ordained into the priesthood; that is, he or she was not "crowned." After having been so empowered, he or she could perform cleansing rituals, divination, offerings, and other rites for the compound or community, rites that elsewhere were typically performed by an ordained *olorisha*. Upon the individual's death, a relative previously chosen by the deceased or determined in divination would inherit the deity. This type of worship in Cuba was called *santo parado* (standing saint), or *santo de dotación* (workgang's saint).[92]

In contrast, the ordination of an *olorisha* in urbanized areas around Havana was much more complex, as it followed the intricate and highly ritualized patterns that had been used in the courts and royal palaces of Oyo and Oyo-influenced areas of ancient Yorubaland. All the areas in West Africa that had come under Oyo influence — Egbado among them — had been inculcated into the worship of Shangó, Oyo's patron *orisha*, and by extension, had been influenced by Oyo's rituals.[93] The Lukumí ordination ceremony, *kariosha*, is referred to as "crowning." In the words of Efunshé's daughter, Odé Deí: "Hacer santo es hacer rey. Y kariocha es una ceremonia de reyes, como las del palacio del Obá Lucumí" (To make saint [to be ordained to an *orisha*] is to make royalty. And *kariocha* [the ordination ceremony] is a royal ceremony, like those from the palace of the Lukumí [Oyo] king).[94]

Traditionally, when devotees spoke of ordination, they commonly referred to it as *coronar santo* (crowning the saint). In fact, even today, on the second day of the Oyo-centric Havana ordination ritual, the ritual garments include a very elaborate crown that is placed on the novice's head by the godparent or sponsoring *olorisha*. Most important, Havana's *orisha* rituals revolve around the Obá Oriaté, the master of ceremonies for all rituals, an indispensable religious specialist who performs the majority of ordination and consecration rites in the religion. While it is still unclear whether the Obá Oriaté existed in African tradition, in all probability this role would have fallen to the priestesses who served the Alafín in the Oyo palace.[95] The word *obá* (king) in the title Obá Oriaté is a clear reflection of the importance of this rank, and the religious dictates of the individual who holds this rank, like the Alafín's secular proclamations, are considered "law."

As Oyo natives displaced Egbados, the Havana rite of ordination into Regla de Osha became extremely Oyo-centric, and Havana became the center for the later dissemination of these traditions to other areas of the island. Not surprisingly, Havana practitioners sought to maintain their predominance by making the royal Oyo coronation ceremony the only legitimate ordination ritual of Lukumí religion on the island. Illustrative of such attempts to enforce Oyo hegemony is the case of Octavio Samá (Adeosun), better known as Obadimejí. Samá, born of Lukumí parents, became one of the most controversial and influential individuals in the history of Lukumí religion on the island. When he arrived in Havana from his native Sabanillas in the early twentieth century, Samá sought to establish his religious practice in the city by identifying with the Lukumí religious community there. He claimed to have been ordained to Oshún, the Lukumí *orisha* of sensuality and beauty, in Sabanillas by his Lukumí family. The Havana community refused to recognize his claim and insisted that he submit to initiation in Havana's Oyo-centric ordination rite. Samá was definitely well versed in Lukumí rituals and even spoke the Lukumí language fluently. In fact, his Lukumí was much better than his Spanish. Although he was a Creole, it is said that he spoke Spanish like a *bozal,* a derogatory term that was used to describe newly arrived slaves.[96]

Latuán, who by this time had established a strong reputation as one of the most respected and powerful Lukumí *olorishas* and Obá Oriatés in Havana, insisted that Samá's ordination in Sabanillas had not been orthodox. By her decree, Samá was ordained in Havana, not to Oshún but to Aganjú, *orisha* of the deserts and patron of travelers. Latuán performed the ordination herself. On the third day of the ordination, in a ceremony during which divination is performed for the novice and the *orishas* express their prescriptions and proscriptions through the oracles, it was revealed that Samá had not lied about his earlier ordination. As a result, he was given the name Obadimejí— "he who is crowned twice." Actually, the term translates literally as "king becomes two," but in Cuba it is interpreted as I have given it here.

In the years following this controversy, any resentment that may have developed between Latuán and Obadimejí as a consequence of her challenge to his legitimacy was put aside, and until her death in February 1935 they remained great friends. Indeed, one of Cabrera's informants told her that Obadimejí and Latuán were inseparable. In fact, the informant hinted at a conspiracy between the two to reordain and/or limit the functions of *olorishas* from the Cuban countryside.[97] It is known that Latuán often boycotted the rites of *olorishas* whose ordinations she considered doubtful by Havana standards, by refusing to lend her services as Obá Oriaté.[98] If Latuán refused to participate, no other Obá Oriaté would dare to challenge her authority by performing a rival ceremony. Apparently, despite the deference she enjoyed from most of her contemporaries, Latuán continued her power struggles for leverage and hegemony well into the twentieth century.

Obadimejí became Latuán's only recognized male disciple, working alongside her and serving as her arms and eyes after she became too old to perform rituals herself. Interestingly, after Latuán's death, the position of Obá Oriaté became dominated by men, who gradually displaced the women who until that time had exercised the office. By the time of Obadimejí's death in October 1944, the Obá Oriaté position was an almost exclusively male function. Obadimejí trained two known disciples, Tomás Romero (Ewín Letí) and Nicolás Valentín

Angarica (Obá Tolá). Despite having been mentored by some of the greatest *iyalorishas* in Lukumí religion, he never trained a woman.[99]

La division de la Habana

The coronation of Obadimejí and his subsequent leadership within the Cabildo, contrasts sharply with the rivalry that developed between Latuán and Obá Tero. Theirs grew out of the variations that existed between Egbado rites and those of the growing Oyo-centric groups. At the heart of the controversy was Obá Tero, who opposed the new reforms or variations that had been brought to Havana, which stressed the already contentious relationship that existed between Obá Tero and the rest of the community.[100] Obá Tero was an Oní Shangó[101]; she had been ordained in what seems to have been an Egbado palace tradition and was obviously influenced by Oyo, although her practice entailed significant regional differences. Although many of Obá Tero's Egbado ritual practices did not conform to the growing Oyo-centric Havana tradition, her ordination and status, in effect, her legitimacy as an *iyalorisha*, were never questioned. Because of common beliefs, her ordination was considered valid by Oyo, and thereby Havana, standards. By itself, her ordination to Shangó, her tutelar *orisha*, was sufficient proof that her coronation conformed to Oyo tradition.[102] She definitely was recognized as a valid and orthodox *iyalorisha*.

While avoiding any overt challenge to Obá Tero's legitimacy, Latuán, at the forefront of the Oyo Court tradition in Havana, did challenge certain procedural aspects of Obá Tero's Egbado rites that were uncommon among the Oyo, and this was the basis of the rivalry between the two. Moreover, Obá Tero contended that Latuán was reforming the religion to cater to other Africans and to the growing presence of whites and mulattos.[103]

Efunshé sided with Latuán against Obá Tero, introducing many adaptations to the Lukumí religion in Havana as well as some rituals that had not been known before her arrival. Some informants say that, before Efunshé came to Cuba, it was the case that during a new *olorisha*'s consecration she would be provided with two *orishas*: Elegbá, the *orisha* of the crossroads, as well as the specific tutelar deity that had been identified for the initiate by the oracles. This custom was typically referred to as *pie y cabeza* ("feet and head"), as the novice was provided with her/his tutelary *orisha*—the "head" *orisha*—as well as the *orisha* of the crossroads, which represented the "feet" with which one would travel along life's road. If the individual needed any other *orishas*, the oracles would determine that on the third day of the ordination ceremony. Oral tradition claims that when Efunshé came to Cuba, she introduced a number of additional *orishas* into the ordination ceremony. Perplexingly, in spite of Efunshé's Egbado origin, the Lukumí consider that most of these *orishas* have strong ties with Shangó, and thereby Oyo, not Egbado, tradition. Four *orishas*—Obatalá, Yemojá, Oshún, and Shangó—along with Elegbá, are often considered the principal pillars of the Lukumí ordination.[104]

On the one hand, variations in ritual practices were not uncommon in Lukumí religion; each Lukumí group brought its own traditions to the island. Traditions varied considerably from one group to another, and distinctions often existed even within members of a single group. In all probability, these differences had their origins in Yorubaland and were then strongly enforced by the Lukumís in Cuba, who needed to reinforce a sense of connection with their lost homeland. The members of the Cabildo Iyesá Moddún in Simpson, all blood relatives, provide an excellent example of this type of tenacity. To this day, the Cabildo continues to follow the African traditions from its territory of Ijeshá, and they have not acceded to either Oyo or Egbado pressure. It should be noted that Ijeshá territory was never penetrated by the Oyos' cavalry because of its location in a heavily forested area of the country where horses were ineffective. Although they paid yearly tributes, the Ijeshá were never considered Oyo subjects. Indeed, the Ijesha were typically mocked by the Oyo as an inferior people, which was possibly a way to divert attention from the embarrassment occasioned by the Oyos' inability to penetrate the Ijesha forests.[105] Perhaps the refusal to accept Oyo-centric religious influences as practiced in Cuba reflects a continuation of the Ijesha's historical resistance to Oyo hegemony.

On the other hand, what constituted the exact procedure for the *pie y cabeza* rite is contested. While the rituals inherent in *pie y cabeza* in all likelihood reflect the older, rural *santo parado* tradition, there is no evidence that the *pie y cabeza* consecration was limited to only two *orishas*. This custom of receiving various *orishas* seems to have African antecedents, for it is paralleled by similar practices in Brazilian Candomblé.[106] It does not seem likely, then, that Efunshé introduced additional deities to the ordination. Rather, what is most probable is that she introduced the Oyo-centric palace tradition of the crowning ceremony, the *kariosha*, which then gradually supplanted the rural, *santo parado* tradition.[107]

Obá Tero refused to practice according to the new standards or alter her rites in any way. She, too, may have introduced some Oyo influences from Yorubaland, but apparently they were not sufficient to placate Latuán. Indeed, one of the fundamental traits of Obá Tero's character was her unyielding nature, and the controversies in Havana earned her a disparaging nickname: la Reina de Quitasol (literally, the "Queen of Take-Away-Sun," or the one who makes the day cloudy). Eventually, Obá Tero came to be seen as a heretic whose rituals varied from those of the more powerful faction; in other words, Obá Tero's rituals "clouded" the rites of the contending faction by flying in the face of the system Latuán and her supporters were trying to impose. This perception worked in Latuán's favor, as many *olorishas*, both deliberately and unintentionally, used the disagreement between the two priestesses to foment additional tensions. It is worth noting that Latuán did not have any difficulties with the other Egbado *olorishas* who practiced in Havana; perhaps this was because not all Egbados were as contentious and rigid as Obá Tero.

Obá Tero in Matanzas

As a consequence of the bad blood between the two reigning priestesses, Obá Tero relocated to Simpson, where she introduced the unknown Oyo-Egbado ordination ritual to the residents of Matanzas. She is therefore credited with having brought the *kariosha* ceremony to Matanzas, from whence it spread to other areas of the island.[108] Controversy followed Obá Tero to Simpson. Soon after her arrival, she once again found herself engulfed in a religious conflict with a Matanzas *olorisha* over the legitimacy of the ordination of Fermina Gómez (Oshabí). Oshabí was a Creole, born on a sugar plantation, where her mother María Elena Gómez (Balagún) had been brought as a slave from the Kalabar area of West Africa. Balagún was ordained to Oshosi in Cuba by Obá Tero. Oshabí's father, Florentino Gómez, was an Egbado. He was apparently involved with Egúngún worship in Matanzas, and was called Elepirí, a name that may reflect some ties with the Yoruba Egúngún cult.[109] Some sources say that he was in charge of the masks used for Egúngún rituals in the city.[110]

Oshabí had been ordained to Oshún in the 1870s by Ño José (Ikudaisí), in what seems to have been the rural *santo parado* tradition. One source insists that Ikudaisí was Oshabí's paternal grandfather.[111] Oshabí's paternal family was Erómele, an obscure Egbado subgroup that in all probability are the Egbado Imálà.[112] One researcher has said that the Imálà were mostly Egbados who migrated south from Oyo during the middle and latter part of the eighteenth century.[113] Presumably, Ikudaisí, who is alleged to have also lived in Regla, was responsible for having brought Oro dancing and Egúngún masks and dancing to Matanzas.

Ironically, Oshabí's life took a terrible turn soon after her ordination ritual. Word of the situation reached Obá Tero, who sent for Oshabí and, through divination, determined that the calamities she was facing had occurred because her ordination had been improper. To correct the mistake, the ordination had to be revalidated. To make matters worse, Obá Tero claimed that Oshabí had been ordained to the wrong *orisha*! Obá Tero reordained her, this time to her "true" *orisha*, Yemojá.[114] Needless to say, the decision to reordain Oshabí brought Obá Tero serious problems with Ikudaisí, and in a stark reminiscence of *La división de la Habana,* soon after, the two *olorishas* were at war. But this time Obá Tero was determined to win, and in so doing, she established an unassailable reputation in Simpson as an extremely powerful and knowledgeable priestess.

A few days after Obá Tero had concluded Oshabí's reordination, sometime after midnight, Ikudaisí came to the Cabildo's door and began to perform a ritual that he boasted would teach his rival a lesson. But Shangó, Obá Tero's *orisha*, had other plans. The unsuspecting *iyalorisha* was already asleep when Shangó possessed her, and she ran to the door and caught Ikudaisí in the act. Ikudaisí was shocked. Dumbfounded, he stumbled and fell, then immediately jumped to his feet and deliriously ran down the street, fearing Shangó's wrath. The commotion awakened Obá Tero's neighbors, who came out to see what was going on. Immediately, Shangó performed a ceremony in the doorway to overturn Ikudaisí's *ogú*. When she returned from her possessed state, Obá Tero was puzzled and wanted to know what had happened to her. When her neighbors told her what had occurred, she was outraged![115]

Hostilities between the two *olorishas* lasted for months. Whenever Ikudaisí had to walk down Obá Tero's block, he would cross to the opposite side of the street to avoid any encounters with his feared rival. Nevertheless, Ikudaisí continued to discredit Obá Tero wherever he went and persisted with his spiritual attacks against her. Although he never dared return to her doorstep again, he sent envoys to throw medicinal powders and other *ogú* in her doorway. At first, Obá Tero simply chose to ignore Ikudaisí's futile threats and remedied the situation with minor rituals to protect her house against him and his magic. Shangó was another issue, though, and he was losing patience. One day, just before noon, the enraged *orisha* again possessed Obá Tero. Tradition insists that she behaved like the dark, menacing clouds raging with lightning flashes that roam the sky at the onset of the violent storms that are so typical both in Africa and the Caribbean.

Shangó dashed out to the wooden bowl that rested atop the inverted mortar where Obá Tero kept his attributes and took one of his most sacred emblems, the lightning stone (*edún ará*), from the bowl. Myth says that such stones accompany the bolts of lightning that the *orisha* propels from the heavens to castigate the wicked. Shangó ran out the doorway with the stone, and then walked to Ikudaisí's house and stood in his doorway. Holding the stone in his hand, Shangó performed a rite with the stone and yelled to the heavens. Soon after, the skies darkened and an ominous thunderstorm ensued. Lightning strikes were reported all over the town, but one very symbolic bolt struck right in front of Ikudaisí's door, in the same spot where Obá Tero, possessed by Shangó, had stood a while earlier. Mysteriously, Ikudaisí died the following day and Obá Tero was hailed as the victor.[116]

In spite of the teleological echoes in this story, believers are convinced that *La división de la Habana* and Obá Tero's subsequent relocation to Matanzas were the result of a supernatural intervention, whose intentions reached beyond the petty human issues involved in the disputes. In the thirty years that she lived in Simpson, Obá Tero revolutionized the practice of Regla de Osha in the town, and by extension, the entire province. She completely reformed Matanzas Lukumí practices by introducing her Egbado ordination rituals as they had been practiced in the ancient Yoruba palaces and in Havana. Before her arrival in Simpson, there had been no orthodox ordinations in that city, at least not the type of ordination that would have been considered orthodox by Havana's criteria, the *kariosha*. That ritual eventually became the acceptable ordination rite for the entire island. Additionally, after her clash with Ikudaisí, Obá Tero's reputation as a powerful priestess and mount of Shangó was unassailable. No one dared to doubt her knowledge, and any skeptics that may have had their reservations were too impressed — possibly intimidated — to dare to voice them.

Obá Tero's arrival in Matanzas had one other important repercussion. Although the details are a bit vague, she was the principal influence in reuniting two African ethnic groups that had been archenemies in West Africa: the Lukumís and the Arará, so-called by traders because their origins were at the port of Allada in the ancient kingdom of Dahomey. Since its inception as a state on the West African coast, the kingdom of Dahomey had had a significant impact on neighboring coastal areas. Dahomey often disrupted the flow of slaves from the interior, as well as sowing seeds of disruption at the compounds where slaves were held awaiting European slave ships. Eventually, these disruptions affected the trade of neighboring peoples so much that the Oyos decided to take action against the younger kingdom. Francisco Pereyra Mendes, the director of the Portuguese slaving port of Whydah, reported that around April 1726, the Oyos began a series of devastating invasions into Dahomey.[117]

Oyo attacks continued for the remainder of the decade, so that by 1730 the Dahomeans came under the domain of the northern empire, agreeing to pay Oyo a yearly tribute. But Dahomey encountered difficulties in fulfilling the terms of their agreement with Oyo, which brought further Oyo hostilities down upon them. Finally, in 1748, both states reached an agreement that would stay in force until the onset of Oyo political unrest in the late 1770s. By that time, Oyo had also incorporated much of northern Yorubaland and was receiving considerable revenue in the form of tribute from various other Yoruba states (including Owu, Egba, Ketú, Sabe, Egbado, Ilesha, Ilá, Ijebú, and Dahomey). One result of the Oyo invasions of Dahomey was that many Arará found themselves on slave ships bound for the Caribbean. Their arrival in Cuba preceded that of their Oyo-Lukumí foes by almost one hundred years.[118]

Resentment and bitterness, legacies of Africa, marked the relationship between the two groups on the island. This clash, which probably existed since at least the late eighteenth century, intensified during the nineteenth century with the increased presence on the island of enslaved Lukumís. As the number of liberated Lukumís grew, a confrontation between the two groups became inevitable. By the nineteenth century, emancipated Lukumís andArarás had been forced by circumstance or necessity to live in the same cities or towns, and sometimes even in adjacent houses or *solares* (housing complexes). Tradition emphasizes that although the two groups exhibited some level of tolerance for one another, for the most part they tried to keep their distance. Although the Lukumí and Arará religions are sister religions, and many Lukumí deities had been adopted by the Arará in West Africa, the religious rituals of one group were often declared off limits to the other and seldom would an Arará visit a Lukumí *cabildo* or vice-versa.

Oral tradition emphasizes that at some point, possibly around the 1890s or early 1900s, at the behest of the deities, the Lukumí began to share their knowledge with the Arará. Before that time, Cuban Arará religion had not been as heavily influenced by the Lukumí as it is at present. Evidence indicates that Lukumí influence on Arará religious practices was born in Matanzas during this particular period.[119] Any initiate familiar with the current Arará ordination ritual will find an unmistakable Lukumí influence that is a definite Cuban product and not something brought over from Africa. The Obá Oriaté, an important hierarchical figure in the Lukumí priesthood, now plays an important role in Arará rituals as well. The Obá Oriaté — a master of ceremonies who directs and presides over all rituals — is considered the utmost source of ritual knowledge. Likewise, the Lukumí oracles, the use of divination with sixteen cowries *(Dilogún)*, and divination using four pieces of coconut *(Obí)* have all achieved importance in Arará rites.[120] The Obá Oriaté's participation in Arará ordination rites has become as indispensable as it is in Lukumí ritual. For this fusion to have occurred, the Lukumís and Ararás had to declare a truce in their embittered relationship. In all probability, as suggested by testimony from various sources, this truce was influenced by Obá Tero after her arrival in Simpson because of her reputation as an orthodox and powerful priestess that she so ardently fought to maintain.

According to oral testimony, sometime at the turn of the century, an important religious celebration took place in Simpson. The exact nature of the ceremony is no longer recalled, though it was possibly a *wemilere* — a festivity that involves drumming and chanting and possession by the deities — and that it had been requested by the oracles at the annual divination ritual.[121] The exact location of the observance is not known. Both Lukumís and Ararás were present, which perhaps indicates that the tension between the two groups had already started to abate. Present at the celebration were Obá Tero and Micaela Arzuaga (Melofo), an important Arará priestess who had founded the Cabildo Arará Sabalú in that city. It was on that day that Flora Heredia's life — and by extension all of Arará culture — would take an interesting and highly significant turn. Subsequent events, whose seeds were planted at that particular *wemilere,* would create a strong alliance between the two groups and change Heredia's life forever.

Heredia, or Florita, as her descendants know her, was a Creole of partial Lukumí descent. From birth, the oracles had identified her as a daughter of Oshún, the Lukumí Venus, but at the time of the celebration she had not yet been ordained. She was a young woman, possibly in her twenties, and that day Florita was enjoying the celebration, dancing somewhere toward the back of the room where the drums were playing, as the uninitiated are required to do. At some point, Towossi (an Arará *vodún* related to death) and Oshún joined the faithful in possession and were dancing to the beat of the drums. If there was tension among the human worshippers, there seems to have been none among the deities, for they shared the same ritual space without any semblance of animosity whatsoever. Towossi turned and caught a glimpse of Florita and then suddenly turned to face Oshún, asking, "Oshún, may I have your daughter?" Oshún, according to the story, answered unhesitatingly, "Sure," — and kept on dancing. But then, possibly because of Towossi's relationship with death, Oshún's worst enemy, it struck her and she asked: "Towossi, what do you want with my daughter?" To which the other deity answered, "I do not want to harm your daughter in any way. Instead, I want to take her somewhere where the people have no leader, no direction. Somewhere she has never been, where I will make her a queen and give her more than you could ever imagine. Give her to me and I'll bring her to rule over my people, and together, our people will know peace." "Let us take her there together, then," answered Oshún.[122] If the gods ordained it, the devotees could do little but abide by their deities' wishes and accept their guidance.

Soon after, in the first of its kind, Florita was ordained to Towossi in a ritual directed by both Arará and Lukumí priestesses and priests. In the ordination, she was named Afoare. Obá Tero directed the ritual, functioning as the Obá Oriaté, and in so doing, she began the process of teaching the *kariosha* ceremony and the use of Lukumí oracles to the Arará who would eventually incorporate much of this knowledge into their own rituals. Like the Lukumí *olorishas* initiated in the *santo parado* tradition, prior to Florita the Arará had not "crowned" their priests and priestesses. Rather, they had consecrated a *fodún* (*vodún*), as dictated by individual necessity, preparing and instructing the devotee in the particulars related to that deity so that he or she could attend to it properly.

Obá Tero's gifts to the Arará were numerous. The geographical proximity of these two peoples in West Africa cannot be ignored, and it is highly probable that diffusion preceded their reencounter in Cuba. Many of the ceremonies that Obá Tero is believed to have shared may not have been new to the Arará. Possibly, the rituals practiced by Obá Tero may have simply reawakened dormant Arará rituals in Matanzas, allowing them to thrive and coexist with Lukumí rituals. One of many possible examples of this revitalization is the current Arará use of cowries and coconuts for divination. Though the Arará had used cowries and coconuts for ritual divination in Dahomey, sources stress that they had not made use of these oracles in Cuba, at least not until the Lukumí shared them with the Arará. Until then, they had been strictly Lukumí possessions.[123] Following the patterns of the Lukumí ordination ritual, the Arará now consecrate a set of *dilogún* for each *fodún* at the time of the ordination of the *asió* (the Arará novice), and on the third day of the ordination, like the Lukumí *orishas*, each *fodún* now communicates the prescriptions and proscriptions through the *dilogún* oracle.

Obá Tero continued working as an Obá Oriaté for the Arará, in many ways bridging the differences between them, until her death in 1907, at which time her religious progeny, Oshabí, took over. The first Arará Oriaté, trained by Oshabí, did not arise until shortly before her death in 1950. As foretold by Towossi, Afoare grew to become the most renowned Arará priestess in Simpson, revitalizing the Arará rituals and invigorating them with a new energy provided by the Lukumí transfusion. Like the unification of power in Havana, for the most part the Arará and Lukumí in Matanzas put aside their political rivalries born of conflict in Africa and allowed similarities in belief to fuse in the New World. In so doing, they gave birth to a new manifestation of Arará religion. By the 1950s, when Cabrera was conducting fieldwork in Matanzas, the relationship between the two groups was definitely amicable, so much so that in Cabrera's legendary study, *El Monte,* the Arará often seem to be just another Lukumí ethnic group and not an individual nation. Cabrera even mentions an Arará informant named Salakó, clearly a Lukumí name, given to a child who is born in a caul.[124] At present, there is a strong unity between the two religious communities in Simpson that has overcome tensions that existed between them in the past. Many Lukumí actively participate in Arará ceremonies, and vice-versa, something that both groups say was unheard of until Obá Tero's arrival in Matanzas.

Conclusion

In a century of rapid expansion and constant change, Africans and their descendants in Cuba were not very different from the rest of Cuban society in that they attempted to transform their world and lay the foundations for their permanence on the island. In all respects, it was a contest in which all participants sought one thing and one thing only: power. Those who had it were not willing to part with it, even if this power was in the limited realm allowable to Afro-Cubans. Those who sought power used whatever means they had available in a society that placed limitations on them because of the color of their skin. Lukumí natives such as Obá Tero, Latuán, Efunshé, and others, no strangers to power and power struggles themselves, reflected the dominant trend of the society and attempted to carve out their niche on the island, a sort of refuge that for Afro-Cubans was impossible to separate from the religious realm.

For most Africans, and especially the Lukumí, religion is not an element in their life but rather a *way* of life, one that is constantly present, and one where worship is not relegated to a specific and detached building or a chosen day of the week. African religion is lived and experienced daily and the supernatural is always in constant relation with humankind. John S. Mbiti summarized this notion when he stated, "Because traditional religions permeate all the departments of life, there is no formal distinction between the sacred and the secular, between the religious and non-religious, between the spiritual and the material areas of life. Wherever the African is, there is his religion."[125]

La división de la Habana is just one of the many struggles that Afro-Cubans confronted in making the best possible use of the resources they had available in Cuba. Nowhere is the importance of women in the larger struggle more evident than in this contest for territory and power. Obá Tero, Latuán, Efunshé, and countless other women whose names and contributions have been lost to the historical record were fundamental protagonists in the perpetuation and propagation of Lukumí religion in Cuba. In turn, religion played a central role in Afro-Cuban society because it was the only thing that was truly theirs, the only remnant of their pride and identity that the dominant society could never extirpate, as religion was totally inseparable from the African worldview. *La división de la Habana* and the reunification of the Lukumí and Arará in Matanzas are just two examples of the various impediments that Africans had to overcome in Cuba to preserve an identity and a sense of self-worth, two important contributors in allowing a degree of power to an otherwise disenfranchised group. In so doing, power struggles of this sort laid strong foundations for the evolution of Regla de Osha in the island and its eventual diffusion in Cuba and abroad.

NOTES

1. Brazil was the major importer of African slaves in the New World, with Cuba trailing close behind. Nonetheless, Cuba was the major importer among all of Spain's colonies in the New World (see Philip D. Curtin, *The Atlantic Slave Trade—A Census* [Madison: University of Wisconsin Press, 1969], 46). See also Basil Davidson, *The African Slave Trade* (Boston: Little, Brown, 1980); Herbert S. Klein, *Slavery in the Americas: A Comparative Study of Virginia and Cuba* (Chicago: Ivan R. Dee, 1967); Pablo Tornero Tinajero, *Crecimiento economico y transformaciones sociales: Esclavos, hacendados y comerciantes en la Cuba colonial (1760–1840)* (Madrid: Centro de Publicaciones Ministerio de Trabajo y Seguridad Social, 1996); Manuel Moreno-Fraginals, "Africa in Cuba: A Quantitative Analysis of the African Population in the Island of Cuba," in *Comparative Perspectives on Slavery in New World Plantation Societies,* ed. Vera Rubin and Arthur Tuden (New York: New York Academy of Sciences, 1977); Manuel Moreno-Fraginals, *El ingenio: Complejo económico social cubano del azúcar,* 3 vols. (Havana: Editorial de Ciencias Sociales, 1978); Jose

Luciano Franco, *La diaspora africana en el nuevo mundo* (Havana: Editorial de Ciencias Sociales, 1975); Robert L. Paquette, *Sugar Is Made with Blood: The Conspiracy of La Escalera and the Conflict between Empires over Slavery in Cuba* (Middletown: Wesleyan University Press, 1988); Louis A. Pérez, Jr., *Slaves, Sugar, and Colonial Society: Travel Accounts of Cuba, 1801–1899* (Wilmington: Scholarly Resources, 1992); Enrique Pérez-Cisneros, *La abolición de la esclavitud en Cuba* (Tibás, Costa Rica: Litografia e Imprenta LIL, 1987); Juan Pérez de la Riva, "Cuadro Sinoptico de la Esclavitud en Cuba y de la Cultura Occidental," *Suplemento de la Revista Actas del Folklor* (May 1961); Juan Pérez de la Riva, *Para La Historia de la Gente Sin Historia* (Barcelona: Editorial Ariel, 1976); Juan Pérez de la Riva, *¿Cuantos Africanos fueron traidos a Cuba?* (Havana: Editorial de Ciencias Sociales, 1977); and Juan Pérez de la Riva, *El barracon: Esclavitud y capitalismo en Cuba* (Barcelona: Editorial Crítica, 1978).

2. Isabel Castellanos and Jorge Castellanos, *Cultura Afrocubana,* 4 vols. (Miami: Ediciones Universal, 1988); Arturo Lindsay, ed., *Santeria Aesthetics in Contemporary Latin American Art* (Washington, D.C.: Smithsonian Institution Press, 1996); Katherine J. Hagedorn, *Divine Utterances: The Performance of Afro-Cuban Santeria* (Washington, D.C.: Smithsonian Institution Press, 2001); Alejo Carpentier, *Music in Cuba* (Minneapolis: University of Minnesota Press, 2001); María Teresa Vélez, *Drumming for the Gods: The Life and Times of Felipe García Villamil, Santero, Palero, and Abakuá* (Philadelphia: Temple University Press, 2000).

3. Well-known examples of such Afro-Cuban men are Antonio Maceo, Juan Gualberto Gómez, Martín Morua Delgado, and Plácido (Gabriel de la Concepción Valdés), among many others, while only Mariana Grajales comes immediately to mind when recounting the achievements of Afro-Cuban women.

4. William R. Bascom, *The Yoruba of Southwestern Nigeria* (New York: Holt, Rinehart, and Winston, 1969), 1.

5. Miguel Barnet, *Biography of a Runaway Slave,* 2d ed., trans. Nick Hill (Willimantic: Curbstone Press, 1995); Daisy Rubiera Castillo, *Reyita, sencillamente* (Havana: Instituto Cubano del Libro, 1997).

6. Rubiera Castillo, *Reyita,* 27.

7. Much of this research was conducted over a period of thirty years as part of my own interest, as a priest, in the religion. I am indebted to a considerable number of *olorishas*, both living and deceased, and too many to list here. *Modupué ó!* I must also recognize the importance of the grant that I was awarded by the Ford Foundation and Florida International University's Cuban Research Institute in 1999, which allowed me to spend time researching primary documents in Cuba's Archivo Histórico Nacional.

8. I cannot proceed without giving recognition to two individuals who read and edited this article, and without whose input the article would have been weaker. First of all, I must thank Dr. Sherry Johnson, historian at Florida International University in Miami. Dr. Johnson recognized the importance of this article as a contribution to the growing body of significant research on Afro-Cuban women and Lukumí history and encouraged me to publish it. I am further indebted to Dr. Akinwumi Ogundiran, also of FIU, who read the original draft and provided much valuable input and clarity. To both of you, *modupué ó.*

9. A. J. Aşiwaju and Robin Law, "From the Volta to the Niger, c. 1600–1800," in *History of Africa I,* 3d ed., ed. J. F. Ade Ajayi and Michael Crowders (New York: Longman, 1985), 426.

10. Robert Smith, *Kingdoms of the Yoruba,* 3d ed. (Madison: University of Wisconsin Press, 1988), 37; Robin Law, *The Oyo Empire c. 1600–c. 1836: A West African Imperialism in the Era of the Atlantic Slave Trade,* 2d ed. (Brookfield: Gegg Revivals, 1991), 211.

11. Olfert Dapper, quoted in Law, *Oyo Empire,* 219; Snelgrave, quoted in ibid., 219.

12. Dapper, qutoed in Law, *Oyo Empire,* 219; Snelgrave, quoted in ibid., 219.

13. Robin Law, "The Atlantic Slave Trade in Yoruba Historiography," in *Yoruba Historiography,* ed. Toyin Falola (Madison: University of Wisconsin Press, 1991), 127.

14. Samuel Johnson, *The History of the Yorubas* (London: Routledge and Kegan Paul, 1921), 70–72, 178–87.

15. Ibid., 187–88.

16. De Chenevert and Abbé Bullet, *Réfléxions sur Juda* (1776), in Robin Law, *Contemporary Source Material for the History of the Old Oyo Empire, 1627–1824* (Ibadan: Institute of African Studies, University of Ibadan, 1992), 47.

17. Johnson, *History of the Yorubas,* 187; Law, *Oyo Empire,* 232, 236; Aşiwaju and Law, "From the Volta to the Niger," 445.

18. The Oyo Empire acted primarily as a sort of middleman between northern traders and Europeans on the coast. Prior to the nineteenth century, the scale of slave raiding within the Yoruba heartland was limited; strong proscriptions were in place that shunned the forcible enslavement of Yoruba people (see Law, *Oyo Empire,* 223; Law, "The Atlantic Slave Trade in Yoruba Historiography," 127).

19. J. A. Atanda, *An Introduction to Yoruba History* (Ibadan: Ibadan University Press, 1980), 30–31.

20. I would like to express my gratitude to Isabel Castellanos for guiding me in the right direction regarding the term Lukumí. She provided me with a copy of an early, undated French map of the Kingdom of Oulcoumi. The map also appears in an article by Dr. Castellanos ("From Ulkumí to Lucumí: A Historical Overview of Religious Acculturation in Cuba," in *Santería Aesthetics in Contemporary Latin American Art,* ed. Arturo Lindsay [Washington, D.C.: Smithsonian Institution Press, 1996], 39–50).

21. There are records of Yoruba slaves being in Peru in the seventeenth century but not in great numbers. Between 1605 and 1650, of 635 Afro-Peruvians, 17 were registered as Lukumí. Between 1615 and 1630, 5 Lukumí slaves entered Peru (see Frederick P. Bowser, *The African Slave in Colonial Peru, 1524–1650* [Stanford, Calif.: Stanford University Press, 1974], 41–43).

22. Moreno-Fraginals, "Africa in Cuba," 190–91.

23. Yoruba religion is also known in the Caribbean island of Trinidad, and there are Yoruba influences in Haitian Vodou as well, although to a lesser degree. For additional information on Lukumí religion in Cuba, see Mercedes Sandoval, *La religion afrocubana* (Madrid: Playor, 1975); and Castellanos and Castellanos, *Cultura Afrocubana.* For Brazil, see Edison Carneiro, *Religiões negras: Notas de etnografia religiosa* (Rio de Janeiro: N. p., 1936); Edison Carneiro, *Candombles da Bahia,* 5th ed. (Rio de Janeiro: Civilização Brasileira, 1977); and Pierre Verger, *Notes sur le Culte des Orisas et Vodun* (Dakar: L'Institut Francais d'Afrique Noire, 1957). For Trinidad, see George E. Simpson, *Religious Cults of the Caribbean: Trinidad, Jamaica, and Haiti* (Rio Piedras: Institute of Caribbean Studies, University of Puerto Rico, 1980).

24. The important place given to women in Yoruba religion has been examined recently by J. D. Y. Peel, "Gender in Yoruba Religious Change," *Journal of Religion in Africa* 32, no. 2 (2002): 136–66. Anthropologist Ruth Landes may have been one of the pioneers in this respect. Landes's research focused on the importance of women in Yoruba religion in Brazil (see *The City of Women* [New York: Macmillan, 1947]). J. Lorand Matory also looks at some of these issues in his study of gender in the Oyo-Yoruba religion, *Sex and the Empire That Is No More: Gender and the Politics of Metaphor in Oyo-Yoruba Religion* (Minneapolis: University of Minnesota Press, 1995). See also Henry J. Drewal and Margaret T. Drewal, *Gelede Art and Female Power among the Yoruba* (Bloomington: Indiana University Press, 1982); Babatunde Lawal, *The Gelede Spectacle: Art, Gender, and Social Harmony in an African Culture* (Seattle: University of Washington Press, 1996); and Oyeronke Oyewumi, *The Invention of Women: Making an African Sense of Western Gender Discourses* (Minneapolis: University of Minnesota Press, 1997).

25. Literally, "mother of [an] *orisha*." The term denotes a priestess that has ordained others into the Lukumí priesthood.

26. In the past, I (and others) spelled her name Efuché, Efushé, or Fushá, among various other

alternatives. It has come to my attention that the proper spelling is Efunshé, which may be an abbreviated version of Efunshetan, the name of an Ibadan palace wife, considered a great female entrepreneur in the nineteenth century (see Matory, *Sex and the Empire That Is No More*, 18–19).

27. An *orisha* is a deity in the Yoruba/Lukumí religious system. As used in the text, the uppercased "Orisha" refers to the religion and the lowercased and italicized *"orisha"* to the deities.

28. Literally, "owner of [an] *orisha*." The term is non-gendered and is used to refer to any individual ordained into the Lukumí priesthood.

29. Osvaldo Villamíl, interview by author, Matanzas, 6 October 1999; Antonio David Pérez, interview by author, Matanzas, 11 October 1999, 16 August 2000 (Pérez is better known as "El Chino" and is a religious descendant of Obá Tero).

30. See David Murray, *Odious Commerce: Britain, Spain, and the Abolition of the Cuban Slave Trade* (Cambridge: Cambridge University Press, 1980).

31. Evangelina Torres Crespo (Lusimí), Soledad's granddaughter, interview by the author, Havana, 25 June 1998.

32. Pérez, interview.

33. Oshabí became one of the most revered and respected *iyalorishas* in the history of the religion in Cuba; her importance in perpetuating Obá Tero's traditions will be discussed in greater detail later in this essay.

34. Egguadó is the Hispanicized pronunciation and spelling of the Yoruba term.

35. *Ilé*, literally, "house," can also refer to the *ilé osha* — "house of the *orishas*," the Lukumí equivalent of a temple. The *ilé osha* serves both as a residence for the *olorisha* and as a place for religious worship.

36. Of these, the most widely known are Oduduwá, Yewá, and Olokún. Olokún is most often associated with Obá Tero, and even more so with her religious progeny Fermina Gómez (Oshabí), who was influential in the dissemination of this *orisha* to other areas of the island.

37. Peter McKenzie, *Hail Orisha! A Phenomenology of a West African Religion in the Mid-Nineteenth Century* (Leiden, Netherlands: Koninklijke Brill, 1997), 28.

38. As defined earlier, an *iyalorisha* is a priestess who has ordained others into the priesthood. She is seen as the individual's religious mother. *Babalorisha* is the equivalent term for a priest. The terms differ from the generic *olorisha* ("owner of an *orisha*"), which is used to denote any priest or priestess.

39. The drums known in Cuba as "Egbado," or Geledé, drums are recognized in many areas of Yorubaland and West Africa and are not exclusively Egbado. Lawal described the drums used for Geledé dancing in southwestern Yorubaland as an ensemble of four wooden, pot-shaped, or cylindrical drums (see *Gelede Spectacle*, 87–88). The Cuban Egbado drums likewise consist of four single-headed drums with tubular, chalice-shaped bodies. The membranes are kept in place by means of a loop made from a strong vine or metal, or the use of hemp cord or rope. These are supported by hardwood pegs that keep the loop and cords in place (Centro de Investigación y Desarrollo de la Música Cubana [CIDMUC], *Instrumentos de la música folclórico-popular de Cuba*, 2 vols. [Havana: Editorial de Ciencias Sociales, 1997], 250).

40. Fernando Ortiz, *Los instrumentos de la música afrocubana 3* (Havana: Dirección de Cultura del Ministerio de Educación, 1951), 412; CIDMUC, *Instrumentos*, 1:247.

41. Fernando Ortiz, *Los bailes y el teatro de los negros en el folklore de Cuba*, 2d ed. (Havana: Editorial Letras Cubanas, 1981), 451. Unfortunately, Ortiz does not give his source. It is not clear whether he actually saw the Olokún dance or whether informants interviewed during the research told him of its existence.

Oral tradition recounts that the Egbado drums that Ortiz discussed were brought to Matanzas by Obá Tero when she left Havana. In the 1970s Cuban investigators concluded that the drums had been in Matanzas, in a house at 57 Salamanca Street, since at least the first decades of the twentieth century, but that they were probably brought there much earlier. After Obá Tero's passing, the drums were inherited by Oshabí, who attended to them until her death, at which time they were passed down to her children. Victor Torrientes, the oldest child, was in charge of them. After his death, they were subsequently passed on to other family members until they ended up with Eugenio "Pucho" Lamar (Eshú Dina). Oshabí and her daughter, Celestina Torrientes (Olufandeí) had ordained Eshú Dina in the 1940s. By the time they came into Eshú Dina's possession, the drums were in a very precarious state due to a variety of factors. Eshú Dina removed them from Oshabí's house because he feared that the house might one day come tumbling down. During his lifetime, he kept the drums in his own house.

Eshú Dina passed away in 1998, and after much, often-heated debate among various groups who were interested in taking possession of them, the drums were returned to Oshabí's home on Salamanca Street. Currently, Antonio Pérez, better known as "El Chino," resides there. Pérez, who is not ordained, has experienced a great deal of animosity from the religious community, and especially the drummers. Pérez has been adamant about the proper care of the drums and covers them with a white cloth, as they are supposed to be treated when not in use. Not only does he reside in Oshabí's house, but he has also been charged with caring for Obá Tero's *orishas* that remain in the house as historic and religious relics and are much valued by her descendants. Customarily, when an *olorisha* dies, a mortuary rite known as *etutu* (*itutu*) is held to allow the oracles to determine if the departed's *orisha* will accompany her or remain with a religious or blood descendant. *Orishas* have been known to stay with the *ilé osha,* that is, in the physical house where the deceased lived, and not with any specific individual. This was the case with Obá Tero's and Oshabí's *orishas*.

42. *Cabildos de nación,* or African ethnic associations, were greatly influential in the retention of African culture in Cuba. *Cabildos* were based on the Spanish *cofradías* (guilds or fraternities) that were first organized in Seville around the fourteenth century. These *cofradías* were placed under the tutelage of a Catholic saint and held their meetings in the saint's chapel. Fernando Ortiz states that the guilds were originally organized during the reign of Alfonso el Sabio, who, after the creation of the Spanish legal code known as Las Siete Partidas, wanted to "give order to matters ecclesiastical and civil" (see Ortiz, "Los cabildos y la fiesta afrocubana del Dia de Reyes," *Revista Bimestre Cubana* 16 [January–February 1921]; reprint, Havana: Editorial de Ciencias Sociales, 1992, 5). See also Isidoro Moreno, *La antigua hermandad de los negros de Sevilla: Etnicidad, poder y sociedad en 600 años de historia* (Seville: Universidad de Sevilla, 1997). Like Ortiz, Moreno agrees that these associations were the precursors to the Afro-Cuban *cabildos*. Philip Howard has also adopted this view and has pointed to the existence of comparable institutions in Africa (Philip A. Howard, *Changing History: Afro-Cuban Cabildos and Societies of Color in the Nineteenth Century* [Baton Rouge: Louisiana State University Press, 1998]).

43. Both are believed to be the progenitors of the Oyo *batá* drumming tradition in Cuba.

44. Fernando Ortiz, *Los Tambores Batá de los Yorubas* (Havana: Publicigraf, 1994), 147.

45. Milagros Palma (Kashé Enjué), interview by author, Matanzas, 6 October 1999.

46. Ortiz, *Los Tambores,* 147.

47. Pérez, interview.

48. Personal communication with Israel Moliner, official historian of the city of Matanzas, 6 October 1999.

49. The *babalawo* (literally, "fathers of the mystery") are the priests of Orunmilá, patron divinity of the Ifá oracle. One of the *babalawo*'s roles is divining for Orisha devotees. For further reading on Ifá, see William Bascom, *Ifa Divination: Communication between Gods and Men in West Africa* (Bloomington: Indiana University Press, 1969).

50. Other scholars have identified Adeshina as an Ijeshá (see John Mason, *Olookun: Owner of Rivers and Seas* [Brooklyn: Yoruba Theological Archministry, 1996], 18). My sources insist that he was Oyo and not Ijeshá. Esther Piedra, currently the oldest member of the Ijeshá *cabildo* in Matanzas, was married to Adeshina's grandson, Rolando Cartalla, who passed away in 1999. This

is probably why he has been mistakenly associated with the Ijeshá people. Rolando's widow confirms that Cartalla was related to the Ijeshá *cabildo* through his marriage to her, and not by birth (Esther Piedra, interview by author, Matanzas, 18 August 2000).

51. Esther Piedra, interview.

52. Ortiz, *Los Tambores*, 146–47; and Pedro Cosme, interview by author, Regla, 30 September 1999.

53. Archivo Histórico Nacional de Cuba, Fondo de Gobierno General, legajo 268, numero 13545: "Padron de Contribucion Extraordinaria para Subsidio de Guerra . . .Correspondiente al Pueblo de Regla, 1872–1873."

54. *Censo de 1881 – Regla, Tomo II*, Museo de Regla, Havana (consulted September 1999).

55. Most sources agree he was well over one hundred years old when he died.

56. Personal communication with Israel Moliner, official historian of the city of Matanzas, 6 October 1999.

57. Esther Piedra, interview; Julio Suarez Oña (Ewi Moyó), interview by the author, Matanzas, 6 August 1999 (Ewi Moyó is a priest of Aganjú and Olubatá [literally, "one who owns drums"]).

58. Pérez, interview. Another variant states that Obá Tero was the *ojigbona*, or second sponsor, and that Ña Inés (Yeyé T'Olokún) was the ordaining priestess (Angel de León [Oloyadé], interview by the author, Regla, 24 September 1999).

59. Esther Piedra, interview. Piedra says that she believes he resided there until 1892, when he moved to Havana.

60. R. C. Abraham, *Dictionary of Modern Yoruba* (London: Hodder and Stoughton Educational, 1946), 21.

61. The term "Santería" has gained acceptance in the last fifty years; earlier it was considered derogatory and had denigrating connotations. Still, I prefer the older term Regla de Osha (or simply, the Lukumí religion), which is more in line with the religion's dogma and ideology.

62. John Mason was told by his sources that she was an Egbadó native, but when I interviewed the grandchildren, they insisted that she was from Oyo. Mason, *Olookun*, 18.

63. Congo is a generic term used in Cuba to refer to Africans of Bantú origin.

64. Manuel Fernández Santalices, *Las calles de la Habana intramuros: Arte, historia y tradiciones en las calles y plazas de la Havana Vieja* (Miami: Saeta Ediciones, 1989), 37. Albear died in 1887 and was never able to see the final result of his massive project.

65. Candelario Zurria Albear and Martin Zurria Albear (Latuán's grandchildren), interview by the author, Buena Vista, Cuba, 20 March 2001.

66. Candelario Zurria Albear and Martin Zurria Albear, interview. See also Franklin W. Knight, *Slave Society in Cuba during the Nineteenth Century* (Madison: University of Wisconsin Press, 1970), 176–77. This comment most likely refers to the period 1880–1888. The abolition law passed in 1880 established 1888 as the date for the termination of slavery. It was during this period that an apprenticeship system was implemented, which was supposed to lay the foundations for the eventual emancipation of the slaves. Slaves were to pass through a transitory stage that would prepare them for their eventual entrance into society as salaried workers by 1888. The system was unsuccessful, though, and by 1883, only 10 percent of the total population of the island was registered as slaves.

67. Candelario Zurria Albear and Martin Zurria Albear, interview.

68. Candelario Zurria Albear and Martin Zurria Albear, interview.

69. Literally, "king, head of the oracle." The title applies to a specific category in the Lukumí priesthood. The Obá Oriaté is the master of ceremonies for Lukumí rituals, and especially for ordination rituals.

70. Candelario Zurria Albear and Martin Zurria Albear, interview.

71. The Obá Oriaté Lázaro Ramos (Okandenijé), interview by the author, Miami 2000.

72. The Obá Oriaté Rodolfo "Cuco" Rodriguez (Igbín Koladé), interview by the author, Havana, 1977; Obá Oriaté José Manuel Grinart (Oyá Dina), interview by the author, New York, September 2000.

73. Lydia Cabrera, *Anagó-Vocabulario Lucumi (El Yoruba que se Habla en Cuba)* (Miami: Ediciones Universal, 1970), 101.

74. Hugo Cárdenas (Obá Oriaté Eshú Miwá), interview by the author, Havana, June 1998.

75. Manuel Mederos (Obá Oriaté Eshú Onaré), interview by the author, Miami, 27 January 2000; Pedro García (Obá Oriaté Lomí Lomi), interview by the author, Pogolotti, Cuba, 13 August 2000.

76. Roque "El Jimagua" Duarte (Obá Oriaté Tinibú), personal communication, Miami, June 1998.

77. Lusimí, interview. Soledad Crespo's descendants, five generations later, continue to employ Lukumí names extraofficially.

78. This would explain the lack of other descendants. Odé Deí was also childless. Nonetheless, both Efunshé and Odé Deí had many religious offspring, which possibly compensated for the lack of biological children. Like her mother, Odé Deí became a very respected *olorisha*. In the 1950s, Cabrera called Odé Deí the last *apuonlá* ("great singer") of that era. Odé Deí was the *ojigbona* — assistant to the *iyalorisha* — at the time of Nemensia Espinoza's (Oshún Miwá) ordination in 1926. Efunshé participated in the ordination and died shortly thereafter. Affected by a period of dementia in her latter years, Odé Deí lived with Oshún Miwá until her death in the 1970s because she had no children or relatives to care for her.

79. Pedro García (Obá Oriaté Lomí Lomi), interview by author, 13 August 2001; Nina Pérez, (Igbín Koladé), interview by author, Cudahy, California, December 2000.

80. My *orisha* lineage descends directly from Efunshé. In 1983, when I interviewed my *orisha* grandfather, Eladio Gutiérrez (Obá Oriaté Eshú Bí), he stressed that our lineage descends from Yewá. The association with Yewá may have been influenced by her direction of the Cabildo San José 80, which sources indicate was under the tutelage of Yewá.

81. Mason, *Olookun,* 18.

82. Rodolfo "Cuco" Rodriguez (Obá Oriaté Igbín Koladé), interview; José Manuel Ginart (Obá Oriaté Oyá Dina), interview.

83. María Eugenía Pérez (Oshún Niké), interview by author, Havana, September 1999. Pérez was ordained by one of Efunshé's *omó orisha* in 1923. Efunshé was present at the ordination, one of the last ordinations she attended, and Latuán acted as Obá Oriaté.

84. Amador Aguilera (Omí Laí, Obá Oriaté Olubatá and priest of Orishaokó), interview by author, San Miguel del Padrón, June 1998; Oshún Niké, interviews, September 1999 and March 2001.

85. This *cabildo,* located on 80 San José Street in the Jesús María section of Old Havana, is known by its physical address (Gilberto Martinez [Babá Funké], interviews by author, Carolina, Puerto Rico, 1982 and 1983; Babá Funké traces his lineage to Latuán).

86. Lazaro Ramos (Obá Oriaté Okandenijé), interview.

87. Hugo Cárdenas (Obá Oriaté Eshú Miwá), interview.

88. Amador Aguilera (Omí Laí, Obá Oriaté Olubatá and priest of Orishaokó), interviews by author, San Miguel del Padrón, Havana, June 1998 and September/October 1999.

89. Johnson, *History of the Yorubas,* 226–27; Law, *Oyo Empire,* 92–95; Law, "The Atlantic Slave Trade in Yoruba Historiography, " 113–17.

90. Ibid.

91. Rodolfo "Cuco" Rodriguez (Igbín Koladé), interview by Angel Riana (Talabí), Havana, 1977.

92. Adelfa Teran (Obá Oriaté Igbín Koladé and Priestess of Obatalá), interview by author, Miami, 26 December 1999; Francisca Sotomayor (Osha Inle, Priestess of Obatalá), interview by author, Jovellanos, Cuba, 14 August 2000 (Ines Sotomayor Sotomayor is the granddaughter of one

of Lydia Cabrera's principal informants in Jovellanos, who is herself an *olorisha* of *santo parado*); Armando Cabrera (Obá Oriaté Eshú Tolú and Priest of Elegbá), interview by author, Cárdenas, Cuba, 14 August 2000; Felix "Cheo" Gonzalez (Oshún Yumí), interview by author, Cárdenas, Cuba, 15 August 2000.

93. Law, *Oyo Empire,* 104, 139–40.

94. Cabrera, *El Monte,* 24 n. 1. Use of the word "saint" by Lukumí *olorishas* is very common and results from the parallelisms between Yoruba *orishas* and Catholic saints, a process often referred to as *syncretism*. This is a subject for future discussion, as past literature has often equated syncretism with religious fusion, something that is obviously not necessarily so in the case of the Lukumí. For similar reasons, I decline to use the term "Santería" in my writing, since it has pejorative connotations.

95. See Miguel Ramos, "The Empire Beats On: Oyo, Batá Drums, and Hegemony in Nineteenth-Century Cuba," Master's thesis, Florida International University, 2000; Abraham, *Dictionary,* 21; Johnson, *History of the Yorubas,* 63.

96. Raul Mojica (Obá Oriaté Osha Inle and Priest of Obatala), interview by author, Jesús María, Havana, 19 September 1999. Sadly, Mojica passed away in January 2001 after a long battle with cancer.

97. Lydia Cabrera Collection, Cuban Heritage Collection, Otto G. Richter Library, University of Miami, Miami, Fla. This was one of hundreds of notes taken by Cabrera that she apparently had to take hastily, as it is probable that many of her sources were hesitant to contribute to her research due to the many stigmas of the era.

98. Angel de León (Obá Oriaté Oloyadé), interview by author, Regla, 24 September 1999.

99. Raul Mojica (Obá Oriaté Osha Inle and Priest of Obatala), interview.

100. Unfortunately, these differences cannot be elucidated without revealing ritual secrets that can only be disclosed to the duly ordained.

101. Oní, literally meaning "owner of," is a title given to Shangó's and Yemojá's *olorishas*.

102. Law, *Oyo Empire,* 104, 139–40.

103. Rodolfo "Cuco" Rodriguez (Igbín Koladé), interview by Angel Riana (Talabí), Havana, 1977.

104. Lukumí myths portray Obatalá and Yemojá as Shangó's parents, and Oshún as his favorite wife.

105. Johnson, *History of the Yorubas,* 21; Law, *Oyo Empire,* 127–29.

106. Personal communication with Candomblé *olorishas,* especially Maria Mello, *iyalorisha* of Obatalá, and Gilberto Ferreira (Ogan), consecrated to Eshú (Elegbá).

107. Most of the elders interviewed throughout the years, including some ordained in the *kariosha* tradition at the turn of the century, were provided with various *orishas* at the time of their ordination. María Eugenía Pérez (Oshún Niké), the oldest *iyalorisha* in Havana, was born in 1904. Oshún Niké was ordained on 23 July 1923 by Luisa Arango (Shangó Ladé), herself one of Efunshé's *omó orishas*. Latuán was the Obá Oriaté. Oshún Niké was provided with Elegbá, Ogún, Oshosi, Obatalá, Yemojá, Shangó, and Oshún, her tutelar *orisha*. Deceased *olorishas,* all ordained during the same period, including Aurelia Mora (Omí Dina), Basilia Cárdenas Massip (Omí Dina), and Nemensia Espinoza (Oshún Miwá), were also provided with various *orishas* at ordination. José Roche (Oshún Kayodé) and Josefina Aguirre (Oshún Gere) were ordained by Tranquilina Balmaseda (Omí Sanjá) in 1896 and 1906, respectively, and were also provided with various *orishas*. All these *olorishas* descend from Efunshé. Sadly, Oshún Niké passed away this spring.

108. Osvaldo Villamíl, interview; Pérez, interview.

109. R. C. Abraham, in his *Dictionary of Modern Yoruba,* refers to the "most senior titleholder everywhere among the Egungún" as Aláàpinni (50).

110. Bárbaro Cansino (Ojulenso), conversation with author, Simpson, Matanzas, August 2001.

111. Ojulenso, conversation.

112. I must recognize the valuable input given by Babalorisha Temujin Ekùnfeó (Obalorún). He suggested the possible link between Eroméle and Imálà and pointed me in the right direction, as I was at a loss. Obalorún studied anthropology at the University of Pittsburgh and researches African and African American folklore and culture.

113. Abraham, *Dictionary,* 177.

114. Some sources have testified that in Cuba some Erómeles had ceased to worship Yemojá and Olokún altogether. What is clear from all sources is that Ikudaisí refused to acknowledge these two *orishas* and blamed them for his lot and enslavement in Cuba. In fact, when he replaced his *orishas* in Cuba, he did not replace his Yemojá or his Olokún. Though he knew through divination that Oshabí was a child of Yemojá, he refused to ordain her to her "true" *orisha* and chose to ordain her to Oshún. At that time, it was inadmissible for an *om'orisha* to question the decisions made by their *iyá* or *babálorisha.* Oshabí had no input whatsoever in the matter.

115. When possession ends, the mount will not remember anything that took place.

116. Pérez, interview.

117. Letter from Francisco Pereyra Mendes, director of the Portuguese port at Whydah, 22 May 1726, quoted in Law, *Contemporary Source Material,* 15.

118. For more in-depth accounts, see Robin Law, *The Slave Coast of West Africa, 1550–1750: The Impact of the Atlantic Slave Trade on an African Society* (Oxford: Clarendon Press, 1991); Law, *Oyo Empire;* and Law, *Contemporary Source Material.*

119. The shared practices were later extended to Havana, where a similar diffusion was reluctantly taking place, although at a much slower pace. In Havana the Arará presented a stronger resistance to the foreign influence. According to sources, varied degrees of friction between the two ethnic groups continued in Havana essentially until the eve of Fidel Castro's revolution and possibly beyond Abelardo Hernández [Oshún Funké], interview by author, Miami, January 2000.

120. Interestingly, these two oracles were known to the Arará in Africa, though in Cuba, oral tradition strongly affirms that the Arará obtained these from the Lukumí. It would seem that by this period, possibly the Arará had lost knowledge of these oracles. In theory, this is a sensible assumption, as in all probability Arará soldiers outnumbered the members of the Arará priesthood among the slaves brought to the island. In all probability, then, the Arará ritual knowledge may not have been as vigorous.

121. To this day, the Lukumí perform an annual divination rite on the first of January to consult the deities on the nature of the coming year. Often, the oracles prescribe *ebó* (sacrifice) to, whenever possible, appease the negative forces of the universe and avoid misfortune.

122. Hector Hernandez (Obá Oriaté Omó Oshosi), interview by author, Matanzas, 5 October 1999; Milagros Palma (Kashenjué and Arará priestess of Makeno, the Arará equivalent of Obatalá), interview by author, Matanzas, 4 October 1999 and August 2000. Presently, Palma is the oldest Arará priestess in Matanzas.

123. Bernard Maupoil, *La Géomancie à l'ancienne côte des esclaves* (Paris: Institute D'ethnologie, Musée de l'Homme, 1943).

124. Cabrera, *El Monte,* 313.

125. John S. Mbiti, *African Religions and Philosophy,* 2d ed. (Oxford: Heinemann Education Publishers, 1989), 2.

K. LYNN STONER

Militant Heroines and the Consecration of the Patriarchal State: The Glorification of Loyalty, Combat, and National Suicide in the Making of Cuban National Identity

ABSTRACT

The female combatant, a common icon of Cuban nationalism, is found in every historical period from independence through the post-Soviet period. Unlike most other nations, Cubans have eulogized women who have defended their nation with their own lives and with those of their husbands and children. Yet, for all the fanfare these heroines have received in the nationalist discourse, few scholarly treatments of their lives exist. Instead, their heroism has been used to exalt male leaders and to uphold a patriarchal state. Their martyrdom has served as a model of sacrifice unto death for all citizens to follow. This article examines the nature of Cuban combatant iconography that followed the Cuban wars of independence, the Early Republic, and the Cuban Revolution, and connects that iconography to the purposes of state building in each era.

RESUMEN

La mujer combatiente, ícono tradicional del nacionalismo cubano, se encuentra en cada período histórico desde la independencia hasta la etapa post-soviética. A diferencia de la mayoría de las naciones, los cubanos han alabado a las mujeres que han defendido sus naciones con sus propias vidas y las de sus esposos e hijos. Sin embargo, pese a toda la atención que estas heroínas han recibido en el discurso nacionalista, existen pocos estudios académicos sobre sus vidas. Por el contrario, su heroísmo ha sido utilizado para exaltar a los líderes masculinos y sostener el estado patriarcal. El martirologio ha servido como un modelo de sacrificio hasta la muerte que todos los ciudadanos deben seguir. Este artículo examina la naturaleza de la iconografía combatiente después de las guerras de independencia, los primeros años de la República y la Revolución de 1959, y relaciona esta iconografía a los propósitos de la construcción de la nación en cada período.

Female allegiance to male leadership and *la patria*, so frequently present in Cuban nationalist discourse, is a cultural artifact that transcends the island's historical periods and ruling ideologies. Women's heroism and sacrifice glorified the brave and recalcitrant Mambí Army,[1] condoned the subversives who

71

eroded President Gerardo Machado's corrupt second term,[2] resonated with the guerrillas' daring acts in the Sierra Maestra,[3] and today defends Castro's revolution in the post-Soviet world.[4] No other symbol so permeates Cuban nationalist lore than that of the stalwart and feminine combatant, willing to sacrifice her home, family, and wealth for her nation and its patriarchal leaders. The ubiquitous image of the female warrior also convinced Spain and the United States of the Cuban resolve to fight to the death, if need be, for its right to be free from foreign control.

Imaging women as patriotic, nationalist symbols is only one aspect of national identity formation, to be sure, but one that achieves a particular logic. The qualities it conveys are loyalty, sacrifice, combativeness, recalcitrance, ingenuity, courage, strength, and the equal distribution of suffering. Women's exceptional suffering on the battlefield has symbolized the torment of a nation constantly at war with colonizers from without and traitors from within. It has represented national resolve to be victorious at all costs. Men's sacrifice and bravery were also exemplary, and they composed the majority of eulogized, national heroes. But loyalty, suffering, and sacrifice of the lives of women and their children have been most effectively conveyed by the deeds of female combatants, because they have equaled men's bravery outside the traditional protection of the home, and they have consecrated the nationalist cause by bringing the home onto the battlefield and transforming the war theatre into a moral arena.

Embedding the image of the female warrior into the national ideal also has a dark side, for it sanctifies insurgency and the highest form of commitment to sovereignty: national suicide. By placing women and children within the heroic struggle, the Cuban myth has glorified heroic sacrifice of its men, and also its women, children, and its future. Cuban nationalists throughout the twentieth century have revered martyrdom in ways that are unique. They have not invoked God, as Mexicans have with their Virgin of Guadalupe, for the consecration of their national cause. The Cuban passion of faith lies in personal martyrdom. The violation of women, which Cubans have made inevitable by literally and figuratively fielding female soldiers, has been the clarion call for the country to unite and fight. By extension, honoring women capable of killing the sons of an enemy has condoned political violence and embedded it in a nationalist consciousness as a potential way of being. Militancy and death have become properties of a civil religion and aspects of national identity.

This article is an inquiry into the nature of combatant iconography that followed the Cuban wars of independence, the Early Republic, and the Cuban Revolution of 1959. Such a study begs to be done if for no other reason than the sheer weight of cultural ephemera that exalts the woman warrior in the post-independence and revolutionary periods. Such evidence calls for an analysis of historical artifacts that projected the female patriot into public consciousness.

The article, then, will comment on the quantity and quality of heroic biographical legends that are embedded in the national consciousness. It will point out similarities and differences in the ways early republican and revolutionary publicists appropriated feminine militancy to authorize patriarchal systems and construct social order. Finally, it will link female soldiering with concepts of martyrdom, national suicide, honor, and militant faithfulness to male family members, national leaders, and the state. That said, the paper does not intend to suggest an essential Cuban political culture, but it will discuss the consequences of public use of heroic biographies for the purpose of state building.

La Mambisa

Leading up to and during the independence campaigns against Spain, Cuban leaders and intellectuals attempted to unify rebels around symbols of patriotism to solidify a nationalist spirit. Heroism took on extraordinary dimensions, with tales of soldiers' brave and cunning deeds and civilians', women's, old people's, and children's endurance of concentration camps, malaria, malnutrition, and battle wounds for "Cuba Libre." Tales and cultural artifacts of legendary female combatants boosted patriotic morale during the wars of insurgency and justified national sovereignty for future generations. The substance of the symbols lay in their subtext. The woman warrior, or rebel, assaulted the barriers of colonial laws just as the Mambi Army wore down Spain's colonial army. To secure nationalist ideals, male publicists created the image of the female warrior and used women's bravery to instruct a nation in new values, such as loyalty and sacrifice to the state. Women warriors *a la cubana* could fight as men, nurture as women, and stand beside their men in refusing to surrender to the Spanish Crown, all the while asking little for themselves. These women were not remembered for their individual circumstances, ingenuity, philosophical understanding of independence, or female-centered objectives. *Mambisas* became inspirational fetishes and examples of nationalist will and a modern orientation, but not individuals in their own right.

In their time, women who resisted Spanish colonialism set the patriotic example for the independence campaigns. Between 1807 and 1810, young women cut their long hair, for which they were famous, as a means of distinguishing themselves from the wives and daughters of Spanish colonizers. Already, Cuban women were aligning a militant attitude with nationalism and their bodies with national identity, even as Cuba did nothing to overthrow 309 years of Spanish rule. By mid-century, demonstrations of repudiating of all things Spanish spilled over into sporadic battles and death, extremes for women in any era, when women involved themselves in Narciso López's filibustering campaigns. Marina Manresa became a legend before the first war of independence and stood as an example of sacrifice for the next generation of women who would be the *mambisas*. She was remembered for her fidelity both to a free Cuba and her fiancé, who aligned himself with López's 1851 invasion. The lovers had cooperated with the invasion, and José Alonso fought in the weeks' long battle. Both Marina and José were captured, but she was given the opportunity to condemn both the invasion and her fiancé's treasonous act to spare her own life. Marina refused to do either and was executed along with her lover. Perhaps Marina's execution was the first example of female heroism that set the tone for those to follow: women were the ultimate patriots, as they simultaneously sacrificed themselves and their potential offspring for their country and their men.

As the first of three wars of independence opened in 1868, two women in particular inspired the notice of patriots. Mariana Grajales Cuello, the mulatta mother of eleven sons, one of whom was the great commander General Antonio Maceo, was memorialized in her day by José Martí for her willingness to sacrifice her children and herself for Cuba. She taught her sons how to use the machete as a fighting weapon, and she instilled in them dreams of an independent Cuba devoid of slavery. As the legend goes, with all but her youngest son on the war front, she received news of the death of her oldest, Miguel. Reportedly, she turned to the youngest and said, "Y tú, muchacho, empíñate, que ya es la hora de que pelees por tu patria" (And now, son, stand tall, for it is time for you to fight for your country). Mariana Grajales embodied all that was Cuba at that moment. She was a woman of color who symbolized that Cuba would be a nation of racial harmony. She was willing to sacrifice all that was most dear, the flesh of her flesh, for her nation. Cubans would never surrender. No sacrifice was too great, not even the prospect of genocidal wars or, by extension, national suicide.

Mariana Grajales became the mother of Cuban independence.[5] She was recognized by José Martí as La Leona. Her example, along with the bravery of many other Cuban women, prompted his praise: "With women such as these, it is easy to be heroes."

Ana Betancourt de Mora, who failed in her attempt to secure citizenship for women under the revolutionary government that met to write the "Bases de revolución" in 1869, nevertheless raised the awareness of women's contributions to independence and the inevitability of full rights for women under a democratic government.[6] Attending the constitutional congress in the place of her ailing husband, Ignacio, Ana pointed out that Cubans had declared that the Negro was the Cuban's brother and that slavery had no place in a new republic. She concluded that women had made the same sacrifices as men and so they too should be considered full citizens in the emerging nation.

Women's work in revolutionary clubs, both within Cuba and in foreign countries, stoked the independence flame through periods between the wars,

Militant Heroines and Consecration of Patriarchal State : 75

and during conflict itself women fought in the armies, working as spies, gun runners, money raisers, propagandists, conspirators, and saboteurs. Their efforts were recognized and added urgency to the campaigns and morality to the cause. All subsequent governments found in the *mambisa* the soul of their own political challenges.

The Early Republic: Creating *Mambisa* Legends

As the republican era opened, commemorating independence heroines fell to publicists, playwrights, composers, sculptors, and politicians, all of whom dedicated themselves to formulating a national identity. Their work began at the dawn of a new century when modern nations were confronting the question of citizenship: could women be citizens with rights and responsibilities equal to those of men? The fighting traditions of the *mambisas* answered that question in the affirmative and formed the basis for women's demands for expanded constitutional rights that placed a commitment to social justice at the heart of national objectives. The female combatant, then, was an integral part of the consecration and enactment of national ideals and social justice.

Along the Malecón in Havana, European-inspired statues from the Romantic era were erected to glorify Cuba's nationalist champions and martyrs. The monument to the medical students who were executed by the Spanish for raising the cause of independence takes a central site on Havana's coastal drive. Generals Máximo Gómez and Antonio Maceo are honored with statues along the Malecón, but Gómez does not stand alone in his defiance of Spain and march toward independent statehood. Sculptures of intrepid women standing with Mambí soldiers and protecting Cuba's children and the nation grace the podium of Gómez's monument to remind the onlooker that the three wars of independence were fought by all Cubans. In El Vedado, on 23rd Street and F, a heavily traveled street only two hundred yards south of the Malecón, a more modest park is dedicated to Mariana Grajales, the mother of Cuban independence. Her effigy kneels by a boy and points the way to battle and freedom. And in Santo Suárez, a suburb of Havana, another park statue commemorates Emilia Córdoba y Rubio, a soldier and exile, who returned to Cuba after independence to become the first female federal employee.

Music was composed and legends were embellished to accompany the newly erected statuary. *La Bayamesa,* a *serenata,* or romantic song, designed to inspire nationalist pride was based upon the life of Adriana del Castillo Vázquez. She had been a conspirator for the rebel forces during the Ten Years' War and had died of distress when she saw the carnage wrecked upon the guerrilla fighters. Composed by Antonio Gumersindo Garay García, the *serenata* was a nostalgic reminder of the cost of independence. A woman is distressed beyond endurance for her country, which she blesses with the purity of her heart and all of her virtues. But no matter how the battle will break her, independence is her only belief and her only religion:

> Lleva en su alma la bayamesa
> tristes recuerdos de tradiciones
> cuando contempla sus verdes llanos
> lágrimas vierte por sus pasiones
>
> Ella es sencilla, le brinda al hombre
> virtudes todas, y el corazón
> pero si se siente de la patria el grito,
> todo lo deja, todo lo quema,
> ése es su lema, su religión.[7]
>
> (In her soul, the Bayamo woman carries
> sad memories of old traditions
> When she looks at her green pastures
> tears well up in her eyes
>
> She is simple, she offers mankind
> all virtues and her heart
> But if she hears her homeland's cry
> she leaves everything, she burns everything
> That is her life, her religion.)

Daily newspapers and weekly magazines created a collective memory about the *mambisas*. *Bohemia* and *Diario de la Marina,* the most popular weekly magazine and daily newspaper, respectively, compromised objective reporting by writing legendary vignettes about the heroines of Cuban independence. Passionate testimonies and nationalist sagas of extraordinary bravery filled their pages, making Cubans mindful of their heritage. Emphasis upon female heroism, loyalty, and sacrifice rang out against humiliation at the hands of the United States and the limitations on sovereignty set by the occupation forces. By demonstrating a collective will to fight to the death for independence, publicists restored some national self-respect and reminded Cubans that they were capable of an unyielding militancy, if only they would refer to the past.

One of the first popular press articles about martyred women was the publication of a letter from General Máximo Gómez to his daughter that recounted her mother's flight from a hidden farm only a few weeks after her birth during the Ten Years' War (1868–78).[8] The Spanish Army had spies who knew where Bernarda Toro Pelegrín de Gómez was convalescing, and they knew that the General had moved on with the patriot army, leaving Bernarda in the care of her brother. A squadron attacked the tiny ranch where she was staying, which was defended by only her brother, two other men, and a soldier who happened along at the moment of the attack. The General's account is about the unspeakable tragedy of a postpartum mother running barefoot ahead of armed Spanish soldiers who wanted to capture her and the child so as to compromise Máximo Gómez's leadership. They ruthlessly killed three of Bernarda's defenders, and she wandered for several days in the dry interior with neither water nor food. Her brother tracked her and finally rescued the mother and child. The tone of the letter exalts the mother's bravery and the extreme cruelty of the Spanish. It also praises the bravery of the men who defended Bernarda. Gómez names them and commemorates their deeds, since they were his daughter's benefactors, the ones who saved her life. Bernarda's tenacity and strength, even in her weakened condition, bespeaks the defiance of Cuban patriots framed within the realm of the feminine world. Bermarda was a mother protecting her daughter, her husband, and her country. Men were glorified also. They gave their lives to protect the Gómez family and their nation. Gómez concluded his letter with heroic hubris, declaring that no sacrifice, including the bloody martyrdom of the men under his command, his family, and possibly himself was too great for independence. The epistle was also a self-declaration of honor. Gómez's authority rested on the commitment of many women and men who were willing to die for his vision of Cuba Libre. One of his greatest defenders was his wife, and her story glorified his honor.

Similarly, Enrique Ubieta's series on women and independence memorialized María Cabrales, the wife of General Antonio Maceo, for her determination to save her wounded husband's life in August 1897.[9] Maceo had been fatally wounded when he led a charge through one of the lines of a Spanish ambush. For ten days, the Spanish and patriot forces had continued the clash, for the sheer purpose of capturing the moribund Maceo. María never left her husband's side, and with the help of Maceo's brother José, she established a mobile hospital bed and mounted an armed defense of it against Spanish horsemen.

Ubieta also reported on other female combatants, of Afro-Cuban and white backgrounds, and from all classes. One story is both humorous and heroic. Inés Morillo, a resident of Villa Clara, manufactured independence flags and hat insignia and ran messages for the rebels. Turned in by another Cuban, she stood trial in the infamous and informal Spanish courts for captured patriots, and she was condemned to death by firing squad. Her family's connections with a Spanish general spared her life, but she was sentenced to life imprisonment in Havana's Women's Prison. Her family then arranged for her to travel to her Havana prison in an elegant coach rather than in the railroad car for political prisoners. As her cortege took several days to reach Havana, word went out of her arrest, and supporters flocked to the road to accompany her carriage into Havana. When she was placed in a cell with common criminals, her family

Table 1
**Characteristics of Iconographic Artifacts about the *Mambisas*,
1900–1958**

Characteristic	Number of Representations	Percentage
Club organizers	22	14.29%
Combatants	13	8.44
Conspirators	13	8.44
Educators	9	5.84
Exiles	11	7.14
Flag makers	2	1.30
Fund raisers	12	7.80
Gun runners		
Martyrs	7	4.55
Messengers	6	3.90
Relatives of patriot leaders	24	15.58
Nurses/herbalists/doctors	9	5.84
Prisoners	13	8.44
Propagandists	9	5.84
Smugglers	3	1.95
Spies	1	0.65
Totals	154	100.00%

Material for this analysis consists of popular biographies, statuary, a stamp, and patriotic songs. Counted are characteristics of the *mambisa(s)* in each piece, not the *mambisa* herself or the single articles. Many ambiguous effigies exist, and they were not counted. If a representation conveyed more than one characteristic, then all characteristics were counted.

once again protested and gained improved living quarters for her. Inés Morillo was released from prison during a general amnesty in 1877 after serving nearly two years for her efforts on behalf of Cuban independence.[10]

When Mercedes Varona, the mother of Cuban educator and philosopher Enrique José Varona and a recognized independence patriot, died in 1911 in New York, her life was remembered in Havana in published statements written by Cuban military and political leaders alike. In her name, all *mambisas* were honored for their contributions to nationalism. Enrique José Varona dedicated a memorial to her and to all Cuban women who had fought in the Ten Years' War:

> The bravery of Cuban men during the Ten Years' War was heroic, but the valor of Cuban women was stupendous. The word heroism does not adequately express their soulful courage that was put to the test. It is more appropriate to call their bravery patriotic stoicism. Everything was denied them all at once, in the blush of their youth, as they were falling in love, they turned their attention to war and they endured all fear-

lessly. They faced the orphaning of their children, widowhood, misery, and they were the tearful companions to their husbands. Yet reproaches never escaped their lips. They accepted sacrifice in silence, they elevated it, they consecrated it, as an obligation to the liberation of their country.

H. Lincoln de Zayas, a commander in the Liberation Army, Epifanio Alvira, Alvaro Llona, and F. Gonzalo Marín also wrote poetry about Mercedes Varona's imprisonment and exile for her faithful support of the independence campaign.[11]

A review of the literature, iconic statuary, and other cultural ephemera offers a profile of women's lives and of how male publicists, artists, and mythmakers perceived their valor. More than one hundred heroines were immortalized in published records, and the more famous were also represented in song, poetry, music, statuary, and photographs, which underscores the ubiquity of the female icon in patriotic lore. The telling and retelling of independence sagas reveals the style and content of national myths. National heroines were revered for their daring, intelligence, recalcitrance, defiance, loyalty, and willingness to suffer alongside their men. Table 1 presents a content analysis of the heroic qualities of these women as represented by male mythmakers. The significance of these stories lies not in their veracity, but in the values propagandists projected for a Cuban public about national identity. Most revered was the patriot mother who violated all prescribed decorum for women and braved the male domain of brute strength, combat to the death, and vile barbarism to defend the nation. In essence, the *mambisa* symbolized Cuban determination to sacrifice all that was decent and beautiful to resist colonization. For women to send their children to the war front, to suffer exile and imprisonment, to become conspirators or international public speakers, or to place themselves squarely before Spanish fire was a commitment to either Cuba Libre or death.

The Making of Early Republican Heroines

Images of the female combatant served as a rhetorical means of marking connections between the noble past (independence), an uncertain present, and a desired future (democracy, prosperity, and social justice). During the Early Republic, however, the *manigua* ceased to be the battleground and nationalist militancy moved to the streets. Accordingly, the icons of female warriors had been transformed by 1914 to portrayals of female nationalists who dedicated their lives and resources to modernization, national defense, social justice, and a more inclusive democracy. Popular depictions of patriotic women included the wives of public officials, educators, and philanthropists. Counterheroines, who were no less prominent representatives of patriotism, included feminists, labor activists, and student insurrectionists. While some might argue that the modern women of the Early Republic lost the soldier identity, I maintain that the female warrior was reincarnated as a militant bourgeois nationalist or a mobilized political activist. Both sets of women were aware of or engaged in some level of heroic militancy that addressed the inadequacies of the present in order to gain a more perfect statehood.

Perhaps the most notable deviation from the *mambisa* legacy was the slightly reduced degree to which early-twentieth-century feminists pledged allegiance to a patriarchal leadership. Through militancy, feminists demanded women's rights, even though Cuban feminism rarely foresaw the demise of the patriarchy. All other groups pledged their loyalty to a male directorate. Most women who were in the public eye retained some aspect of nationalist militancy and were loyal to the male leadership of their political factions. Only the feminists altered, without destroying, women's reverence for the patriarchy.

Popular photojournalism recorded the activities of women who committed themselves to the construction of the new state. Associated with powerful men, white, elite women involved themselves in public works, education, health, and international affairs. Their work was no less romanticized in the popular press than the sacrifices of the *mambisas* who had preceded them. Themes of independence, sacrifice, loyalty to husband and country, philanthropy, and elite bearing, for example, converged in the person of Marta Abreu. The heiress of a sugar refinery near Santa Clara, Marta had involved herself in the independence movement as early as 1885 by building an electric plant for her city without the assistance or permission of Spain. Bringing light to the colonial town was understood by the citizens and the Spanish mayor to be a sign of Cuban self-reliance and of Marta's personal support for national sovereignty. When hostilities broke out in the War of 1895, Marta and her husband Luís Estévez y Romero traveled to Europe and the United States, where they conspired with the government-in-exile and helped fund the patriot army. When the war ended, the couple returned to Santa Clara, where Marta initiated and funded public works. Luís Estévez was tapped for public service, and his first appointment was as Justice Secretary under the occupational administration of General Leonard Wood. Estévez served only four months because he disagreed with the foreign command. When the United States recalled its military government and Cubans began selecting their own national leaders, Estévez ran as Tomás Estrada Palma's vice-president and served the first four-year term. When Estrada Palma's government was charged with corruption in 1905, Estévez urged the president to step down and separate himself from corrupt members of the government and U.S. control. Estrada Palma refused to take Estévez's advice, so the vice-president resigned in March 1905.

Marta Abreu was a reluctant political wife, but she made it clear that she would leave her beloved Santa Clara because she supported her husband and her country. She was above all a faithful wife to a noble patriot. Marta was most comfortable in Santa Clara, so their return in 1905 afforded her the opportunity to raise her family and restore her city. Her patriotic philanthropy included building a public library and a school for the arts and vocations. Her contributions to civic life were viewed by the citizens of Villa Clara and the entire island as a public covenant, a sacred act, that advanced the hope of democracy in a new nation.

Marta Abreu was an exemplary wife, nationalist, patriot, and philanthropist. She was white, educated, and self-sacrificing for husband and country. She was widely acclaimed by the nation and publicists.[12] Straddling, as her life did, the independence and republican periods, she was both a legendary and contemporary heroine. She was tested during independence, and she tried to build a sovereign nation during the Republic. Yet her voice was rarely recorded, and she did not participate in the many biographical accounts that extolled her feminine patriotism. Through benign neglect, she cooperated with her own iconization, since hagiographic tales beatified an ideal, not the real, republican lady of high society.

Accounts of María Luisa Dolz's life fall somewhere between heroic biography and accurate journalistic reports.[13] Cuban publicists and educators of the Early Republic extolled her girls' school, founded during the colonial period, for its modern curriculum and teaching excellence. Her voice was also recorded for posterity, since she made speeches on behalf of women's education and national independence, but the militancy of her message was preserved mostly by feminists, not the popular press or mythmakers. What was missing from this popular literature was her insistence that national democracy would be invalid so long as women remained outside the voting polity, and that women's education was fundamental for universal suffrage. Thus, women's education, feminism, democracy, and nationalism were a systematic whole in Dolz's way of thinking. Dolz attended and spoke at the First and Second National Women's Conferences held in 1923 and 1925, respectively.[14] Her efforts were to educate and liberate, and therefore women were the ones who were eulogized as heroic contributions to the nation. But for the general public, feminism went too far and threatened the patriarchy, a violation women could not commit and be good Cubans.

Mariana Sava de Menocal, the wife of Cuba's third president Mario Menocal, revived the image of militant patriotism in a most unexpected way. Her two terms as the first lady of Cuba began inauspiciously enough. She was an advocate of personal acts of charity in a nation that was on its knees economically. She organized women's charitable activities throughout her husband's two presidential terms. For her, democracy *a la cubana* meant providing for the poor through philanthropy, so she opened orphanages, girls' schools, and hospitals, and she distributed toys and candy to indigent children.[15] Rather than campaigning for federally funded social programs, she felt that setting an example of compassion and charity was the way to achieve social altruism, a value ingrained in Cubans through their national saint, La Virgen de la Caridad del Cobre (the Copper Virgin of Charity). As the incarnation of charity and goodness, Mrs. Menocal was the perfect complement to the patriarchal head of state.

World War I and Cuba's membership in the Allied Nations transformed Mrs. Menocal's charity into a national war campaign and kept Cuban female militancy alive. The war interrupted Cuba's evolution into a modern state by threatening trade agreements with the United States. The Great War also provided an opportunity for Cuba to join the Allies in the deadliest of all modern wars to date. European hostilities were a test for the young nation, and the greatest public standard bearer for Cuba was Mrs. Menocal.

Mrs. Menocal recast her domestic philanthropy projects into a visible war effort as she led high-society women into Red Cross cadres. The press lavishly reported her efforts and photographed her and the Red Cross ladies in their uniforms.[16] Their job was to pack bandages and medical supplies and to knit socks and scarves for the Allied soldiers. Mrs. Menocal assisted the Allies, and through her efforts Cuba proved it belonged with the victorious allies in the War to End All Wars. When many intellectuals clucked their disapproval in newspapers and journals for the horror of the war and the failure of world leaders to avert global carnage, Mrs. Menocal took a public stand for the Allies. She was Cuba's doughboy. Once victorious, Cuban jurists (all male) signed the Treaty of Versailles, a privilege earned by Cuba's declaration of war, of course, but physically warranted by Mrs. Menocal's passionate efforts.

Ofelia Domínguez Navarro,[17] Ofelia Rodríguez Acosta,[18] and Mariblanca Sabas Alomá,[19] among others, countered personalistic and at times self-serving models of charity and fidelity to the patriarchy when they equated democracy with women's right to suffrage, sexual expression, self-definition, the exalting of motherhood, and equal rights with men. They engaged in militant acts, as the *mambisas* had, but they included in their campaign the rights of women. All three women were radicals and ardent critics of the leading families. They were feminists and single women, unattached to individual men or male leaders. They were members of the avant-garde that destabilized the very lifestyle and national image that Mrs. Menocal projected. They organized feminist, labor, and student demonstrations, and they professed variant forms of socialism. All were journalists, all had more than one lover, and none ever married. Ofelia Domínguez Navarro was jailed for her radical activities as a labor organizer and legal defense lawyer for arrested labor and student activists. While they were not generally accepted as national heroines, they were acclaimed as exemplary women within radical and intellectual circles — groups that had extraordinary authority in the 1930s. Perhaps they were antiheroines, who inverted female standards by taking strong stands and who suffered harsh consequences not so much for defending women's rights as for living without men.

Ofelia Domínguez Navarro was the daughter of the independence activist Florentino Domínguez, who was twice arrested by the Spanish and finally exiled to Mexico. Ofelia and her mother lived briefly in one of the horrendous concentration camps where many Cubans perished for lack of food and medicine. The young Ofelia remembered the refusal of her parents to bend to Spanish demands, even when their lives and those of their children were at risk. As a young woman, she began her professional life as a grade-school teacher in Jorobada, a small rural village outside Aguas Bonitas in Las Villas. Her classroom was a single-room shack, and she had to jury-rig the seats and tables. In the rural setting, she learned a great deal about the folkways that limited peasants' access to health, education, power and self-determination. She observed how parents expected girls to leave school sooner than boys. She served as a reader for an illiterate community, so that the citizens might understand how issues were decided that influenced their livelihood. She also witnessed the arbitrary arrest and torture of rural people by the rural police force.

Ofelia's father supported her desire to seek an advanced degree, but he favored pharmacy, then an approved female occupation. But Ofelia chose law. She was driven from a young age to defend the unfortunate. Many of her clients were criminals, to be sure, but they were people she believed had been brought to crime by their desperate circumstances. The women she defended were, by and large, prostitutes and petty thieves.

When she moved her law office to Havana in 1924, she quickly joined the emergent feminist movement, but in 1928 she broke with the powerful Alianza Nacional Feminista over issues of workers' rights and the rights of illegitimate children. In 1930 she formed her own organization, the Unión Laborista de Mujeres, and became absorbed in the radical overthrow of President Gerardo Machado. In the midst of the 1933 revolution, she served the interests of the students and workers and formed a strong, personal alliance with Julio Antonio Mella, the founder of the Cuban Communist Party.

Between 1931 and 1933 Ofelia was jailed twice, and in 1933 she became a refugee in Mexico. She returned to Cuba in 1934, but was jailed two more times by Fulgencio Batista, and in 1935 she once again sought refuge in Mexico. While in jail in Cuba, she lived among the women she had previously defended, and she wrote brilliantly about conditions in the Guanabacoa Women's Prison during the 1930s. Under both the Machado and Batista military governments (1934–40), Ofelia witnessed the torture of political prisoners and saw the desperation, drug addictions, diseases, and superstitions of poor common criminals. In Mexico, she lived with radical Cuban expatriates, a virtual colony at the time, who found comfort in President Lázaro Cárdenas's prolabor government. When Leon Trotsky was assassinated in Mexico by an avid Marxist-Leninist,

Ofelia formed part of the murderer's defense team. Yet, in 1939, when she returned to Cuba, she immediately participated in the preparation of the democratic 1940 Constitution, the most progressive in the Western Hemisphere.

Ofelia Domínguez Navarro was a committed feminist, socialist, and activist. Her picture appeared in newspapers and weekly journals during the 1930s, as did printed records of her speeches and arrests. She also wrote for mainstream weeklies, and she regularly submitted columns for the more radical paper ¡Alerta! She was present at most commemorations of radical heroes, and she nearly always delivered speeches or organized demonstrations that drew attention to social injustices of the time. Few in Cuba, literate or illiterate, did not know her name.

Mariblanca Sabas Alomá presented her activism through the popular press. She belonged to the most influential intellectual group, El Grupo Minorista, and she wrote regular columns in *Social* and *Carteles*, two leftist but widely read periodicals. Her consistent social views focused most on liberating women from patriarchal domination through divorce and employment, supporting women's own sexuality, and freeing illegitimate children from social prejudice. Some referred to her as "The Red Feminist" because of her socialist inclinations, a label she bore with some pride. Mariblanca did not carry her activism to the streets; rather, she lived more of a bohemian life in which she practiced her interest in free love and avant-garde literature.

Ofelia Rodríguez Acosta, a journalist and novelist, wrote a regular column in Cuba's best-known weekly journal, *Bohemia*. She engaged the public in the debate about women's rights since her readers often responded to her positions, and their letters were printed in her column. Rodríguez Acosta largely agreed with Mariblanca and sympathized with Ofelia Domínguez, but she was also a philosophical thinker. Her most famous novel, *La vida manda*, which was acclaimed when it was released, was pessimistic about women's ability to find happiness and self-expression in Cuban society. Male dominance permeated all aspects of life, including even a woman's ability to be a mother. She finally left Cuba in the 1950s to live out her life in Mexico. She, like her two contemporaries, commanded audiences in Cuba, and together they projected an example of a female intelligentsia, a querulous avant-garde, an intellectual militancy, and even street violence and arrest, molding them into the Cuban sense of self.

Images of the female nationalist diversified during the Early Republic. While the *mambisa* retained her sacred place as an historical icon that unified a nation, new images of female militancy presented new ideals. Most repeated allegiance to state and patriarchy with examples of self-sacrifice. But the republican woman's military combativeness was muted, and her new modes of dedication spanned the spectrum from political wife to educator, philanthropist, feminist, journalist, worker, student, and political radical. All nationalist heroines and antiheroines claimed loyalty to the state, and all wished to mold

Table 2
Comparison of Early Republican and Revolutionary *Mambisa* Iconography

Characteristic	Republic	Percentage	Revolution	Percentage
Club organizers	22	15.49%	18	9.28%
Combatants	13	9.15	39	20.10
Conspirators	13	9.15	10	5.15
Educators	9	6.34	5	2.58
Exiles	11	7.75	29	14.95
Flag makers	2	1.41	2	1.03
Gun runners			3	1.55
Martyrs	7	4.93	10	5.15
Messengers	6	4.23	1	0.52
Relatives of men	24	16.90	30	15.46
Nurses/herbalists	9	6.34	10	5.15
Prisoners	13	9.15	24	12.37
Propagandists	9	6.34	8	4.12
Smugglers	3	2.11	4	2.06
Spies	1	0.70	1	0.52
Totals	142	99.99%	194	99.97%

As in Table 1, the memorabilia come from journal essays, funeral eulogies, and emblems. Counted are the characteristics of the *mambisa* in each commemorative piece and not those of the woman herself. Many ambiguous effigies exist, and they were not counted. When a representation conveyed more than one characteristic, all were counted.

the national character to their concept of state and society. The feminists were the only women to question whether undaunted loyalty to the patriarchy was a necessary element of patriotism. By 1930, all were recognized as protagonists and shapers of public opinion.

The Insurgency Period: The Making of Guerrilla Heroines

Early republican leaders, with U.S. support, subdued revolutionaries for nearly fifty years without entirely extinguishing the flames of nationalist rage that smoldered and occasionally flared in public demonstrations and protests. When Fulgencio Batista vacated constitutional law in 1952 and became a dictator president, seasoned radicals formed revolutionary resistance groups determined to overthrow him and restore the 1940 constitution. Violence, sabotage, and guerrilla warfare were their weapons of choice and among the cadres were women.

Between 1953 and 1958 a small number of women adopted violence as a means of returning the nation to Martí's promises of sovereignty and social justice, and, like their *mambisa* grandmothers, they pledged allegiance to male leaders. Resistance groups varied in their political orientation and tactics, but women served as conspirators, messengers, intelligence gathers, strategists, saboteurs, and armed guerrillas in all of them. Female militancy was a well-known fact that had a romantic currency. Thus, women revolutionaries were captured, tortured, and killed by Batista's secret police with little leniency given because of gender.

On 26 July 1953, a young rebel, Fidel Castro, led a band of angry revolutionaries in an attack on Santiago de Cuba's Moncada Barracks. His purpose was to announce an insurrection against the dictatorship of President Fulgencio Batista and to mobilize dissidents behind his leadership. Among the rebels were several women, the most famous of whom were Haydeé Santamaría[20] and Melba Hernández.[21] Both women were outfitted and received orders on a ranch just outside of Cuba's second largest city, and they rode into combat with one of the columns directed to take the barracks. Haydeé's brother Abel was an ardent supporter of Fidel Castro, and the brother and sister had worked with the underground to prepare for the attack. Melba was drawn to the insurrection along with her boyfriend.

The plan of attack included storming the barracks, taking the radio station, announcing the existence of the insurrection, and then receding into the Sierra Maestra to launch a guerrilla campaign. Breaching the walls of the barracks cost many rebel lives, as those who were not shot in combat were captured, tortured, and either jailed or executed. Some rebels, including Fidel Castro, never made it into the barracks, but Haydeé and Melba did. They were captured in Moncada's hospital, along with Abel and the rest of the men who had penetrated the military quarters. Haydeé and Melba were subjected to interrogation and torture, and Haydeé was presented with her brother's eyeballs as a means of breaking her will to keep silent. She was reputed to have replied that since Abel had never given information, she could not capitulate to such inhumanity. Both women were imprisoned for their participation in the attack, and both were released in the 1956 general amnesty. In November 1956, when Castro gathered his revolutionary troops to invade Cuba's southern coast, both women worked in the underground that supported him, and Haydeé went into the mountains to fight as a guerrilla soldier.

In the Sierra Maestra, Fidel Castro amassed a guerrilla army, and a group of women volunteered for battle duty. As the legend goes, Castro refused to place women on the battlefield, using the same excuse as Rosa La Bayamesa's commander had used nearly a century before: women did not have guns, and so they could not go to war. Castro pointed out that his male guerrillas had scant supplies and arms, so it was impossible to arm the women. The Sierra Maestra women took his argument to its logical conclusion and pledged to capture their own arms with which they would fight.

Approximately thirty women supplied their own guns and ammunition, most of which they captured in surprise attacks on Batista's military rural guards in Oriente province. Once armed, they participated in hostilities and fought with the second and third divisions of the Twenty-Sixth of July Army. On 31 December 1958, Fulgencio Batista boarded a plane and left Cuba to the revolutionaries. As Fidel Castro organized his cavalcade to march from Santiago to Havana in the first week of January 1959, he invited the female combatants to join him. These women rode atop tanks and trucks beside their *compañeros*, their faces lit with hope for the country and love for their countrymen. The sight of the victorious youth, men and women, taking over a nation long subjected to the control of a bourgeois elite and foreign interests ignited national pride and consecrated the Revolution. Triumphant female soldiers enshrined militancy as a national trait. Fidel Castro, once circumspect about female combatants, glorified their importance to the Revolution and used the new icon to keep Cubans on perpetual military alert and politically loyal.[22] In a gallant gesture of gratitude and respect, Castro benighted them by awarding them a permanent ceremonial position in military reviews. Since 1959, the Pelotón Mariana Grajales has led military parades and been the first squadron to present arms to their *comandante en jefe*. In this single act, female soldiers were seen by an entire nation as a beloved symbol of loyalty, militancy, and sacrifice to a male leader and a nation. Conversely, for their loyalty, militancy, and sacrifice, Fidel Castro honored and recognized them symbolically, but without surrendering power, autonomy, or authority to them.

Revolutionary Symbols: Appropriation of the *Mambisa*

Resurrecting the *mambisa* figure and linking her to the Revolution was one of the first acts of revolutionary mythmakers. Their mission was to root the 1959 Revolution in an authentic past. The remains of famous independence fighters were transferred to tombs of honor in the Colón Cemetery in Havana. New biographies of old heroines appeared, this time emphasizing their militancy and combativeness, traits that had not been remembered during the Early Republic (see Table 2 for a comparison of revolutionary depictions of the *mambisas* with those of the Early Republic). After the Revolution, new representations of the *mambisas* furnished a historical legacy to the actions of the Pelotón and female soldiers. In some cases, biographies of the *mambisas* were retold with a new emphasis on militancy and violence. In other cases, new research uncovered material and testimony about the *mambisas* and their soldiering activities. In still other cases, post-1959 biographies transferred attention from women's revolutionary club work to stories of physical danger and defiance of colonial authority. Whereas early republican propagandists had softened the picture of the combatant with images of conspirators and militant educators, revolutionary mythmakers emphasized physical danger and battlefield action. Both sets of propagandists eulogized women martyred by the enemy and praised them as loyal wives, mothers, daughters, and sisters of patriots. In fact, during the Early Republic, *mambisas* were mostly praised for their kinship with patriots. Most interesting is the comparative interpretation of exile by revolutionary narrators. Despite living in the context in which only traitors left the Island, they considered going into exile during the independence period to have been a major sacrifice for the nation.

Both generations of Cuban nationals appropriated the example of the *mambisas* as antecedents to the installed governments. During both periods, memorializing the *mambisa* constituted a rhetorical means of making links between the past, present, and future. Neither set of mythmakers devoted themselves to validating information about the independence combatants, but instead used their presumed actions in a rhetoric of national unification and credibility for the incumbent governments.

The two periods produced different interpretations of the *mambisas*, however. During the Early Republic, publicists used them as symbols of pride, sacrifice, and devotion. Few believed that women in Cuba Libre should continue with the same kind of sacrifice, but the hope was that the heirs of independence would be grateful to their mothers and understand that all Cubans, including women, were capable of such militancy should the nation be threatened. Since independence heroines' loyalty to family and country distinguished their actions and enriched popular passion for the state, citizens, both female and male, embraced the notion of fidelity and took emotional stands for patriarchal leadership. A by-product of *mambisa* history was the use of familial association as a means of ascending to higher circles of national society.

Revolutionary memorializing consolidated the image of the *mambisa* into a means of bringing a living definition to the state—that is, a model worthy of emulation in daily life in revolutionary Cuba. The fighting tradition of otherwise innocent young women and their complete loyalty to their men and country were reincarnated into a socialist image of revolutionary citizenship. Through the past, Cuban leaders applied revolutionary principles of unwavering loyalty to Fidel Castro, exemplary sacrifice, combat readiness, and exceptional fighting ability. The connection between the *mambisas*, the Pelotón Mariana Grajales, and the daily *lucha* of nearly all Cuban women has been to encourage the common woman to accept austerity and constant struggle as part of the nationalist state of being. By militarizing many aspects of life, Castro has made heroines out of all women and consecrated the Revolution by making the least militaristic members of society the greatest revolutionaries. Thus, he has succeeded in framing Cuba as a nation in constant struggle, in a constant state of rebellion, and never in a posture of orderly development or secure sovereignty.

Revolutionary Symbols: *Las Guerrilleras*

Once Castro assumed power, revolutionary iconography became a cottage industry, and artifacts appeared in the form of pins, posters, songs, funeral services, biographies, stamps, and banners presented to national and international observers of the Revolution. Romantic revolutionary songs performed by Nueva Trova, Silvio Rodríguez, Pablo Milanés, Sara González, and El Grupo Moncada exalted the female revolutionary, referring to her as a *compañera* in tender as well as political tones.[23]

In addition, all aspects of life were militarized, and each mission involved female combatants. Women, for instance, participated in literacy brigades, housing-construction brigades, agricultural work fronts, healthcare campaigns, and voluntary labor brigades, in addition to the Cuban Armed Forces, Rapid Response Squads, and militias. Women went to Angola and Central America as nurses, doctors, and teachers in the midst of open warfare to prove Cuba's alliance with revolutionary societies throughout the world. They also lent credence to Cuba's commitment to the humane treatment of combatants, even captured enemy troops. The female *militante* embodied militancy, the Revolution, and the idealization of Fidel Castro. It is instructive, then, to examine how the Revolution presented legendary stories of women who fought and died for the Cuban Revolution.

Unlike the immortalizing of the *mambisas* during early republican period, the *militantes* had a hand in writing their own histories, and their actions have served as living examples of how to be "good Cubans" or "good revolutionaries." Celia Sánchez[24] and Haydeé Santamaría became the grandes dames of the Revolution. Celia was Fidel's administrative advisor and constant companion until her death from cancer in 1980. Haydeé Santamaría married Armando Hart, the Minister of Culture, and she directed Cuba's prestigious Casa de las Américas until her suicide in 1981.Vilma Espín, the former wife of Raúl Castro and the first lady of Cuba, is the president of the Federation of Cuban Women. Public testimonials about their bravery have come in the form of articles in news magazines and newspapers, popular biographies, speeches, and eulogies. Fidel Castro himself spoke at both Celia's and Haydeé's funerals, lauding these two intelligent and unyielding revolutionaries whose devotion to him was beyond doubt. Biographical information appears primarily in the magazines *Mujeres* and *Muchachas,* through interviews with the revolutionary heroines about their roles in the overthrow of the Batista regime. In short, the powerful women of the Revolution have not released their papers for lengthy biographical study, and they have controlled the flow of information about themselves. Only Fidel Castro independently contributes information for public consumption. Besides Tiffany Thomas's work on this issue, no sophisticated biography

90 : K. Lynn Stoner

Table 3
Characteristics Conveyed by Iconographic Literature on
Revolutionary Women, 1953–1959

Characteristic	Number of Representations	Percentage
Combatants	25	38.46%
Conspirators	10	15.38
Educators	2	3.08
Exiles	2	3.08
Gun runners	1	1.54
Martyrs	11	16.92
Messengers	4	6.15
Nurses	1	1.54
Prisoners	1	1.54
Propagandists	4	6.15
Saboteurs	3	4.62
Spies	1	1.54
Totals	65	100.0%

has been written about these women, and their papers are classified and not readily available to biographers.

The members of the Pelotón Mariana Grajales have had limited authority in recording their war histories. To be sure, articles about them have been written by men and women and have appeared in national newspapers such as *Granma*, *Trabajadores*, and *Joven Rebelde* for political purposes. But the documents of greatest value are the as yet unpublished interviews that reside in the FMC Archive and that will be the primary documents for scholarly biographies.

The stories of some of the first martyrs of the Revolution have been made into popular histories by the leadership, particularly when these women have fit the image of the dedicated and sacrificial heroine. Clodomira Acosta Ferrals and Lidia Doce, both of peasant backgrounds from Oriente province, ran messages for Fidel Castro's guerrilla army and fought with the Pelotón Mariana Grajales. Clodomira was captured by Batista's secret police, tortured, and then executed without revealing important information about the clandestine operations of the Twenty-Sixth of July Movement. Lidia Doce, an armed combatant and messenger for the guerrilla forces, died in an ambush while on a combat mission. Che Guevara offered Clodomira's eulogy, and the Cuban Communist Party published pamphlet-length biographies of the two women.[25] The authors' intentions were to disseminate patriotic passion, revolutionary ideology, and examples of total loyalty to the revolutionary experiment.

According to a statistical review of iconography (presented in Table 3), the greatest contribution women made to the revolutionary guerrilla campaign was as combatants, and the second was as conspirators. Whether these women were related to male revolutionaries was not given as much prominence as in the independence period. What was always noteworthy was their unshrinking devotion to Fidel Castro, Ché Guevara, or the Twenty-Sixth of July Movement. Women's support roles as messengers, spies, fundraisers, and conspirators were less important, even though the women were vital to gun running, creating an underground with safe houses, supplying and provisioning the troops, and raising funds. No revolutionary praise or pity went to women who exiled themselves. Instead, such women must endure the epithet *gusanos* (worms), and worse.

Despite efforts to preserve the voices of revolutionary heroines, most attention has been focused on their war heroics, to the exclusion of personal introspection, uncertainty, serendipity, romance — in short, the subjective aspects of these women's lives. So, the women of the Sierra Maestra and the underground movement share a similar militant sainthood with their Mambí grandmothers, because they are more icons than real women. They are projected, perhaps even more than the *mambisas*, as examples of the ultimate *compañeras* — women willing to die not only for their own *compañeros*, but for the *comandante en jefe* and the Revolution.

Interpretation of the Iconography of Female Combatants in the Formation of Cuban National Identity

Throughout the twentieth century Cubans have used the iconic figure of the female combatant as a means of generating intense national identification. The method has been effective because it has unified souls behind the tragic/heroic figure of the female soldier by mixing psychological identification with nationalist pride. It has also portrayed the unspeakable violation of the most helpless and yet most defiant members of society.

Violence has its allure in national identify formation. It inspires unity against an enemy and stories of bravery in the face of a superior force that go directly to the heart. The citizenry can identify with female combatants, because they recognize in them their own vulnerability and they admire their refusal to surrender. This collective compassion and admiration initiate a social awareness of nation. The lived, moral experiences of the combatants in both the Early Republic and the Revolution, but especially during the Revolution, has taken on the public role of a religion. It has given a moral purpose to civic society that asks citizens to transcend individual necessity for the good of the whole. It is the example of a people willing to commit national suicide by risking the lives of young women for sovereignty. Female combatant imagery has become an aesthetic, a moral precept, and a ritualization of values.

The heroic female combatant also links the honor of male rebel leadership with the honor of a nation. In Cuban society, prerevolutionary and revolutionary, honor is the cornerstone of social consciousness. Male leaders depend upon public adulation and uncontested loyalty. Glenn Dealy argues that Latin American male honor depends upon individual male status within a group of potential competitors.[26] He is especially recommended by the adoration of women, which he cultivates for public display, which indicates his domination of all other potential contenders. The absolute loyalty of women who are willing to die for nation and the male leadership is a strong symbol of the worthiness and honor of both. Female loyalists stand between the honor and shame of a nation as well as the male leadership. Their example also justifies bloodletting and violent resistance to immoral and cruel foreign domination. The integrity of women recommended and recommends the honor of men and country. The sacrifice of the *mambisas* themselves and their witnessing of the deaths of members of their families without surrendering to the cruelty of the Spanish army was a source of humiliation for the Spanish and an endorsement of the honor of the nationalist leadership. The resilience of the women of the Pelotón to Batista's armed forces and even to Castro's prejudice against fielding them in battle diminished Batista's honor and exalted Castro's, for the women were willing to die, even for a man and a revolution that did not understand their worth. The continuing sacrifice of Cuban women on the domestic and international fronts constitutes one of the strongest foundations upon which Fidel Castro relies to remain in power.

The female soldier has given definition to Cuba's national character. Female sacrifice and loyalty to the nation and patriarchy have caused Cubans to transcend colonialism and truncated sovereignty by exalting national will, female heroism, and male honor. It has constructed what Dirkheim calls "the sacredness of the whole," a pious sentiment and not a reality. The sacredness of national identity has been used in both periods to humiliate foreign enemies and exclude Cubans unwilling to commit to the same cause. Ironically, the female warrior icon has also become a symbol of intolerance, exclusion, violence, and even struggle unto death — a war without limits.

NOTES

Lesbia O. Varona aided the research of this paper by producing information on the Cuban national anthem and the opera "Patria." Uva de Aragón directed my attention to the distinction between early republican and revolutionary interpretations of the female combatant. Both women are colleagues and friends who guide, criticize, and sustain me *en un ambiente de cubanía femenina.* Funding for this project was provided by the Rockefeller Fellow-in-Residence Grant, furnished through Florida International University in 1998.

1. For bibliographic citations about the nineteenth-century struggle for national independence, see Biblioteca Nacional José Martí, *Bibliografía cubana* (Havana: Instituto del Libro, 1968); Biblioteca Nacional José Martí, *Bibliografía de bibliografías cubanas* (Havana: Editorial

Organismos, 1973); and K. Lynn Stoner and Luís H. Serrano, eds, *Cuban and Cuban American Women: An Annotated Bibliography* (Wilmington, Del.: Scholarly Resources, 2000).

2. Déborah Betancourt Milanés and Maricela Molina Piñeiro, *La lucha de la mujer por sus derechos: Indice temático (1941–1945)* (Havana: University of Havana, 1987); Dania de la Cruz, *Movimiento femenino cubano: Bibliografía* (Havana: Editora Política, 1980); Instituto de Literature y Lingüistica de la Academia de Ciencias de Cuba, *Diccionario de la literatura cubana* (Havana: Editorial Letras Cubanas, 1984); Lucila Quinteiro Pacheco and Zunilda Rodríguez Santiago, "Procesamento y automatización del fondo: Club Femenino de Cuba," Escuela Nacional de Técnicos de Bibliotecas, Centro Nacional de Escuelas de Arte, Ministerio de Cultura, Havana, 1993; Stoner and Serrano, *Cuban and Cuban American Women*.

3. Louis A. Pérez, "Women in the Cuban Revolutionary War, 1953–1959: A Bibliography," *Science and Society* 39, no. 1 (Spring 1975): 104–8; Nelson P. Valdés, "A Bibliography on Cuban Women in the Twentieth Century," *Cuban Studies* 4, no. 2 (1974): 1–31; Stoner and Serrano, *Cuban and Cuban American Women*.

4. Teresita de Barbieri, "El feminismo y la Federación de Mujeres Cubanas," *Fem* 4, no. 15 (July–August 1980): 65–69; Tomás Fernández Robaina, *Bibliografía de la mujer cubana* (Havana: Ministerio de Cultura, 1985); Araceli García-Carranza, "Homenaje: XV aniversario de la Federación de Mujeres Cubanas, nuestra bibliografía sobre la mujer," *Revista de la Biblioteca Nacional José Martí* 18, no. 1 (January–April 1976): 91; Stoner and Serrano, *Cuban and Cuban American Women*. For commemorations of heroines of the Cuban Revolution, the magazines *Bohemia, Mujeres,* and *Muchachas* frequently run special articles on individual women who sacrificed in some extraordinary way for the Revolution. See also speeches made by Vilma Espín, president of the Federation of Cuban Women.

5. Victoria de Carturla Brú, *La mujer en la independencia de América* (Havana: Jesús Montero, 1945); Matilde Delfina Rodríguez Danger, *Mariana Grajales* (Santiago de Cuba: Editorial Oriente, 1977); Nydia Sarabia, *Historia de una familia mambisa: Mariana Grajales* (Havana: Instituto Cubano del Libro, Editorial Orbe, 1975); Nydia Sarabia, *Mariana Grajales* (Havana: Editorial Gente Nuevo, 1976).

6. Nydia Sarabia, *Ana Betancourt* (Havana: Editorial de Ciencias Sociales,) 1970; Mirta Aguirre, *Influencia de la mujer en Iberoamérica: Ensayo* (Havana: Imprenta P. Fernández y Cía., 1947).

7. Robert Solera, "Tres eran . . . las tres bayamesas," 16 September 2002, http://sites.netscape.net/robertsolera/bayamesa.html.

8. Enrique Ubieta, "La mujer en la revolución cubana: La familia del General Máximo Gómez," parts 1–3, *Bohemia* 1, no. 30 (26 November 1910): 347; no. 31 (3 December 1910): 359; no. 32 (10 December 1910): 370.

9. Enrique Ubieta, "La mujer en la revolución cubana: Mariana Grajales, viuda de Maceo," *Bohemia* 1, no. 33 (17 December 1910): 383.

10. Enrique Ubieta, "La mujer en la revolución cubana: Inés Morilla Sánchez," *Bohemia* 2, no. 9 (26 February 1911): 506.

11. Enrique Ubieta, "La mujer cubana en la revolución: Mercedes Varona," *Bohemia* 2, no. 20 (14 May 1911): 146.

12. Aguirre, *Influencia de la mujer en Iberoamérica*; Mirta Aguirre, "Marta Abreu, (1845–1909)," *Mujeres cubanas* 13 (November–December 1951): 5; Panfilo D. Camacho, *Marta Abreu: Una mujer comprendida* (Havana: Editorial Trópico, 1947); Juan José Casasús, *La inmigración cubana y la independencia de la patria: Primer premio en el concurso de la Asociación de Emigrados: Comenoración del Centenario de Martí* (Havana: Talleres Tipográficos de Editorial Lex, 1953); José Alvarez Conde, "Marta Abreu, El Naturalista y Villacara," *Magazine Social* 4 (April 1951): 8–9, 28–29; Manuel García Garofalo y Mesa, *Marta Abreu Arengibia y Dr. Luis Estévez y Romero* (Havana: Imprenta y Librería La Moderna Poesía, 1925); Elena Mederos de

González, "Women of the Americas: IV. Marta Abreu, Cuba," *Pan American Bulletin* 76, no. 1 (1942): 32–35; Vicentina Elsa Rodríguez de Cuesta, *Patriotas cubanas* (Pinar del Río: Talleres "Heraldo Pinareño," 1952); José A. Rodríguez García, *De la revolución y de las cubanas en la época revolucionaria* (Havana: Imprenta El Siglo XX, 1930); Emilia Romero, *Mujeres de América* (Mexico: Secretaría de Educación Pública, 1948); Antonio J. Vidaurreta Casanova, "Marta Abreu de Estévez: 3 facetas de una vida extraordinaria," in *Un año de periodismo,* ed. Mirta Aguirre (Santa Clara: Ediciones Culturales Publicidad, 1952), 12–24.

13. Alfredo Miguel Aguayo, *María Luisa Dolz, educadora de la mujer cubana* (Havana: Imprenta Cultural, 1937); Pastor del Río, *María Luisa Dolz: El maestro y su apostado* (Havana: Imprenta de "El Fígaro," 1929); Emilio Roig de Leuchsenring, "La muerte de una gran patriota," *Social* 10 (July 1925): 7; Dora Jiménez, *Las revoluciones del feminismo* (Havana: Molina, 1930); Juan Manuel Planas and Manuel J. Mesa, *La liberación de la mujer cubana por la educación* (Havana: Oficina del Historiador de la Ciudad, 1955); María Luisa Dolz y Arango, *La liberación de la mujer cubana por la educación: Homenaje de la Ciudad de la Habana en el centenario de su nacimiento, 1854–1954* (Havana: Oficina del Historiador de la Ciudad, 1954); María Luisa Dolz y Arango, "Las precursoras," *Mujer Moderna* 1, no. 1 (November 1925): 21–24; "Colegio María Luisa Dolz," *El Hogar* 7 (27 March 1904): 4–6.

14. Federación Nacional de Asociaciones Femeninas de Cuba, *Memoria del Primer Congreso Nacional de Mujeres: Abril 1–7, 1923* (Havana: Imprenta de la Universal, 1923); Federación Nacional de Asociaciones Femeninas de Cuba, *Memoria del Primer Congreso Nacional de Mujeres* (Havana: Imprenta La Universal, 1924); Federación Nacional de Asociaciones Femeninas de Cuba, *Memoria del Segundo Congreso Nacional de Mujeres organizado por la Federación Nacional de Asociaciones Femeninas, Abril 12–18, 1925* (Havana, 1927); Federación Nacional de Asociaciones Femeninas de Cuba, *Memoria del Segundo Congreso Nacional de Mujeres, Abril 12–18, 1925* (Havana, 1925); Federación Nacional de Asociaciones Femeninas de Cuba, *Primera serie de conferencias de divulgación cívica* (Havana: Talleres Gráficas Cuba Intelectual, 1927); Federación Nacional de Asociaciones Femeninas de Cuba, *Programa oficial del Segundo Congreso Nacional de Mujeres organizado por la Federación Nacional de Asociaciones Femeninas de Cuba* (Havana, 1925).

15. The popular press covered Marianita Sava de Menocal's work on at least a weekly basis. Social columns, frontpage stories, and current events are the sections of *Bohemia, Social,* and *Diario de la Marina* that were reliable sources of information about the political leadership. The following citation is but one example of such reporting: "Actualidades," *Bohemia* 5, no. 28 (12 July 1914): 333.

16. For extensive coverage of Mrs. Menocal's war effort, see Conde Kostia, "Marianita Seva de Menocal," *Social* (May 1916): 23–25, 36–37.

17. For a brief biographical sketch on Domínguez Navarro, see K. Lynn Stoner, "Ofelia Domínguez Navarro: The Making of a Cuban Socialist Feminist," in *The Human Tradition in Latin America,* ed. William Beezley and Judith Ewell, 119–40 (Wilmington, Del.: Scholarly Resources, 1990). See also K. Lynn Stoner, *From the House to the Streets: The Cuban Woman's Movement for Legal Reform, 1898–1940* (Durham, N.C.: Duke University Press, 1991). Domínguez Navarro's personal papers are in the Cuban History Institute in Havana, Cuba. Domínguez Navarro published frequently in the press. For many of her references, see Stoner and Serrano, *Cuban and Cuban American Women.* Domínguez Navarro also published two autobiographical books: *De seis a seis: La vida en las prisiones cubanas* (Mexico City, 1937), and *Cinquenta años de una vida* (Havana: Institute Cubana del Libro, 1971).

18. Ofelia Rodríguez Acosta wrote a regular column on Cuban feminism for *Bohemia* between 1927 and 1932. A listing of some of her more outstanding essays may be found in Stoner and Serrano, *Cuban and Cuban American Women,* 92–95. She was also a novelist and short-story

writer, and her literary works are also listed in the above bibliography. She suffered from mental instability in her last years and died in Mexico. For a brief treatment of her life, see Stoner, "The Feminist Journalists," *From the House to the Streets*, 87–107.

19. Mariblanca Sabas Alomá, known as the Red Feminist for her socialist feminist views, wrote regularly for *Social* and *Carteles*. She was a member of the Grupo Minorista, an intellectual group of writers and artists who had enormous influence over radical perceptions of national identity during the 1920s and 1930s. She wrote one novel, *La Remora* (Havana: Imprenta El Siglo XX, 1921). Many of her best articles on feminism appear in *Feminismo: Cuestiones sociales– Crítica literaria* (Havana: Editorial Hermes, 1930). For a more extensive, although not complete, listing of her essays, see Stoner and Serrano, *Cuban and Cuban American Women*, 96–98.

20. See biographical files in the Federation of Cuban Women's Archives. Celia Sánchez's file contains recorded conversations between Haydeé Santamaría, Celia Sánchez, Vilma Espín, Melba Hernández, and Fidel Castro about their activities in the clandestine movement. See also Graziella Méndez, "Mujeres de la Revolución," *Mujeres* 4, no. 7 (July 1964): 48; Graziella Méndez, *Mujeres ejemplares* (Havana: Editorial Orbe, 1977); Graziella Méndez, *Mujeres en revolución* (Havana: Sección de Historia de la Dirección Política de las FAR, 1974); Iris Dávila, "Compañeras," *Mujeres* 13, no. 7 (July 1973): 4; Vilma Espín, "Habla de Haydeé y Celia," *Bohemia* 73, no. 10 (6 March 1981): 36–39. Haydeé Santamaría's personal papers are not available for public use. Some messages from the period of the insurrection can be found in Stoner and Serrano, *Cuban and Cuban American Women*.

21. The Federation of Cuban Women houses a file on Melba Hernández that consists of two short articles. Besides the articles on Haydeé Santamaría that frequently mention Melba, see Carol Robb and Alice Hageman, " 'Let Them Be Examples' . . . ," *Cuba Review* 4, no. 2 (1974): 19–21.

22. The Federation of Cuban Women has created an extensive archive on the Pelotón, which includes transcribed individual and group interviews. It also contains files on the individual women who participated in the Sierra Maestra revolutionary army. The only published account of the Pelotón is found in a 1960 publication entitled *Las mujeres en la Revolución Cubana*, found in the History Institute Library. For an extensive listing of references, see Stoner and Serrano, *Cuban and Cuban American Women*, 185.

23. An example of the romanticization of the revolutionary woman is Silvio Rodríguez's song "Mujeres," which exalts the woman who sends her children into combat, referring to Mariana Grajales. Rodríguez worships the other mother who marches toward the star, referring to Bernarda Toro de Gómez, who kept the star of Máximo Gómez's uniform with her. These women, he sings, buried their men with their own hands. He trembles before the woman who confronted the *caudillo* (Weyler), who always lurked in the shadows, by spreading fire in his path. He shivers before the woman who is willing to leave her home on the ferocious continent and come to live in another house (perhaps referring to women willing to change from capitalism to socialism or women leaving the United States to live in Cuba). He is in awe of many women, women of fire and of snow. He trembles before women who are recognized in history and those who have been forgotten, for no book is large enough to contain their stories. Rodríguez collapses the independence past into the revolutionary present, and he dares the historian to gather their names.

24. Celia Sánchez was Fidel Castro's confidant and aide-de-camp during the guerrilla period and administrative advisor after he assumed power. She died in 1980 of cancer. Some of her records are with the Federation of Cuban Women, and an entire archive is devoted to her papers.

25. Gaspar González-Launaza Rodríguez, *Clodomira Acosta Ferrals* (Havana: Comité Central del Partido Comunista de Cuba, 1983); Departamento de Orientación Revolucionaria del Comité Central del Partido Comunista de Cuba, *Presencia de Lidia Doce* (Havana: Comité Central del Partido Comunista de Cuba, 1974).

26. Glen Claudill Dealy, *The Latin Americans: Spirit and Ethos* (Boulder, Colo.: Westview

Press, 1992); and Glen Claudill Dealy, *The Public Man: An Interpretation of Latin American and Other Catholic Countries* (Amherst, Mass.: University of Massachusetts Press, 1977). For a general treatment of the use of honor, shame, and humiliation as forces in identity construction, see William Ian Miller, *Humiliation and Other Essays on Honor, Social Discomfort, and Violence* (Ithaca, N.Y.: Cornell University Press, 1993).

MAYRA BEERS

Murder in San Isidro: Crime and Culture during the Second Cuban Republic

ABSTRACT

This article uses the murder of a well-known politician in Cuba, Alberto Yarini y Ponce de León, who was also a celebrated pimp, to delve into questions of national identity and nationalist discourse. The theoretical framework relies on the importance of gender images and prostitution in nation-building rhetoric, arguing that these matters have been used in support of political interests. Its methodology analyzes the tensions and ambivalence surrounding Cuban national identity in the first two decades of the republic. The murder of Alberto Yarini catalyzed a seemingly odd convergence of Havana elites, underworld figures linked to prostitution, and the social and cultural layers in-between. The confluence of class and culture displayed the duality that was — and some argue remains — a fundamental feature of Cuban national identity. However, this article questions the extent to which national identity — *cubanidad* — was the product of a nativist counterculture that contested elite nationalist discourse. The romantic version of Yarini was the embodiment of that developing consciousness. In the midst of endemic institutional corruption and graft, his most cited attribute was his "honor," within the nuanced context presented by the environment of popular classes and their sense of esteem. This work will, therefore, examine the sociocultural milieu that produced this tension, which formed part of the identities and solidarities that energized Cuban popular culture, thus providing new ways of observing an emerging national identity and drawing important but hidden connections between gendered discourse and popular leadership.

RESUMEN

Este artículo utiliza el asesinato de un conocido político cubano, Alberto Yarini y Ponce de León, que también era un célebre proxeneta o "chulo", para incursionar en cuestiones sobre la identidad nacional y el discurso nacionalista. El marco teórico se basa en la importancia de las imágenes de género y la prostitución en la retórica para construir una nación. Arguye que estos asuntos han sido utilizados para apoyar intereses políticos. Su metodología analiza las tensiones y ambivalencias sobre la identidad nacional cubana durante las dos primeras décadas de la República. El asesino de AlbertoYarini sirvió de catalizador de una aparentemente extraña convergencia de la elite habanera, figuras del bajo mundo relacionadas con la prostitución, y las capas culturales en el medio. La confluencia de clases y culturas mostró la dualidad que era — y algunos dirán que aún es — parte fundamental de la identidad nacional cubana. Sin embargo, este artículo cuestiona hasta que punto la identidad nacional — la cubanidad — era el producto de una contracultura nacional que retaba el discurso nacionalista de la elite. La versión romántica de Yarini es la encarnación de esa naciente conciencia. En medio de los chanchullos y la corrupción nacional endémica, la característica que más se le atribuía era su "honor," en las sutilezas del contexto que ofrecía el ambiente de las clases populares y su sentido de respeto. Este trabajo, por tanto, examina el medio sociocultural que produjo esta tensión que formaba parte de las identidades y solidaridades que alimentaban la cultura popular cubana, dándonos nuevas formas de observar la naciente identidad nacional, y estableciendo importantes aunque escondidas conexiones entre el discurso de género y el liderazgo popular.

"Not since the funeral of Máximo [Gómez]," reported the Associated Press, "[has] Havana witnessed such a tremendous demonstration of popular sympathy and respect as that which attended the funeral of Alberto Yarini."[1] On 24 November 1910, thousands of spectators lined the sidewalks and men quietly tipped their hats in respect as Yarini's funeral cortege made its way through Havana's main boulevards; many in the somber crowd joined the procession as it passed by.[2] Led by a police escort under the command of General Armando Riva, the city's chief of police, the procession included a band of musicians who walked behind the officers while mourners rhythmically marched to their somber tune.[3] Behind them came the hearse, drawn by eight plumed horses, each draped in the yellow and black finery of the city's most expensive funeral house.[4] Several men jockeyed in the street for an opportunity to carry the bier on their shoulders. Yarini's father and brother, dressed in mourning clothes, solemnly followed the young man's coffin.[5] Next came four wagonloads of flowers, with numerous wreaths hanging from the coaches, their purple ribbons with gold-lettered dedicatories streaming in the breeze.[6] A procession of several thousand (one estimate calculated the crowd at more than ten thousand), including delegations from Havana's various political and commercial bodies, followed the flower-coaches.[7] More than a hundred carriages, carrying representatives of the best society figures in the city, government officials and dignitaries, and officers from the army and navy ascended the knoll known as "El Bosque" on the road to the Cementerio Colón. Also in the throng that inched its way along Galíano Street that November morning were "all the elements of the 'red light' district," "gaudily attired women," and members of "vodoo societies." Few pimps have ever been interred with such pomp.[8]

The spectacle must have been impressive since coverage of Yarini's funeral was picked up by the Associated Press and featured on the pages of U.S. metropolitan dailies the day after Thanksgiving. The *New York Times* ran the story under the headline, "Laud Yarini as a Patriot." The *Tampa Tribune* headline read "Demonstration over Remains of Bad Man." The *Washington Post* story heralded the death of a white slaver and included his connection to vodoo societies.

Images conjured by the funeral cortege of the young Cuban and by the U.S. headlines were contradictory and portentous. Although a member of Havana's elite, Yarini was nevertheless involved in the demimonde of prostitution. Honored by multitudes but condemned by newspaper editors, lauded as a patriot yet denigrated as a "bad man," the contrasts and contradictions enveloping Yarini illustrate the social flux and political chaos that accompanied the first decades of Cuban independence, when the country reeled in the aftermath of revolution, two U.S. interventions, and a second attempt to found a republic.

Historiography

In recent decades the demimonde of prostitution has served historians as an analytical device to explore gender issues and nation building in both Europe and the Americas. The groundbreaking work of Judith Walkowitz for Victorian England and Donna Guy for Argentina focused attention on gender issues associated with female prostitution at the turn of the twentieth century.[9] The paucity of sources, however, makes the principal actors in these studies a cadre of male politicians, criminologists, sociologists, doctors, and other professionals. The males, at times aided by elite female activists, are shown as impinging upon the institution in their attempts to sanitize its practices and eliminate or minimize its presence. The voices of participants in the trade are often inaudible. In addition, this growing body of work has focused on Europe, and especially on studies of fin de siècle Paris, London, and New York.[10]

A small number of feminist historians dealing with Spanish America, however, have been particularly concerned with the import of gender images and prostitution in nation building. Supporting the findings of Guy, Sueann Caulfield's research on Brazil argues that gender and prostitution issues were invoked in support of "particular political interests."[11] Invariably, the studies conclude that the debate over state regulation of prostitution and weak efforts toward its abolition were part of an orchestrated attempt by the new Spanish-American nations to be recognized as a part of a "modern" world.[12] Few studies, however, address the apparent cleavage between official rhetoric about, and popular responses to, prostitution.[13]

By the second half of the nineteenth century, prostitution and its control had become hotly debated topics both in Europe and the Americas. The massive immigration from Europe during the last two decades of the century renewed the zeal of "enlightened" nations to "clean up" the urban centers and "protect" their citizens. Prostitutes were targeted in morality and public health campaigns on both sides of the Atlantic, but for Latin America the added incentive for elites was in luring foreign capital. For example, Caulfield argues, "the aims of urban authorities [in Spanish America] included transforming the capital cities into showcases of dynamic modern nations." She concludes that "liberal professionals believed that their policies would accelerate progress, understood as a linear process through which both urban space and the culturally and ethnically diverse Latin American populations would come to resemble those of white, industrialized Europe."[14] Often, as in the case of Cuba, however, elite ideals for the nation ignored popular sentiment and contrasted sharply with the reality of the streets.

Few studies of the mechanisms of prostitution in Cuba have been published, and, except for an anecdotal history by Tomás Fernández Robaina, they deal with prostitution in the post-Revolution years.[15] After examining the barrage of newspaper stories, police reports, judicial proceedings, and subsequent dramatic depictions of the Yarini episode, I conclude that the political expediency of modernization and nation-building rhetoric was hard-pressed to find popular support. This apparent paradox mirrors the Cuban quandary in crafting a national identity and attempting to present itself as one of the modern and independent nations of the world. Having come late to independence, Cuba struggled to "catch up" to the rest of Latin America as it sought to define "Cuban" in white, Northern European terms. At the state level this meant consolidation of the nation, although, as Aline Helg argues, European immigration was seen as the "salvation of the nation," as it had been in Argentina.[16] At the cultural level, following Martí-style nationalism, a new kind of anti-imperialist and populist nationalism surfaced.

The Second Time Around

The young Cuban nation struggled physically and ideologically to establish a place among the progressive countries of the world. Havana's officials tore down sections of the old colonial city walls only in 1853; a Republican Cuba completed the job in the early twentieth century in an effort to show the world its commitment to modernity.[17] As Spain's last colony in the Western Hemisphere, and stinging from imposed U.S. control, Cuban society underwent traumatic transformations during the first decade of the republic. Louis A. Pérez Jr. has argued that with intervention, "a Cuban war of liberation was transformed into a U.S. war of conquest," and that even the terminology, the Spanish-American War, denied Cuban participation in achieving independence and deprived the Cuban people of agency.[18] Such symbolic emasculation deeply affected expressions of nationhood. *"Por el bien de Cuba"* (for the good of Cuba) was the compelling force of both the *independentistas* and those favoring continued U.S. control. Perhaps it was only during such a time of crisis that a man like Yarini could have emerged as a cultural icon for the Cuban people, providing fodder for what has been termed the Cuban Republic's first myth.[19] In part, this essay argues that in early republican Cuba the prostitution debate, illustrated by the contrasting responses to Yarini's death, is indicative of the failure of Cuban elites to craft a national vision that garnered and maintained popular support during the first decades of independence.

In 1898, as the United States engaged Spain in an imperialist war, thirty years of revolutionary rebellion against the Spanish Crown by the Cuban people abruptly ended. Although characterized by President McKinley in an announcement to Congress on 11 April 1898 as "a forcible intervention . . . as a neutral stop to war," in reality the intervention measures established U.S. claim to the island by virtue of arms.[20] Observers in the United States noted the lackluster military operations of the Cubans in their independence struggles as indicative of the irresolute Cuban character. Cubans were excluded from the peace talks with Spain while the United States negotiated a unilateral peace. In addition, claiming to have ended Spain's colonial rule over Cuba, the United States asserted its own right to govern the Cubans. After four hundred years of Spain's colonial rule, official U.S. occupation of the island began on 1 January 1899.

The Cuban people, however, actively challenged U.S. intervention. While an ascendant bourgeoisie welcomed the occupation with relief and gratitude, *independentismo* resurfaced as the most formidable challenge to North American control and hopes of eventual annexation of the long-coveted island. The "better-classes," U.S. officials assumed, were for annexation and only the "rabble," singularly unfit to govern, demanded independence. U.S. officials hoped that over time, the Cubans would "come around" and clamor for annexation, having realized the benefits of being a part of the United States "Empire." As General Wood noted, "The real voice of the people of Cuba has not been heard. . . . When they do speak, there will be more voices for annexation." But in the elections of 1900, the Cubans did not elect the U.S.-sponsored candidates and instead opted for what occupation officials termed "demagogues" and "emotional candidates," thus proving their "inadequacy for self-government."[21]

In view of the Cuban people's reluctance to submit to U.S. demands, by 1901 the occupation quickly became an expensive burden for the United States — some half a million dollars a month. The Platt Amendment, passed by Congress in 1901, while guaranteeing an end to the occupation, imposed U.S. controls on Cuban self-government, especially in the area of foreign relations and debt restrictions.[22] After several months of sometimes violent protests and demonstrations by the citizenry, the delegates of the Constitutional Convention convened in Havana acquiesced and by a single vote the Platt Amendment became a part of the Cuban Constitution of 1901.[23] After the military occupation ended in 1902, Tomás Estrada Palma, an "ultraconservative" and a U.S. ally, became the first president of the republic. His reelection in 1906 provoked an armed uprising in Cuba and, after a desperate plea from Cuba's president to Washington, renewed U.S. occupation ensued from 1906 to 1909. Estrada

Palma's reelection and the subsequent U.S. occupation once again stoked the fires of the *independentismo* movement.[24]

In *Cuba: Between Reform and Revolution*, Pérez argues that "rather than expressing economic interest in any one class, the separatist movement was expected to open up opportunities for a heterogeneous social amalgam."[25] The movement appealed to Cubans of all classes who expected independence to create a new society. However, Pérez also contends that in 1902 "Cuba entered nationhood with its social order in complete disarray and its class structure totally skewed."[26] The dominant Creole bourgeoisie of the late nineteenth century had toppled in the wake of the sugar crisis and of revolution. The economic vicissitudes of the planter elite also produced a dispossessed peasantry. In an agricultural economy, agriculture was at a virtual standstill and economic opportunities in every sector stifled. Foreigners — including U.S. citizens with over $200 million in investments on the island — controlled sugar production, land speculation, mining, railroads, utilities, and banking. Foreign capital funded the island's limited industry, and few Cubans were willing to invest in manufacturing in the absence of a viable market as cheap, U.S.-manufactured goods flooded the island.[27]

A new elite looked to politics — including graft, bribery, and embezzlement — for their livelihood.[28] For example, in 1909, after the U.S. relinquished control of Cuba for a second time, the Liberal Party candidate, José Miguel Gómez, ran on a platform that assured the restoration of cockfights and the lottery; he handily won the election.[29] The Gómez presidency (1909–1913) was notorious for graft and corruption.[30] Irene Wright, a U.S. journalist living in Havana during the first decades of independence, noted in 1910 that government "offices [were] considered plums, [they] fall not to the fit, but to the favorites of the Great Paternal Power — the central government."[31]

Adding to the political and economic turmoil, as in most of Spanish America, immigrant workers from Europe (usually young, male, and single) arrived in Cuba in large numbers after 1900.[32] Competing with Cuban labor in all sectors, some 30 percent of immigrants remained in the capital city. Foreigners usurped economic opportunities in every field and *peninsulares* quickly replaced Cuban women as domestics.[33] This added displacement deeply affected *criollas* who already faced social restrictions and economic hardships on the island.

The Women and the Trade

In Cuba, the ideology of appropriate roles for women, both within the family and the community, restricted employment opportunities, especially for white women. A double standard existed in Cuban society: "The woman is at home and the man is on the street."[34] Carefully constructed public and private spaces insured that women's influence was relegated to traditional roles within private space. Motherhood and female domesticity were revered in Cuba's moralistic, romantic tradition for women. Traditional cultural values that excluded women from occupations requiring contact with men effectively undermined female agency.[35] Except for teachers, employment outside the home was not acceptable for married women and left the vast majority of female wage earners as single or widowed. This distinction crossed lines of race and class.[36]

War and reconcentration efforts of the 1890s displaced many women from the countryside. Widows in postwar Cuba represented 50 percent of the adult female population. "The life of a woman is very sad here in Cuba," Wright commented. "The only right a woman had was the right to starve to death when her support failed."[37] Nevertheless, more than 2,440 women engaged in prostitution, the "fourth largest source of employment" for women on the island. The occupation government did not act expeditiously in issuing prostitution restrictions. It was not until 27 February 1902 that Military Order #55 adopted a General Decree (Reglamento General) in an attempt to regulate the practice of prostitution both in the capital and throughout the island, and further sought to segregate the prostitution trade within the city of Havana.[38] Within the approved zones, prostitutes catered to the vibrant maritime traffic, the large number of mostly single, male immigrants who arrived regularly, and to military personnel both Cuban and U.S.

The prostitute community of Havana was unique in Spanish America. Ramón Alfonso, Secretary of the Special Hygiene Commission, in his 1902 annual report, offered a detailed demographic analysis of the island's prostitutes.[39] Unlike the large number of immigrants among the prostitute sector in countries such as Brazil and Argentina, in Cuba the vast majority of prostitutes were *hijas del país* (585 of the 744 counted for Havana were Cuban-born). The prostitutes concentrated in the capital, where the 1899 census listed more than 700 prostitutes living in some 338 brothels.[40] More than half of Havana's prostitutes had been born in the capital, while most of the rest had emigrated from provincial capitals or other national urban centers.[41] These women worked in Havana's *zonas de tolerancia* in the oldest parts of the city by the wharfs and industrial sectors. Alfonso also noted that unlike the statistics published by Benjamín de Céspedes in 1888, who found that 60 percent of Havana's prostitutes were black, by 1902 white prostitutes were in the majority (64 percent). In addition, Alfonso found that prostitutes from the western half of the country (Pinar del Río, Havana, and Matanzas) were less educated than those from the eastern half (Las Villas, Puerto Principe, and Santiago de Cuba), although the majority from all regions were illiterate.[42] Foreign-born prostitutes included Spaniards, Mexicans, and Puerto Ricans, with a few other nationalities represented in small numbers. Of the 744 surveyed, 425 were white, over 300 were illiterate, and a majority had held previous occupations as servants; a few had been laundresses and seamstresses (the most common occupations for women in Cuba according to the 1900 census). These women, generally between the ages of 18 and 25, poor and illiterate, represented the most marginalized sector of the economy.[43]

Nevertheless, prostitution had a long and celebrated history in Cuba, and in particular, in the capital city. Céspedes, in his 1888 study of prostitution and disease, noted that as early as 1493, the crew members who accompanied Columbus had "prostituted" Indian women and introduced syphilis to the New World.[44] The subsequent arrival of large numbers of young, single men as conquistadors and colonists was accompanied by that of *mujeres de mal vivir*, who, according to Céspedes, had escaped from the clutches of the Inquisition.[45] In a letter to the King, dated 23 December 1584, Governor General Gabriel de Luján accused the mayor, the town's chief military officer, and a sergeant of "housing" several women. By 1657, the accusations sent to the Spanish Crown included charges against the Bishop of Havana, J. Manuel Montiel, and various priests and friars, contending that the poisoning of the previous Bishop, Diez Vara, resulted from disputes over prostitution among the clerics of the city. According to Céspedes, with the introduction of African slaves to Cuba, the prostituting of black women became a viable and profitable enterprise throughout the island, as slave-owning entrepreneurs catered to the large numbers of white, single men who constituted the vast majority of Cuba's population.[46] Céspedes noted that during the eighteenth century, while several governors of the island made sweeping reforms toward "good government," none addressed the issue of prostitution, so inculcated was its necessity for the economic interests of the island. A move toward reform was made in 1776 when the Marquis de la Torre established La Casa de Recogidas to house the large numbers of "delinquent and rowdy" women who lived on Havana's streets.[47]

The first attempt to regulate prostitution in Cuba materialized in 1873. In April of that year, Governor Pérez de la Riva ordered that a hospital be opened to treat the large numbers of syphilitic prostitutes in the capital. Prostitutes were to be registered and licensed, with proceeds used to pay the expenses of the Sanitation Hospital (Hospital de Higiene) that opened in June 1873. On 27 December 1873 the first regulations and laws governing prostitutes were published. Four hundred prostitutes were listed in the registers for the inaugural year.[48] Using the revenue from the 30 peso, 80 centavo annual "license" fee, these women were to be examined at home twice weekly, once for a general external exam and once internally by use of a speculum. Many prostitutes, however, unable to pay the heavy fee, became *fleteras* (streetwalkers), often living and performing services between parked carriages and rail cars or in the alleys of the city.[49]

By 1875, military authorities, complaining that 10 percent of the armed forces were infected with syphilis, demanded that the government issue more-stringent regulations. That year, Dr. Claudio Delgado was appointed Director of Physician Hygienists and drafted a new study of the prostitution "problem," which called for more-stringent enforcement of existing regulatory decrees.[50] On 9 September 1888, *La Cebolla*, a Havana newspaper reportedly published by and for prostitutes, protested the new regulations in an editorial. "It is sinful," the editor complained. "It is unconstitutional. It is a miscarriage of justice against unfortunate women who seek to carry out their business under the auspices of the law, for which they pay a hefty fee."[51] Two weeks later, the paper published an unsigned letter, supposedly from a prostitute, which further denounced the new reforms and regulations:

The Mayor, who is old and cranky, so that not even a fly dares to land on him, has decreed that we cannot exhibit ourselves in the doorways of our own establishments.... Is this fair? What country prohibits the businessman from showing the public his merchandise? The "horizontals" of this city pay more contributions to the state than necessary. Yet, although we contribute more than any other sector to bolster the revenues of the state with the sweat of our . . . brows, we are treated as if we were slaves; as if we were outlaws. In other words, we are considered citizens so as to meet our obligations, but not to enjoy the rights of citizenship.[52]

Each edition of *La Cebolla* also included a tantalizing centerfold labeled simply La Guajira, La Madrileña, or some other similar description.

In spite of such protestation, the movement for regulation and abolition of prostitution continued in Cuba as elsewhere. Increasing cases of disease among prostitutes and their clients in the 1880s and subsequent decades and the inability of government to pass meaningful regulatory measures had spurred Céspedes to join many of his contemporaries in conducting "scientific" studies of prostitution. This coincided with many analyses of prostitution produced at a time when proving modernity was a priority for many nations. At the turn of the twentieth century, in countries such as France, Spain, England, Argentina, Brazil, and the United States, doctors, scientists, and women activists "studied" prostitution, its causes, and its regulation, and especially its danger from disease.[53] A second concern, culminating in a League of Nations inquiry and subsequent resolutions aimed at solving the problem, was the traffic in "white slaves."[54]

Historical inquiries, however, have largely ignored the internal workings of prostitute communities at the local level. After the turn of the century, the prostitute community, both inside and outside the *zonas de tolerancia* in Havana, boasted a strict moral and social hierarchy. Especially in San Isidro, the most well-known prostitution barrio in the capital, there existed a "manifest camaraderie, true friendship, and solidarity. . . . The barrio had its ethical and moral standards and whoever did not tow the line was criticized and looked down upon."[55] Named after an ancient colonial church and hospice, the street of San Isidro gave its name to the entire prostitute community. Wright reported, "There are districts in Havana—one street, in particular—where, I am told, indecency beggars the average man's imagination . . . [and] inspires many visiting women to drive, with their husbands, through this section."[56] Incidents reported in local newspapers simply read "lo de San Isidro" in identifying prostitute problems.[57] Located close to the wharfs and in the oldest part of the city, San Isidro gained fame as a place for prostitutes, pimps, free living, and for harboring Afro-Cuban religious syncretism.[58] San Isidro was described as a place where "the strongest of human passions [found] a counterpoint in racial co-existence, popular religion, and even in politics."[59]

Within San Isidro and other prostitution zones, the residents recognized an ordered social system. As Reay Tannahill argues for France, the hierarchy of prostitution depended on the established nature of the prostitute; the more mobile she was, the less the respect she commanded within the prostitution community.[60] In San Isidro, members of the community were differentiated among established prostitutes and *fleteras*. Matrons and pimps who kept their own houses and had several women working for them were at the top of the social order; independents who rented a room by the month came next; and *fleteras* ranked lowest in the female community.[61] Those prostitutes who had a room or a house were held in highest regard, for even though they were at the mercy of policemen bent upon extortion, they had some protection under the law. *Fleteras*, on the other hand, were regularly rounded up and often beaten in the streets before being sent to the *vivac*, or local prison.[62] Whether these distinctions were a result of the differentiations originally imposed by government officials in the regulations or originated within the community itself is difficult to ascertain.[63]

Several additional distinctions were evident among the prostitutes. Ethnic and racial discrimination existed, although apparently not between prostitutes; it was in the clientele that racial differentiation became an issue. While "Consuelo," a prostitute who lived in the Zona Colón and later in San Isidro during Yarini's time, reportedly would sleep with men of all races, many of the other women would only sleep with white men.[64] French women who arrived in San Isidro after 1900 were seen as a threat to the social order, especially by Cuban women, since they were supposedly more sensuous and created a new standard for the barrio.[65] "Religion" was also important for established prostitutes in San Isidro, and it was common to see a prostitute cross herself for good luck before her first trick each night. None were beyond consulting a Santería practitioner if things were not going well.[66] Race, ethnicity, and *buena suerte* defined the most desirable prostitute.

The pimps of San Isidro also held different positions and demanded varying degrees of respect within the community. There were the "working" pimps who were employed on the wharfs, in banks or industry, or as white-collar workers, depending on their social status. Another group, the "delinquent" pimps, sold drugs and committed burglaries or petty thefts. "Real" pimps did no work at all. The most respected, such as one Suavecito ("Easy Does It"), had several women, while others had but one each, with whom they lived in common-law relationships. On the lowest rung of Havana's social ladder within the prostitute community were the *"café con leche"* pimps. These men were distinguished as the poorest and least respected. Unlike most of the "respectable" pimps, who owned apartments and cars, the *café con leches* lived in the parks; they had to hang out in the streets, waiting for their "woman" to finish with a customer, as they had nowhere else to go. One prostitute noted with indignation that one could easily differentiate between pimps, since *café con leche* pimps had to suffice with cheap watches, while the more "respectable" ones flashed expensive gold watches, bracelets, and large diamond rings. The worst insult one prostitute could hurl at another was that she belonged to a *café con leche* pimp.[67]

Political turmoil, graft and patronage, legalized vice and prostitution, all characterized the capital city, where in 1910 the lottery was in full swing and cockfights were scheduled every Sunday.[68] In San Isidro, however, life was ordered and honor well defined, even if under a unique rubric.

Lo de San Isidro

It was during the unsettled decade of independence and U.S. occupation that Alberto Yarini came of age. Born in 1882, Yarini was a member of one of the island's prominent families. His father was a highly respected dental surgeon and professor at the University of Havana and his brother, José de Jesús Yarini, became a successful Havana surgeon and dentist.[69] Thus, the young aristocrat had the political, social, and cultural connections to ensure a prominent and lucrative career in whatever field he chose. As a member of one of the island's most prominent families, the U.S.-educated Yarini would have been a most desirable catch for a Havana socialite. But, as Wright noted, Cuba was the "land of topsy-turvy . . . where life runs, not like reality, but after the style of librettos of stage plays."[70] In fact, Yarini became the young republic's most celebrated and respected pimp.

By the end of the second U.S. occupation in 1909, Yarini had already acquired a reputation as a brave and honorable man, despite his sideline. Consuelo la Charmé, a prostitute who began to ply her trade at that time, remembered that Yarini "not only was a good man, but a friend, yes, sir, a good friend; the kind that when one was really in trouble [*jodida*] you could count on for help, without any conditions; he expected nothing in return, even though he was a politician, and a Conservative." She boasted that "he would not greet you because you were a somebody. No! He would speak with a negro; or a Chinese; with anyone. He did not tolerate anyone who put on airs."[71] He was highly respected among the inhabitants of San Isidro because of his aristocratic and political connections, which he used regularly to help his friends and acquaintances, and for that matter, anyone who asked for his help. It was reported that Yarini offered financial assistance to anyone who was out of work; he was, according to Consuelo, "the first to open his bag and the last to close it."[72]

It seems that Yarini first gained widespread notoriety when at age twenty-six he provoked an altercation in a local café. When he overheard two officials from a U.S. warship stationed in Cuba's harbor in 1906 denigrate Cuba and Cubans, he challenged them to a fistfight. Consuelo described the incident — U.S. newspapers in 1910 reported it as an "assault on J. Cornell Tarler, charge d'affaires of the American legation" — as a patriotic defense of the integrity of the Cuban people.[73] The two officers had been eating in one of the numerous corner cafes that dotted the streets in Havana. Speaking English, the pair objected to the Cubans because, "in this country blacks and whites hang out together and there are blacks everywhere." Yarini, who apparently spoke fluent English, was in the café with General Jesús Rabí, a prominent Afro-Cuban military leader, but shortly thereafter he left the bistro accompanied by a group of friends. Yarini then excused himself from the group, saying that he had left something behind at the table. Returning to the café, the Cuban "yelled insults at the Americans," screaming that General Rabí had fought like a lion, along with many other blacks, for Cuba's independence, and "who the hell did they think they were saying such things [about Cubans and blacks]." With that, Yarini jumped on the men and a fistfight ensued. Onlookers and friends who wanted to avoid trouble with the U.S. authorities stopped the fight, which Yarini reportedly was winning.[74]

During his short life, Yarini enjoyed wide popularity in San Isidro. The prostitutes were "fascinated as he rode by on his immense steed, as majestic as he was. It was also said that he was very special in the 'other.' "[75] Several women, seven or more, were "with" Yarini, but often, because of his involvement in politics — he was president of the Conservative Party Committee for San Isidro — he would not visit them for three or four days.[76] Their most-often-heard complaint was that Yarini would sleep with them only once a month. After the young pimp's death, other prostitutes boasted that they had been with Yarini and that he had paid them and "made love" to them.[77] It was a mark of honor to have slept with Yarini or to have been one of his women because "they were happy." The young politician gained legendary status among the prostitutes and other residents of San Isidro, who viewed him as their protector.[78] For example, when Consuelo's French pimp, Pierre le Doux, threatened to cut her up with a knife, she ran to one of Yarini's establishments for protection; only there did she feel safe since no one would dare to challenge the young Cuban.[79]

According to *Diario de la Marina*, Havana's ultraconservative newspaper, problems between Cuban pimps (*guayabitos*) and French pimps (*apaches*) had long existed. Several altercations — knifings and fights — involving the two groups had taken place in the barrio streets.[80] Generally, French pimps in Havana handled women that had been recruited in France. And on occasion, with permission from the well-bribed Havana city officials, the French pimps would travel to France to bring back fresh women for the trade. It was allegedly during one such trip by the *apache* Louis Lotot, in 1910, that the prostitute Berta Fontaine left his establishment for that of Yarini. This was the worst infraction that an "intern" prostitute could commit; switching houses and pimps was considered overstepping her "place."[81] When Lotot returned, however, perhaps sizing up Yarini's political and social connections, his "bravery," and his support within San Isidro, he apparently thought twice about provoking a confrontation. He reportedly concluded that he had "come to Cuba to exploit women, not to die for them. It was his professional ethic." According to one report, the other French pimps pressured Lotot to make an example of Yarini for the good of their group; after all, "what would the *apaches* do if all their women, both French and Cuban, were to leave them?" Later, a report by the Havana secret police noted that several French nationals had met at a café on the corner of Habana and Desamparados Streets. There they had been overheard plotting Yarini's murder. But it was also rumored at the time that the Liberals had fostered the confrontation, for they wanted to have Yarini out of the way in the upcoming elections.[82] The favorite in the race, Yarini was widely supported in Havana by the prostitution sector, the Conservatives, and by the *ñáñigos*, the secret cult of Abakuá. This Afro-Cuban society was especially powerful because its practitioners held to a code of honor and brotherhood that supported and protected its members against "outsiders."[83]

In any event, what followed was a carefully planned ambush, although at first the authorities thought it was a crime of passion. On the appointed night, 21 November 1910, shortly after seven o'clock in the evening, five of Lotot's compatriots stationed themselves on the rooftops opposite the house where Yarini visited with Elena, one of his "women."[84] Lotot and Jean Petijean arranged to "bump into" Yarini as he left Elena's house at number 60 San Isidro.[85] According to Consuelo, Lotot already had his pistol drawn, a .38-caliber Smith, when he encountered Yarini. Realizing it was an ambush, Yarini drew his weapon and fired off several rounds against Lotot and Petijean. The men stationed on the rooftops, however, wounded Yarini, who apparently never saw them. Pepito Bastarrechea, Yarini's companion who was in the house next door, heard the shots, ran outside, and fired at the pair of Frenchmen in the street. One round felled Lotot immediately. Firing at the men on the rooftops, Bastarrechea forced them to run away, and he, too, took flight out of San Isidro, disposing of his revolver in the street. Eight French and two Cuban women were held as material witnesses and fourteen others were arrested in connection with the shooting, including Bastarrechea.[86]

Both Yarini and Lotot were seriously wounded, and both were taken to a nearby hospital. Lotot had been shot five times, once in the head, twice in the left hand, and once in each arm.[87] He was pronounced dead on arrival and was later identified as a twenty-eight-year-old chauffeur by Jennie Fontaine, his concubine.[88] While Yarini was being treated, Berta Fontaine, Cecília Martin, and Elena Morales, "his favorites," paced in the waiting room.[89] Dying of his gunshot wounds, Yarini became aware that Bastarrechea was being accused of having murdered Lotot. In what some describe as the last honorable deed of an honorable man, Yarini made a deathbed confession in which he took sole responsibility for Lotot's death; it read, "Concerning the shots that killed the Frenchman, I am solely responsible; I shot him in self defense." Written on hospital stationery, the pencil-scribbled confession was witnessed by a distinguished *habanero*, Licenciado Freyre Andrade.[90] No one expected less from the politician/pimp. "After all," Consuelo noted, "that is how true men act."[91]

The following morning, 22 November, Yarini was still hanging on to life. Havana's morning newspapers carried the story of the shooting and Lotot's death on their front pages. *Diario de la Marina* noted that the events that had taken place in San Isidro the previous evening were reminiscent of a picaresque novel by Cervantes—an appropriate, if unintentional, reference, in view of Yarini's almost Quixotic reputation in Havana. That afternoon, a group of Cubans of "all races" ambushed the mourners who had attended Lotot's burial as they were returning from the cemetery.[92] Later that night, shortly before 11 p.m., Yarini finally died. The following morning, Havana's mayor ordered several brothels in the city closed permanently. However, an editorial by José Viera, published in *Diario de la Marina*, doubted that the mayor's order would have much effect. "Instead of paying for their lawlessness with a jail sentence," noted Viera, "they [the pimps] put on the airs of great gentlemen. Today, any miserable person who lives off of prostitution . . . looks down upon decent people with disdain and speaks with pride of his many spheres of influence. . . . The world belongs to murderers and prostitutes." The piece ended with "We'll see, we'll see."[93]

Announcements of Yarini's death were circulated throughout the city:

R.I.P.
ALBERTO YARINI Y PONCE DE LEÓN HAS DIED
 Subscribers, Presidents, Delegates, and Secretaries of the National Conservative Party, plead that all affiliated with the Party and all the population in general attend the viewing, Calzada de Galiano, No. 22, tomorrow, Thursday, the 24th of this

month, at 9 a.m., to accompany the body to the Colón Cemetery, this favor will be greatly appreciated.
Havana, 23 November 1910

The notice was signed by some of the most prominent men in the city, including General Andrade and José Bastarrechea.[94]

Answering the call, "whores, *guayabitos*, *ñáñigos*, and people of all social classes" attended the viewing and burial of Yarini. Dressed in their most somber clothes, trying not to attract undue attention, most of the prostitutes of the city went to pay their last respects; a few were accompanied by their "husbands."[95] Even some of the *apaches'* prostitutes went to the Yarini family home at Galiano 22. Many of the women in the crowd wept quietly throughout the night, but in the morning, when it came time to remove the coffin from the house to assemble the funeral procession, most wept openly and loudly.[96]

During the all-night wake, so many people converged on 22 Galiano Street that crowd control became an issue.[97] The men present formed a human barricade, creating a path for mourners who wished to express condolences to make their way to the home's front door. The family received visitors throughout the night in their living room; Consuelo described it as "full of wreaths and other flowers." The dedicatory ribbons indicated the variety of classes that were represented in the crowd:

"To my unforgettable Alberto Yarini, from Mercedes Tamayo."
"R.I.P. Alberto Yarini, with fond memories from Sara López."
"To her unforgettable Alberto, with fond memories from la Johly."
"To Alberto, the National Conservative Party."
"To our unforgettable President, the Conservative Committee of San Isidro."

Amid the messages and flowers, and "next to the door in the room where the coffin stood sat the deceased's family. In four enormous silver candelabra burned an equal number of candles, their flames dim in the somber air." A steady line of visitors passed by the coffin until its departure for the Colón Cemetery.[98]

The funeral cortege that left Galiano at 9 a.m. on Wednesday was more than three city blocks long.[99] As already described, the procession was varied and impressive, growing longer as it made its way down Havana's most important boulevards. When the body of the young man passed in front of the headquarters of the Conservative Party, flowers rained down on the coffin from every window. Police monitored, reportedly without incident, the minor scuffles that took place over who could carry Yarini's coffin on their shoulders. Many mourners awaited the cortege at the cemetery, where military commander Miguel Coyula gave the eulogy.[100] The *ñáñigos* also had a farewell ceremony, *el enlloró*, for Yarini in the field beyond the cemetery.[101]

While pimping in Havana's barrios often involved violence and even death, the murder of Yarini had important repercussions for the city of Havana. Both Cuban and French pimps sought revenge, and the subsequent assaults, knifings, and shootings put the entire city on guard for several weeks. The ambush of Lotot's mourners by Cuban pimps had injured several Frenchmen and killed one, resulting in several arrests; in response, Frenchmen assaulted Cubans randomly in the streets of San Isidro.[102] Consuelo remembered that the revenge was spontaneous: "A Cuban had been murdered by the apaches [the ambush took place before Yarini died], and complete justice was not to be expected from the authorities." After all, she noted, "the deceased was a conservative, the liberals were in power and had amiable relations with the apaches, who not only procured for them 'good women,' but also bags of money in order to continue with the traffic and engage in trade in the area."[103]

On 24 November, *Diario de la Marina* reported that the chief of police was proceeding to "clean-up" San Isidro with an iron hand, moving against all those who were violating existing immigration and prostitution laws. His draconian measures were directed against both pimps and prostitutes. Even some members of the police force were reprimanded. Police captain Ledón of the 10th precinct, for example, was dismissed for negligence in not having prevented the incidents associated with Lotot's funeral.[104] But prostitutes, who were indiscriminately rounded up and sent to the *vivac,* felt the brunt of the measures imposed by the police chief. Establishments and businesses in San Isidro were "inspected," heavy fines were levied, and many were ordered to close down.[105] Several citizens were falsely accused and arrested, and many women had to resort to *fletear* (turning tricks in the streets) in order to subsist.[106]

From all provinces of the country, newspaper editors, too, reacted, firing off editorials that demanded government action.[107] The initial response of *Diario de la Marina* was to blame the United States for what had happened. "The Americans outlawed cock fights, bullfights, and the lottery," complained editor Joaquín N. Urumburú. "Why then did they leave public prostitution? In the United States it does not exist, it is not permitted, and neither is it permitted in other civilized countries."[108] In fact, during the initial occupation, both in 1899 and again in 1902, the United States had not outlawed prostitution, but had tried instead to guide reform efforts toward the enactment and enforcement of reforms, organizing the Department of Hygiene as an independently supported authority and outlawing all unregistered prostitutes.

Interestingly, although it thoroughly covered the arrests and the "clean-up" campaign associated with the murders, and through it published many editorials against legalized prostitution and in support of the police, *Diario de la Marina* did not carry any description of the funeral procession, only noting that police had been on hand in case of disturbances. The newspaper's coverage of the events largely took the form of editorials and official reports. For example, a two-part editorial appeared under the headline "Por el bien de Cuba" in the morning editions for 25 and 26 November. The editorials criticized the administration and called for the abolition of the trade. In the afternoon edition of 25 November, in a front-page editorial, the newspaper lambasted the city's image as immoral, regressive, and a cause of shame for Cuba in the international community: "Where such things happen, how can one expect the regeneration and prosperity of collective honor and national strength?"[109]

The afternoon editions of the paper featured *baturillos,* or random thoughts, on the "bloody occurrence" in San Isidro. The murder of Yarini and the two Frenchmen had "revealed, through the power of scandal, a terrible evil, a hub of moral corruption, against which [the editors] have been incessantly clamoring, although society, in whose interest we cry out, has not paid attention." The article continued: "Three men are dead... others are injured; some are in prison; a respectable home is draped in mourning; the gray hairs of a learned old man and the decorum of an honest family stand in contrast against the irrational acts of a son, already a corpse; new crimes are committed daily; and all eyes, frightened and curious, turn to that diseased zone where *chulos* and *horizontales* [prostitutes] disgrace our country, while the authorities stand by complacently."[110]

The moralistic editor of *Diario de la Marina* also pointed out the prevalence of "an interminable series of pornographic stories and illustrations, postcards and epigrams, and impudent tales printed in newspapers read by women." Such publications, according to Urumburú, had made vice acceptable for Cuban society.[111] At the same time that the newspaper denounced the public's indifference to vice, it also published letters received from readers who voiced similar concerns, although they numbered only "six or eight." One letter, in particular, from a "Galician," generated a long and pointed response from the editor. The writer contended that while regulation of prostitution was necessary in modern society, he doubted that prohibition was effective, and thought that it was actually immoral. Urumburú's response sharply criticized both society's acceptance of "immoral vices" and the corrupt government officials who "told prurient anecdotes" in some of the most respectable living rooms of the capital and winked at the increase in prostitution.[112]

The response of Cuba's national government to the crime was ambivalent. On 28 December 1911, Decree #1158 closed San Isidro as a *zona de tolerancia* and moved its operations to the barrio Luyanó.[113] Under pressure, the government nullified the move to Luyanó some ten months later.[114] One year later, on 23 October 1913, the legislature suspended the regulations on prostitution that had been in force since 1899 and eliminated all specified zones for prostitution, thus relaxing all controls. Claiming that the social and public health benefits that had been promised by the regulations had not materialized, the decree, sponsored by the Secretaría de Sanidad y Beneficiencia (Department of Health and Welfare), contended that the opposite had occurred. State regulation had merely fostered pimping, had criminalized women, and had discredited public administration. The decree further stated that obligatory medical exams and hospitalization had proved ineffective in controlling venereal disease and had instead offered the public a false sense of security. After noting the probable world opinion of a country that allowed prostitution to continue and the anti republican nature of the current system of regulated prostitution in Cuba, the decree stipulated the abolition of all regulatory measures.[115] Twelve years later, on 30 September 1925, Cuba would ratify resolutions adopted by the International Convention for the Suppression of the Traffic in Women and Children. Under international pressure, the Cuban government would also subscribe to the accords published previously, in 1904 and 1910. From 1911 until 1915 more than twenty new immigration decrees were enacted by the Cuban government that restricted women traveling alone internationally, set the minimum age for women immigrants, required fingerprinting, and generally tightened controls for all immigrants. In particular, National Decree #384 ensured Cuba's support of the Convention by prohibiting and punishing the introduction of any women into Cuba for the purpose of prostitution, gradually aligning Cuban policies with international sensibilities.[116]

Réquiem por Yarini

For all the governmental and media hyperbole and publicity, little permanent change actually ensued after 1910. Prostitution issues in Cuba took a back seat to the continued convulsions of nation building for several decades after Yarini's death. No new prostitution-related legislation was passed until the 1950s. However, renewed campaigns for moral reforms followed the debates over the new Constitution drafted in 1940. On 7 January 1951, the magazine *Bohemia* carried an extensive photo-spread of recent murders in the barrio Colón, where a drug-dealing pimp had been murdered. The magazine lauded police action in breaking up the vice and drug cartels that were entrenched in Colón. In a related article, university professor Francisco Carone offered his opinion that "prostitution was as old as humanity, and satiated many primordial social, economic, and even doctrinal needs, [but] it also carried consequences—including the existence of pimps." In the same article, however, Cardinal Manuel Arteaga of Havana publicly commended government officials of the Secretaría de Gobernación for having "attacked the empire of corruption and vice, [and] for turning off all the 'red lights' of moral infection. It is what Cuba expects."[117] He also commended them for having passed a new resolution that forbade the creation of new *"zonas"* in the republic.[118]

By the mid-1950s, however, Cuba was once again in a state of crisis, buffeted by as much political, economic, and social instability as it had experienced in its first decade of nationhood.[119] Organized crime, in partnership with the government of President Fulgencio Batista, enjoyed revenues from payoffs and bribes in the millions of dollars.[120] Batista relied heavily on his cut from gambling profits and on the corrupt officials and police officers who also practiced bribery and extortion to fill their pockets. Nationally, labor problems and a falling standard of living further undermined the economic and social structure. Most Cubans perceived themselves worse off in the 1950s than they had been in 1920. The protests that ensued expressed "social frustration, economic loss, and political anger."[121]

The stress of political and economic uncertainty was singularly evident in the capital city. With money from U.S. organized crime figures and with the protection of Batista's corrupt officials, Havana had become an international center of legalized vice. Drugs, gambling, pornography, and prostitution flourished. By 1958, there were 270 brothels in Havana and more than 11,500 women engaged in prostitution.[122] The growth of the industry was noted in an editorial published by *El Mundo* on 15 March 1956: "The famous barrio Colón, whose ambience was provided by two or three streets, has so grown in these last few years, that it is now impossible to clearly establish its limits. ... It now borders on the most elegant and luxurious commercial establishments . . . conducting its business with unprecedented civility."[123] The editorial also criticized the laxity of law enforcement by the police but stopped short of citing complicity.[124] Advertisements, like those that appeared in the magazine *Información* in January 1958, lured women into prostitution with promises of high earnings: "Wanted, young women with a pleasant appearance for the new Happy-Land Club . . . Salary $90. Plus, commission and good tips."[125] Another advertisement, published in December of that same year for the Centro Bar, offered similar enticements, but this one specifically requested that rural girls apply for work. The ad included directions for appropriate bus routes to the bar.[126] On the streets, solicitation was commonplace. One writer recalled that U.S. citizens who traveled to Havana for a big weekend of carousing would reel through the streets, "picking up fourteen-year-old Cuban girls and tossing coins to make men scramble in the gutter."[127]

A significant difference separated the 1950s from the 1910s, however, at least in the view of the prostitute community of Havana. There was no Yarini to protect them from abuse, to bail them out of jail, or to influence and bribe politicians. In the 1950s, no pimps emerged who could be described as "honorable;" they were only exploitive.[128] Prostitutes were not able to maintain their "status," and *fleteras* were everywhere. Foreign, and especially U.S., capitalist interests, and not the "community," ruled in barrios such as San Isidro. Resulting anxieties and conflicts echoed the tensions that had existed between foreigners and Cubans during the 1910s.

It is significant that during the 1950s the Cuban playwright Carlos Felipe made the much discussed personage of Alberto Yarini the title character of what was to become his most famous play, *Réquiem por Yarini*. Lovingly dedicated to "my people of the barrio of San Isidro," Felipe worked on *Réquiem* between 1955 and 1960. However, with the "Triumph of the Revolution" in December 1958, there followed still another period of dramatic political, social, and economic change for Cuba.[129]

Felipe's body of work has been characterized by one critic as "a constant criticism, explicit or suggested, of [Cuba's] sociopolitical reality controlled by . . . insatiable plutocrats."[130] Invariably, the playwright portrays powerful elites in a negative light. But perhaps Felipe's most important contribution to Cuban theater has been the uniquely Cuban flavor of his plays, which depict scenes set close to the harbors of Havana. "No [Cuban] dramatist," note José Escarpenter and José Madrigal, "has been able to portray more eloquently the transfigured and phantasmagorical world of the Havana wharfs, where with rare articulation the vestiges of a colonial past, perpetuated in stone, mates with the cosmopolitan steam of foreign seaborne business."[131] In particular, *Réquiem* had been singled out as Felipe's most important and most "Cuban" play. Two themes that appear often in Felipe's plays are also prevalent in *Réquiem*: the search for happiness and the recovery of the past. In the San Isidro brothel, which is the setting for the action, Felipe's characters try desperately to relive the past only to find that happiness, through its chimerical changes, eludes them.

Although not a biographical work, *Réquiem por Yarini* takes place in San Isidro on the night of 21 November 1910, and the action parallels the real events of that night. The interior spaces are those of a brothel in that district, which is described as clean, decorous, and well-appointed, making it what the stage directions call "an extraordinary place."[132] The play's main characters include Alejandro Yarini,[133] "king of the proxenetas in Havana"; La Jaba, Yarini's *mulata* manageress who is totally dedicated to him; Luis Lotot, French pimp and Yarini's rival; Bebo la Reposa, a priestlike character; La Dama del Velo (the Lady of the Veil), a mysterious veiled figure from outside San Isidro; la Macorina, the beautiful (but dead) Queen of the prostitutes; and la Santiagüera, a prostitute for whose love Yarini is killed.[134]

As was the case in the real barrio, Felipe's San Isidro is a closed society where values are inverted in relation to the outside world. Yarini's fictional barrio is a microcosm where order reigns, where every member knows his or her role and where life is carefully orchestrated under the efficient tutelage of La Jaba. "My business is order," declares Yarini in the play. "There exists a Regulation that my interns must know and respect."[135] Within that "pure universe of negative values," the beautiful and seductive Santiagüera, who is deeply in love with Yarini, represents disorder.[136] It is because of her that the great lord of the pimps falls victim to disorder. He is a prisoner of love, just like

La Santiagüera, and because of it dies at the hands of his rival, Lotot, whom la Santiagüera has abandoned. In this case, "disorder . . . leads to death."[137]

Felipe characterizes Yarini as a politician, gambler, and pimp. For example, La Jaba's opening dialogue expresses her adulation for Yarini: "Yarini the politician means nothing; Yarini the gambler is no big deal . . . but Yarini the pimp (*chulo*) . . . Yarini the pimp is the King! I would have conquered the world for him, and it would have not been enough; he deserves much more."[138] This description, however, also sets up the supernatural image of the man. In *Réquiem*, pimping and prostitution are shown not as a social evil, but as an activity with religious overtones. Bebo La Reposa acts as a sort of pastor of the San Isidro congregation. He uses *caracoles* (shells) to predict Yarini's death yet is powerless to prevent it. Throughout the play, the action is imbued with images of *santería,* as the characters call upon Changó and Eleguá, gods of the Yoruba pantheon.[139] For example, when Yarini's death is predicted, all the practitioners of Afro-Cuban religion on the island intercede before their gods with prayers on Yarini's behalf. Around him rallied many disparate entities of Cuban society. In the world of prostitution, Yarini was a king; for his "interns," a god. Men in his service imitated his dress and his mannerisms; La Santiagüera rendered him homage.

Another character in *Réquiem*, the Lady of the Veil, has been explained as representing Yarini's fame outside of San Isidro, beyond prostitution and the "Zone."[140] A woman of high society who wants to meet Yarini out of curiosity, in *Réquiem* she speaks of Yarini as the talk of all Havana, who generates great curiosity and admiration among high society. Indeed, his dress and style are mimicked by men in all social circles.[141] "They tell me," muses La Dama, "that he is the handsomest man in Havana. And he is; and I know men . . . the *danzón* [Cuba's national dance] was invented for [Yarini]."[142] Yarini's importance in Havana's collective psyche is evidenced in how Carmen, a resident of San Isidro, characterizes him: "Ah, yes! He was the most beautiful man to have lived in Havana."[143]

Escarpanter and Madrigal have offered two explanations for Felipe's use of Yarini as the hero of this tragedy. In the first, Yarini projects the subconscious mentalité of the Cuban people. He combines the island's sensualness and Iberian machismo to generate the admiration of society. The historic Yarini was young, handsome, seductive, with potent sexual attributes, intelligent, and self-assured, who "in his short life apparently enjoyed life to the fullest, and made the most beautiful women of his time enjoy it also."[144] In his controversial analysis of the Latin American "Public Man," Glen Caudill Dealy argues that "public virtues such as grandeur, generosity, and manliness are useful because they help in the aggregation of followers and it is this which makes them virtues."[145] The second explanation is based on Felipe's socio-historical commentary of what he perceives to be the Cuban reality. In the play, the anarchy and political scandals of Cuba are described as "an era of dust and mud."[146] It is these, and not prostitution, that are regarded as the truly demoralizing forces of Cuban society. For Felipe, the Cuban republic is but the sum of decades of corruption wrapped in grandiose words. This, then, is reflected in the microcosm of *Réquiem*'s San Isidro, where the only honor and order are to be found among pimps and prostitutes.[147]

To possess San Isidro was to posses the heart and soul of Havana. Thus, Yarini was the mythic prototype whom many wanted to imitate. In *Réquiem*, however, his death is necessary to transform him into a myth.[148] According to María del Carmen González, Yarini becomes a sacrificial victim for the government, for his profession, and even for his country.[149]

Conclusion

Réquiem por Yarini has often been described as the embodiment of Cuba's first national myth under the structure of the classic Greek tragedy. Yarini is the tragic hero who makes a mistake in judgment and struggles against forces more powerful than he (love and the government); ultimately, however, he is greater than earthly power and finds the long-sought love and order only beyond the grave.[150] Felipe wrote that "the Cuban artist should create his own myths. With Yarini I think that I have created a myth about a person who has become legendary in San Isidro."[151] Yarini was already a legend that only needed codification. In the Catholic Church, a Requiem is "a mass for the dead, or the music for such a mass;" its less-used definition is that of "rest, quiet or peace." Through Felipe's words and characterization in *Réquiem for Yarini*, the legendary pimp found a kind of "rest;" Yarini emerged from the world of rumor and innuendo and became a part of Cuba's mainstream culture. Felipe ends the play with the line, "Rest in peace, Yarini."[152]

During the last two decades, *Réquiem* had been produced several times in Madrid, New York, and Miami, and at least twice on the Cuban stage.[153] Although the play addresses themes of prostitution and Afro-Cuban religion, both opposed by Fidel Castro's revolutionary ideology, the production was well received in Cuba and critics lauded what they perceived as its moralistic themes: the young republic was corrupt and engaging in prostitution carries severe consequences. In 1986, Graciela Guzmán, entertainment reporter for *Bohemia*, noted in her review that *Réquiem* revealed the problem of "corruption and opportunism of that period . . . the erotic and passionate world with a creole essence, that now has found expression in new ways to enhance our development."[154] In another review, published in *Trabajadores*, the workers' magazine of Cuba's Communist Party, the first decades of independence are described as a "pseudo-republic" where "pseudo morals" prevailed.[155] Thus,

Yarini served to validate revolutionary propaganda in Cuba some seventy years after his death. Interestingly, one of the best documented developments of the 1980s in Cuba is the proliferation of prostitutes in the tourist sectors of Havana.[156] One *jinetera*, as prostitutes are known in Cuba, complained that they "are living in a time of no kindness. That doesn't exist here. Everywhere there is envy, and people value things that are not true, and everyone is selfish now, and it is very scary in my heart. . . . Everything in the country is for sale. There is no moral center to life now."[157]

In *Foundational Fictions*, an analysis of Latin American fiction in the nineteenth and early twentieth centuries, Doris Sommer argues that during those decades, "romance and republic were often connected. . . . [Novels] fueled a desire for domestic happiness that runs over into dreams of national prosperity; and nation-building projects invested private passions with public purpose."[158] Perhaps for neo-independent Cuba, Yarini provides a similar image. In 1986 a Cuban theater critic described Yarini as "a well-known character in his time, and not because of his great merit exercised in our historic development, on the contrary, because he was one of the most celebrated pimps of neo-colonial Havana at the dawn of the twentieth century, a city and era of contrasts, where everything or nothing could happen."[159] However, it was precisely because he could successfully navigate between the contradictory spheres of Havana's social and political strata that Yarini emerged as a cultural memory for Cuba, embodying the coalescence of elite and popular conceptions of patria.

Irene Wright, writing in 1910, described Havana as a city of contrasts. On the one hand, the morals of a very Iberian and moralistic culture forbade elite and middle-class women from going out alone in public; they could not attend funerals or even shop unaccompanied. When young women walked down Havana's streets in tight-fitting gowns, they were chaperoned everywhere they went. Men of all social classes, on the other hand, would position themselves on the narrow streets so that women passing by would have to come very close and would sometimes be forced to brush up against them.[160] Such double standards allowed men (especially those among high society) who felt constrained by the restrictive social norms that valued chastity in women and sexual prowess in men to make their way to the streets of barrios like San Isidro. According to Wright, "The most notorious street in town [was] within a block or so of the most fashionable church and of the American Legation, opposite it. In short the 'old city' [was] a grab bag — its contents unsorted."[161] From such "disorder" emerged Yarini.

Yarini remained fixed in the collective memory of the capital. It was not socially acceptable to admire Yarini openly, unless one was a member of the prostitution community, but his prowess made him a sort of hero for many Cuban men who imaged themselves to be like him, the most "public" of men.

In a society where reputation and connections were all-important, he was the god of the double standard; Yarini acted in the open, not caring about what others thought. His memory long survived through gossip and popular stories, only to be openly resurrected by Carlos Felipe at the close of the 1950s. When Felipe's play was published (more than a decade would pass before it was produced in Cuba), it validated in print the gossip and stories that Consuelo said had been much discussed in Havana for many decades.[162]

Yarini the patriot, the socialite, and Yarini the pimp coexisted with dignity in a Cuba that convulsed in the throes of nation building. Politicians capitalized on the powerless, and their moralization campaigns were criticized by Felipe's mulatta madam, La Jaba, as the "moralizing of [politician's] pockets, full of scruples without risks."[163] In the midst of such corruption and graft, Yarini's most important quality was honor; his ordered "regulations" for San Isidro, his patriotic comportment, his beneficence, and even his deathbed confession made him respected and admired. While after his death some said that he had been mad, to others the twenty-nine-year-old martyr of San Isidro became a unique symbol of nascent *cubanidad*. Thus, the politics of prostitution and of independence created a truly Cuban "hero," who was also very human—not a hero crafted by elites for international interests, but one hand-picked by the common people. More than a Don Juan or a Casanova, Yarini emerged as the Don Quixote of San Isidro.[164] For its prostitutes, the barrio represented an ordered world offering respite from the social disorder that prevailed beyond its borders. In that "public" space, the *mujeres públicas* of the barrio gave birth to the young republic's first myth.

NOTES

1. *Tampa Tribune*, 25 November 1910. Irene Wright described Gómez's funeral in much the same terms as news accounts described Yarini's cortege (Irene Wright, *Cuba* [New York: Mac-Millan, 1910], 78–79). For descriptions of Yarini's funeral procession, see *Diario de la Marina* (Havana), 25 November 1910; *New York Times*, 25 November 1910; and *Washington Post*, 25 November 1910. The *Tampa Tribune* carried the story of the viewing on 24 November 1910, and the next day offered coverage of the funeral.

2. Tomás Fernández-Robaina, *Recuerdos secretos de dos mujeres públicas* (Havana: Editorial Letras Cubanas, 1983), 40.

3. Fernández-Robaina, *Recuerdos secretos*, 39.

4. Wright, *Cuba*, 78–79.

5. Yarini's mother was noticeably absent from the group, and Consuelo la Charmé, a prostitute, noted her absence (Fernández-Robaina, *Recuerdos Secretos*, 39). Irene Wright wrote that Cuban women did not attend funerals, since it was not acceptable conduct in "good society" (Wright, *Cuba*, 45). A study of nineteenth-century travelers' accounts of life in Havana confirms the limited exposure of middle- and upper-class women on Havana's streets (see Luis Martínez-Fernández, "Life in a 'Male City': Native and Foreign Elite Women in Nineteenth-Century Havana," *Cuban Studies/Estudios Cubanos* 25 [1995]: 27–49).

6. Wright, *Cuba*, 79.
7. Fernández-Robaina, *Recuerdos secretos*, 46. The population of Havana province was estimated to be 538,000 in 1907, while that of the island as a whole was 2,048,980 (José L. Luzón, *Economía, poblacíon y territorio en Cuba, 1899–1983* [Madrid: Ediciones Cultura Hispánica del Instituto de Cooperación Iberoamericana, 1987], 83).
8. For a description of a typical Cuban viewing, funeral, and burial, see Wright, *Cuba*, 43–48.
9. Donna J. Guy, "Prostitution and Female Criminality in Buenos Aires, 1875–1937," in *The Problem of Order in Changing Societies: Essays on Crime and Policing in Argentina and Uruguay, 1750–1940*, ed. Lyman L. Johnson (Albuquerque: University of New Mexico Press, 1990), 89–116; Donna J. Guy, *Sex and Danger in Buenos Aires: Prostitution, Family, and Nation in Argentina* (1991; reprint, Lincoln: University of Nebraska Press, 1995); Donna J. Guy, "White Slavery, Public Health, and the Socialist Position on Legalized Prostitution in Argentina, 1913–1936," *Latin American Research Review* 23, no. 3 (1988): 60–80; Judith R. Walkowitz, *City of Dreadful Delight* (Chicago: University of Chicago Press, 1992); Judith R. Walkowitz, *Prostitution and Victorian Society: Women, Class, and the State* (Cambridge: Cambridge University Press, 1980).

10. For Paris, see Alain Corbain, *Women for Hire: Prostitution and Sexuality in France after 1850*, trans. Ann Sheridan (Cambridge, Mass.: Harvard University Press, 1990); Susan P. Conner, "Public Virtue and Public Women: Prostitution in Revolutionary Paris, 1793–1794," *Eighteenth-Century Studies* 28, no. 2 (winter 1994): 221–41; and Susan R. Grayzel, "Mothers, Marraines, and Prostitutes: Morale and Morality in First World War France," *International History Review* 19, no. 1 (February 1997): 66–86. For Great Britain, see Linda Manhood, *The Magdalenes: Prostitution in the Nineteenth Century* (New York: Routledge, Chapman, and Hall, 1990); and Trevor Fischer, *Prostitution and the Victorians* (New York: St. Martin's Press, 1997). For New York City, see Marilyn Wood Hill, *Their Sisters' Keepers: Prostitution in New York City, 1830–1870* (Berkeley: University of California Press, 1993); and Timothy J. Gilfoyle, *City of Eros: New York City, Prostitution, and the Commercialization of Sex, 1790–1920* (New York: W. W. Norton, 1992).

11. Sueann Caulfield, "Getting into Trouble: Dishonest Women, Modern Girls, and Women-Men in the Conceptual Language of Vida Policial, 1925–1927," *Signs* 19, no. 1 (autumn 1993): 147. See also Sueann Caulfield, "The Birth of Mangue," in *Sex and Sexuality in Latin America*, ed. Daniel Balderston and Donna Guy (New York: New York University Press, 1997). Other studies that engage the demographics of prostitution have focused on specific regions within a country to observe community trends in dealing with prostitution. For Argentina, see Liliana Graciela Isabello, "La prostitución y la trata de blancas: 1874–1886," *Todo es Historia* 18, no. 223 (November 1985): 83–92, which notes the lack of enforceable prostitution regulations in Buenos Aires at the close of the nineteenth century; for a demographic analysis of prostitution in the Territorio Nacional de la Pampa, see María Herminia Di Liscia, María Silvia Di Liscia, and Ana María Rodríguez, "Prostíbulos y control estatal en el Territorio Nacional de la Pampa," and Lilian Diodati, "Prostitutas, burdeles y reglamentos en la ciudad de Colón (Provincia de Buenos Aires)," both in *La mitad del país: La mujer en la sociedad argentina*, ed. Lidia Knecher and Marta Panaia (Buenos Aires: Centro Editor de América Latina, 1994). For Mexico, James R. Curtis and Daniel D. Arreola argue for a spatial rather than a moral segregation of *zonas* on the U.S.–Mexican borderlands (see "Zonas de Tolerancia on the Mexican Border," *Geographic Review* 81, no. 3 [1991]: 333–44; and William E. French ("Prostitutes and Guardian Angels: Women, Work, and the Family in Porfirian Mexico, 1876–1911," *Hispanic American Historical Review* 72, no. 4 [November 1992]: 529–54) argues that Mexico followed a North American/European pattern in addressing prostitution issues as part of their efforts toward modernity. Cf. K. Lynn Stoner, who argues that the women's movement in the early Cuban Republic was uniquely Cuban in its motivation, demands, actions, and outlook and did not follow Anglicized models (*From the House to the Streets* [Durham, N.C.: Duke University Press, 1991]).

12. Caulfield, "Birth of Mangue," 86.
13. Even fewer studies have focused on the male procurer's role in defining the forms of prostitution or its politics. For the twentieth-century United States, see, e.g., Neal Kumar Katyal, "Men Who Own Women: A Thirteenth Amendment Critique of Forced Prostitution," *Yale Law Journal* 103, no. 2 (1993): 791–826. For an early and sympathetic look at procurers, see E. M. S. Danero, *El Cafishio* (Buenos Aires: Fontefrida Editora, 1971.)
14. Caulfield, "Getting into Trouble," 149.
15. Julia O'Connel Davidson, "Sex Tourism in Cuba," *Race and Class* 38, no. 1 (1996): 39–50; and, tangentially, Lois M. Smith and Alfred Padula, "Twenty Questions on Sex and Gender in Revolutionary Cuba," *Cuban Studies* 18 (1988): 149–58.
16. Aline Helg, "Race in Argentina and Cuba, 1880–1930: Theory, Policies, and Popular Reaction," in *The Idea of Race in Latin America, 1870–1940*, ed. Richard Graham, 37–69 (Austin: University of Texas Press, 1990).
17. Manuel Fernández Santalices, *Las calles de La Habana entramuros: Arte, historia y tradiciones en las calles y plazas de La Habana Vieja* (Miami: Saeta Ediciones, 1989), 26.
18. Louis A. Pérez Jr., *Cuba: Between Reform and Revolution*, 2d ed. (New York: Oxford University Press, 1995), 178–79.
19. José A. Escarpanter and José A. Madrigal, *Carlos Felipe: Teatro* (Boulder, Colo.: Society of Spanish and American Studies, 1988), 50.
20. President William McKinley, quoted in Pérez, *Cuba: Between Reform and Revolution*, 178.
21. General Leonard Wood, quoted in ibid., 181.
22. News of the Amendment sparked anti–U.S. demonstrations, and on 2 March 1901 a torchlight demonstration descended on General Wood's house. The populace was in an uproar, as telegraph lines jammed with protests from every corner of the island. Officials in Washington countered that there would be no compromise or concession to Cuban independence unless the amendment was accepted (see Geoff Simons, *Cuba: From Conquistador to Castro* [New York: St. Martin's Press, 1996], 211).
23. Simons, *Cuba: From Conquistador to Castro*, 208–14.
24. Raúl M. Shelton, *Cuba y su cultura* (Miami: Ediciones Universal, 1993), 205–11; see also Louis A. Pérez Jr., *Cuba under the Platt Ammendment, 1902–1934* (Pittsburgh: University of Pittsburgh Press, 1986).
25. Pérez, *Cuba: Between Reform and Revolution*, 213.
26. Ibid., 193.
27. Ibid., 193–220.
28. Pérez argues that Cuban independence was the last in a series of events that effectively toppled the planter class. In its place emerged a bourgeoise that looked to U.S. largess to guarantee national political and economic stability and thus promote U.S. hegemony (see Louis A. Pérez Jr., "The Collapse of the Cuban Planter Class," *Inter-American Economic Affairs* 36, no. 3 (Winter 1982), 3–22.
29. Wright, *Cuba*, 187. More than 372 indictments were brought against public officials from 1909 to 1916 (Pérez, *Cuba: Between Reform and Revolution*, 217). The Cuban lottery was under the direct control of the government, and the officials who ran it personally benefitted from its revenues (see Charles Chapman, *A History of the Cuban Republic: A Study in Hispanic American Politics* [New York: Octagon Books, 1969], 547–63). Perhaps cockfighting was seen as a uniquely Cuban pastime, much as bullfighting was associated with Spanish imperialism by many Cubans. Bullfighting was also outlawed by the U.S. military government on 10 October 1899, and was not reinstated by republican Cuba (Louis A Pérez Jr., "Between Baseball and Bullfighting: The Quest for Nationality in Cuba, 1868–1898," *Journal of American History* 81, no. 2 [September 1994]: 493–518).

Crime and Culture during the Second Cuban Republic : 123

30. Chapman, *History of the Cuban Republic*, 231; 297–317.
31. Wright, *Cuba*, 142. The control of resources and revenues was the "central, if unstated, issue of politics at all levels of the republic." As economic conditions worsened during the Cuban republic's first decade, so did corruption and patronage. According to Pérez, by 1903, 20,000 Cubans were on the public payroll, with 40 percent (8,000) of those in the city of Havana; by 1911 the number had risen to 40,000 federal employees, which required that two-thirds of the budget be expended for payroll. In Cuba at the turn of the twentieth century, politics was a matter of "economic and social urgency" (Pérez, *Cuba: Between Reform and Revolution*, 205, 220).
32. Simons, *Cuba: From Conquistador to Castro*, 221.
33. During occupation, e.g., U.S. plumbers contracted to work in the capital organized a local union that excluded Cubans. In addition, Spanish merchants hired their relatives (nephews) from Spain rather than Creoles, so that the term *sobrinismo* quickly came into common usage (Pérez, *Cuba: Between Reform and Revolution*, 203).
34. María del Carmen González, "La cultura popular en el drama cubano del siglo XX," Ph.D. diss., University of Florida, 1984, 8.
35. E.g., Martínez-Fernández argues that "of all the major cities in the New World, nineteenth-century Havana placed the most stringent limitations on the female population" (Martínez-Fernández, "Life in a Male City," 44).
36. Pérez notes the predominence of single and widowed women in most female occupations by citing the ratios of single or widowed women to the total female workforce. In the professional ranks, 518 of 646 teachers were single or widowed and most were white. Among the occupations where women of color predominated, the single and widowed again were in the majority: 15,388 out of 20,980 laundresses; 19,970 out of 22,807 servants; 1,362 out of 1,580 cigarworkers; and 342 out of 419 seamstresses (Pérez, *Cuba: Between Reform and Revolution*, 210).
37. Wright, *Cuba*, 101.
38. Milo Adrián Borges, ed., *Compilación ordenada y completa de la legislación cubana, 1899–1950*, 2d ed. (Havana: Editorial Lex, 1952), 1:94.
39. Although the colonial government provision that established the Comisión de Higiene in 1873 required annual reports, I was only able to locate reports for 1888, 1902 (when by military order, the regulations were adopted by the military government and were later extended to the republic until 1951), 1912, and 1914. In 1899 the *Reglamento de la prostitución en la ciudad de La Habana* was published by the Comisión de Higiene Especial; it adopted the colonial legislation for "independent" Cuba. See also Benjamín de Céspedes, *La prostitución en la ciudad de la Habana* (Havana: Establecimiento Tipografico O'Reilley, 1888); Ramón M. Alfonso, *La prostitución en Cuba y especialmente en la Habana: Memoria de la Comisión de Higiene Especial de la Isla de Cuba* (Havana: P. Fernández, 1902); Ramón María Alfonso, *Reglamentación de la prostitución, breves apuntes como debe ser en Cuba* (Havana: Imprenta el Siglo XX, 1912); and Matías Duque, *La prostitución, sus causas, sus males, su higiene* (Havana: Rambla, Souza, y Compañía, 1914).
40. *El Censo de Cuba* (Washington: Imprenta del Gobierno, 1900). The number of brothels is cited by Pérez; compare the 1990 figures with the 270 brothels in Havana by the late 1950s (Pérez, *Cuba: Between Reform and Revolution*, 305).
41. Ibid., 207–8; Céspedes, *La prostitución*, 157–59. For figures on Brazil, see Caulfield, "Birth of Mangue," 89; on Argentina, see Donna Guy, *Sex and Danger*, 104–5.
42. Alfonso, *La prostitución*, 18–33.
43. Pérez, *Cuba: Between Reform and Revolution*, 207–8.
44. Céspedes, *La prostitución*, 62–64. In a wide-ranging look at changing attitudes to syphillis, Claude Quétel argues that by the close of the nineteenth century doctors used the fear of venereal disease to extend their influence. With growing secularization of society, they became not only a kind of public health police, but also set themselves up as the arbiters of the new morality. Quétel is not emphatic, but concedes that syphilis was transmitted to Europe from the Americas

sometime after Columbus's return (see Claude Quétel, *History of Syphilis*, trans. Judith Braddock and Brian Pike [Oxford: Polity Press, 1990]).

45. Céspedes, *La prostitución,* 66.

46. A majority of the men who came to the New World, and to Cuba, in particular, wanted to make their fortune (*hacer America*) and then return to Europe as quickly as possible. Thus, Céspedes argues, prostitution became the most practical means for this transient population to fill its sexual needs (Céspedes, *La prostitución,* 71).

47. Céspedes, *La prostitución,* 66–71.

48. Ibid., 74–75.

49. Ibid., 79; Fernández-Robaina, *Recuerdos secretos,* 85–86.

50. Claudio Delgado, "La Higiene especial de la prostitución en la Habana, su estado actual y reformas que exige el ramo," in Céspedes, *La prostitución,* 80–81.

51. *La Cebolla* (Havana), 9 September 1888.

52. *La Cebolla* (Havana), 23 September 1888.

53. See, e.g., Constancia Bernaldo de Quirós and Jesús María Llanas Aguilaniedo, *La mala vida en Madrid: Estudio psico-sociológico* (Madrid: B. Rodríguez Serra, 1901); Paulina Luisi, *El problema de la prostitución: Abolicionismo o reglamentarismo* (Montevideo: Sindicato Médico del Uruguay, 1926); George Jackson Kneeland, *Commercialized Prostitution in New York City* (New York: The Century Co., 1913).

54. The "white slavery scare" gripped progressive nations during the early decades of the twentieth century. Readers were titillated with exotic tales of kidnapped innocents and their misadventures at the hand of the slavers. Mark Connelly, in a study of the profusion of white slavery tracts that appeared in the United States between 1908 and the 1920s, argues that "the indignation and concern over white slavery was intense, widespread, and often hysterical" (Mark Connelly, *The Response to Prostitution in the Progressive Era* [Chapel Hill: University of North Carolina Press, 1980], 114–15). For contemporary accounts, see Ernest A. Bell, *Fighting the Traffic in Young Girls, or War on the White Slave Trade* (Chicago, 1910); Jane Addams, *A New Conscience and an Ancient Evil* (New York: Macmillan, 1923); Albert Londres, *The Road to Buenos Ayres* (London: Constable and Co., 1928); Nylian Molinari Calleros, *La trata de blancas* (Buenos Aires, 1933). Cuba passed legislation to show its compliance with the League of Nations recommendations in 1925 (*Reglamento de la ley de inmigración y de las trata de blancas* [Habana: Imprenta y Papelería de Rambla, Bouza, y Cía., 1925]).

55. Fernández-Robaina, *Recuerdos secretos,* 41.

56. Wright, *Cuba,* 97.

57. See *Diario de la Marina,* morning edition, 22 November 1910.

58. The barrio San Isidro was bounded by Acosta on the north, Habana on the south, Desamparados to the east, and Egido to the west (Santalices, *Calles de La Habana,* 24).

59. In a city notorious for changing street names often and with little provocation, San Isidro early on was renamed Calle de las Tenazas (Street of the Forceps) because of its proximity to the gate of the same name in the old city wall. Following independence, it was renamed Emilio Núñez, after a war general who later became governor of Havana. Unlike what occurred with the names of many other streets in the city, neither new name stuck; with a sense of pride, the street and the barrio are still called San Isidro (Santalices, *Calles de La Habana,* 131–32); see also Francisco Rojo García, *Plano de La Habana* [Havana: N.p., 1951]).

60. Reay Tannahill, *Sex in History* (New York: Stein and Day, 1980), 357–64.

61. Fernández-Robaina, *Recuerdos secretos,* 29.

62. Ibid., 15, 17.

63. The *reglamentaciones* of 1899 listed several categories of prostitution, each with a different maximum monthly tax: "casas con pupilas," 35 pesos; "casas de aisladas," 12 pesos;

Crime and Culture during the Second Cuban Republic : 125

"casas de citas," 35 pesos; "meretrices ambulantes," 5 pesos. Each of these categories was further subdivided into five levels, each with different tax (*Reglamento*, 20).

64. Fernández-Robaina, *Recuerdos secretos*, 72. The memoir published and edited by Fernández-Robaina intermingles the recollections of two prostitutes, Consuelo and Violeta la Charmé. Since it is at times almost impossible to distinguish which of the two is speaking, throughout the rest of the essay Consuelo's name will be used as representative of the two.

65. One French matron, waiting in Cuba for a visa to immigrate to New Orleans, is said to have left the island with thousands of dollars in profits (Fernández-Robaina, *Recuerdos secretos*, 72).

66. Fernández-Robaina, *Recuerdos secretos*, 55, 90.

67. Ibid., 30.

68. Wright, *Cuba*, 187.

69. See Fernández-Robaina, *Recuerdos secretos*, 33. The tenure and promotion records for Yarini's father, José Leopoldo Yarini, are in the Archivo Historico Nacional (AHN), Madrid; see AHN, Folio Ultramar, 263, expediente 11, 14. The elder Yarini received tenure in 1884 and promotion in 1890. The Yarini and Ponce de León family names are linked in marriage in 1859. Although this union is probably too early to be Alberto's parents, it nevertheless indicates the close relationship of the two families (see Fernando Suárez de Tangíl y de Angúlo, conde de Vallellano, *Nobiliario cubano: O, las grandes familias isleñas, por el conde de Vallellano* [Madrid: F. Beltrán, 1929], vol. 2). With residence and offices on Galiano Street, No. 16, it seems likely that this Yarini was Alberto's "doctor brother" (*Bohemia*, November 1920, 72).

70. Wright, *Cuba*, vii.

71. Fernández-Robaina, *Recuerdos secretos*, 26.

72. Consuelo noted that the term "bag" was used because during this period Cuba had no national currency and gold and silver coins from various countries, including Spain, France, and the United States, were in common circulation (Fernández-Robaina, *Recuerdos secretos*, 50; and Wright, *Cuba*, 67).

73. The correspondent noted that Yarini had taken the opportunity to confront Tarler in the "absence of Minister Edward V. Morgan." Exemplifying the moralizing campaigns being waged in the United States, the paper reported in the same issue on one of a series of purity meetings, where speakers "exhorted the people of Tampa to wage a fight against the forces of immorality," especially those in "the district" (*Tampa Tribune*, 24 November 1910).

74. Fernández-Robaina, *Recuerdos secretos*, 26.

75. Ibid., 51. The first automobile arrived in Cuba at the time of its occupation in 1898.

76. Fernández-Robaina, *Recuerdos secretos*, 33.

77. Ibid., 51.

78. Consuelo la Charmé stated that she, too, would have been happy if she had been one of Yarini's "women," and she regretted that she had not slept with him (Ibid., 50).

79. Ibid., 33.

80. *Diario de la Marina*, morning edition, 22 November 1910. The *Diario* was Havana's most conservative newspaper, with close ties to Spain and the colonial order. Its editor and staff saw themselves as "the sole zealous support of Mother Church in the Americas" (Wright, *Cuba*, 142–43).

81. Using boarding-school euphemisms, Section 8 of Article 20 of the 1899 Reglamento stated that prostitutes living in a brothel, with a female madame or a male pimp, would be called *pupilas* (*Reglamento para el régimen de la prostitución*, 12).

82. Fernández-Robaina, *Recuerdos secretos*, 34; *Diario de la Marina*, morning edition, 24 November 1910.

83. Escarpanter and Madrigal, *Carlos Felipe*, 60. Ñáñigos were members of a secret Afro-

Cuban cult that practiced its religion in Cuba. *Ñáñigismo* worshipped the spirit of Abakuá and its slogan was "partner and friend." Members were generally considered *orilleros*, or marginalized, and were usually from the ranks of the poor and socially ostricized, although some very prominent Cubans have been leaders in the sect, which is still active in the north-central part of Cuba, including Havana. Cuban children were frightened into obeying their parents with threats that the *ñáñigos* would get them (a Cuban version of the "bogeyman"). One of *Ñáñigismo*'s characteristics, which surfaced in popular culture, was the use of colloquialisms such as *mayimbe* for a leader or chief; *parna* for friend; and *la jara* for the police. According to Consuelo (or Violeta) la Charmé, prostitutes in San Isidro generally called the police *la jara*, a *ñáñigo* term (Gisela Arandia, Rockefeller Fellowship Scholar, interview by author, 2 April 1997, Florida International University, Miami; and Fernández-Robaina, *Recuerdos secretos*, 40–45; see also Jorge Castellanos and Isabel Castellanos, *Cultura afrocubana* [Miami: Ediciones Universal, 1994]).

84. Consuelo remembered that there were two assailants on the rooftops (Fernández-Robaina, *Recuerdos secretos*, 50). *Diario de la Marina* identified five men who had been on the rooftops: Jean Boggio, César Mornan, Ernesto Laviere, Cecilio Bazzout, and one known simply as Valetit; and several witnesses testified to hearing footsteps on their rooftops on the night of 22 November (*Diario de la Marina*, morning edition, 24 November 1910). The seven o'clock time was published in *Diario de la Marina*, as part of the official report of the incident of 21 November, which was signed by Fransisco F. Piñero and Jesús Olive (*Diario de la Marina* morning edition, 25 November 1910).

85. Consuelo identified the companion as (Jean) Boggio (Fernández-Robaina, *Recuerdos secretos*, 50; *Diario de la Marina*, morning edition, 24 November 1910).

86. *Diario de la Marina*, morning edition, 22 November 1910; Fernández-Robaina, *Recuerdos secretos*, 50.

87. *Diario de la Marina*, morning edition, 22 November 1910.

88. Lotot's place of residence was given as Desamparados, no. 42; (*Diario de la Marina*, 22 November, 1910).

89. *Diario de la Marina*, afternoon edition, 13 November 1910.

90. *La Lucha*, 23 November 1910.

91. Fernández-Robaina, *Recuerdos secretos*, 39.

92. *Diario de la Marina*, afternoon edition, 23 November 1910.

93. *Diario de la Marina*, afternoon edition, 23 November, 1910.

94. The names listed were: Federico G. Morales, Domingo J. Valladares, General Fernando Freyre de Andrade, Commandante Miguel Coyula, Commandante Armando André, Antonio León, Capitán Emilio Sardiñas, Federico Caballero, Raúl Busquet, Pedro Quiñones, Ambrosio J. Hernández, José Bastarrechea, and Eduardo Infante (Fernández-Robaina, *Recuerdos secretos*, 36).

95. The prostitution regulations of 1899 restricted garish dress outside the zones (*Reglamento*, Capitulo I, Articulo 10, Numero 5).

96. Fernández-Robaina, *Recuerdos secretos*, 45.

97. Noting that the police were needed for crowd control, the *Tampa Tribune* first reported the large numbers assembled at the Yarini home for the all-night vigil (*Tampa Tribune*, 24 November 1910).

98. Fernández-Robaina, *Recuerdos secretos*, 36–46.

99. The Associated Press report of 24 November anticipated that there would be crowd-control problems during the funeral procession that day (*Tampa Tribune*, 24 November 1910).

100. Fernández-Robaina, *Recuerdos secretos*, 36; see note 1 above for newspaper coverage of the Yarini viewing and funeral.

101. Fernández-Robaina, *Recuerdos secretos*, 40.

102. An official report of the details of the Cuban ambush of the French group at "El Bosque" was published in *Diario de la Marina*, morning edition, 26 November 1910.

103. Fernández-Robaina, *Recuerdos secretos*, 50.
104. *Diario de la Marina*, morning edition, 24 November 1910.
105. *Diario de la Marina*, afternoon edition, 30 November 1910.
106. *Diario de la Marina*, morning edition, 28 November 1910; morning and afternoon editions, 29 November 1910.
107. *Diario de la Marina* mentions other newspaper coverage, including that of Havana's *El Mundo* and Camagüey's *El Comercio*, and repeatedly refers to the "immoral press," which sensationalized the events to increase circulation: "Almost all Havana newspapers turn into epic tales the accounts of the day's repulsive crimes" (*Diario de la Marina,* morning edition, 27 November 1910).
108. *Diario de la Marina*, morning edition, 22 November 1910.
109. *Diario de la Marina*, afternoon edition, 25 November 1910.
110. *Diario de la Marina*, afternon edition, 25 November 1910.
111. *Diario de la Marina,* afternoon edition, 25 November 1910.
112. *Diario de la Marina*, afternoon edition, 2 December 1910.
113. The barrio Luyanó was bounded by the following streets, which were set aside specifically for prostitution: Pérez, Arango, Juan Alonso, and Rosa Enríquez. In addition, the decree moved regulatory and enforcement powers from the Comisión de Higiene Especial to the Secretaría de Gobernación y Sanidad. The decree was signed by President Gómez and Gerardo Machado, then minister of the Secretaría de Gobernación (see Secretaría de Gobernación, Decreto No. 1158, *Gaceta Oficial de la Republica de Cuba* 10: 151 [27 December 1911]: 6653).
114. Decreto No. 883, *Gaceta Oficial de la Republica de Cuba,* 4 October 1912: 4014. The Secretary of the Ministerio de Gobernación was by then Federico Laredo Bru.
115. Signed by President Menocal, Decreto No. 964 voided existing regulations, except for minors; made the treatment of syphilis the responsibility of local, not national authorities; eliminated the restriction of the trade to *zonas*; gave police greater power to arrest anyone engaged in "public" prostitution; allowed two months for the "public" image of brothels to be altered; moved the treasury of the Servicios de Higiene under the jurisdiction of the Secretaría de Sanidad y Beneficiencia; turned over all records of the Servicio to the Negociado de Higiene Especial de la Dirección de Sanidad; and entrusted the enforcement of the new decree to the secretaries of Sanidad y Beneficiencia, Gobernación, y Justicia. The decree was signed by President Menocal and the secretary for Sanidad y Beneficiencia, Dr. Enrique Núñez (Decreto No. 964, *Gaceta Oficial de la Republica de Cuba*, 23 October 1913: 5453–54).
116. Immigration laws did not again command such attention until the period between 1940 and 1944 (*Compilación*, 3:428–31).
117. Manuel de J. Zamora, "Hasta donde llegara la acción de la policía en el barrio Colón?" *Bohemia* (Havana), 7 January 1951, 68–74; Jorge Mañach, "La decadencia del pudor," *Bohemia* (Havana), 7 January 1951, 49. See also Fernández-Robaina, *Recuerdos secretos*, 43, 53.
118. Fernández-Robaina, *Recuerdos secretos*, 45, 53.
119. Pérez, *Cuba: Between Reform and Revolution*, 295.
120. Simons, *Cuba: From Conquistador to Castro,* 263; see also Shelton, *Cuba y su cultura,* 351.
121. For union problems during the 1950s, see Pérez, *Cuba: Between Reform and Revolution,* 300–3.
122. Pérez, *Cuba: Between Reform and Revolution,* 392–93. The population of Havana province had tripled between 1907 and 1953, growing from 538,000 to 1,500,000 inhabitants; the percentage of the population of the island living in Havana province remained stable, at about one–fourth of the total: 26.3 percent in 1907 and 26.4 percent in 1953. The number of brothels decreased, however, but the number of prostitutes showed a dramatic increase, to 11,500. This figure is still impressive, even if one believes that the 1902 figures of 744 prostitutes in the city

were vastly underreported (see Luzón, *Economía, poblacíon y territorio en Cuba,* 83). Alain Corbain argues that the decline in brothels and the growth of independent practicioners were not the result of police measures, but rather a change in the patterns of male sexual desire that resulted from socioeconomic change (Corbain, *Women for Hire,* Introduction).

123. Quoted in Fernández-Robaina, *Recuerdos secretos,* 61; see also *Bohemia,* 7 January 1951.

124. *El Mundo* (Havana), 15 March 1956.

125. *Informacion* (Havana), 1 January 1958, cited in Fernández-Robaina, *Recuerdos secreto,* 71.

126. Fernández-Robaina, *Recuerdos secretos,* 71.

127. Arthur Schlesinger Jr., quoted in Pérez, *Cuba: Between Reform and Revolution,* 305.

128. The 1951 article in *Bohemia* reported the gang-related activities of pimps who also worked the drug trade. The photo layout included a Yarinesque picture of a pimp who had been killed in a drug-related altercation (*Bohemia,* 7 January 1951).

129. In 1964 a second dramatic work based on the life and death of Alberto Yarini was published in Havana. *El Gallo de San Isidro,* by José R. Brene, however, did not receive the acceptance and accolades afforded Felipe's work. The events of 21 November 1910 are also the focus of *El Gallo,* but Alberto Yarini is characterized as a shrewd politician who is "working" the barrio. His largess is explained as a politician's ploy to win votes. In the play, one of the pimps boasts that "Cuba has produced the best pimps in the world. Rum, sugar, tobacco, and pimping, in these no one can best [the Cubans]" (José R. Brene, *El Gallo de San Isidro* [Havana: Ediciones R., 1964], Act I).

130. Felipe, quoted in Escarpanter and Madrigal, *Carlos Felipe,* 22.

131. Escarpanter and Madrigal, *Carlos Felipe,* 24.

132. Carlos Felipe, *Réquiem por Yarini: Drama tragico en tres actos de Carlos Felipe* (Miami: Ediciones Calesa, 1978), 10.

133. Note that in *Réquiem* the author changed the protagonist's first name from Alberto to Alejandro. If Felipe were consciously trying to create a myth in the style of the ancient Greeks, could this change have been an allusion to Alexander the Great?

134. "La Macorina" was Havana's most famous prostitute. She plied her trade in the early decades of the twentieth century, after Yarini's time (Felipe portrays her as having lived before Yarini.) She has been immortalized in poems, such as Alfonso Comin's "La Macorina," and in popular songs like "Ponme la mano aquí Macorina" (Put your hand here, Macorina). Disfigured in a car accident, after which she was left destitute, Macorina lived out her life in obscurity in a small apartment on Jovellar Street in Habana (Escarpanter and Madrigal, *Carlos Felipe,* 60 n. 81; Editorial, *El Nuevo Herald* [Miami], 10 January 1983, 7).

135. Cf. the Reglamento of 1899.

136. Escarpanter and Madrigal, *Carlos Felipe,* 40.

137. Ibid., 41.

138. Ibid., 26–27.

139. Ibid., 48.

140. González, "La cultura popular," 32.

141. Ibid., 41.

142. Felipe, *Réquiem por Yarini,* 45; see also Wright, *Cuba,* 61.

143. "Carmen," interview by author, 31 January 2001, Havana.

144. Escarpanter and Madrigal, *Carlos Felipe,* 1, 48.

145. Glen Caudill Dealy, *The Public Man* (Amherst: University of Massachusetts Press, 1970), 41.

146. Act I of Carlos Felipe's play, quoted in Escarpanter and Madrigal, *Carlos Felipe,* 47.

147. Escarpanter and Madrigal, *Carlos Felipe,* 48–49.

148. González, "La cultura popular," 43–45.
149. Ibid., 45.
150. Escarpanter and Madrigal, *Carlos Felipe,* 49.
151. Felipe, quoted in González, "La cultura popular," 23.
152. Felipe, *Réquiem por Yarini,* 65.
153. In Miami, the play was produced in November 1984, October 1990, and, most recently, in June 1998. It was scheduled to open in Madrid and Havana later in 1998 as part of the Festival Internacional de Teatro Hispano (*El Nuevo Herald,* 27 November 1984; 25 October 1990; and 4 June 1998).
154. Graciela Guzmán, "Irrumpe Yarini," in *Bohemia* (Havana), 5 September 1986.
155. Mercedes Santos Moray, "Réquiem por una puesta," *Trabajadores* (Havana), 15 May 1980.
156. See Lynn Darling, "Havana at Midnight," *Esquire,* May 1995, 96–106.
157. Ibid., 2.
158. Doris Sommer, *Foundational Fictions: The National Romances of Latin America* (Berkeley: University of Califormia Press, 1993), 7.
159. Guzmán, "Irrumpe Yarini," 25.
160. Wright, *Cuba,* 95–97.
161. Wright, *Cuba,* 10.
162. Fernández-Robaina, *Recuerdos secretos,* 34.
163. Felipe, *Réquiem por Yarini,* 19.
164. Ibid., 39.

KIRWIN SHAFFER

The Radical Muse: Women and Anarchism in Early-Twentieth-Century Cuba

ABSTRACT

Following independence from Spain in 1898, Cuba's anarchists focused attention on what they regarded as elite hypocrisy regarding the larger social problems besetting Cuba. In the hope of drawing Cuba's popular classes into the global anarchist movement, their critique addressed the manner in which industrial, bourgeois society victimized women, especially those of the working class. Cuban radicals used the image of women and women's issues as foils to analyze and criticize health, workplace, and family issues. They also used women as symbols of obstruction to anarchist-defined notions of progress. Finally, they showed how women could aspire to be female heroines, by promoting an ideal type of "noble woman" and the concept of "revolutionary motherhood" to which women should strive. Anarchists directed their messages to women and men through the movement's popular cultural forms. Newspapers, novels, short stories, plays, and social gatherings in which plays were performed or revolutionary songs were sung all played a part in anarchist appeals to female followers and functioned as a form of education.

RESUMEN

Después de la independencia de España en 1898, los anarquistas en Cuba pusieron su atención en lo que consideraban la hipocresía de la elite sobre el problema social mayor que acosaba a Cuba. Sus críticas sostenían que las mujeres, especialmente las de la clase trabajadora, eran víctimas de la sociedad industrial burguesa. Al enfatizar estos problemas, los anarquistas tenían la esperanza de atraer a las clases populares cubanas al movimiento anarquista global. Los radicales cubanos emplearon la imagen y los problemas de la mujer como una forma de analizar y criticar temas laborales, familiares y de salud pública. Los anarquistas también usaron a las mujeres como símbolos que obstruían las nociones de progreso, según las definiciones de los anarquistas. Finalmente, pintaron cómo la mujer podía aspirar a ser una heroína femenina al promover el tipo ideal de "mujer noble" y "madre revolucionaria" al que debían aspirar las mujeres. Los anarquistas dirigieron su mensaje a mujeres y hombres a través del movimiento cultural popular. Periódicos, novelas, cuentos cortos, obras de teatros y reuniones sociales en las que se desarrollaban estas obras teatrales o se entonaban canciones revolucionarias, contribuyeron a atraer a las mujeres al anarquismo y funcionaron como una forma de educación.

How could it happen? Independence from Spain was supposed to usher in a new Cuba filled with justice, freedom, equality — in short, a social revolution was to have taken place. Yet to anarchists, the most radical leftists on the political spectrum, reality had fallen far short of this revolutionary ideal. In the decades following political independence from Spain in 1898, anarchists claimed that the social goals for which they and others had fought had been abandoned by the elite. This political and social elite promoted patriotism while allowing the island to be carved up by urban and agribusiness industrialists. Anarchists charged that the elite and their industrial partners were turning Cuba into a cesspool of vice and exploitation that differed little from the days of colonial rule.

The island's anarchists repeatedly focused attention on what they regarded as elite hypocrisy and the larger social problems besetting Cuba in the first three decades of independence. Within this critique they regularly addressed women's issues and how industrial, bourgeois society affected women, especially of the working class. Women's victimization moved anarchists to address interlocking gender, race, and class issues as they reflected Cuban reality. By highlighting these issues, in which women played a central role, anarchists hoped to draw Cuba's popular classes into the global anarchist movement. These Cuban radicals employed the image of women in several ways. First, they used women and women's issues as foils to analyze and criticize health, workplace, and family issues. In essence, if women could be treated inhumanely in an increasingly capitalist Cuba, then men and children would also suffer, both at work and at home. Second, anarchists used women as symbols of obstruction to anarchist-defined notions of progress. Many women were members of class and religious groups that opposed anarchism. Other women were portrayed as mothers lacking revolutionary and working-class consciousness. These women and mothers exploited children or aped the bourgeoisie. As such, they became symbols for the type of behavior women should avoid — and what men and women should try to correct. Finally, while anarchists portrayed women as victims and reactionaries, they also showed how women could aspire to be female heroines. Anarchists promoted an ideal type of "noble woman" and the concept of "revolutionary motherhood," to which women should strive. Such women and mothers would help lead society to recover a world of mutual aid, cooperation, and harmony, which anarchists believed industrial capitalism, politics, and religion were destroying. Not only did these heroic images offer a vision of how women should act, but also the images reflected how anarchists idealized family relationships. Nevertheless, this view of women and motherhood, while challenging bourgeois society, failed to blame the patriarchy for women's problems and in fact tended to incorporate patriarchal notions of women as mothers.

Cuban anarchists directed their messages to women and men through the movement's popular culture, which functioned as a form of education. Thus, anarchist newspapers, novels, short stories, plays and the social gatherings in which plays were performed or revolutionary songs were sung all contributed to anarchist appeals to female followers. Besides trying to attract women to the movement, these cultural forms expressed the very images of women that anarchists used to criticize bourgeois society and to promote revolutionary motherhood. For anarchists, "woman" became a radical muse in the traditional sense of the word. That is, "woman" inspired anarchists. They portrayed these different images of women throughout Cuba's public and private spheres, at work, in schools, on the streets, and in the home. Anarchists used "woman" as a source of inspiration to illustrate the shortcomings and "unnatural" qualities of Cuban bourgeois society, while also showcasing an anarchist idealized future for the island.

Anarchism, Health, and Women

Despite waves of health and sanitation reforms created under the U.S. military occupations of 1898–1902 and 1906–1909, numerous health problems persisted, both in the general populace and within the workplace, with tuberculosis leading the way. Anarchists argued that the only solution for tuberculosis was prevention, but this required large investments from the government and/or factory and tenement owners. All were reluctant to make such investments. Thus, more Cuban adults died from tuberculosis year after year than from any other single disease (see Table 1).

In 1886, 1,187 *habaneros* died from TB. By the close of the war in 1898, these figures had escalated, due to the hideous sanitary conditions experienced by the great masses of Cubans forced to live in what amounted to refugee camps during the war. In that year, 2,795 people in Havana died of the disease. Over the next two decades, poor living and working conditions facilitated a continued high occurrence of TB, so that even by 1919 TB was a leading cause of death (1,209 deaths in Havana alone).[1]

Anarchists regularly complained about this disease, which they saw as synonymous with the growth of bourgeois industrial society. Besides frequent discussion of the disease in the anarchist press, creators of Cuban popular culture merged TB and gender in a form of social criticism. In his two novels, Cuban anarchist and labor union leader Antonio Penichet wrote about tuberculosis deaths, especially the deaths of working-class women, to illustrate the painful reality experienced by the working class. In Penichet's *La vida de un pernicioso*, the main character Joaquín is in jail for anarchist activities. While he is imprisoned, his *compañera,* Natalia, a former prostitute, is forced to live in unsanitary conditions and eat poorly. Ultimately, she becomes ill and dies from tuberculosis.[2] A similar situation befalls the main character, Rodolfo, in

Table 1
Ten Leading Causes of Deaths in Havana during 1901

Cause	Number of deaths	Death rate/1,000
Tuberculosis of lungs	833	145.62
Diarrhea/enteritis (under 2 years)	742	129.70
Organic disease of the heart	447	78.14
Affections of the arteries (atheroma, aneurism, etc.)	336	58.74
Diarrhea/enteritis (2 years and older)	304	53.14
Simple meningitis	273	47.72
Bronco-pneumonia	193	33.74
Cerebral congestion/hemorrhage	166	29.02
Tetanus	148	25.87
Intermittent fever and malarial cachexia	135	23.60

Table adapted from W. C. Gorgas, "Report of Deaths in the City of Havana during the Year 1901," in Leonard Wood, *Civil Report of Brigadier General Leonard Wood: Military Governor of Cuba* (Washington, D.C.: U.S. Government Printing Office, 1902), 14–17.

Penichet's *¡Alma Rebelde!, Novela histórica*. In this novel Rodolfo's girlfriend likewise succumbs to the disease.[3]

In both novels, the deaths of women associated with anarchists, and who were themselves anarchist supporters, illustrated several things. First, working-class readers recognized the common sight of one of their own falling to TB. By 1920, 61 percent of the total population ten years old and older was literate. Generally, whites had higher literacy rates, with foreign-born white men and women the highest (77.3 percent and 69.3 percent, respectively). Still, despite one's color, sex, and place of origin, over half of the people in all categories in the 1919 census could read. As a result, large numbers of men and women of all colors and classes could receive these anarchist messages and note how the novels' characters reflected the readers' own reality.[4] Second, anarchists characterized women, especially anarchist women, as representations of a noble womanhood to which all women should aspire, but who often fell victim to the elite and conditions in capitalist industries. These women were on the road to being, if not already, in harmony with nature and had developed a working-class consciousness. That these women could succumb to such a disease as TB illustrated the truly horrendous, antinatural, life-endangering features of contemporary bourgeois Cuban society. Third, in both cases, the deaths prompted Joaquín and Rodolfo to reinvigorate their struggles to fight for improved health conditions, but more importantly, to fight for an anarchist future that would bring society more in line with nature and justice.

Besides using female characters as tools to discuss larger health issues in Cuba, anarchists used the real-life situations of female factory workers to draw attention to what they regarded as antihuman, and especially antifemale, conditions in capitalist Cuba. This was best seen within the female workforce employed in the tobacco industry. Women tobacco factory workers had specific health and economic dilemmas to overcome in addition to the dust and lack of fresh air in the factories. The destemmers (*despalilladoras*) of tobacco leaf were mostly women, and they suffered some of the lowest wages in the industry.[5] Beyond this economic issue was an important health issue. From six in the morning to five in the afternoon, these women would stoop over a barrel of tobacco leaves with little rest, fresh air, or sunlight. Anarchists charged that due to the combination of poor diet, the necessity of eating in filthy workplace surroundings, and constantly working in a bent over position, women suffered from bad digestion as well as intestinal and uterine problems.

Anarchists further alleged that the youngest female stemmers were particularly vulnerable. Quoting an unnamed health practitioner, the writer Adriano Lorenzo noted that the girls "who have not begun to menstruate, usually find their development retarded, her reproductive system corresponding to the overall development of her body. Her chest narrows, her back contorts, her breasts do not develop, her hips narrow — in a phrase: her whole body stops developing."[6] Another writer asked what would happen when these girls, whose bodies were not adequately developed, began to have babies — assuming they could become pregnant or carry a fetus to term?[7]

The anarchist concern with female laborers' health had less to do with keeping women out of production, as later labor codes throughout Latin America would do, and more to do with concerns over safety for female workers who might be future mothers. These mothers-to-be would have to be healthy and strong to rear the next generation of enlightened children and future workers. When health and safety standards in the workplace threatened women, they threatened the next generation of the working class. This concern with health, children and working-class motherhood was certainly justified. Infant mortality was a very serious issue in Cuba and one with which anarchists regularly concerned themselves. In 1901 diarrhea and enteritis (inflammation of the intestinal tract) was a leading cause of death among Havana's children. Children under two years old died at a rate of 129.70 per 1,000 population, and children two years old and older died at a rate of 53.14 per 1,000 population. Of 5,720 reported deaths in Havana that year, more than one-fourth (1,453) were children under one year old and more than one-third (1,940) of total deaths were children ten years old and younger.[8] Eighteen years later, the islandwide 1919 census would show a slight worsening of these figures for the youngest children (see table 2).

Thus, by the late 1910s, more than one-fourth of reported deaths islandwide were of infants under one year old and nearly half of all deaths (47 percent) were of youth under twenty years old. These figures merely give an

Table 2
Deaths by Age Group (population based on
1919 figures and deaths registered in 1916)

Age	Population	Number of deaths	Deaths/1,000
Less than 1 year	74,918	11,206	149.6
1–4	335,340	6,400	19.1
5–19	1,110,250	1,705	1.5
20–39	839,666	6,580	7.8
40–59	390,185	6,121	15.7
60+	138,645	8,931	64.4
Total	2,889,004	40,943	14.2

Censo de la República de Cuba Año de 1919, 249.

aggregate overview of something truly dismal occurring in Cuba in the decades after independence. Not only did anarchists blame infant mortality on women's workplace conditions but also on dietary issues related to motherhood. In 1903 one anarchist commentator suggested that high infant mortality and disease were in large part caused by nutritional problems. According to the anonymous author of the column "Por la raza," which appeared in the pages of the anarchist weekly newspaper ¡Tierra!, it was increasingly rare to see mothers nursing their young. Of course, wealthy and middle-class mothers could and did resort to employing wet nurses, but obviously this was not an option for poor families. Poorer families were resorting to bottle feeding. However, "especially in Havana, the milk that was sold generally was impure," and the purest milk available was too expensive. While families living on the outskirts of town were able to get fresh milk from nearby cattle barns, most families, the author argued, were reduced to buying condensed canned milk imported from the United States. The writer concluded that such a practice, besides being expensive and making the poor that much more dependent on imports (and less so on what was available naturally!), was leading to high infant mortality and later childhood diseases, especially tuberculosis.[9]

Childbirth provided a venue for anarchists to address their concerns over the growing use of injections by the Cuban medical community. Anarchists considered injections dangerous to women during childbirth. True to the theories of what later practitioners would label "natural childbirth," one writer criticized doctors for their continual search for pain-relieving substances to inject into birthing mothers. Obstetricians could not safely use ethyl-bromide or ethyl-chloride, and chloroform and ether were too dangerous to use except in the final stages of pushing out the baby. Instead, obstetricians increasingly relied on opiates for pain relief, even though the same doctors acknowledged that these drugs were "inconvenient" because they tended to paralyze the mother's intestines. Instead of so quickly deciding to give injections to deaden the pain of contractions, the writer suggested that doctors should consider a series of hydrotherapy treatments, such as hot water and steam baths, to relax muscles and ease tension. To better prepare for childbirth, mothers should adopt a vegetarian diet, which would cause less stress on the digestive and intestinal organs "and effectively prepare the mother to better raise the child."[10]

Elsewhere, writers challenged the supposed health-threatening women's fashions of middle-class culture, which anarchists claimed many working-class women were trying to emulate. In 1918 the writer "Apolonio" warned girls and young women of the health dangers associated with fashion, particularly the wearing of corsets, high heels, and makeup. Corsets and heels not only led to disfigurement of the natural human body, but also impeded blood flow, the writer warned. As for makeup, it was worse. Not only did makeup disfigure the natural face, it also caused premature aging of the skin and blocked pores that were necessary "for the flow of oxygen through the body in order to fortify the blood and enrich our life."[11]

Anarchists' concerns with women's health issues expanded to a larger concern for all of Cuban society. If women's health was jeopardized, then all of society was jeopardized. Anarchists saw several threats to women's health, especially that of working-class women: the temptations of antinatural bourgeois fashion, the injection-happy state of the professional medical community, the increase in reliance on canned as opposed to breast milk, infant mortality, and poor workplace conditions. Anarchists were generally concerned with the health of working-class women. After all, these were their wives, lovers, daughters, and friends. Some of these women were anarchists themselves. In addition, by focusing on women's health concerns and issues, anarchists used female images as a foil to criticize the larger culture. In so doing, they focused light on the poor conditions facing Cuba's masses after independence and thus illustrated how the goals of independence had been subverted for both men and women alike.

Women, Social Events, Anarchist Theater, and Education

For anarchists, education went beyond schoolhouse walls, extending into public gatherings (*veladas*) and the home. While anarchists started their own schools in the decades following independence, these schools could only reach a small number of children during the day, as well as an equally small number of male and female workers at night. Anarchists used their popular culture as a form of education to reach a larger audience. By examining the content of anarchist novels, plays, and short stories, one discovers that women and women's issues were constant themes in this literature and, by extension, that women were a primary audience for this education.

Whether they were on a propaganda tour or participating in weekly gatherings, anarchists regularly held *veladas*. These were social events where workers and their families could come, usually on Sunday evenings, to hear lectures on anarchism, health, education, and family-oriented topics. From a cultural standpoint, the *veladas* were important acts of revolutionary popular culture where men, women, and children also sang revolutionary hymns, performed libertarian plays, and recited anarchist poetry. All ages and both sexes attended, so that these anarchist cultural events became important educational tools for critiquing Cuban and global politics while suggesting an imaginable anarchist future.

Women were very prominent in the audience at the *veladas*, and newspaper descriptions usually reported that large numbers of them were seated in the front areas closest to the stage and podium. This was confirmed after 1910 when anarchists began to publish photographs of audiences in their newspapers. U.S. military intelligence also noted the presence of women and their children at these gatherings. For instance in January 1908, a Capt. John Furlong wrote to U.S. Military Governor Charles Magoon that the "meetings are being attended by women as well as men. The women bring their children and the meetings seem to be part of an educational system established by these anarchists."[12]

On occasion, noted Cuban female anarchists would appear as speakers at the gatherings. These included anarchist women like Teresa Faro, Emilia Rodríguez, and María Luisa Bustamante.[13] These women had prominent roles in anarchist propaganda illustrating women's revolutionary abilities to women and men alike. They demonstrated their rejection of traditional gender roles and highlighted the capabilities of rationally inspired women. Besides large female attendance and occasional female participation in the talks, speakers often discussed the role of women and the family.

While the speeches were important elements of the *veladas*, the truly invigorating cultural work was found in the songs, poetry, and plays. A typical *velada* began with either an opening speech or a band piece followed by a speech. Speeches then were interspersed with poems with titles like "Himno al pueblo," "La libertad," "A la anarquía," "Los parías," "Una limosna," "El sol perdido," and "Las dos grandezas." Children always recited the poetry. Most often, the children were the sons and daughters of anarchists, such as the son of Miguel Martínez Abello who recited poems at *veladas* from 1905 to 1907, or Rafael García's daughter Celia who did the same in 1913.[14] In a discussion of his brief stay in 1911 with the family of Havana anarchist Jesús López, the noted labor organizer and later government official and celebrated novelist Carlos Loveira also observed how anarchists employed their children in cultural events. López had seven children, one of whom (Jesuito) was a public speaker; the others (all with good anarchist names: Germinal, Rebeldía,

Aurora, Libertad, Igualdad, and Fraternidad) recited poetry and performed songs at meetings and *veladas*.[15]

Anarchist plays were important cultural ingredients at the *veladas* and were thus important sources of popular education aimed particularly at women. From 1904 until the 1920s, no other play was performed as frequently as *Fin de fiesta,* written by the Spanish-born but Cuban-resident anarchist playwright and novelist Palmiro de Lidia (Adrián del Valle). This brief, seven-scene play captured most of anarchism's central themes: worker solidarity, exploitative capitalists, and backward religious or social customs, particularly regarding marriage and its effects on women. In the play, Elena, the daughter of wealthy factory owner Don Pedro, is in love with her poor, struggling, working-class lover Julián. However, Don Pedro wants to marry her off to an old friend. When Elena tells her priest about her predicament, the priest reminds her that she must follow the wishes of her father no matter what. By the end of the play, the audience discovers that Don Pedro intends to close the factory. But workers have gone on strike and set fire to the building, preventing him from liquidating his assets. In the final scene, with his factory in flames, Don Pedro confronts the strikers with pistol in hand. However, Elena charges in and places herself between her father and the workers just as the pistol is fired, killing her. For women audience members the play illustrated the crippling role of traditional marriage and patriarchal authority that anarchists imagined were the lot of women. Yet it also offered women a female martyr—someone who, inspired by love and justice, threw herself between a capitalist and workers to defend the workers, one of whom she loved, and who paid the ultimate price for her sacrifice.[16]

While audience members saw the heroine Elena die for a higher revolutionary cause, they also saw a women who lacked a revolutionary or working-class consciousness. This is clear in Antonio Penichet's play *¡Salvemos el hogar!* in which Matías is the father in an anarchist-defined dysfunctional family. Matías, a worker who regularly attends meetings and talks at the Workers' Center, increasingly becomes convinced of the justness of the workers' revolutionary message. Meanwhile, his wife and children have completely different interests. The son Daniel is primarily interested in the sporting and gaming scene. Daughter María echoes the bourgeois and religious dogma of the middle classes, whose trappings she and her mother strive to emulate. The entire family views their father with contempt, believing that he is wasting his time at the Workers' Center. In one scene, the mother Magdalena wants Matías to accompany her to the baptism of a friend's child, but Matías declines because he must go to the Center, where an assembly on an upcoming strike is to be held. Matías's friend Domingo arrives to escort Matías to the assembly and berates him for the condition of his family, which is "like a summary of current society, all its prejudices, all its errors and all its fanaticisms." To top it off, Matías's youngest son has even joined the Boy Scouts — a youth paramilitary organization to prepare soldiers!

In the play's third and final act, the strike has been violently repressed, with fights breaking out between strikers and strikebreakers. Magdalena, María, and Daniel are smugly pleased with themselves for having recognized what they see as the foolishness of working-class actions because there will always be rich and poor. But Magdalena is bitter, too, yelling at Matías and Domingo that because of the strike and the lack of income coming into the home, "Now I will not be able to buy the ribbons and scalloped lace to adorn my dress for the dance!" Ultimately, for Matías, it is almost too much to stand, and he threatens to abandon the family, but Domingo convinces him to stay. "No, don't drive yourself to despair, Matías. Calm down. What is happening to you is happening to the majority of workers." Workers, Domingo argues, must educate the family to save it, by bringing home books, pamphlets, and other materials and by taking the family to the Workers' Center to hear talks and see performances. Domingo closes by explaining to Matías, and, by extension, to all workers and especially their wives or *compañeras*, "In the harmonious home, there must exist an affinity for ideas so that through a clear explanation all family members come to understand the humanity of our mission."[17]

Women were the special targets of anarchist educational and popular theater initiatives for two important reasons. First, anarchists regularly commented on the religious inclinations of Cuban women. From this perspective, women were the ones who attended mass and filled the confessionals. Through this interaction, the Church was able to influence the religious, and thus the political, beliefs of Cuban mothers. Operating under this influence, mothers would indoctrinate the children in *jesuitismo*, with all its mysticism, emphasis on the soul and an afterlife, and antirational dogma. If this was allowed to continue, then children and the family would not be prepared to lay the groundwork for the coming social revolution.

Second, and completely opposite of this first scenario, was the concept of "woman" occupying an almost reverential place in anarchist discourse. Women were portrayed as liberated beings who had broken the chains of slavery. Women were likewise shown as leading the light of progress in a social climate full of deception, struggle, and vice. Most importantly, women were valued for their roles as mothers and nurturers of children. It was as a revolutionary mother that a woman could best lay the foundations for not only her children but also for social progress. However, before fully exploring the anarchist notion of the "noble woman" and the "revolutionary mother," we should look a bit more at the anarchist-defined negative roles women were to avoid and the ways in which plays dramatize this.

Prostitutes and Bad Mothers

Prostitution was widespread in Cuba, particularly in the capital city. For instance, from 1912 to 1931, the number of prostitutes in Havana alone rose from 4,000 to 7,400. Historical accounts and travelogues tell of the sexual free-for-all that a person with disposable income could enjoy. One such "treat" was enjoying the bodies of girls and young women.[18] Anarchists incorporated this reality into their fiction as a critique of the larger culture. The prostitution of girls and young women appears in a particularly disturbing scene in Penichet's *¡Alma Rebelde!* In this story, the Cuban-born Rodolfo makes his way to Havana near the end of Cuba's War for Independence. Along his way, Rodolfo confronts the evils caused by the war and its lingering effects, which have been exacerbated by a hypocritical elite. He meets a judge whose daughter sleeps with a priest; a pharmacist's daughter who sleeps with two different men, one of whom was paid by yet another man to sleep with his own wife; the two sons of "Don Daniel" and "Don Domingo," who are caught in "una posición repugnante"; and Petrona, the madam of a whorehouse where, in the last days of the war, business has slowed. Petrona hears about a military encampment nearby, and in order to raise much needed cash, she entices the soldiers to the bordello, where two girls begin to service them. After the tenth pair of soldiers, the girls are unable to continue "because the girls were spewing forth blood from all over, especially the mouth." Both girls die, but there is little scandal because Petrona herself lives with the chief of police. Petrona simply finds new girls as replacements.[19]

In Adrián del Valle's short story "En el hospital," the heroine Marta's mother and father die before she becomes a teenager, so she travels to Havana to live with her poor aunt who works as a laundress. While living at her aunt's house, Marta's cousin rapes her. When the aunt loses her job due to illness, she and her son arrange to prostitute the girl. After several years as a prostitute, Marta leaves the house and enters a bordello, where she contracts syphilis and eventually must go to the hospital. While del Valle's description of events leaves very little sympathy for the aunt and her son, he argues that they are not entirely to blame, having acted out of economic necessity.[20] Consequently, the story is not only about the fall of a pure spirit (Marta) but also the larger social environment that drove family members to exploit a young female relative in order to survive.

As these two examples illustrate, the girl-turned-prostitute either dies or becomes incapacitated. At times, anarchist writers portrayed how turning girls into money-making enterprises often resulted in them committing suicide. In Penichet's *La vida de un pernicioso,* Joaquín is a Spanish soldier who switches sides to fight with the Cubans in the War for Independence. After independence, he resumes his trade as a shoemaker and begins anarchist agitation. In a strike aimed at the Havana shoe workshop owned by Rosendo, Joaquín is arrested, and while he is in jail his live-in companion Natalia dies from tuberculosis. The noble free-union relationship between Joaquín and Natalia is held up as an ideal. Penichet contrasts Joaquín and Natalia's relationship with that of Rosendo and his young live-in servant, the orphan Rosa María. Rosendo sexually molests Rosa María before arranging her marriage to Rosendo's friend and confidant Gumersindo. Appalled at the prospect, Rosa María clips from the newspaper an article titled "Aburrido de vivir," which describes how a girl soaked her clothes in alcohol and then lit them, killing herself. Rosa María believes that suicide is the only way out of the sexual abuse she has already experienced and a future life of misery: "That was her only means of freeing herself. How sad that she found herself in such a situation! To be born, to live, and then in the prime of her life, to have to end her life before Nature had fulfilled its mission." One day, Rosendo returns to his home only to find the girl's charred remains.[21]

Penichet's short story "La venta de una virgen" is even more sinister in discussing a mother's exploitation of her first child Lucía. The mother, Jacinta, wants a child but does not care who the father is. What is important is that she give birth to a child so that her breast milk can come in. Then she can sell herself as a wet nurse to a rich couple to nurse their child. She, in fact, succeeds at both of these endeavors after giving birth to Lucía, and then has two sons so that she can continue to make money as a wet nurse. However, after several years of this, Jacinta recognizes that her body is wearing out and she desperately thinks up new schemes to earn a living. As Lucía is approaching puberty, her mother begins to recognize that the young girl's striking blue eyes and blond hair can be used for economic advantage. Jacinta begins to take Lucía to work with her, in the hope that some rich man will lay his eyes upon her and pay handsomely for "the enjoyment of her angelic, tender body."[22] Ultimately, Jacinta conspires with Godínez, a wealthy man who apparently has a history of taking the virginity of many young girls. He brings presents to Lucía, who rejects his advances. Frustrated, Jacinta and Godínez entrap Lucía one day, and this culminates with Godínez raping the girl. Fraught with despair, Lucía flees from her mother and leaps to her death into the crashing sea waves along Havana's Malecón sea wall. Jacinta, thoroughly distraught, begins to cry upon hearing the news of her daughter's death. Yet, the tears are not because she has lost her daughter, but because she has lost her "business."[23]

Anarchists did not damn prostitutes for their activities. Rather, anarchist blame fell more squarely on the pimps and hustlers who coerced young women or girls to sell or trade their sexual services. Women and girls who fell victim to prostitution and other exploitative sexual situations were more frequently portrayed as innocents caught in a larger world of deceit, vice, and corruption. In this sense, "prostitutes" (women exploited for someone else's economic advantage), like the girls at Petrona's, or even Lucía, were held up as noble figures who had been victimized by other women, such as the madame Petrona or the "bad mother" Jacinta. Ultimately, fictionalized prostitutes symbolized the suffering of the popular classes under the weight of postindependence bourgeois Cuban society. Their female exploiters (particularly when they were mother figures) represented what women had to avoid but also illustrated how a corrupt, postindependence Cuba could drive women away from their noble mission to be strong, progressive mothers and noble women.

Noble Women, Family, and Revolutionary Mothers

The image of the "noble woman" and "revolutionary mother" are familiar symbols in the history of twentieth-century Latin American revolutionary struggles. One recalls the famous images of female soldiers with bandoleers slung over their shoulders during the Mexican Revolution. Revolutionary movements in Cuba in the 1950s and in El Salvador in the 1980s also promoted the image of an armed female militia or revolutionary brigade. Likewise, millions of people around the world have seen the famous image of a young Nicaraguan mother with a rifle hanging from her shoulder while an infant suckles at her breast. The antecedents of such twentieth-century images can be found in early-twentieth-century anarchist images of women. To anarchists, the ideal woman was an enlightened mother who educated her children in the revolutionary ideals of equality, justice, and mutual aid. She also attended and participated in anarchist social gatherings or taught in anarchist schools. She was strong, in tune with the highest ideals of Nature — equality, freedom, and cooperation — and she considered herself an equal partner with her male companion. She struggled against capitalist exploitation and rejected religion as antirational.

On the surface, this ideal of woman as "noble" and as "mother" in many ways appears to resemble the ideal of the dutiful homebound wife that was essential for the development of a Latin American middle class in the late nineteenth and early twentieth century. Throughout Latin America, such a middle-class ideal sought to reinforce the notion that women should be restricted to the private realm of the home. There, she would educate her children and purify her husband, who daily ventured into the filth and vice of the public sphere.[24] In Cuba, middle-class women both challenged and expanded this construction of motherhood after independence. As Lynn Stoner has illustrated, feminist organizations formed between 1902 and 1940 were primarily composed of middle-class members. These organizations influenced legislation, challenged the U.S. military occupations, and rejected the individualist tendencies of U.S. feminism. In their quest to expand democracy in Cuba, the island's feminists sought to retain their femininity and their roles as mothers. They believed that as Cuban "matriarchs" they could bring forth a fuller notion of democracy in Cuba. These feminists, though, were not revolutionaries. They did not seek to end patriarchy or even to achieve complete social equality. Rather, Cuban feminists sought to use their femininity to gain recognition of the importance of motherhood as a divine right. Motherhood would then play a role in creating a "feminine space" within the government where women could use their traditional roles as "mothers and guardians of morality" to oversee welfare programs for children, women, and families.[25]

The anarchist ideal of motherhood challenged these middle-class notions. The anarchists' "revolutionary mother" came from the working class and had nothing but contempt for bourgeois society and values. In addition, anarchists completely rejected the idea of working within the government. Rather, anarchists held up the working-class mother as a symbol to which all women should aspire. As such, the "revolutionary mother" was not just a revolutionary alternative to bourgeois values but a condemnation of those values and their effects on Cuban women. In addition, the "revolutionary mother" was the guiding force of the family unit. Cuban anarchists, while denouncing the legal and religious institutions of marriage, held the family in high regard. In fact, anarchists came to argue that the family was the basis for an anarchist form of communism, in which the "revolutionary mother" was both the leading caretaker and the leading symbol.

For anarchists, "marriage" and "family" were not synonymous. While anarchists belittled marriage as an entrapping institution sanctioned by the state and the Church, they emphasized the importance of the family for the development of a communistic society of free, equal, cooperative individuals. One such anarchist was Antonio Penichet. In his widely disseminated pamphlet "Tácticas en uso y tácticas a seguir" (1922), Penichet used five of his forty-five pages to outline this idea. "First, it is necessary to triumph in the home and then triumph in society," he advocated.[26] However, the home and family were more than just the first battle zone in the larger social struggle. The home and the family were actually the bases for communism. Penichet saw the basic familial relationship as nothing short of a small-scale form of communism:

> An individual, who appears to have no obligations toward anyone else, meets someone with whom he wants to enter a conjugal life. And we see that this individual, who did not know this person earlier, comes to share with her all his sadness, all his joy, and the product of his labor. Then from here is born a familiarity with other family members, parents, brothers, uncles, nieces, etc. and a bond forms between all of them — something that indicates the march toward communism. . . . The home, then, is the most pronounced origin of communism and its best field for experimentation.[27]

Penichet's idea of communism was anarchist in nature. For Penichet, the roots of communism do not derive from a revolutionary state that imposes communism downward upon the masses. Rather, communism arises out of peoples' everyday lives. The family, then, served as the most basic grouping of people and the site for the development of human sentiment and cooperative actions. The development of this "natural" process of cooperative relationships was the seed from which larger forms of communist cooperation would emerge. Ultimately, the family was crucial in this development—a development that required a strong, noble, revolutionary mother to guide it and serve as an example of the virtues of a cooperative, just, and humane Nature.

Noble Women, Revolutionary Mothers, and Cuban Anarchist Fiction

The notion that women could embody the noble sentiments of humanity in a hypocritical social environment occurs throughout anarchist literature.[28] In the novella *La eterna lucha* Adrián del Valle describes a bar scene where two men, who are getting drunk, persuade a beautiful, artistic woman to sit with them. One man, a poet, continues drinking and eventually falls asleep at the table. His companion, however, listens intently to the woman, who speaks about struggling for "the ideal." Struggling, she argues, is never in vain when it is for an ideal, but struggling for survival is a truly horrible thing. Still, she notes, struggle is part of Nature's law; the problem is that humans have misinterpreted it to mean struggling against each other. The Russian anarchist Peter Kropotkin was del Valle's most important intellectual influence, and in this novella del Valle is clearly drawing upon Kropotkin's book *Mutual Aid*, when he has his revolutionary female character describe her ideal: "My ideal, the ideal of all generous hearts is this: To replace the brutal struggle of man against man with mutual aid, with mutual love and to see that the eternal struggle to which Nature condemns us has as its final goal the conquest of a free, beautiful, happy life." With that, the young man joins her and both leave the bar; the drunk poet rises to protest, only to fall forward on the table in front of him.[29]

In *La flor marchita*, del Valle continued this theme in a conversation between an unnamed man and woman. As the couple walks, she picks up a fallen rose and begins plucking it apart petal by petal. The man asks his female companion, "What is woman, but the '*flor humana*' whom bad and weak men pick for their own adornment and to enjoy the fragrance." When a man is done with a woman, our narrator continues, the woman (like the flower) is thrown out. Still, the man notes that women have a special characteristic. Unlike the flower, women can rebel against the brutal hand that picks them and thus against human brutality. It is not that the flower and the woman were born to suffer. To the contrary: "Woman, like the flower, was born to enjoy life."[30]

While women may have been born to enjoy life, as were all people, the social environment in which they lived often prevented this. Such simple enjoyment of life was difficult to come by in postindependence Cuba, anarchists argued. As noted earlier, women suffered from joblessness or from working long hours as *despalilladoras* in tobacco factories or as laundresses and seamstresses in homes and shops. They had few educational opportunities, and they lived in an environment that anarchists described as deceptive and antirational. Consequently, when some women found the strength to perform noble acts in such a degenerate setting, anarchists saw them as embodying the noble revolutionary sentiment that would guide humanity into the future.

One such woman appears in del Valle's novella *En el mar: Narración de un viaje trágico*. Though not set in Cuba, the story is poignant. A ship at sea is engulfed in flames and all but the captain go to the life boats. One passenger, Lord Vilton, who clearly represents the aristocracy and upper classes with his diamond-encrusted tooth and pompous affectations, tries to bribe his way onto a lifeboat ahead of the women and children. Once safely away from the burning ship, one young mother becomes hysterical and jumps overboard with her infant child, but another female passenger, described only as La Rusa, saves the baby. At sea, hunger sets in among the survivors, a fact made unbearable by the continuous cries of the starving infant. In a moment of true noble revolutionary motherhood, La Rusa bares her virgin breasts and offers her milkless nipples to the child. In contrast, Lord Vilton is so hungry that he pays a sailor five thousand pounds sterling so that Vilton can make a gash in the sailor's arm and suck the sailor's blood. After three days at sea, the baby dies from hunger and dehydration. Lord Vilton tries to wrestle the infant from La Rusa's hands in order to eat it. In the ensuing struggle, La Rusa throws Vilton's suitcase full of money into the sea, shouting, "Get it. . . . Buy some shark's blood with it!" Then someone hits Vilton over the head and dumps him into the sea. Upon being rescued some time later, La Rusa is still holding the little corpse.[31]

La Rusa's actions reflect the anarchist notion of the noble woman struggling against the rich. In addition, her unselfishness regarding the starving infant exemplifies a quality associated with revolutionary motherhood that Cuban anarchists praised as an ideal capable of saving society. Society had to stop seeing women as merely furniture, money makers, or playthings. Their gifts of motherhood and a nurturing instinct, bestowed on them by Nature, had to be rescued from the downward spiral of society and the dogma of the Church. Women were not merely fallen flowers tossed aside when their sexual charms wore out. Neither were women the embodiment of original sin and the fallen Eve. Women, when their "true" sentiments and proclivities were recognized and employed, were the guiding forces for steering society in accord with the dictates of an anarchist-defined Nature. Women, in fact, had the capacity to be the true revolutionaries in a despoiled age, as well as the standard bearers of what Nature held for humanity. Only by reasserting their true, noble gifts could women then teach their children truth and justice, as anarchists defined these ideals.[32]

While many women practiced what they believed to be their anarchist calling as women, anarchist popular culture sought to convince those who did not practice these beliefs (or whose commitment was shaky) to abandon bourgeois ambitions and actions. Anarchists urged women to look toward more noble sentiments and actions as revolutionaries and mothers. In ¡Alma Rebelde!, Penichet describes Rosa, the mother of the main character Rodolfo's best friend Miguel. Rosa is a widow, a strong woman raising her sons and continuously thwarting the advances of middle-class men. Midway through the novel, Miguel gets his girlfriend pregnant. While the young woman wants to terminate the pregnancy, Miguel says no and Rodolfo agrees. Rosa, too, rejects the idea of an abortion, telling her son that once she too had considered it, but she is now thankful that she had the child, for that child was Miguel.

Abortion raises an important issue concerning the anarchist ideal of women's natural role as mother. While anarchists supported birth control, terminating a life was unacceptable, as Penichet clearly expressed through his character Rodolfo. No one had the right, notes Rodolfo,

> to commit those mysterious murders that frequently occur with impunity. The child ought to be preserved, for nobody knows what its designated mission is on Earth. It seemed to be an abomination to destroy the child brought forth from a woman's vital organs, and the common excuses many used to avoid social gossip were neither reasonable nor humane.

Ultimately, anarchists believed that bourgeois Cuban society used abortion and *casas de beneficencias* (orphanages) for the same reason: to remove the evidence of "passionate moments." The unborn child became the victim of an immoral society made up of "traficantes de conciencias" (traders in consciousness) and "asesinos autorizados" (authorized murderers).[33] When we understand that in anarchist thought children have the same rights as adults, even abortion of the unborn child amounts to murder. Abortion also challenged the natural role of mother and nurturer, which anarchists found so fundamental to a woman's true nature. Abortion, then, was more than murder. It destroyed a little bit of Nature and undermined anarchist progress toward reestablishing the natural order of mutual aid.

Perhaps the strongest female character in Cuban anarchist literature, and thus the character that most embodies the noble woman and revolutionary mother, is del Valle's Soledad in his novel *La mulata Soledad*. Soledad is a working-class mulatta in Havana who comes from an interracial anarchist household. The story begins with Carlos, a young medical student, encountering Soledad on the long tram ride from the Vedado section of Havana to the city's old town shops and factories. Carlos is first initiated into anarchist ideas through his mentor Dr. Anaya, who not only devotes time to working with the poor but also urges Carlos to consider the ideas of anarchism, especially those of Kropotkin. Then, because of Soledad's attempt to live according to the anarchist ideal, Carlos embraces anarchism for the first time. When Soledad begins to date the white Carlos, her family expresses a number of different race and class concerns. Her brother sees whites as the enemy, while her sister questions the intentions of a white man toward a darker woman. Soledad's working-class father Jaime also questions his daughter's actions, not because Carlos is white but because he is a doctor-to-be from the bourgeois class. Still, Jaime leaves the decision to his independent, rationally minded daughter. Carlos and Soledad join in free union and establish a home together. However, Carlos represents the ambivalence of someone from the middle class. He struggles between meeting societal expectations and doing what he knows is right. He leaves Soledad so that he can marry a white woman of his own social rank on the very night after Soledad tells him that she is pregnant. Soledad eventually gives birth to a son.

From this point in the story, we see two anarchist views of Cuban women. Carlos's white wife Estela merely wants the legal recognition of a marriage to enjoy social privilege and middle-class materialism, but she does not want children. In essence, Estela rejects her natural calling of motherhood for the hypocritical, unnatural world of bourgeois social graces. Meanwhile, Soledad continues sewing in the home, a common practice for working-class women, while never abandoning her principles. She continues to raise her child in difficult circumstances but with the solid support of her anarchist parents. When Carlos discovers that his wife has cuckolded him, he returns to Soledad. Meanwhile, his family had disinherited him and he suffers the social repudiation of living outside of marriage with a nonwhite woman. With his savings drying up, Dr. Anaya reappears and offers his clinic to Carlos for treating the poor. After an official divorce from Estela, Carlos and Soledad move in together and jointly raise their son.

Ultimately, *La mulata Soledad* exemplifies how anarchist popular culture could focus on the debilitating social environment that shaped people's behavior, while also illustrating how average people could cooperate and live up to the ideals of anarchism in preparation for the social revolution. As noted previously, anarchists used women as metaphors for both good and ill, and *La mulata Soledad* reflects this. Through the character of Estela, the novel portrays the type of woman and habits to be avoided. Just as important, the novel offers an example of a woman — a revolutionary mother — living a life full of love for humanity and children while striving for justice in her own and others' lives.

Race, Women, and Free Unions

As noted, *La mulata Soledad*'s heroine was of mixed race. Del Valle characterizes one of her strengths as her ability to reject "using" white men for social advancement. Early in the novel, Soledad is seen doing piecework in a shop where her fellow black and mulatta workers discuss how they hope to seize the first white man who will take them away from their working-poor lives. Soledad rejects this sentiment, noting how *mulatas* have always sold themselves to whites in hopes of social advancement. One of Soledad's colleagues responds by arguing that linking up with whites is preferable. From her viewpoint, she might then have a lighter-skinned child, which, she believes, would advance the black race. Soledad has been taught by her white father and black mother to reject such discussions of race and racial characteristics. Race merely divides people, whereas anarchism seeks to unite them. Soledad answers her coworker by saying that when she speaks of love she means the love that is in all humans and that the love must be mutual.[34]

In del Valle's novella "Jubilosa," a very light-skinned mulatta female character becomes another venue to address anarchist notions of race and class. "Jubilosa" in many ways resembles *La mulata Soledad*. A young law student, Gonzalo, dreams of giving up his studies in order to take a job and move in with his girlfriend Jubilosa. Jubilosa responds that Gonzalo's parents would never let him marry the seamstress daughter of a mulatta. In time, Jubilosa confesses to Gonzalo that she is pregnant, but when Gonzalo offers marriage, claiming that Jubilosa could "pass" as white, the following exchange takes place:

> Jubilosa: Mulattas who love whites know how rare it is to find themselves standing before a judge or in a church.
> Gonzalo: But you're not a mulatta.
> Jubilosa: Neither am I white, even though you say that I appear to be. And I am not going to renounce the African blood that runs through my veins.

Jubilosa makes Gonzalo promise not to marry another woman so that they may at least live together.

Breaking his promise to Jubilosa, Gonzalo runs off to marry his wealthy white cousin, but continues to send money for his and Jubilosa's child. She refuses the money. Meanwhile, a black anarchist named Perucho is living in Jubilosa's home, having rented a room there for ten years. Perucho becomes the child's "grandfather," helping out financially as well. Then one evening, as Perucho walks to his room, he passes by Jubilosa's door. He hears a soft voice call his name from inside the room. He walks through the open door, feels two arms wrap around him and lips press against his mouth. The forty-three-year-old anarchist "grandfather" becomes the lover of twenty-one-year-old Jubilosa and the new "father" of the child.[35] The themes in "Jubilosa" echo those of *La mulata Soledad*. A mulatta meets and has a baby with a white male who is studying to enter a bourgeois profession. In *La mulata Soledad*, the woman is betrayed but her lover eventually returns to her, inspired by the anarchist influences of both his mentor and his mulatta lover. In "Jubilosa," the woman is betrayed by her white lover, but finds love and redemption in a black male anarchist.

This confluence of race and gender is important for understanding the dynamics of postindependence Cuba. By the time of independence, slavery had formally been abolished on the island for only a generation. People of African descent, as well as increasing numbers of black and mulatto Caribbean laborers, made up a significant portion of the Cuban population. Any social movement hoping to make inroads into the collective consciousness and imagination of such a racially diverse population would have to appeal to the Afro-Cuban and mixed-race peoples on the island. Adrián del Valle, with the publication of *La mulata Soledad*, clearly recognized this. Yet Soledad represented more than just the black and mixed-race populations playing a role in a future anarchist Cuba. Soledad represented the blending of African and European influences that by the 1920s increasingly characterized what it meant to be Cuban. This notion of *cubanidad*, though, is not only associated with a nationalist identity. Instead, del Valle merged Soledad's anarchist principles and revolutionary motherhood with her mixed-race and Cuban female worker status.[36] Soledad, the mulatta heroine, came to represent a female working-class Cuban who was part of a larger international anarchist movement.

In addition, del Valle's focus on women of color allowed him to address directly the importance of free, consensual unions outside of marriage. It is significant that both Soledad and Jubilosa are of mixed race, have anarchist links, and live in free unions. Anarchists rejected the institutionalized slavery, as they saw it, of legal marriages sanctioned by the state and Church. Thus, men and women should be free to live together outside of these institutional encroachments on individual freedom. Since independence, the proportion of all Cubans living in what the government classified as "illegitimate unions" had declined. For instance, from 1907 to 1919 the percentage of people living together outside of marriage had fallen from 8.6 percent to 6.1 percent of the island's population, whereas in 1919, 23.1 percent of the population was legally married.[37] However, while the overall percentage of popular free unions (the anarchist term for unions outside legal sanction) may have fallen, the practice was still widespread among the nonwhite population. In 1919, 6.1 percent of the population lived in *uniones ilegítimas* (the government term). If one breaks this statistic down by racial categories, as the 1919 census did, one sees that a far larger number of nonwhites than whites lived together outside of legal marriage. Among whites, only 3.5 percent, or 73,000 persons, were in consensual unions. In contrast, 13 percent of the nonwhite population (104,310 persons) were in such unions. The 1919 census also reveals the following ratios, which show a more dramatic contrast: whereas there were only 13 consensual unions per every 100 legal marriages among whites, the ratio was 95 per 100 among nonwhites.[38]

Obviously, nonwhite adults more frequently cohabited without legal sanction, or in anarchist terms, they more frequently engaged in free union than their white counterparts. The ratios suggest that there were nearly as many nonwhite illegitimate unions as there were legal unions in 1919. When broken down by province, the census shows that in Pinar del Río and Matanzas more nonwhite couples lived together outside of legal sanction than within legal marriage (112 and 172 illegitimate unions per 100 legal unions, respectively). In Oriente there were 95 illegitimate unions for every 100 legal ones. Consequently, when in the 1920s del Valle wrote these stories of nonwhite women in free unions, he was acknowledging an obvious fact in Cuba's nonwhite population and based his stories in Cuban reality: nonwhite couples lived in anarchist-defined free unions almost as commonly as they lived in formally recognized legal marriages. By blending racial and gender realities explicitly into his stories, del Valle put a Cuban face on the international anarchist movement. Bringing together gender, race, and free-union status was a way to appeal for increased black, mulatto, and female participation in the anarchist movement, because doing so reflected the diversity of Cuban reality. In anarchist fiction, women of color and the relationships they had with men of different colors provided a means by which to celebrate anarchists' preferred relationships, and as a means of propaganda, to attract followers of all races.

Conclusion

Depending on the message they tried to put forth, Cuba's anarchist movement portrayed women either as victims, misguided reactionaries, or noble revolutionaries. Drawing upon Cuban social reality, anarchists showcased how female workers suffered in the capitalist workplace, in exploitative commercial settings, and in the home. Such victimhood existed in all races and in all classes, reflecting how a focus on gender issues mirrored larger exploitation issues revolving around class and race. At the same time, anarchists depicted some women as deceivers and reactionaries. These women's actions, whether as church-going mothers, deceptive parents, or enterprising brothel owners, impeded the march to transform society. Still, at other times, anarchists put forth the ideal of women as revolutionaries. These women joined with men as equals, raised their children in a spirit of rational cooperation at home and ventured into the public realm to teach and speak.

Undoubtedly, these images of women's true destinies as noble partners, and especially as revolutionary mothers, reflected a certain patriarchal bias imbedded in Cuban anarchism. Mostly male authors dominated the Cuban and international movements, and their writings of idealized women sound almost reactionary to the modern ear. In addition, it is difficult to estimate how many women actively joined the movement. Certainly, there were women who rejected the promotion of motherhood as an ultimate destiny, which they had no desire or ability to fulfill. Even more women embraced motherhood and believed in its sacred mission, and they preferred to live it out within the sanctions of formal marriage and traditional sex roles. Other Cuban women, like socialists and feminists, wanted state support for motherhood and saw women's mothering natures as beneficial reasons for why women should be in the government. In addition, anarchists appealed to some of the most marginalized sectors of Cuban society: poor women of all races. Almost by definition, these were some of the least politicized people on the island and quite naturally this would result in limited numbers of female adherents.

In addition, many obstacles blocked the path of women living and working an anarchist ideal. Poor-quality jobs and unsafe working conditions, inappropriate health care, problems surrounding high infant and child mortality, the world of prostitution, and the lack of a working-class consciousness all impeded women's development. Also, anarchists competed with feminists, socialists, and trade unionists, all of whom had their own programs designed to benefit poor women and liberate them from overbearing men. Undoubtedly, women moved in and out of these different groups, and there was little that would prevent a woman from participating in any combination of groups at the same time.

Still, we know from press reports, photographs, and intelligence reports that many women regularly attended meetings and actively took part in plays, readings, and singing at anarchist social gatherings. Periodically, a few would write for the anarchist press. In Cuba during the first three decades following independence, many women actually came to live the anarchist ideal—women like Teresa Faro, Emilia Rodríguez, María Luisa Bustamante, and Blanca Moncaleano. These revolutionary women spoke at rallies, taught in anarchist schools, and raised a brood of free-thinking children.

Ultimately, though, "woman" was a radical icon of Cuban anarchism. While anarchists hoped to use their popular culture to attract female followers, the image of woman was primarily used as a muse for anarchist ideals. Readers of anarchist newspapers, novels, and short stories, or viewers of anarchist plays could gain an internationalist, nonracist, working-class consciousness from seeing the way women were treated and victimized in Cuban society and at the workplace. Yet women also inspired anarchists to put forth an ideal for women and the family that could serve as a model for Cuba's popular classes. Those same readers and viewers, who recognized how Cuban reality victimized women, could also observe ideal types of female behavior that could be encouraged in spouses, daughters, and friends. Likewise, men were exposed to strong, noble women whom they would have to respect as intellectual and emotional equals. That was the anarchist agenda for Cuba—equality and freedom in all manifestations, whether racial, gender, or class. When anarchists discussed women in their newspapers, at talks, or in their popular culture, they made a conscious and conscientious choice to use images of women not only to reflect reality but also to inspire social change.

NOTES

1. *Censo de la República de Cuba, Año de 1919* (Havana: Maza, Arroyo y Caso, S. en C., 1919), 253.
2. Antonio Penichet, *La vida de un pernicioso* (Havana: Avisador Comercial, 1919), 130.
3. Antonio Penichet, *¡Alma Rebelde!, Novela histórica* (Havana: El Ideal, 1921), 90.
4. *Censo de la República de Cuba, Año de 1919*, 366–67.
5. Jean Stubbs, *Tobacco on the Periphery: A Case Study in Cuban Labour History, 1860–1958* (Cambridge: Cambridge University Press, 1985), 77–78.
6. *El Nuevo Ideal*, 25 February 1899, 3.
7. *¡Tierra!* 17 October 1903, 2.
8. "Report of Deaths in the City of Havana during the Year 1901," in "Report of W. C. Gorgas," *Civil Report of Brigadier General Leonard Wood, Military Governor of Cuba, 1901* (Washington, D.C.: War Department), 17.
9. *¡Tierra!* 24 October 1903, 2.
10. *Pro-Vida*, February 1915, 1–2.
11. *Pro-Vida*, 30 April 1918, 4.
12. Memo for the Chief of Staff from John W. Furlong, Captain, General Staff, Chief, Military Information Division, 3 January 1908, Records of the Provisional Government, Record Group 199, National Archives, Washington, D.C.
13. *¡Tierra!* 12 June 1907, 2; 10 August 1907, 2, 4.
14. *¡Tierra!* 11 November 1905, 4; 30 November 1907, 1; 8 August 1913, 3; *El Dependiente*, 20 August 1913, 1; 17 September 1913, 4.
15. Carlos Loveira, *De los 26 a los 35: Lecciones de la experiencia en la lucha obrera (1908–1917)* (Washington, D.C.: Law Reporter Printing Company, 1917), 78. The use of children for revolutionary cultural events is still popular in Cuba today. In a public forum with a local Committee for the Defense of the Revolution in Camagüey in 1989, a group of scholars and librarians and myself were treated to several children reciting memorized revolutionary poems.
16. Palmiro de Lidia, *Fin de fiesta, cuadro dramático* (New York, 1898).
17. *Nueva Luz*, 10 April 1925: 4–6.
18. Louis A. Pérez Jr., *On Becoming Cuban: Identity, Nationality, and Culture* (Chapel Hill: University of North Carolina Press, 1999), 193. See also Rosalie Schwartz, *Pleasure Island: Tourism and Temptation in Cuba* (Lincoln: University of Nebraska Press, 1997); and T. Philip Terry, *Terry's Guide to Cuba* (Boston: Houghton Mifflin, 1929).
19. Penichet, *¡Alma Rebelde!* 25.
20. Adrián del Valle, "En el hospital," in *Por el camino* (Barcelona: F. Granada y Comp., 1907).
21. Penichet, *La vida de un pernicioso*, 139.
22. Penichet, "La venta de una virgen," in ibid., 193–210 (quote is on p. 198).
23. Penichet, "La venta de una virgen," in ibid., 193–210 (quote is on p. 210).
24. To understand how this functioned in various parts of the Americas, see, in particular,

William French, "Prostitutes and Guardian Angels: Women, Work, and the Family in Porfirian Mexico," *Hispanic American Historical Review* 72, no. 4 (November 1992): 529–53; and David McCreery, "'This Life of Misery and Shame': Female Prostitution in Guatemala City, 1880–1920," *Journal of Latin American Studies* 18, no. 2 (November 1986): 333–53. As McCreery states, "Attempts to regulate prostitution must be understood as a part of a liberal drive to mobilize and control society as a whole in the interest of a class-defined vision of national development" (334).

25. See K. Lynn Stoner, *From the House to the Streets: The Cuban Women's Movement for Legal Reform, 1898–1940* (Durham, N.C.: Duke University Press, 1991).

26. Antonio Penichet, *Tácticas en uso y tácticas a seguir* (Havana: El Ideal, 1922), 38.

27. Ibid., 40–41.

28. *¡Tierra!* 5 June 1925, 4. In fact, the Barcelona-based La Novela Ideal series, which published many of del Valle's short stories in affordable booklet forms, explicitly aimed "to make the hearts of women and children pulsate." Del Valle's *Mi amigo Julio* was the series' first installment.

29. Adrián del Valle, "La eterna lucha," in *Cuentos inverosímiles* (Havana: Nuevo Ideal, 1903), 110. Del Valle was a great admirer of Kropotkin's works, even publishing a brief biography of the anarchist intellectual.

30. Adrián del Valle, "La flor marchita," in *Cuentos inverosímiles*, 193.

31. Adrián del Valle, "En el mar: Narración de un viaje trágico," in *Cuentos inverosímiles*, 163.

32. In Cuban reality, one found this in the work of women like Blanca de Moncaleano, who taught in anarchist schools with her husband while raising her children with anarchist sentiments. Likewise, Emilia Rodríguez, a female anarchist agitator in Matanzas, was a leading anarchist figure; she organized the 1912 Cruces Congress and in 1913 directed a school in Yabucito while raising her four children—all after her partner's deportation (*¡Tierra!* 12 June 1907, 2; 10 August 1907, 2, 4; 8 June 1912, 3; 14 January 1913, 2).

33. Penichet, *¡Alma Rebelde!* 91–92.

34. Adrián del Valle, *La mulata Soledad* (Barcelona: Impresos Costa, 1929), 50.

35. Adrián del Valle, "Jubilosa," La Novela Ideal series, no. 10 (Barcelona: La Revista Blanca, n.d.), 6–7.

36. For more on the anarchist notion of revolutionary motherhood and Soledad's role in it, see Kirwin Shaffer, "Prostitutes, Bad Seeds, and Revolutionary Mothers: Imagining Women in the Anarchist Fiction of Adrián del Valle and Antonio Penichet, 1898–1930," *Studies in Latin American Popular Culture* 18 (1999): 1–17.

37. *Censo de la República de Cuba, Año de 1919*, 348–49.

38. Ibid., 353. Censuses taken in Cuba combined all nonwhite populations into the category "de color." These included blacks, people of mixed race, and Asians. The ratios concerning legal and nonlegal cohabitation do not delineate unions between people of different races, e.g., a white and black or a black and mulatta—the two examples from del Valle's fiction.

TIFFANY A. THOMAS-WOODARD

"Towards the Gates of Eternity":
Celia Sánchez Manduley and the
Creation of Cuba's New Woman

ABSTRACT

This article traces the contours of the complex set of public and private acts of memory that have emerged in the twenty years since the death of Cuban revolutionary Celia Sánchez Manduley (1920–1980). National leaders, government institutions, and individual men and women have articulated a complex, and at times contradictory, array of memories of Celia's life and contributions to the revolutionary cause. In turn, these memories have shaped a much larger national discourse concerning the relationship of the individual to the body politic, the definition of an ideal revolutionary *cubanidad* (Cuban nation identity), and the proper role for women within Cuban society.

RESUMEN

Este artículo traza los contornos del complejo grupo de actos de recordación, públicos y privados, que han surgido en los veinte años desde la muerte de la revolucionaria cubana Celia Sánchez Manduley (1920–1980). Líderes nacionales, instituciones gubernamentales así como individuos —hombres y mujeres— han articulado un intrincado, y a veces contradictorio, abanico de memorias de la vida de Celia y sus contribuciones a la causa revolucionaria. A su vez, estas memorias han moldeado un discurso nacional más amplio sobre la relación del individuo con el corpus político, la definición de una "cubanidad" revolucionaria ideal, y el papel de las mujeres dentro de la sociedad cubana.

Nadie que este en el recuerdo,
Nadie muere si allí está.
Nadie que viva en el pueblo,
Se muere ni morirá.
— Mirta Aguirre

(No one who exists in memory,
No one dies if they are there.
No one who lives in the people,
Dies or ever will die.)

Sánchez Manduley and Cuba's New Woman : 155

In his seminal work *Imagined Communities: Reflections on the Origin and Spread of Nationalism*, Benedict Anderson states that "the deaths that structure the nation's biography are of a special kind."[1] The death of Cuban revolutionary and Secretary to the President, Celia Sánchez Manduley on 11 January 1980,[2] was one such special historical event that has earned its place in the biography of Cuba. For a nation coming to terms with a turbulent and often violent history, Celia has become the symbol of a revolutionary ideal. The various "sites of memory"[3] that were produced subsequent to Celia's death, by national leaders, government institutions, and individual men and women, present particular memories of her contributions to Cuban society. In turn, these memories have shaped a much larger, multifaceted national discourse concerning the relationship of the individual to the body politic, the definition of an ideal revolutionary *cubanidad* (Cuban national identity), and the proper role for women within Cuban society.

As a study of the intersections of gender, revolution, and memory,[4] this essay will highlight the fact that memories are gendered and that the gendering of memory both reflects and shapes social spaces and expressive forms. Following the work of Miriam Cooke and Angela Woollacott, I contend that the experience of the Cuban revolution, more than any other event of the twentieth century, has influenced the discourse of masculinity and femininity in Cuban society at both the individual and collective levels.[5] Utilizing official and unofficial memories of Celia Sánchez Manduley's contributions to the Cuban revolution as a case study, I will demonstrate that the act of memorializing deceased individuals is one key element of the politics of remembrance. As we shall see, the act of memorializing Celia's death was causally linked to her subsequent mythification, and this process has had a tremendous impact on both official and popular imaginings of the ideal socialist revolutionary. In short, this essay is an attempt to highlight the array of memories that have emerged about Celia and the shaping force they have exerted on Cuban society. By tracing the contours of the complex set of public and private acts of memory that have emerged in the twenty years since Celia's death, we can begin to establish the links between gender, revolution, and memory. Specifically, we gain new insights into the ways in which the mythologized biography of an individual can become the embodiment of a geographical place, a collection of ideal human characteristics, and a way of life.

Because of the particular limitations of the sources concerning the life of Celia Sánchez Manduley — namely, their relative paucity and their commemorative nature — this essay necessarily approaches her biography through the lens of memory. Thus, this discussion begins with an examination of some of the methodological difficulties incurred when embarking upon a study of gender and national memory. The second section then explores the process by which national leaders and government institutions created an official or public memory of Celia's role in the revolution in the years following her death. In order to draw comparisons and contrasts, the third section highlights the array of memories of Celia that exist at the private or individual level. It should be noted here that the decision to divide the essay into official memory and private memory sections was made purely for the sake of organization, and is not meant to imply that these two categories are mutually exclusive. In fact, as we shall see, the two kinds of memory are highly interactive.[6] In order to clarify the process by which this interaction takes place, the concluding remarks will reflect on the various intersections and/or fissures between these public and private memories of Celia and the impact this process has had on the construction of a national blueprint for Cuba's New Woman.[7]

Memory Trouble: Exploring the Boundaries of Fact and Fiction

Although it is not the intention of this essay to provide a complete or definitive biography of Celia Sánchez Manduley, some discussion of what is considered common knowledge about her life seems merited. Little is known about Celia's early childhood, but it is generally accepted that she was born and raised in the small town of Media Luna, a rural suburb of the municipality of Manzanillo, in the eastern provinces of Cuba. Notwithstanding the fact that the socioeconomic status of the Sánchez family is rarely mentioned in Celia's popular biography, there is some evidence to suggest that as the daughter of a dentist who also owned several sizable properties, Celia enjoyed a relatively affluent lifestyle.[8] If little is known about Celia's early childhood, even less is known about her ideological formation as a young woman. While Celia's father is frequently identified as having been her primary intellectual influence, there is a gaping hole in our knowledge of why Celia became committed to the revolutionary cause. Typically, popular knowledge of Celia's biography begins with her official incorporation into the revolution in her early thirties, initially as an arms runner and later as a combatant. In terms of her participation in the armed phase of the revolution, Celia is commonly referred to as the first woman to fire a weapon in battle, an achievement that earned her the unofficial title of "first female guerrilla of the Sierra Maestra." Additionally, Celia is credited with organizing the first battalion of female combatants, known as the Mariana Grajales Brigade.[9] Following the triumph of the revolution in 1959, Celia was appointed Secretary to the President, a position to which she was reappointed in 1964. In her capacity as a government official, Celia is credited with the creation of several large public institutions and tourist centers, including the Oficina de Asuntos Históricos (Office of Historical Affairs), the Palacio de la Revolución (Palace of the Revolution), Havana's 1,900-acre Lenin Park, and the famed "Coppelia" ice cream parlor.

While the above information represents what is considered common

Sánchez Manduley and Cuba's New Woman : 157

knowledge about the trajectory of Celia's life, it bears mentioning that there are other elements of Celia's biography that are not so well entrenched or openly discussed. Perhaps no aspect of Celia's life has received more attention from the international academic community than her relationship with Fidel Castro. In fact, this is frequently the only context in which she is mentioned within the general histories of the Cuban revolution. As Secretary to the President, it is clear that Celia wielded a considerable amount of personal and political power. What is less clear is whether or not Celia's relationship with Fidel was purely professional—and neither Fidel nor Celia ever publicly addressed this issue. Within Cuba, the question of the nature of Fidel and Celia's relationship is most often either addressed at the level of rumor—"se dice que fueron amantes" ("they say they were lovers")—or it is not spoken of at all. A more common response, however, is an uncomfortable silence followed by the claim that Celia never married in order that she might fully devote herself to the needs of the Cuban people.[10] It is important to note here, however, that the mere prevalence of a set of memories about an individual does not mean that they will be universally upheld. The Cuban exile community in the United States has proven to be a major source of countermemories of Celia. Several of the histories of the Cuban revolution published in the U.S. derisively refer to Celia as the "proverbial lion at [Fidel's] door" who also happened to be "sharing his double bed,"[11] or as "Fidel's long-term companion."[12] While it is difficult to measure the impact (if any) these sources have had on the popular memory of Celia within Cuba, their mere existence is interesting to note, as they expose the tender underbelly of national mythology.[13]

Despite the popular discretion with which Celia's personal life is treated, it is clear that within Cuba's national mythology Celia Sánchez is widely recognized as an important revolutionary figure. Beyond the basic biography sketched above, however, it is difficult to find any specific information about who Celia was as an individual. Unbelievably, the card catalog at the José Martí National Library in Havana contains no listing for Celia, and, ironically, the archival contents of the Celia Sánchez Library would actually be more relevant to a biography of one of the male revolutionary leaders. This relative absence of official documentation of Celia's contributions to Cuban society leads one to question why a woman openly spoken of as Cuba's First Lady does not have at least one biography written about her life.[14]

While Celia's multiple achievements would seem to belie her relative elision from official history, there is an element to Celia's story that explains the way that her voice resonates today in the lives of the Cuban people. The exercises of official history in Cuba (namely commemorative speeches and public monuments) have created a space in which the Cuban people create their own memories of Celia—memories that may not always correspond with official history. Thus, through poetry, storytelling, and other forms of mythmaking, a space has been claimed for Celia in the unofficial history, or *intrahistoria,* of the Cuban revolution. The importance of this position cannot be ignored. According to Julián Marías, this *intrahistoria* represents that which is permanent and definitive in history.[15] Marías claims this space specifically for women precisely because they are so often omitted from the official record of history. This complication does not, however, in any way excuse scholars from including women in analyses of historical events and processes. In order to exhume this *intrahistoria,* it becomes necessary to consider different kinds of sources. In her work on women and social change in Latin America, Elizabeth Jelin speaks to the "urgent need to retrieve historical memory."[16] It is crucial, she contends, to "build-up a micro-history based on the retrieval of popular recollections and the recollections of the actors themselves and of their own movements."[17] Critical to this process is personal testimony. Jelin maintains that "because there are few written traces from the past concerning women . . . reconstruction of history through personal testimony is a priority."[18]

In the case of Celia Sánchez this approach becomes more of a necessity than a methodological choice because when she died in 1980, Celia left no diary, had few surviving siblings, had never married, and had no children. Thus, poetry, commemorative speeches, memoirs, periodical sources, photography, monuments, and oral testimony become the key primary sources for tracing the contours of Celia's enigmatic biography. These sources prove both intriguing and problematic, as they perhaps better reflect the vagaries of individual purposes or the broader philosophy of nationalistic projects than a commitment to establishing verifiable historical truth.[19] Of the multiple periodical sources cited in this study, almost all were written subsequent to Celia's death and are based heavily on interviews conducted by the various authors. Likewise, all of my own interviews were conducted after Celia had been deceased for almost twenty years. Therefore, it is difficult to assess how much of the information presented in these sources is based in historical fact and how much of it has undergone a process of individual and/or communal memory censorship. It seems that articles such as "Como eterna flor del lomero" ("Like the Eternal Flower of the Hills") in the January 1983 edition of *Trabajadores* (the Cuban communist workers' daily paper) and "La niña que fue Celia" ("The Child That Was Celia") in the 1985 edition of *Revista Pionero* (the newspaper for members of Cuba's Communist Youth) served a didactic purpose. Depending on the intended audience, these periodical sources concentrate on certain aspects of Celia's real or imagined biography as a means for encouraging Cubans to aspire to Celia's level of revolutionary conviction and commitment.

The multiple interviews I conducted with Cubans who had known Celia personally or who had fought with her in the Sierra Maestra must also be critically evaluated. In the same way that information contained within the periodical sources was more or less crafted depending on the nature of the publication as well as the intended audience, we must also consider that my informants might have constructed and crafted their narrative according to their own personal or political agendas.[20] Lourdes Sang, who currently holds a position as an organizer of women's work in the Federation of Cuban Women (FMC) — and who herself chooses to forgo an office and desk in favor of a more personal daily contact with the women workers of Havana — focused her testimony around Celia's similar reputation as a "woman of the people." In comparison, Nirma Cartón, now a prominent lawyer in Havana who is highly involved in several of the large bureaucracies of the Cuban government, presents Celia as a political official who used her positions within the postrevolutionary government to further her political goals of constructing the Office of Historical Affairs and several other government-sponsored facilities. Similarly, Nirma is exceedingly proud of her own military participation in the battles that took place during the early years of the revolution, and thus made repeated references to Celia's role in the Sierra Maestra. Finally, it is also possible that the tense economic situation between Cuba and the United States, which came to a fore with the Helms–Burton law of 1996,[21] only months before my arrival in Havana, influenced what my informants were willing to share with me. There may have been elements of the story that they withheld in order to avoid any subject that might be sensitive for one or both of us. On the other hand, they may have felt protective of certain aspects of their national history and decided not to share them with me, a citizen of Cuba's great political "enemy."

Finally, it bears mentioning that Celia herself may well have been one of the primary architects of the official silence surrounding the particularities of her lived experience. At the heart of socialist ideology is the belief that all people are equal, and Celia is said to have believed firmly in this notion. She was, in the words of Aira Morelo Fonseca, a woman who has worked at the Office of Historic Subjects for twenty-five years, a *"compañera* of ideals."[22] Celia's commitment to the teachings of José Martí — namely, his belief that "all the glory in the world fits inside one grain of corn" — is frequently offered as an explanation for her "allergic" reaction to cameras and the press and for the lack of any known personal diary or journal. Additionally, it is used to explain why Celia chose to be buried among her compatriots in a modest grave, marked only with the number "43," in the mausoleum dedicated to the Armed Revolutionary Forces (FAR) in the Colón Cemetery in Havana. In short, many believe that Celia's silence was self-imposed. Thus, perhaps, Celia's belief that her deeds were no more laudable than those of her compatriots provides an additional explanation for why so few details of her life are known.[23]

As we will see, what is said about Celia depends heavily on who is doing the remembering, and the conflation of the political and the personal in these sources has, without doubt, influenced the production of our knowledge about Celia. Yet, despite the possibility that the sources cited in this essay present a mythologized version of Celia's life, she is no less real to those Cubans who guard her memory.[24] Though the sources often temper reality with myth, and may consciously or unconsciously fashion Celia's memory in specific, and at times contradictory, ways, each one contributes a piece of the puzzle that is Cuba's own "biography" of Celia.

Remembering a Revolutionary: A Memory from Above

The funeral procession for Celia Sánchez Manduley, member of the Central Committee of the Communist Party of Cuba, diplomat to the National Assembly of Popular Power and Secretary of the Council of State, will depart today, Saturday, at 3:00 in the afternoon, from the base of the Monument to José Martí in the Plaza of the Revolution where her body is currently on view.[25]

One of life's great ironies is that death can mark both an ending and a beginning. On 11 January 1980, Celia Sánchez's life ended, only to then spark the beginning of a national project to resurrect her spirit in the name of rekindling Cuba's revolutionary fires. In many ways, the timing of her death could not have been better. Two decades of significant economic problems, caused in part by an increasing level of Soviet–Cuban dependency and a failure to diversify Cuban exports, had left their mark on the nation in the form of mounting social and political tensions. While the Cuban government did not yet know that this rising anxiety would eventually result in the mass exodus of thousands of Cubans to the United States during the Mariel boatlift,[26] rising levels of worker absenteeism and the declining participation of women in work were becoming cause for alarm.[27] It may come as no surprise, then, that in his 12 January eulogy to Celia, Armando Hart Dávalos, member of the Political Bureau of the Central Committee of the Communist Party of Cuba, stated:

Celia, with her valor, her constancy, her *laborious nature,* and her highly effective *work* next to Fidel entered definitively into History. In the Sierra, Celia was the heroine not only of the war, but also of *work*. In her, legend acquired real form and content.[28]

Thus, only one day after her death, officials were already constructing a nationalist memory of Celia as the quintessential symbol of work and dedication to the communist cause in Cuba. This was only the first of several symbolic purposes Celia would serve over the following months and years.

"The people know how this symbol was created, but in this moment we are participating in the duty of remembering."[29] These were the words pronounced by Armando Hart Dávalos as the body of Cuba's national heroine was being interred in the mausoleum dedicated to the Armed Revolutionary Forces in the

Colón Cemetery in Havana on 12 January. On that day, "hundreds of thousands" of Cubans came to pay their respects to "the woman who [had] been and [would] forever be an image of the Revolution."[30] In the week following Celia's death, two major Cuban periodicals, *Granma* (the official newspaper of the Central Committee of the Communist Party of Cuba) and *Bohemia*, dedicated full issues to mourning the loss of the nation's revolutionary heroine. These initial commemorative acts mark critical moments in the creation of Cuban national memory, as they established the tone for what would become the official memory of Celia. On 12 January, *Granma* published an assortment of editorials, photographs, and poetry reflecting on the life of Celia and documenting the overwhelming sadness that consumed all those who had known her directly or indirectly. Included also were official statements from the Federation of Cuban Women (FMC), as well as statements from officials in each of Cuba's fourteen provinces. While the former demarcated a gender-specific arena of mourning, the latter symbolized a unified sense of national loss.

On 18 January, *Bohemia* likewise published an entire issue in commemoration of Celia's death, entitled "Para siempre en el corazón del pueblo" ("Forever in the Hearts of the People"). The *Bohemia* issue, like the *Granma* issue a few days earlier, resembled a collage of memories. A multiplicity of sources were published, including dozens of photos, several editorials, a sampling of letters sent between Fidel and Celia during their years in the Sierra Maestra, and a complete transcript of Armando Hart Dávalos's eulogy at Celia's funeral. The selection of photos displayed in the issue is particularly striking, as it attempts to re-create a basic chronology of Celia's life. The chronology begins with her trip to the highest peak in Cuba, Turquino Peak, in 1953 (at the age of thirty-three), where she, her father Manuel Sánchez Silveira, and a close female friend paid homage to a large bust of José Martí, the hero of Cuban Independence.[31] The final picture depicts Celia's coffin being interred in the mausoleum dedicated to the FAR. Interestingly, of the thirty-five photographs of Celia included in the issue, nineteen (a little over half) show her standing directly at Fidel's side. That the first thirty-two years of Celia's life were visually omitted from this montage seems to imply that her life prior to the inception of the revolution is of little or no consequence. Conspicuously absent are any photographs documenting Celia's relatively affluent childhood; instead, Celia's life is presented as one of unwavering sacrifice and dedication to the cause of the Cuban revolution and to its leader.

While these two issues dedicated explicitly to the memory of Celia are important sites of memory in and of themselves, a more detailed examination of a few of their component parts reveals some fascinating patterns in language, symbolism, and imagery that merit our attention. The text of the Federation of Cuban Women's official statement on Celia's death, for example, asserted:

> Today our people lost a glorious figure who elevated the name of women during the revolutionary struggle, one who knew how to win the love and respect of the sons of our country with her simplicity, modesty, exemplary attitude and with her participation in every task necessary to the construction of a new society.[32]

Yet another contributor to the issue, Marta Rojas, echoed this emphasis on love and respect as a reward for absolute devotion to the revolutionary cause. In a lengthy tribute to Celia entitled "Hemos perdido un centinela a toda prueba" ("We Have Lost a Proven Sentry"), Rojas stated:

> [Celia's] audacity, valor and optimism; her discipline, modesty and total devotion to the leadership of Fidel; her tact, discretion and intelligence earned her the respect of the entire Revolutionary Army, of the troops of the Movement and of the rural people during the insurrection as with the triumph of the Revolution.[33]

While describing Celia as "profoundly kind," Rojas was quick to note that Celia, in defense of her cause, could become an "insurmountable concrete wall against which those disloyal to the Revolution and the enemies of Cuba dashed themselves to bits."[34] However, this ideological toughness did not seem to interfere with her fashion sense, as Celia was "made of one solid revolutionary piece, from her feet to the tips of her hair, which she so liked to adorn with flowers, ribbons or combs."[35] Finally, an anonymous editorial bearing the simple title "Celia," stated that while

> her name and image appeared only sporadically in public, she was never missed. The people knew that she was there, where she should be, like the invisible salt in the immense sea of the Revolution. And thus, day after day, she entered more and more in the heart of the Cuban people, conquering that peak which is so hard to scale which is the affection, the admiration and the respect of an entire people.[36]

Reflecting on Celia's personal virtues, the author states simply, "Rarely has such genuine glory marched hand in hand with similar modesty, human sensibility, and loyal and impartial devotion to the service of the revolutionary cause."[37]

While three different authors penned these examples from the *Granma* issue, the similarities of the sentiments expressed are noteworthy. A quick comparison of the adjectives utilized in the descriptions of Celia's personal attributes reveals that the words "respect," "modesty," and "devotion" appear in all three selections. Words like "discipline," "optimism," and "simplicity" are also prominent. Aside from the commonalties in language, all three selections stress images of Celia as a woman who rigorously defended the cause yet sought no personal accolades for the tasks she performed. In fact, it was her status as an invisible element of the revolution — "the invisible salt in the immense sea of the Revolution" — that earned her the love and respect of her compatriots. Over the next several years, this uniquely intimate connection to the Cuban people would become the principal touchstone of Celia's image. The statement by the FMC also hints at a kind of maternal role for Celia — stressing her ability to earn the respect of Cuba's "sons" with her modesty and simplicity — and this type of imagery would become even more pronounced over time. Perhaps even more frequent, however, would be an image of Celia as the ideal embodiment of ideological toughness and fierce determination, on the one hand, and femininity and superb aesthetic sensibilities, on the other.[38]

The language and symbolism employed seven days later, in the *Bohemia* issue dedicated to Celia, was in many ways strikingly similar. In their article entitled "Capitana del Pueblo" ("Captain of the People"), Pedro Pablo Rodríguez and Manuel González Bello posed an intriguing rhetorical question to those Cubans mourning the loss of their beloved compatriot:

For, what better example is there of living after death than Celia? If, as a poet said, life is a river that gives itself onto the sea, which is death; Celia, the one who forever gives an image of strength and permanence beyond the short space of human life, has gone to the sea. Into the sea of the Revolution, into the sea of the people, into the sea of the Cuban nation . . . has disembarked the life of Celia.[39]

As mentioned previously, the final pages of the issue are a complete transcription of Armando Hart Dávalos's eulogy to Celia, which was entitled "El ejemplo de Celia: Aliento y enseñanza para continuar el camino y marchar con decisión hacia adelante" ("Celia's Example: Courage and Instruction to Continue the Journey and March Forward with Determination"). At the height of his oratory fervor, Hart proclaimed to the Cuban nation that Celia was:

great in her heroic abnegation, her unconditional loyalty, great in her identification with the people, in her love for the revolutionary project, in her passionate interest in others. Great in her preoccupation for the concrete and decisive elements of every aspect of the Revolution. Great, perhaps, beyond every other virtue, in her modesty and simplicity. Among all her qualities we should certainly single out her rejection of all forms of ostentation and her fondness for simple manners and for the simplicities of life and work. This was, surely, one of her most moving virtues. Celia's character is reminiscent of the words of Martí: "The rivulet of the mountain ridge pleases me more than the sea."[40]

Throughout his eulogy, Hart highlights Celia's exceptional work ethic as a virtue to be emulated by all Cubans. It is this dedication to the advancement of the revolutionary project that provides the inspiration for the fiery conclusion of Hart's speech. Switching abruptly from a lengthy enumeration of Celia's virtues, Hart ends his speech by proclaiming that:

a dignified homage to Celia Sánchez is to ... fortify the work of our mass organizations, improve the workings of the State and all the administrations in labor centers, and elevate the efficiency of our administrative, labor and political organizations ... with the noble purpose of advancing the Cuban Revolution.[41]

This call to action was punctuated with shouts of "Victories against deficiencies! Victories against imperialism! Victories for socialism!"[42]

The many similarities in language and symbolism among the selections discussed above from the *Granma* and *Bohemia* commemorative issue merit our attention. Words such as "loyalty," "modesty," and "simplicity" appear in both. However, the *Bohemia* pieces take the commemorative act one step beyond mere praise to one of action. While the "Captain of the People" piece utilizes a much more symbolic language than Hart's eulogy, there is a common theme in both. Both authors highlight Celia's intimate connection with the Cuban people, but both also stress the responsibility that relationship now carries. With Celia's passing, the burden to continue her life's work now falls on the "sea of the people," for whose benefit her labors were always intended. To this effect, Dávalos quoted Julio Antonio Mella's phrase that "even after death we are useful!" explaining that "Celia should continue being useful, but this no longer depends on her. It will depend on every one of us being capable of understanding and applying the lesson of her life."[43] Thus, Hart's eulogy ends on a highly practical note, in which the needs of the state are projected onto the Cuban people through Celia. For a nation facing increasing economic and social difficulties and desperately in need of both uniting a fracturing society and spurring them toward collective labors, this oratory strategy proved both dramatic and functional. Coincidentally, it would reappear frequently over the next years.

On 16 January 1981, Fidel Castro recognized the first anniversary of Celia's death by dedicating a hospital in her name in her hometown of Manzanillo. The dedication service for the large facility, which contained 630 beds and 16 operating rooms,[44] drew a large crowd. In an exhaustive commemorative speech, Castro outlined the history of medical services in the area and praised the work of all the individuals whose labors had made the construction of the hospital possible. Aside from the obvious health benefits the hospital would offer to the inhabitants of the region, Castro claimed a symbolic purpose for the facility. Encouraged by eager applause from the audience, he proclaimed that the Hospital Celia Sánchez would serve as an

homage to our compatriot Celia Sánchez, on the first anniversary of her death . . . [APPLAUSE] . . . I truly believe that this is the best form of tribute to pay to someone who dedicated herself to duty, without resting for a moment, without forgetting one single detail; and I believe, sincerely, that this is the most heartfelt, profound, and revolutionary homage that one can give to a compatriot who gave her life for the Revolution [APPLAUSE].[45]

In June of that same year, the periodical *Mujeres* published a short article entitled "A Dignified Homage to Celia." The article — whose title bears a striking resemblance to the words employed by Hart in the conclusion of his eulogy to Celia the previous year — praises the work of the 2,900 female members of the "Celia Sánchez Manduley" volunteer labor brigade. The article's author, Gilberto Blanch, relied primarily on interviews and his personal observations in order to reflect on the women's work in the sugarcane fields of Ciego de Ávila. The multiple photos interspersed throughout the article's text depict smiling women proudly wearing the brigade's signature uniform — broad-brimmed palm frond hats and wristbands bearing the image of Celia — driving tractors, cutting sugarcane, and carrying potatoes in large wooden crates. While the women are clearly hard at work under the Cuban sun, the author of the article seemed particularly interested in the women's appearance. He wrote: "To see them in the fields is a feast for the eyes, because all are dressed elegantly in their uniforms."[46] In reference to this commentary, Mirta Benedico, head of propaganda, stated that the women had been instructed that "all the members had to shine prettily, with hats, with the image of Celia Sánchez on our wristbands . . . and with blouses of different colors."[47] The article concluded by proclaiming the honor of the brigade's contribution to the nation's productivity levels and the importance of their labors as a "dignified homage to our beloved Celia."[48]

In both the dedication of the hospital and in the establishment of the "Celia Sánchez Manduley" female volunteer labor brigade, Celia's memory was evoked as a means for encouraging social and economic development. The Celia Sánchez Manduley Hospital — a highly appropriate memorial to a woman remembered for her consistent dedication to the Cuban people — appears to have fulfilled both practical and symbolic functions. The medical care provided by the individual doctors and nurses working at the facility is a symbolic extension of the caretaking Celia performed in life. The female labor brigade is perhaps even more fascinating, as it embodied the qualities most associated with Celia — hard work and selflessness. Interesting also is the focus on the women's appearance, as it resonates with Rojas's description of Celia in the 1980 issue of *Granma* in which she made special reference to Celia's penchant for adorning her hair with flowers and ribbons. Just like Celia, the women of the labor brigade are both fiercely revolutionary and delightfully feminine.

Taken as a whole, these earliest attempts to construct an official or public memory of Celia were about much more than recalling the significant dates, honors, and accomplishments of one woman. The new challenges being faced by the Cuban state throughout the 1970s and 1980s required a new language, a new set of solutions, and a new mythology in order to mobilize the nation for change. In fact, in his book *Political Order in Changing Societies*, Samuel Huntington defines revolution itself as "a rapid, fundamental, and violent domestic change in the dominant values and *myths* of a society, in its political institutions, social structure, leadership, and government activity and policies."[49] As we have seen, the national mythology that emerged in the years following Celia's death was decidedly female-centered and female-directed. Aside from representing the ideal Cuban revolutionary, Celia represented a distinctly female ideal. This role-model status is not perhaps as problematic as the list of characteristics that qualified it: simplicity, modesty, femininity, selflessness, austerity, and devotion. The key point here, however, is that this fairly standardized list of personal virtues represented much more than mere symbolic references to a deceased individual. Rather, they provided a blueprint for Cuba's New Woman. For a country in desperate need of remobilizing its female labor sector, creating a vision of the ideal Cuban woman as someone who was capable of balancing physical labor with caretaking, strength with femininity, and leadership with modesty served a purpose above and beyond the mere commemoration of one woman.

Myth, Mother, Mujer: Celia in Popular Memory

> Celia, you have sung to me the song that I chose.
> You cradle me in your round breast
> Which is a nest of feathers.
> You are the one who exalts me.
> You are the one who knows me.
> — Nancy Morejón[50]

Just as official commemorative speeches and newspaper editorials flourished after Celia's death, so too did more personal reflections on Celia's role in the Cuban revolution. While Celia's intimate connection to the Cuban people may have provided the inspiration for government propaganda, there were those who reflected on their personal memories of Celia in other ways, and did so with, perhaps, other motivations. Among these more individualized expressions of memory, the poetry of the Afro-Cuban poet Nancy Morejón quickly rose to prominence. While Morejón's poetry was public, in the sense that it was widely circulated, it represented a uniquely personal expression of memory. Images of Celia as a tender mother figure, as a friend of the people, and as the embodiment of strength and devotion are prevalent in all of Morejón's poems, just as in the commemorative speeches and public editorials we have already seen. Morejón was clearly familiar with the general tenor of official discourse on Celia's role in Cuban society, and the imagery she employed often contained subtle — and at times not so subtle — references to larger social and political issues. However, the language, symbolism, and message of Morejón's poetry reveal a level of intimacy with the subject that sets it apart from official sites of memory.

Perhaps the most famous of Morejón's poems dedicated to the memory of Celia is "Elegia coral a Celia Sánchez" ("Choral Elegy to Celia Sánchez") that appeared in the January 1984 issue of *Revista Revolución y Cultura*. Utilizing vibrant language and a distinctly Cuban symbolism, Morejón espouses Celia's memory as a national treasure.

> Celia és ágil y fuerte
> y atraviesa una ruta
> de orquídeas, cada día.
> Celia es cubana y nuestra
> como los montes de la Sierra.
> Celia, buena y sencilla,
> entre los pescadores de Niquero
> y el esplendor de la bahía.
> Fusiles, hachas, flechas,
> piedras del río condujo
> hacia el pico más puro.
>
> Llega Fidel de la montaña
> y Ella deshierba helechos
> y lo pone a sus pies
> para avivar el corazón del pueblo.
> Como el viento sutil en Media Luna,
> Celia es así, callada, buena.
> Su boca amanecida
> siempre pronunciará
> la palabra que amamos
> la que necesitamos en la vida.
> Celia es así, como era Celia,
> sonrisa y tempestad,
> y con ella se marcha,
> entre mantos y orquídeas,
> hacia las puertas de la eternidad.[51]
>
> (Celia is agile and strong
> And she traverses a route
> Of orchids every day.
> Celia is Cuban and ours
> Like the mountains of the Sierra.
> Celia, good and simple
> Among the fisherman of Niquero

And the splendor of the bay.
Rifles, hatchets, arrows
River rocks she carried
Toward the purest peak.

Fidel arrives from the mountain
And She plucks ferns
And places them at his feet
To enliven the hearts of the people.
Like the soft wind in Media Luna,
Celia is like that, quiet, good.
Her dawning mouth
Will forever pronounce
The word that we love
The one we need in this life.
Celia is this, as Celia was,
Smile and tempest
And she departs
Between robes and
Towards the gates of eternity.)

Clearly, for Morejón, Celia is a woman of mythic proportions. She is "strong," "sincere," and, above all, devoted to the Cuban people and to Fidel. It is this devotion to others that earns Celia the semidivine status signaled by the capitalized pronoun "Ella." It is interesting to note, however, that it is only in the thirteenth line, where Celia defers to her male compatriot, Fidel, that she is granted her semidivine status. In all the other lines of the poem, "ella" begins with a lowercase "e." The Biblical imagery present in Morejón's poem similarly serves to elevate Celia to a divine status. Celia plucking ferns and placing them at Fidel's feet resonates with Christian images of Mary placing palm leaves before Jesus as he enters Jerusalem. The irony, then, of Celia's power is that she must be willing to surrender it in order for it to be worthy of praise.[52]

While Morejón's poetry was undoubtedly one of the most widely circulated forms of personal reflection on Celia's role within the Cuban revolution, at least one other significant memory text appeared in the years following Celia's death. In November 1985 Julio M. Llanes published a small book entitled *Celia nuestra y de las flores*.[53] Illustrated throughout with brightly colored collages of flowers and butterflies interspersed with photos of Celia and fanciful sketches of idyllic landscapes, the slim volume actually resembles a personal scrapbook more than a scholarly biographical study. The story presented in the book centers around a young Cuban boy from Manzanillo, the boy's grandfather, and an impromptu road trip to Havana. The adventure begins with just five words from the grandfather: "I have to see her."[54] The reader soon learns that the "her" referred to is Celia, and that the purpose of the trip is to lay flowers on Celia's coffin, where it is on display in Havana's Plaza of the Revolution.

The story of the journey is told through the grandson's own thoughts, and the focus of his reflections is primarily on his grandfather's character, habits, and talent for storytelling. In the earliest pages of the book, the grandson recalls:

There are two stories that Grandfather told, time and again, and that I have never forgotten. He told them a thousand times; however, whenever you heard them it seemed like the first time. I remember that he would light his cigar, sit back in his chair, and ask me:
   "Have I told you the stories of Norma [Celia's nom de guerre] and the 'Granma?' " . . .
   "No . . . I don't remember," I would answer him, so that he would tell them again.
   Then, Grandfather would blow the smoke from his cigar through his nostrils and begin very slowly, with the same hoarse voice . . .[55]

The long car ride to the capital becomes a pilgrimage for the bereaved grandfather and a history lesson for the grandson. As they travel through the Cuban countryside, the grandfather recounts all of his personal stories of Celia during the earliest years of the revolution. Using a mixture of both past and present tenses, he shares intimate memories of the first time he met Celia in the Sierra Maestra, of the multiple beautification projects she organized around the rebel base, and of the flowers she always wore in her hair.[56] In an especially emotional segment, the grandfather reflects on Celia's caretaking role:

If someone put on a pair of new boots that were sent from the plains, he/she thought of Celia. We knew that she was the one that had sent them. If a package arrived with uniforms or knapsacks . . . we would go crazy with happiness and think: " 'Celia sent this!' " . . . Such was the level of her help that we loved her like a sister, or like a mother. Because mothers are like that: always worried about the needs of others. And if someone doesn't have something, they leave no stone unturned looking for it, and they deliver it with a smile.[57]

In reference to Celia's character, the grandfather states that "she is quiet. She does a lot and says little. She doesn't like to make noise for anything. She does it all quietly, but she does it."[58] Unfortunately, the grandfather's reactions to seeing the body of his beloved compatriot are not included in the story, and the book ends with a final poignant conversation between the grandfather and his grandson as they begin the journey back to Manzanillo. As the taxi passes through Havana's city limits, the boy suddenly comprehends the finality of Celia's death and asks innocently:

"Grandfather, now we won't see Celia anymore?" I asked him.

He paused for a moment before answering me; then he said:

"Perhaps now we will see her more in photos and we will hear more anecdotes about her. Now, everyone who knows something about her will say it" — he stopped talking, as if thinking . . .

"You know something?" — he asked as he glanced at me out of the corner of his eye — "People die when they are forgotten; but when they are remembered with love, they are alive."[59]

In the final scene of the book, the young boy and his grandfather are clasped in a tearful embrace.

This poignant story of one man's personal memories of Celia is a fascinating example of the ways in which individual and collective, as well as official and unofficial, histories can intersect. In order to grasp the significance of this book as a memory text, we must first set aside the question of "truth." Whether or not the characters in the book represent real people who actually experienced the events described is irrelevant. What is important here is the book's emotive content — the "virtual reality" being created in order to tell a much larger story.[60] While the book presents the memories of one individual's (the grandfather's) personal relationship with Celia, the language and symbols used to relate those memories resonate with other sources we have seen. Descriptions of Celia as a self-abnegating mother figure who was both hardworking and feminine had been in circulation for over five years at the time of the book's publication. Thus, it is at least reasonable to assume that the book's content was produced through the commingling of the personal recollections of the author, Llanes, and the existing public discourses surrounding Celia's memory. If the originality of the book's content is somewhat questionable, its form is nonetheless unique. Presented as an intergenerational dialog, *Celia nuestra y de las flores* becomes the story of storytelling itself — of the dynamic social process in which memory is both transmitted and transformed. From the grandfather, to the grandson, to the reader of the book, these memories of Celia are passed from the imagination of the author to the imagination of the public, only to then be incorporated into new dialogues between different people at other moments in history. It is this cyclical movement of memory, from the public realm to the private realm and then back to the public realm, that permits Celia's memory — with all its attendant lessons, myths, and symbols — to be passed on to the next generation of Cubans.

Clearly, *Celia nuestra y de las flores* is a rich source of individual memory-made-public in and of itself; however, the final exchange between the grandfather and his grandson speaks to the existence of a final "site of memory" that should be addressed — oral testimony. It should be noted here that while oral and written sources come into being through rather different processes, both pass through a number of memory "filters" before their final articulation.[61] In the same way that the written sources we have seen were influenced by the existing discourse surrounding memories of Celia, so too are those memories transmitted through oral testimony. What is important about oral testimony, however, is that it offers an intimate glimpse into the ways in which the language and symbolism of official memory can be integrated into or challenged by individual "truths."

When asked about Celia's contributions to the Cuban state subsequent to the triumph of the revolution, it is neither her titles nor her involvement in large-scale government projects that are remembered. Rather, it is her dedication to answering the most fundamental questions facing the Cuban people that Cubans recall most vividly. Lourdes Sang, an organizer of women's work within the Federation of Cuban Women, recalled:

Celia never really worked within the FMC or in the other large governmental bureaucracies, and she was rarely seated behind a desk. She worked from wherever she was . . . that became her office. She was never seen with a chauffeur, instead she drove her own jeep. Celia was a *campesina*, and was never seen enjoying the smallest privilege. Instead, she concentrated on the Cuban people's most basic needs. In fact, when she heard that my father-in-law died, she even came to our house to be with us in our time of need. She didn't even know us. That's how she was.[62]

Thus, what Sang remembered about Celia is not based on her activities as a public official, but rather as a compatriot who was intimately aware of the hardships of her fellow countrymen. In the same vein, Sergio Rego Pita, an employee of the Provincial Direction of International Relations in Havana, claimed Celia was "a person with great sensitivity toward humanity in general: the elderly, children, and guerrillas."[63] Consequently, when the people had problems, they would write letters to Celia asking for help. Men, women, and children wrote letters soliciting everything from employment, housing, and healthcare to clothing, food, and personal items.[64] Nirma Cartón, a prominent Havana lawyer who fought alongside Celia in the Sierra Maestra, recalled both Celia's generosity and her graciousness:

Everyone came to [Celia's] office to talk to her . . . there was always a line. And when she would go to visit the homes of the peasants in the countryside to attend to their problems, she wouldn't scratch herself when fleas bit her for fear of insulting the people who lived there.[65]

Similarly, Nilda Porot, an employee at the José Martí National Library in Havana who lived across the street from Celia for several years, recalled that "Celia gave houses and cars to people, she even fixed people's roofs. If she couldn't help you, she sent someone who could. We had everything thanks to her ... clothes, everything."[66] Interestingly, Porot also made repeated references to Celia's status as a "believer" who placed fresh flowers at the foot of a small altar dedicated to the Virgen del Merced (the black Virgin of Mercy) that stood at the entrance to her apartment.[67]

It is interesting to note the numerous thematic similarities between these various oral testimonies. In each selection, Celia is presented as a sensitive, caring, and humble woman who placed primary importance upon addressing the daily needs of the Cuban people. Not only did Celia take the time to visit individual Cubans during their time of need, but she also lived a life of relative austerity herself — a further sign of her solidarity with the people. Equally as interesting to note, however, are the discrepancies between the testimonies. First, Sang's comment contains an ambiguous reference to Celia not having an office, whereas Cartón makes special mention of Celia's office as the center of her popular outreach programs. While there are several known photographs depicting Celia working from her office in the Plaza of the Revolution, what is important is that these two women used the existence or absence of Celia's office to make the same point about the nature of Celia's connection to the Cuban people.[68] Yet another intriguing component of Sang's testimony is her reference to Celia as a "*campesina*." In terms of class, Celia was not a *campesina*, as Sang indicates; rather, she was from an affluent family. Thus, there are at least two possibilities for what motivated Sang's comment. Sang may not have been familiar with the true economic situation of Celia's family, or she may have chosen to use the term *campesina* more as an indicator of Celia's solidarity with Cubans of more humble origins than as an indicator of her social class. Finally, Porot's reference to Celia's dedication to the Virgin of Mercy is fascinating in that it is the only such reference to Celia's own religious identity. While it is difficult to assess the accuracy of this statement, it is nonetheless interesting to question why this facet of Celia's personality does not appear in any of the official sites of memory we have seen. The revolutionary government's strict division between church and state, at the level of policy and discourse, may account for the fact that no other mention of Celia's religious beliefs has been encountered. It is important to note, however, that Porot wore the beaded necklace and bracelet of a devotee of santería (Afro-Cuban religion) to her interview. Thus, perhaps Porot's reference to Celia's religious identity was an attempt to draw a link between Celia and herself, as a means for demonstrating the depth of their personal/spiritual relationship, or as a means for Porot to validate her own religious identity. As we have seen, attaching personal meaning onto memory is not an infrequent practice.

While this essay has only presented a small sampling of the diverse forms that individual memory can take, there are a number of conclusions that can be drawn from the above examples. In Morejón's poetry, Llanes's *Celia nuestra y de las flores,* and the oral testimonies of individual Cubans, Celia is described as the epitome of nurturing, devotion, self-abnegation, and hard work. The enumeration of these personal qualities demonstrates the persistence of a relatively standardized language and symbolism to describe Celia, from the time of Hart's eulogy in 1980 to Porot's interview in 1998. However, the focus of the unofficial memories of Celia differs from that of official memory in at least one significant way. The focus of these unofficial memories is on the nature of Celia's relationship to a particular individual and not to a more abstracted "Cuban people." In each of the sources above, the mythology surrounding Celia is grounded in the world of personal experience. At times these real or imagined experiences converge with official memory, and at others times they diverge from it, thus opening up new spaces for memory to exist. The often ambiguous, but always highly interactive, relationship between official memories of Celia and the memories that are transmitted by individuals highlights an important characteristic of national memory. Each story, each experience, and each conversation (whether it exists in written or oral form) that makes reference to memories of Celia is just one thread in the much larger memory quilt of the Cuban people. Over the years, these threads of memory have been woven together by various individuals to serve a range of purposes, from rallying the nation to collective action in the face of an economic crisis to simply recalling the lived experience of the early years of the revolution. However, these memories of Celia, in all their multiple forms, prove that "memory is not a passive depository of fact, but an active process of creation of meanings."[69] The meanings ascribed to Celia's memory have had ramifications far beyond the memorializing of one woman; they have played a crucial role in the creation of Cuban national identity itself.

Conclusion

In the final pages of his article entitled "Collective Memory and Cultural History: Problems of Method," Alon Confino states that "memory as a whole ... is bigger than the sum of its parts."[70] As we have seen in the case of Cuba, an often fragmented set of memories concerning a multiplicity of social, political, and cultural experiences have, over the course of more than twenty years, converged (albeit in contradictory or ambiguous ways at times) in order to create a national blueprint for Cuba's New Woman. This New Woman, embodied most closely in Celia Sánchez Manduley, is the result not simply of an official memory that has supplanted memories that exist at the level of the individual, but rather of a continuous process of commingling and cross-pollination. It is important to note that because "memory is not static but alive," this process is perpetual.[71] Today, official commemorative sites such as Celia's tomb have become creative spaces where visitors exchange memories about Celia, recount stories of their own participation in the revolution, and ascribe their own meanings onto their national heroine. Through the interjection of new voices and experiences, the mythology surrounding Celia is continuously being redefined and reinvented. As Nora states, "Sites of memory only exist because of their capacity for metamorphosis, an endless recycling of their meaning and an unpredictable proliferation of their ramifications."[72]

It would seem that if revolution is a "process," then the process of constructing collective memory is as much a part of revolution as are the battles won and lost.[73] The grand unifying historical events of the Cuban people, their revolution, and the ideal female revolutionary, Celia Sánchez Manduley, become common reference points against which all citizens (but perhaps women especially) are encouraged to measure their revolutionary conviction. Through the expression of various types of collective and individual memories, Celia's life has assumed mythic proportions that far exceed the possibilities of any one woman. In the words of Armando Hart Dávalos, "In the history of every true revolution, legend acquires very real characters."[74] Whether or not popular imaginings of Celia and her life represent the reality of whom she was matters much less than their ability to reflect the ideals of a larger revolutionary discourse—one which Cubans aspire to, reformulate, or reject accordingly. Consequently, the fact that Celia is remembered as both a private and a public figure, as tough but tender, as hardworking but feminine, and as dedicated but humble perhaps tells us less about Celia than it does about the revolutionary values of officials and activists determined to (re)define the parameters of an ideal *cubanidad* in the face of new national challenges.

NOTES

This essay began as my Master's thesis entitled "Myth, Mother, Mujer: Celia Sánchez Manduley, A Cuban Revolutionary" (University of New Mexico, 1999). I am grateful to Judy Bieber, Linda Hall, Elizabeth Hutchison, and Jane Slaughter, and to my colleagues at the University of New Mexico who all offered helpful advice on earlier drafts of this work.

1. Benedict Anderson, *Imagined Communities: Reflections on the Origin and Spread of Nationalism* (London: Verso, 1991), 205.

2. While the date of her death is certain, it is interesting to note that, as is the case with so many details of Celia's life, there is some confusion surrounding the exact year of her birth. While some sources claim that she was born in 1916, others claim 1920. However, 1920 is the date most frequently encountered. The cause of Celia's death was lung cancer.

3. Here, I am referring to the original definition of the term, as coined by Pierre Nora. While his definition of *lieux de mémoire* ("where memory crystallizes and secretes itself") may leave room for interpretation, his three-part definition of their purpose (material, symbolic, and functional) is not only insightful but useful as well (see Pierre Nora, "Between Memory and History: Les Lieux de Mémoire," *Representations* 26 [Spring 1989]: 7–24).

4. Here, I am using the term memory as defined by Confino: "the ways in which people construct a sense of the past" (see Alon Confino, "Collective Memory and Cultural History: Problems of Method," *American Historical Review* 102 [December 1997]: 1386). On a related note, it is important to keep in mind, as Noakes points out, that "this sense of the past is created in

two ways: through public representations and through private memory" (see Lucy Noakes, *War and the British* [London: I. B Tauris, 1998], 12).

5. Miriam Cooke and Angela Woollacott, eds., *Gendering War Talk* (Princeton, N.J.: Princeton University Press, 1993). Noakes defines masculinity and femininity "as related cultural and social constructs. They are not living, breathing men and women but sets of ideas about how living, breathing men and women are expected to act" (*War and the British*, 16).

6. Lucy Noakes has provided us with a succinct definition of "public" and "private" memories, and their interrelationship. She states that "private memories refer to memories that focus, at least in part, on the individual experience and memories of the war years; public memories refer to more general images of the war that appear in public sites of memory." Noakes is also quick to point out the interdependent nature of these two forms of memory. "In the practice of people's everyday lives, of course, public and private memory can be difficult to separate. Public and private memories are essentially interactive: private memories can be validated when they are shared by large numbers of people, thus gaining access to the public field of representation, while dominant public or popular memory has to have a purchase with most people's personal memories of the war years in order to become widely accepted" (*War and the British*, 12–13).

7. Although Celia's contemporaries never expressly referred to her as the "New Woman," I utilize this terminology to refer to an explicitly gendered formulation of the ideal Cuban revolutionary that emerged following Celia's death. The original concept of Cuba's "New Man" was the focus of many of Ernesto "Che" Guevara's writings; namely, his classic essay "Man and Socialism" (1961). The full text of Guevara's essay can be found in Arthur Lothstein, ed., *"All We Are Saying . . .": The Philosophy of the New Left* (New York: Capricorn Books, 1971), 365–81.

8. The only published information on the Sánchez family's economic status that I have encountered thus far was located in a small pamphlet entitled "Celia: Los años de Media Luna," which was published by the Sección de Investigaciones Históricas Comité Provincial in May 1990. The pamphlet claims that the Sánchez family owned three farms ranging in size from 60 caballerías (1,998 acres) to 12 caballerías (399 acres). Unfortunately, the pamphlet does not document its sources for this information. Considering that Celia was a prominent member of a socialist revolution, it seems logical that information concerning her family's elevated economic status has been omitted from Cuban popular memory.

9. The Mariana Grajales Brigade, named after the heroic mother of Cuban independence, was officially inaugurated in September 1958, with Isabela Rielo as the commanding officer. Though consisting of only fourteen women, the Marianas participated in a number of military encounters with Batista's army (Lois M. Smith and Alfred Padula, *Sex and Revolution: Women in Socialist Cuba* [New York: Oxford University Press, 1996], 30–31).

10. The language associating Celia with a form of national motherhood seems to have first been coined by Raúl Castro in the early years of the revolutionary struggle. In an oft-cited letter of April 1957, Castro wrote: "You have become our weeping cloth [and thus] we are going to have to name you the 'Official Godmother of the Detachment'" (see *Celia: Heroína de la Revolución Cubana* [Havana: Editora Política, 1985]; the original Spanish reads "Tú has convertido en nuestro paño de lágrimas . . . te vamos a tener que nombrar 'Madrina Oficial del Destacamento'").

11. Jon Lee Anderson, *Che Guevara: A Revolutionary Life* (New York: Grove Press, 1997), 235, 344.

12. José Llovio-Ménendez, *Insider: My Hidden Life as a Revolutionary in Cuba* (New York: Bantam Books, 1988), 99.

13. Several scholars have attempted to explain the prevalence of the assumption that powerful female figures achieve power through their sexual relationship with a male leader. See, e.g., Jean B. Elshtain, *Public Man/Private Woman: Women in Social Political Thought* (Princeton, N.J.: Princeton University Press, 1981); and Marian Sawyer and Marian Simms, *A Woman's Place: Women and Politics in Australia* (Sydney: George Allen and Unwin, 1984).

14. A cursory search within the Library of Congress's online catalog revealed that there are currently forty-one published official and/or unofficial biographies of Fidel Castro and sixty-five biographies of Ernesto "Che" Guevara.

15. Julián Marías, "La intrahistoria, dominio de mujer," in *La mujer y su sombra* (Madrid: Editorial Alianza, 1986), 63–71.

16. Elizabeth Jelin, *Women and Social Change in Latin America* (London: Zed Books, 1990).

17. Ibid., 8.

18. Ibid.

19. In her work on female resistance during the Spanish Civil War, Shirley Mangini likewise notes that "recounting memories is a slippery task. Questions of truth versus fiction are based on the fickle nature of memory, the passage of time, the need for self-justification, self-compassion, and self-aggrandizement, and so on" (Shirley Mangini, *Memories of Resistance: Women's Voices from the Spanish Civil War* [New Haven, Conn.: Yale University Press, 1995], 53).

20. I believe this type of discussion of the potential effect my own presence had on the production of my knowledge of Celia is important. As Susan Crane states, "Historical research is a lived experience that the self-reflexive historian consciously integrates into collective memory. Historical representation is inadequate to this lived experience only so long as the author remains absent and the textual or site-artifact serves only the function of commemoration" ("Writing the Individual Back into Collective Memory," *American Historical Review* 102 [December 1997]: 1382).

21. On 9 February 1995, Senator Jesse Helms introduced the "Cuban Liberty and Democratic Solidarity (LIBERTAD) Act," which would tighten the U.S. embargo against Cuba. The full text of the law is available in "Legislation and Regulations—United States: Cuban Liberty and Democratic Solidarity (LIBERTAD) Act of 1996 (Helms–Burton Act)," *International Legal Materials* 35, no. 2 (1996): 359–79. For an analysis of the events leading up to the legislation, see Joaquín Ferrao, *Helms–Burton Law: Historical Background and Analysis* (Miami: Endowment for Cuban American Studies of the Cuban American National Foundation, 1998).

22. Aira Morelo Fonseca, interview by author, tape recording, 8 July 1996, Oficina de Asuntos Históricos, Havana, Cuba.

23. In her work on memory in Italy, Luisa Passerini notes that "all those who have collected oral testimonies have noted that one of the constant features of the left-wing activists' life-histories is the 'canceling out of individual private life'" (*Fascism in Popular Memory: The Cultural Experience of the Turin Working Class* [Cambridge: Cambridge University Press, 1987], 41).

24. Elizabeth Van Houts has similarly stated that "if . . . we are interested . . . in the process of remembering and the formation of memories, the criterion of historical reliability is of little or no importance in judging the significance of the memory" (*Memory and Gender in Medieval Europe, 900–1200* [Toronto: University of Toronto Press, 1999], 7.)

25. "Sería transmitida hoy por radio y televisión la despedida de duelo de Celia Sánchez," *Granma* 16, no. 10 (12 January 1980): 8. The original Spanish reads: "El sepelio de Celia Sánchez Manduley, miembro del Comité Central del Partido Comunista de Cuba, diputada a la Asamblea Nacional del Poder Popular y secretaria del Consejo de Estado, partirá hoy sábado a las tres de la tarde, desde la base del Monumento a José Martí, en la Plaza de la Revolución, donde se encuentra su cadáver."

26. For more information on the events surrounding the Mariel boatlift, see Felix Roberto Masud-Piloto, *With Open Arms: Cuban Migration to the United States* (Totowa, N.J.: Rowman and Littlefield, 1988).

27. For a more thorough discussion of the economic problems facing Cuba in the 1960s and 1970s, see Patricia Ruffin, *Capitalism and Socialism in Cuba: A Study of Dependency, Development and Underdevelopment* (London: MacMillan Press, 1990); Carmelo Mesa-Lago, *The Economy of Socialist Cuba: A Two-Decade Appraisal* (Albuquerque: University of New Mexico Press,

1981); and Carmelo Mesa-Lago, *Cuba in the 1970s: Pragmatism and Institutionalization* (Albuquerque: University of New Mexico Press, 1978).

28. Armando Hart Dávalos, *La más autóctona flor de la Revolución* (Havana: De la Cultura, Ediciones, 1990), 13. The original Spanish reads: "Celia, con su valor, su constancia, su abnegación, su *laboriosidad* y su *trabajo* altamente eficaz junto a Fidel entró definitivamente en la Historia. Celia, en la Sierra, no fue sólo la heroína de la guerra. Fue eso y, además, la heroina del *trabajo*. En ella la leyenda adquirió formas y contenido reales" (emphasis mine).

29. Armando Hart Dávalos, "El ejemplo de Celia: Aliento y enseñanza," *Bohemia* 72, no. 3 (18 January 1980): 59. The original Spanish reads: "El pueblo conoce la historia de cómo se forjó ese símbolo; pero en este momento estamos en el deber de rememoria." Interestingly, Nora makes reference to a similar notion of the "impossible debt" of memory each individual feels they must pay to the nation (see Nora, "Between Memory and History," 16).

30. Pedro Pablo Rodríguez and Manuel González Bello, "Capitana del Pueblo," *Bohemia* 72, no. 3 (19 January 1980): 53. The original passage reads: "Es imposible calcular cuántos desfilaron por la base del monumento a Martí o se congregaron en la Plaza de la Revolución y a lo largo de la ruta del cortejo fúnebre. Pero, sin lugar a dudas, fueron cientos de miles. . . . Porque aquel serpenteante río humano que llenó la Plaza desde la tarde del viernes 11 quería dar su último adiós a esa mujer que ha sido y será siempre imagen de la Revolución."

31. The caption from the *Bohemia* photo layout reads: "Cuando al frente de ellos Fidel Castro iniciara la guerra el 26 de julio de 1953, invocando el ideario martiano, la efigie de José Martí, desde la Sierra Maestra, oficiaría el ámbito revolucionario desde las más altas cumbres cubanos. Meses antes, ese mismo año, junto a su padre, el doctor Manuel Sánchez Silveira, Celia Sánchez Manduley había fijado el busto de Martí en la cúspide del Pico Turquino."

32. "Mensaje de la Dirección Nacional de la Federación de Mujeres Cubanas," *Granma* 16, no. 10 (12 January 1980): 2. The original Spanish reads: "Nuestro pueblo pierde hoy una figura gloriosa que puso muy en alto el nombre de la mujer durante la lucha revolucionaria, que supo ganarse el respeto y el cariño de todos los hijos de nuestra Patria por su heroísmo, por su valor a toda prueba, por su sencillez y modestia, por su actitud ejemplar, por su entrega plena a cada tarea necesaria en la construcción de la nueva sociedad."

33. Marta Rojas, "Hemos perdido un centinela a toda prueba," *Granma* (12 January 1980): 5. The original Spanish reads: "su audacia, valor y optimismo; la disciplina, modestia y entrega total a la jefatura de Fidel; su tacto, discreción e inteligencia le hicieron acreedora del respeto de todo el Ejército Rebelde, de los cuadros del Movimiento y de los campesinos durante la insurrección al igual que en la Revolución triunfante . . ."

34. Ibid. The original Spanish reads: "profundamente humana" . . . " infranqueable muralla de concreto contra la que se estrellaban los desleales a la Revolución y los enemigos de Cuba."

35. Ibid. The original Spanish reads: "hecho de una sola y sólida pieza revolucionaria, desde los pies a la punta de los cabellos, que tanto gustaba adornarse con flores, lazos o peinetas."

36. "Celia," *Granma* (12 January 1980): 6. The original Spanish reads: "Su nombre y su figura sólo esporádicamente aparecían en público, pero no hacía falta. El pueblo sabía que estaba allí, donde debía estar, como la sal invisible en el inmenso mar de la Revolución. Y así, día tras día, se adentró más y más en el corazón de los cubanos, conquistando ese lugar tan difícil de escalar que es el cariño, la admiración y el respeto de un pueblo entero."

37. Ibid. The original Spanish reads: "pocas veces una gloria tan genuina ha marchado acompañando de semejante modestia, sensibilidad humana y entrega leal y desinteresada al servicio de la causa revolucionaria."

38. The gendered nature of the language used to describe Celia best comes into focus when compared with the language used to describe one of Cuba's most famous male revolutionaries, Ernesto "Che" Guevara. On 19 October 1967, ten days following Che's untimely death in Bolivia, the Cuban periodical *Granma* dedicated a full issue to espousing Che's status as a theoretical

visionary and fallen hero. Among his personal characteristics were listed his status as an "insuperable soldier; an insuperable commander . . . an extraordinarily capable man, extraordinarily aggressive." Contrasted with the construction of Celia's image as a woman of modesty and simplicity, Che is described as representing the perfect union of "the man of ideas and the man of action" (*Granma* [19 January 1967]: 2–4).

    39. Pedro Pablo Rodríguez and Manuel González Bello, "Capitana del Pueblo," *Bohemia* 72, no. 3 (19 January 1980): 53. The original Spanish reads: "Porque, qué mejor ejemplo de vivir en el morir que el de Celia. Porque si un poeta dijo que la vida son los ríos, que van a dar a la mar, qué es el morir; Celia ha ido a la mar, esa que da siempre imagen de fuerza y de permanencia más allá del corto espacio de la vida humana. En la mar de la Revolución, en la mar del pueblo, en la mar de la nación cubana . . . ha desembocado la vida de Celia."

    40. Hart, "El ejemplo de Celia," 61. The original Spanish reads: "Grande en su abnegación heroica, en su lealtad incondicional, grande en su identificación con el pueblo, en su amor a la obra de la Revolución, en su interés aspasionado por los demás. Grande en su preocupación por los aspectos más concretos y decisivos de cada obra de la Revolución. Grande, quizás, sobre cualquier otra virtud, en su modestia y sencillez. Entre todas sus cualidades debemos efectivamente destacar su rechazo a cualquier forma de ostentación y su apego a las maneras simples y sencillas de vivir y trabajar. Esta era, seguramente, una de sus más conmovedoras virtudes. El carácter de Celia recuerda aquellos versos de Martí: 'El arroyo de la sierra me complace más que el mar.' "

    41. Ibid., 62. The original Spanish reads: "Un homenaje digno de Celia Sánchez está en fortalecer el trabajo de nuestras organizaciones de masas . . . mejorando el trabajo de nuestro Estado y de todas las administraciones en los centros laborales, y elevando la eficiencia de nuestros organismos administrativos, sindicales y políticos . . . con el noble propósito de hacer avanzar la Revolución Cubana."

    42. Ibid. The original Spanish reads: "¡Victorias contra las deficiencias! ¡Victorias contra el imperialismo! ¡Victorias por el socialismo!"

    43. Hart, "El ejemplo de Celia," 61. The original Spanish reads: " '¡Hasta después de muertos somos útiles!' dijo Julio Antonio Mella. Celia debe seguir siendo útil, pero esto ya no dependerá de ella. Dependerá de que cada uno de nosotros seamos capaces de comprender y aplicar la lección de su vida."

    44. Dr. Arnaldo Gómez Satti provided me with this information when I visited the Hospital Celia Sánchez on 27 July 1996.

    45. Fidel Castro, "Fidel en la inauguración del Hospital Celia Sánchez Manduley," *Bohemia* (16 January 1981): 52. The original Spanish reads: "homenaje a nuestra compañera Celia Sánchez con motivo del primer aniversario de su muerte . . . [APLAUSOS] . . . yo creo que realmente ésa era la mejor forma de rendir tributo a quien de manera tal se consagraba al deber, sin descansar un minuto, sin olvidar un solo detalle; y creo, sinceramente, que éso es uno de los homenajes más sentido más profundo, y más revolucionario que se le pueda rendir a una compañera que haya dado la vida por la Revolución [APLAUSOS]."

    46. Gilberto Blanch, "Digno homenaje a Celia," *Mujeres* (June 1981): 8. The original Spanish reads: "Verlas en los campos es una fiesta para los ojos, porque todas visten elegantes uniformes."

    47. Ibid. The original Spanish reads: "todas las integrantes tenían que lucir bonitas, con sombreros, con la efigie de Celia Sánchez en el brazlete . . . y con blusas de distintas colores."

    48. Ibid. The original Spanish reads: "un digno homenaje a nuestra querida Celia."

    49. Samuel Huntington, *Political Order in Changing Societies* (New Haven, Conn.: Yale University Press, 1968), 264 (emphasis is mine).

    50. Nancy Morejón, "Coral del pueblo," *Revolución y Cultura* (January 1984): 59. The original Spanish reads: "Celia, tú me has dicho al oído la canción que elegí / Tú me acunas en tu pecho redondo / que es un nido de plumas / Tú eres quien me enaltece / Tú eres quien me conoce."

51. Nancy Morejón, "Elegia coral a Celia Sánchez," *Revolución y Cultura* (January 1984): 59.
52. The various continuities between Christian and revolutionary imagery have been the focus of several recent studies. Perhaps most relevant to this discussion of the semireligious imagery surrounding Celia Sánchez is J. M. Taylor's work on Eva Perón. Taylor likewise found for the case of Eva Perón that themes of sacrifice, maternal love, purity, and devotion were prominent, both during and after her death, primarily as they related to her image as the Lady of Hope (see J. M. Taylor, *Evita Perón: The Myths of a Woman* [Chicago: University of Chicago Press, 1979], 104–10). For an interesting, albeit fairly controversial, examination of the links between Christian (specifically Catholic) imagery and male public figures, see Glen Caudill Dealy, *The Public Man: An Interpretation of Latin American and Other Catholic Countries* (Amherst: University of Massachusetts Press, 1997).
53. Julio M. Llanes, *Celia nuestra y de las flores* (Havana: Editorial Gente Nueva, 1985).
54. Ibid., 10. The original Spanish reads: "Tengo que verla." It is interesting to note that the book was written with the collaboration of Celia's sister, Acacia Sánchez Manduley, and with Nydia Sarabia of the Oficina de Asuntos Históricos, who, coincidentally, I interviewed eleven years later.
55. Ibid., 25. The original Spanish reads: "Hay dos cuentos que el abuelo hacía, una y otra vez, y que nunca se me han olvidado. Los hacía mil veces; y, sin embargo, siempre que uno los escuchaba, parecían nuevecitos. Recuerdo que encendía su tabaco, se echaba hacia atrás e el sillón, y me preguntaba: '¿Yo te he hecho los cuentos de Norma y el 'Granma?' . . . 'No . . . no me acuerdo' — le contestaba, para que él los volviera a contar. Entonces, el abuelo botaba el humo del tobaco por los huequitos de la nariz, y comenzaba muy despacio, con su voz ronca de siempre . . ."
56. Ibid., 19, 22, 50.
57. Ibid., 47. The original Spanish reads: "Si uno se ponía un par de botas nuevas que enviaban el llano, pensaba en Celia. Sabíamos que era ella quien las mandaba. Si llegaba un paquete con uniformes o mochilas . . . uno se ponía loco de contento y pensaba: "'¡Esto lo mandó Celia!'" . . . era tanto su ayuda, que la queríamos como una hermana, o como una madre. Porque así son las madres: siempre preocupándose por si a uno le falta algo. Y si uno no lo tiene, se lo buscan hasta debajo de la tierra, y lo traen con una sonrisa."
58. Ibid., 73. The original Spanish reads: "Ella es callada. Hace mucho y dice poco. No le gusta hacer ruido para nada. Todo lo hace calladita, pero lo hace."
59. Ibid., 79. The original Spanish reads: "¿Abuelo, ya no veremos más a Celia?— le pregunto. Él se demora un ratico en contestarme; luego me dice: "'Quizás ahora la veamos más en fotos y eschuchemos más anécdotas de ella. Ahora todo el que sepa algo sobre ella lo va a decir' — deja de hablar, como pensando—: "'¿Sabes una cosa?'" — pregunta al mismo tiempo que me mira derechito a los ojos. "'La gente se muere cuando la olvidan; mientras que lo recuerden a uno con cariño, uno está vivo.'"
60. See Susanna Egan, *Patterns of Experience in Autobiography* (Chapel Hill: University of North Carolina Press, 1984); and Shirley Mangini, *Memories of Resistance: Women's Voices from the Spanish Civil War* (New Haven, Conn.: Yale University Press, 1995), 57.
61. Elda Guerra has described the difference between written and oral sources, stating that "written memories are influenced by the weight of past literary models, the conviction of the author, the intended reader and the ambiance in which the text eventually survives. Oral recollections raise these issues and more, being especially coloured by the relationship between the interviewee and the interviewer, and thus by the communicative past which they establish" (see Elda Guerra, "Memory and Representations of Fascism," in *Italian Fascism: History, Memory, and Representation*, ed. R. J. B. Bosworth and Patrizia Dogliani [London: Macmillan, 1999]), 197). The notion of memory "filters" is discussed by Patrick Geary in *Phantoms of Remembrance: Memory and Oblivion at the End of the First Millennium* (Princeton, N.J.: Princeton University Press, 1994), 7, 177.

62. Lourdes Sang, interview by author, tape recording, 8 July 1996, Havana, Cuba. Celia's jeep is on display at the Automobile Museum in Havana. The original quote reads: "Celia nunca realmente trabajaba con la FMC, ni con las grandes burocracias, y ella raramente se sentaba por detrás de un escritorio. Ella trabajaba de cualquier lugar . . . eso transformó en su oficina. Nunca se veía con chofér, ella manejaba su propio yipi. Celia era una campesina, y ella nunca disfrutaba de lo más mínimo privilegio. En vez de eso, ella se concentraba en las cuestiones más fundamentales de la gente. En verdad, cuando ella se dió cuenta de que mi suegro se murió, ella pasó por nuestra casa para estar con nosotros durante nuestras horas de necesidad. Ella no nos sabía para nada. Ella era así."

63. Sergio Rego Pita, interview by author, tape recording, 10 July 1996, Dirección Provincial de Relaciones Internacionales, Havana, Cuba.

64. Smith and Padula have likewise commented on Celia's attentiveness to the daily needs of the Cuban people, stating that Celia "served as a national benefactress, a socialist Eva Perón, who through the years responded to personal appeals for assistance and investigated complaints of injustice from thousands of Cubans" (see *Sex and Revolution,* 32).

65. Nirma Cartón, interview by author, tape recording, 6 July 1996, Havana, Cuba. The original quote reads: "El mundo entero pasó por su oficina para hablar con ella . . . siempre había una cola. Y cuando ella visitaba las casas de los pobres en el campo para atender a sus problemas, ella nunca se rascaba por miedo de ofender a las personas que vivían allí."

66. Nilda Porot, interview by author, tape recording, 26 June 1998, Biblioteca Nacional José Martí, Havana, Cuba. The original quote reads: "Celia siempre daba casas y máquinas a personas, y hasta arreglar techos. Si ella no le podía ayudar, ella mandaba alguien que podría. Teníamos todo gracias a ella . . . ropa, todo."

67. Ibid. The original quote reads: "Celia era creyente. Ella siempre ponía flores por frente de una virgencita al entrar en su casa."

68. It is important to note here that the subtle tensions expressed within these personal testimonies — namely in terms of Celia's simultaneous role as a public official and as a mother figure — are perhaps indicative of broader ambiguities within Cuba's revolutionary project. As Sandra McGee Deutsch has pointed out, various Latin American revolutionary projects (specifically those that occurred in Cuba, Argentina, Mexico, and Chile) struggled over the definition of revolutionary womanhood and encountered difficulties when attempting to rectify the new image of the revolutionary woman with more traditional conceptualizations of gender roles (see Sandra McGee Deutsch, "Gender and Sociopolitical Change in Twentieth-Century Latin America," *Hispanic American Historical Review* 71 [May 1991]: 259–306).

69. Alessandro Portelli, *The Death of Luigi Trastulli and Other Stories: Form and Meaning in Oral History* (New York: State University of New York Press, 1991), 52.

70. Confino, "Collective Memory and Cultural History," 1399.

71. Van Houts, *Memory and Gender in Medieval Europe,* 7.

72. Nora, "Between Memory and History," 19.

73. For a discussion of revolution as "process" (rather than endpoint), see Gilbert M. Joseph and Daniel Nugent, eds., *Everyday Forms of State Formation: Revolution and Negotiation of Rule in Modern Mexico* (Durham, N.C.: Duke University Press, 1994), xii.

74. Hart, "El ejemplo de Celia," 59.

K. LYNN STONER

Conclusion: Enshrined on a Pedestal

Throughout the twentieth century, historians have struggled with two countervailing forces: the magnetic and observable force of nation building and the centrifugal and immeasurable force of micro- and macrocultures extant both within and beyond the boundaries of modern nations. Inherited from the nineteenth century, traditional histories of modernity included works on battles for independence and national survival, nationalist philosophy, governmental actions, economic change and expansion, political groupings and persuasions, scientific inventions, famous personalities, international diplomacy, military technology and strategies, and social organizations. At the turn of the twentieth century, historians turned their attention to the underclasses, the marginalized, and the dispossessed, often employing political/economic explanations of class differentiation and Marxist analysis as their methods of study.[1] Post–World War II historians have recognized that scientific knowledge, modernization, and the objective do not tell the entire story of the human condition. The influence of human sciences such as psychology and anthropology, as well as human rights movements, have encouraged humanists to examine the subjective qualities of human life as well as the objective events that have guided human action. As a result, historians today delve into subjects previously dismissed as unremarkable or useless in explaining national and global events.

In the western world it took the social revolutions of the 1960s and 1970s to open the way for the new social history. Suddenly, the study of minorities and civil rights, women, sexuality, fashion, environmental and urban history, labor history, ethnographies told by laborers or slaves, cultural phenomena such as rock and roll and cultural mentality found legitimacy. Feminist historians claimed that the personal was political, and they set out to prove it by demonstrating how intimate, nonpublic issues could become the driving force behind public acts. Academic disciplines and research methods blended. Historians studied music, for instance, as a way of understanding the discourse of illiterate slaves. Postmodern historians have recognized that nations, regions, and people are complex admixtures of enclaves, local events, and cultural tendencies. The study of the inner workings of societies, then, has become so prevalent that writing grand design history now seems imprecise, simplistic, and perhaps a little suspect.

If nineteenth-century scholars in the western hemisphere and Europe wrote about nation building, and twentieth-century thinkers deconstructed our sense of national unity, then we must now come to terms with the fact that the Cuban experience has been consistently out of step with events and the historical record in the West. Take the example of slavery. As the western world was ending the horrendous practice, Cuba began it in earnest. When the Americas were declaring their independence from European colonizers, Cuba remained faithful to Spain. When Cuba did become independent from Spain, it was forced to sacrifice its sovereignty to the United States, and when sovereignty seemed attainable after the 1959 revolution, dependency upon the Soviet Union was the arrangement that curbed U.S. retaliation. When the nation was threatened from within by corruption or dictatorship, a unified, popular response was less likely than mass emigration. In a very real sense, Cuban national identity never settled down long enough, nor were Cubans left sufficiently alone to determine a grand design, a prevailing sense of self, that would later be broken down into its parts. In short, we can ask whether Cuba has ever had its modern or postmodern age, with its concomitant historical writing. It seems more likely that Cuba has been in a perpetual state of becoming, and that has determined the behavior of citizens, women among them, and the historical record.

Cuban women's history must be understood as part of Cuba's unique path. No one can doubt the consistently extraordinary roles Cuban women have assumed in the construction of their island's history. In fact, the purpose of this volume has been to show that crossing gender boundaries, an event that occurs in all cultures in times of emergency, has been commonplace in Cuba because emergency and drastic change has been the rule, not the exception. As a result, Cuban women's history has followed its own logic. Often it has been appropriated by a male-dominated disciplines and male politicians to consecrate a nation. Women themselves have frequently acted to support a monarchy, a dictatorship, or a male-led democracy or revolution. But they have also used their feminine identity to advance women's issues, interpreted either as their own family interests or more broadly as issues of women as citizens or women as members of classes. In short, Cuban women's actions and history have not particularly followed the models flowing from Europe or the United States, although they have not been totally immune to them either. Rather, Cuban history has held to the insular experience of the Cuban condition in its limbo between colonialism and modernist nationalism, and a postmodernist spin is difficult to apply to the feminine condition.

What has become evident in this volume is that Cuban women were always elevated on a pedestal, often for the good of the patriarchy. Their stories, regardless of the period, were predominantly written by men, and when women did write, only in exceptional cases did they deviate from the official patriarchal canon. By collecting these stories, some official, some not, the authors in this volume have shown how the feminine image has been appropriated by the national story and has become part of a cultural profile called *cubanidad*.

But other stories abound, many recorded in oral traditions and others in historical archives. These stories tell a no less heroic tale, but their messages are somewhat subversive. Common women lived in the same environment of constant alert and social and political instability as official heroines did. They, too, had to rise to the occasion to survive, to raise the consciousness of neighbors to change governmental commitments to the poor, to influence political figures, to find sources of strength in Afro-Cuban religion, and even to subvert state structures by placing their families first. Their lives were not relaxed, and for them, as with the heroines, the extraordinary became the ordinary, and the heroic became the expected. Their stories, however, demonstrate the dark side of life. Triumph was not always theirs. Their stories did not always have a moral, but instead depicted a Cuban reality composed of chaos and the absurd. In such a world, power structures, including patriarchy, had a loose grip on a roiling populace, and the powerless established niches of influence and even authority. Some of the authors in this volume have discovered corners of influence and found that they were presided over by women. While these niches and these women have not been part of the official story, they are nonetheless elements of *cubanidad*.

The authors of this volume would like to invite students of Cuban studies to consider how memory has been constructed in Cuba. Since Cuba is a place where issues of race, cultural identity, class division, and association with colonial and imperial powers have challenged a unified sense of belonging, and since the island has always faced the peril of attack, the national myth has been especially rigid. But we have been able to juxtapose official heroines against the protagonists of the daily struggle. Official heroines aggrandized the nation and the patriarchy, while unofficial heroines highlighted women with a rogue vitality, picaresque humor, autonomy, wiliness, and even a ferocious territorial authority. Through the tales of the official and unofficial historical female figures we can see the elements of Cuba's great dichotomy: loyalty and subversion. These qualities better define the Cuban condition than the historical configuration of the nation state and its subpopulations that command the attention of researchers in U.S., Latin American, and European universities.

This collection, then, challenges non-Cuban historians to see that the Cuban historical trajectory does not fit within the modern or postmodern contexts taught in Western universities. Cuban scholarship and Cuban memory, whether belonging to the colonial, prerevolutionary, or revolutionary periods, have been dominated by the island's vulnerability to outside forces and internal strategies of defense. Women have been required to respond to danger and take extraordinary action, and also have displayed surprising authority in unexpected places because they lived in an unstable world. Thus, in Cuba, women have been subject more to the historical moment than to men's tendency to control them, and women viewed themselves more as part of a grand design than as unique because of their gender.

NOTES

1. Micro- and macrocultures refer to individuals or unique regional groups that challenge positivistic ideals of order, progress, and homogeneous images of national cultures.

ARCHIVES

COMMENT

REPLY

MARISA S. MONTES

Cuba-Related Research Collections in Miami

In Louis A. Perez Jr.'s work, *A Guide to Cuban Collections in the United States,* the author assembled an invaluable reference tool for scholars interested in Cuba. Since the publication of the work in 1991, however, great strides have been made in the development of academic and scholarly resources in the Greater Miami area — the largest area of concentration for Cuban Americans. In recent years, the city has proved to be fertile ground for the support of academic scholarship on Cuba The following is a brief guide to Cuban collections found specifically in the Miami area, as a way to update the information in Professor Pérez's guide. The collections are listed in alphabetical order, by institution.

Barry University
Monsignor William Barry Memorial Library
11300 NE Second Avenue
Miami Shores, Florida 33161–6695
Phone: 305–899–3760

The collection is open to the public from 9:00 a.m. to 5:00 p.m. from Monday to Friday. Researchers are urged to contact Sister Dorothy Jehle, the Pedro Pan archivist, to arrange an appointment to see the collection. The special collections phone number is: 305–899–3027.

Pedro Pan / Monsignor Bryan O. Walsh Papers
Barry University's Barry Memorial Library is the home to this extensive collection of materials donated by the late Monsignor Bryan Walsh, the man who, as director of the Catholic Welfare Bureau, spearheaded the Pedro Pan campaign from its inception. Among the contents of the collection, which are still being processed, are photographs of the Operation Pedro Pan children, newspaper clippings related to the program and the children of Pedro Pan, and articles and convention papers written by Monsignor Walsh regarding the history of Pedro Pan, the program's children, and various topics of interest. The collection houses bound copies of *Miami Voice,* the Catholic diocesan newspaper of Miami, published from 1959 through the 1990s. The collection also contains a number of books related to Monsignor Walsh's fields of interests, including material on the disciplines of sociology/social work, immigration, and the Catholic Church.

**Florida International University
University Park Campus
Green Library
11200 SW 8th Street
Miami, Florida 33199
Phone: 305-348-2461**

The following collections can be found at Florida International University's Special Collections and University Archives Department on the fourth floor of Green Library (GL-425). The collection is available to the public from 8:00 a.m. to 5:00 p.m. Monday through Friday. Researchers are urged to contact the department ahead of time, so as to allow the staff to facilitate your needs. Call 305-348-2412 for more information.

Jorge Bolet Music Collection

The Bolet archives provide information on the professional and personal life of Cuban-born pianist Jorge Bolet. The material cover his time with the Cape Town and Durban Symphonies in South Africa, the Long Beach Symphony, and the Kern Philharmonic Orchestra, among others. The collection includes personal correspondence, family memorabilia, and notes relating to his concerts.

Cuban Living History Project of Miguel González-Pando

Miguel González-Pando, founder and director of the Cuban Living History Project, produced three documentaries: *Y los quiero conocer*, recounting the era of the Cuban Republic; *Calle Ocho: Cuban Exiles Look at Themselves*, based on the Cuban American exile community; and *Ni Patria Ni Alma*, which focuses on the Cuban American struggle to oust the Castro regime. The collection consists of over 114 taped interviews that González-Pando conducted between the years 1990 and 1997. Most of the interviewees, now deceased, were prominent figures in the political and intellectual life of the Cuban Republic. A number of other items, including press articles by Miguel González-Pando, press kits, personal photos, and posters, are included in the collection.

Leví Marrero Collection

Cuban historian Leví Marrero is best known for his fifteen-volume survey of the island's history, *Cuba: Economía y sociedad*. Materials necessary to complete this study, including photo reproductions and transcriptions of documents from the Archivo General de Indias in Seville, Spain, are part of the collection. Manuscripts used in the writing of *La Historia de Cuba*, parts 1, 2, and 3, are found in the collection as well. Personal correspondence between 1960 and 1994, photographs, and maps are also a part of the collection.

Cuban Exile History Project

This collection includes documents and a myriad of materials relating to the Cuban exile experience. The collection includes runs of such Cuban periodicals as *Bohemia, Carteles,* and *El Camagueyano*; publications from the Cuban American National Foundation; and photographs of exiles. Correspondence between project director Miguel Bretos and other exiles, and publications of the Cuban Exile History Project are also included. The Project materials also include a Cuban Pamphlet Collection. Within this collection are a variety of paper series and pamphlets issues by different political movements within the island.

Rogelio Caparros Collection

Cuban photographer Rogelio Caparros captured much of Cuban life on film. The collection holds thousands of photographic proofs taken between 1957 and 1963. The bulk of the collection holds images of the Cuban Revolution and a number of photos taken in New York during Caparros' tenure as a photographer for the United Nations in the early 1960s. Of note among these photos are those taken of Fidel Castro while addressing the United Nations in 1961.

Cristóbal Díaz-Ayala Cuban and Latin American Popular Music Collection

Renowned musicologist and author of *Cuba Canta y Baila: Discografía de la Música Cubana,* Vol. 1, *1898–1925,* Díaz-Ayala donated approximately 100,000 items that span the history of popular Cuban and other Latin music. The collection features 25,000 LPs; 14,500 78rpms; 4,500 cassettes containing radio interviews with composers and musicians; 4,000 pieces of sheet music; 3,000 books; and thousands of other music-related paraphernalia.

Historical Museum of Southern Florida
101 West Flagler Street
Miami, Florida 33130
Phone: 305-375-1492

The Research Center of the Historical Museum of Southern Florida is open to the public from 10:30 a.m. to 4:00 p.m. from Monday to Friday. To access a guide to the Research Center's manuscripts and visual materials, please visit: http://www.historical-museum.org/collect/rc.htm

Historical Museum of Southern Florida Research Center

The Historical Museum of Southern Florida is dedicated to preserving the history, cultures, and archeology of the people of South Florida and the Caribbean. The research center is home of the archives, library, and documentary collections of the Historical Association of Southern Florida. The center houses a number of small, privately donated collections of items related to the people of South Florida, including its Cuban-American population. The research center also houses an impressive picture archive (1,000,000+) of images from South Florida and the Caribbean.

Miami-Dade Public Library
101 W Flagler Street
Miami, Florida 33130
Phone: 305-375-2665

Florida Moving Image Archive

Access to this archive is strictly by appointment only. Appointments can be made from 9:00 a.m. to 5:00 p.m. Monday to Friday by contacting Lou Ellen Cramer at 305-375-1505. The archive staff will also compile a VHS tape of research materials of interest if so requested; there is a research fee for this service. For more information, contact the research staff at info@ia.org

Florida Room

The Florida Room is open during regular library hours, Monday to Saturday from 9:00 a.m. to 6:00 p.m. (Thursday 9:00 a.m. to 9:00 p.m.) and Sunday 1:00 p.m. to 5:00 p.m.. For more information regarding the Florida Room, call 305-375-5023.

Florida Moving Image Archive

The Florida Moving Image Archive is an extensive collection of moving images recorded in South Florida from the 1920s through the 1990s. The archive houses local news broadcasts, films produced privately within South Florida, and news documentaries chronicling local reaction to events of historic significance produced by local television affiliates.

Florida Room

The Florida Room at the Miami-Dade Public Library houses complete runs of a variety of periodicals from across the state of Florida. The Florida Room specifically emphasizes materials from the region of South Florida. The Florida Room also houses a small collection of literary works by Cuban Americans from the Miami area.

University of Miami
Otto G. Richter Library
Cuban Heritage Collection
1300 Memorial Drive
P.O. Box 248214
Coral Gables, Florida 33124–0320
Phone: 305–284–4900; Fax: 305–284–4901

Housed at the new Roberto C. Goizueta Pavilion on the second floor of the Otto G. Richter Library, the University of Miami's Cuban Heritage Collection (CHC) acts as a repository for an impressive collection of materials on the history of Cuba from discovery to the present. The collection is also home to a number of materials related to the Cuban exile community and Cuban Americans. The CHC houses more than 50,000 books (both rare and contemporary), a substantial number of Cuban-exile and Cuban-published periodicals, and over two hundred personal and corporate collections.

The CHC is open to the public from 9:00 a.m. to 4:00 p.m. Monday to Friday. Researchers not affiliated with the University of Miami (its faculty, students, and staff) will have to obtain a visitor's pass from the Richter Library circulation desk. All that is required to obtain a pass is a photo identification. Visiting researchers are also urged to call in advance for the CHC staff to best assist your needs. For a more in-depth overview of the Cuban Heritage Collection, visit the website: http://www.library.miami.edu/umcuban/cuban.html

Also available on the web is the University of Miami's Cuban Heritage Digital Collection. It contains the digitized contents of selected Cuban Heritage Collections. To access the Digital Collection, visit: http://www.library.miami.edu/chcdigital/intro.html

Tomás Estrada Palma Collection, ca. 1880–1999

Tomás Estrada Palma, the first elected president of the Republic of Cuba, served in office from 1902 to 1906. This collection, donated by Tomás Douglas Estrada Palma III in 1995, includes a variety of correspondence, photographs, and other documents related to Estrada Palma and his descendants. The collection also reflects the relationship of the Estrada Palma's government with the United States.

Tad Szulc Collection, 1984–1986

Tad Szulc, the distinguished journalist and author, donated to the CHC the bulk of original research material that he utilized in the work *Fidel: A Critical Portrait*. Among the items in the collection are typewritten transcripts of interviews with Fidel Castro and eighteen of his associates in the Cuban government. The interviews all took place in Cuba between the years 1984 and 1985.

Polita Grau de Agüero Collection

Polita Grau, the former first lady of Cuba, who served fourteen years in prison for conspiring to overthrow Fidel Castro and her role in coordinating Operation "Pedro Pan," donated this collection in 1993. The collection includes letters, clippings, and photographs of Polita Grau, and also clippings and photos of her uncle, the former Cuban president Ramón Grau San Martín.

David Masnata y de Quesada Collection

Masnata was the founder and first secretary of the Cuban Institute of Genealogy and Heraldry. The collection contains research material on Cuban and Spanish genealogy and heraldry. It is arranged in five series: I: Gonzalo de Quesada y Arostegui Family; II: Genealogy (of Masnata's family); III: Genealogy related to other European countries; IV: José Martí (contains materials related to the Cuban poet); and V: David Masmata y de Quesada Papers (contains manuscripts of two of his unpublished works "The Founders of the Cuban Republic" and "Hierarchy of the War of '68").

Cordovés and Bolaños Families Collection, 1878–1999

The Cordovés and Bolaños families were involved in Cuba's Wars of Independence against Spain. The collection, donated by Julio Mestre, contains letters and documents from Cuba's Wars of Independence. The remainder of the collection includes clippings, documents, and photographs regarding the Bay of Pigs invasion, with which the donor was involved.

The Truth about Cuba Committee Inc. Records

The collection houses the official records of the organization, Truth about Cuba Committee, Inc. (TACC), established to publish information regarding Cuba and its role in promoting communism throughout Latin America. The collection includes over 390,000 pages of testimony, membership records, photographs, clippings, correspondence, and visual and audio recordings from 1961 to 1975.

Alberto Arredondo Papers, 1929–1975

The collection consists primarily of economic reports prepared by Arredondo, a Cuban economist. The papers are divided into four series. Series I is composed of biographical information regarding Arredondo. Series II and III contains reports written for the Symposium Nacional de Recursos Naturales de Cuba, the Consejo Nacional de Economía de Cuba, and the Confederación de Trabajadores de Cuba (CTC). Series IV holds material related to issues of particular interest to Arredondo, including Cuban tariffs, tobacco, and employment and salaries.

Cuba: Capitanía General Collection, 1851–1898

Valeriano Weyler and Ramón Blanco were both Captain Generals of the Island of Cuba. The collection is composed of "bandos" or edicts, "Reales Ordenes," and official forms (1896–1898) published during both Valeriano Weyler and Ramón Blanco's tenures.

Lyceum and Lawn Tennis Club Collection

The Cuban women's organization, the Lyceum and Lawn Tennis Club, aimed to promote women's issues, social welfare, and women's athletics. After being shut down by the Castro government in the late 1960s, several members continued meeting in exile in Miami, led by María Luisa Guerrero. The collection includes these members' memorabilia, photographs, newsletters, and yearbooks.

Manuel R. Bustamante Photograph Collection

The collection is composed primarily of photographs taken in Cuba between the early 1900s and the 1990s. The collection also consists of materials related to Bustamante's personal experiences.

Enrique Labrador Ruiz Collection, 1933–1991

Enrique Labrador Ruiz, a Cuban author and journalist, was exiled from Cuba in 1976. During his years of exile, Labrador Ruiz wrote for many literary journals and newspapers. The collection consists of his manuscripts, correspondence, and newspaper clippings.

Gerardo Machado y Morales Collection, 1873–1994

Gerardo Machado y Morales was the fifth president of the Republic of Cuba, from 1925 to 1933. Due to extreme opposition and popular unrest, Machado was forced into exile in 1933. The collection contains correspondence, legal documents, and papers and photographs that chronicle his life in exile.

JAMES G. HERSHBERG
Associate Professor of History and International Affairs
George Washington University

Comment

Professor Anna Kasten Nelson (American University), who rendered a unique service to scholarship on U.S.–Cuban relations through her role in promoting the declassification of pertinent U.S. government records as a consequence of her service on the board created by the John F. Kennedy Assassinations Record Act (1992), also contributed valuable fresh evidence on the subject of the Kennedy Administration's secret military planning and actions vis-à-vis Cuba in her article, "Operation Northwoods and the Covert War against Cuba, 1961–1963," published in *Cuban Studies* 32.[1] Unfortunately, and quite unnecessarily, she chose to highlight the importance of her interpretation by egregiously distorting my own work on the subject, and this brief note serves to correct the record. In particular, in setting up a "straw man" to knock down, Professor Nelson wrote:

> Was Castro wrong [in fearing a U.S. invasion in 1962 prior to the October missile crisis]? Were his fears of an invasion completely unwarranted? In a 1990 article in *Diplomatic History*, James G. Hershberg tries to answer that question with documents obtained through the Freedom of Information Act (FOIA). These documents are incomplete, however, and his answer is tentative. He does remind the reader that the military services always prepare contingency plans and argues that plans for Cuba were quite likely of that variety.[2]

To say I was taken aback when I read these words would be an understatement, because in fact, the entire thrust of my article was precisely the opposite of what Professor Nelson stated.[3] Far from contending that U.S. military contingency plans relating to Cuba in 1962 prior to the missile crisis were "quite likely" routine, I argued forcefully that they were, in fact, quite serious, and could *not* be dismissed (as some former Kennedy Administration officials had tried to do) as simply routine contingency planning. As I noted in that article, a prime inspiration for writing it had been that some other prominent scholars (such as Raymond L. Garthoff and Graham T. Allison) had recently brushed off Soviet fears of a possible U.S. military invasion of Cuba in 1962, prior to the crisis, as groundless, and had described Pentagon military contingency planning toward Castro's regime at the time as routine. Both authors changed their views and took the issue more seriously after reading a draft of my *Diplomatic History* article.

Just to set the record straight as to my own views as reflected in my 1990 *Diplomatic History* article (as well as in a slightly revised version published as a book chapter two years later),[4] here are a few of many passages in which, contrary to Professor Nelson, I emphasized the seriousness of the military contingency planning and its relevance to the concurrent Operation Mongoose covert operations (and assassination plots against Castro):

> It is now clear that throughout the first ten months of 1962, Operation Mongoose, the Kennedy administration's secret program of covert operations against Cuba, was closely coordinated with enhanced Pentagon contingency planning for possible U.S. military intervention to bring about Fidel Castro's downfall. During this period, U.S. officials actively considered the option of sparking an internal revolt in Cuba that would serve as a pretext for open, direct military action. Top officials in the U.S. government initially shied away from the idea of overt military involvement in Cuba prior to the missile crisis. But the Pentagon, acting at the direction of the president and the secretary of defense, dramatically accelerated contingency planning in late September and early October 1962, just as the president was ordering a sharp increase in anti-Castro covert operations. Although the ultimate purpose of these intensified military preparations remains unclear, I argue that one can no longer breezily dismiss, as have some commentators and former officials, the possibility that, under domestic political pressure and even before they learned in mid-October that Soviet nuclear-capable missiles were in Cuba, top U.S. policymakers seriously considered military action — including, if necessary, a full-scale invasion — to overthrow the Castro regime. (163–64)

The article also "raises the possibility that in addition to previously disclosed covert operations and assassination plots against Havana, large-scale U.S. conventional military maneuvers in the Caribbean in the spring of 1962, heretofore ignored in most analyses of the crisis, may have influenced the Soviet leader's perception that an American invasion was in the offing" (164). It also specifically criticized Allison and Garthoff for deriding the significance of these activities, quoting Garthoff's statement in the first edition of *Reflections on the Cuban Missile Crisis* (1987) that Soviet analysts "incorrectly conclude from evidence that there was a policy and firm plan for a new invasion of Cuba by the United States' armed forces." I add: "He then added, somewhat sarcastically: 'No doubt a military contingency "plan" was on file' (the United States in 1941 even had a 'war plan' for conflict with Great Britain), but there was no political decision or intention to invade Cuba before October 1962" (165, quoting Garthoff, *Reflections on the Cuban Missile Crisis*, 5).

Having heard them express incredulity at an October 1987 Harvard University meeting about Soviet claims that Nikita Khrushchev had been influenced by fears of a U.S. attack on Cuba in his decision to deploy nuclear weapons to the island, I wrote that the newly available documents raised questions about the indignant assertions by former National Security Advisor McGeorge Bundy and former Secretary of Defense Robert S. McNamara that the United States had no intention to invade Cuba: "The new evidence does not resolve the question of whether Kennedy, who had personally prodded McNamara to intensify military plans against Cuba, actually intended to attack Cuba. It does suggest, though, that preparations for military action, including active steps to ready an air strike or invasion, had reached a more advanced stage before the 16 October revelation to Kennedy of the Soviet missile deployments than previously supposed or acknowledged" (167).

Explicitly rejecting the argument that routine contingency planning could explain U.S. actions, I wrote that "it should be possible to sort out routine, dog-day-afternoon contingency planning of the 'Suppose Canada goes Communist?' variety from the far more serious brand that is done on orders from the highest level under sharp time deadlines, that leads to concrete actions such as redeployments of forces and equipment, and that suggests, in sum, that actual implementation is viewed as a realistic possibility and a means of carrying out an established policy objective. Much of the Cuban contingency planning, the denials of former officials notwithstanding, clearly falls into this second category" (169).

At the time when the missiles were discovered in mid-October, the *Diplomatic History* article stated, "far from gathering dust in some cabinet, as some former officials would have us believe, Pentagon plans for action against Castro were already being revivified at the express direction of the secretary of defense, who in turn acted at President Kennedy's behest." While I—like Professor Nelson in her article—found insufficient evidence to conclude firmly that JFK had, or would have, ordered an invasion absent the discovery of the nuclear missiles, I argued that "it seems reasonable to conclude, however, that in late September and early October, Kennedy or his top aides seriously considered an air strike, blockade, or other overt military pressure against Castro" (197).

Ironically, given Professor Nelson's statement, I had previously been quite strongly criticized by some defenders of President Kennedy for asserting that one could not blithely dismiss the possibility that he might, indeed, have flirted with a military attack against Cuba prior to the discovery of the nuclear missiles in mid-October. (And, in a mirror image of Professor Nelson's distortion, some scholars have erroneously claimed that I had written in that article, based on the military contingency plans, that in fact JFK had actually decided or intended to attack Cuba even before the missiles were discovered; the article is actually agnostic on that point.)

My article was, so far as I know, the first scholarly analysis to draw attention to the fact that plans for a decisive U.S. military intervention had always been a major component of the "Mongoose" operation approved by JFK in late 1961 and initiated in early 1962—an aspect that was concealed when the covert operations and assassination plots were disclosed and partially described by the Church Committee investigation of the CIA in the mid-1970s.

Therefore, my own views, as expressed then, were not only consistent with, but identical to, Professor Nelson's conclusion that "Operation Mongoose, the covert attempt to overthrow Castro, and Northwoods, the military plans for the invasion of Cuba, were just two sides of the same coin. For that reason alone, plans for invasion cannot be rejected out of hand as just another example of military planning" (152). Professor Nelson hardly needed to invent a disagreement out of thin air to justify publication of her important findings, especially when other scholars and some former Kennedy Administration officials continue to discount entirely the significance of the enhanced U.S. military preparations and covert actions against Cuba in 1962.

NOTES

1. Anna Kasten Nelson, "Operation Northwoods and the Covert War against Cuba, 1961–1963," *Cuban Studies* 32 (2001): 145–54.

2. Nelson, "Operation Northwoods and the Covert War against Cuba," 146. The reference is to my own article.

3. See James G. Hershberg, "Before 'The Missiles of October': Did Kennedy Plan a Military Strike against Cuba?" *Diplomatic History* 14, no. 2 (Spring 1990): 163–98.

4. James G. Hershberg, "Before 'The Missiles of October': Did Kennedy Plan a Military Strike against Cuba?" in *The Cuban Missile Crisis Revisited,* ed. James A. Nathan, 237–80 (New York: St. Martin's Press, 1992).

ANNA KASTEN NELSON
Distinguished Historian in Residence
American University

Reply

I'm not sure why Professor Hershberg has taken umbrage at my article on Operation Northwoods. He certainly magnifies the importance of my half-dozen lines pertaining to his article by declaring that I set him up as a "straw man" to knock down, or to "invent a disagreement." Nothing was farther from my mind. In fact, I placed my reference to his 1990 article in the body of the paper rather than relegating it to a footnote because I recognized its importance.

I had no need for a "straw man" since the purpose of my article was to add to the public knowledge of newly released documents from the Defense Department. Hershberg, on the other hand, writing some thirteen years ago, was refuting some of the early scholarship about the years before the Cuban Missile Crisis. His work, therefore, includes material from an early joint conference on the crisis as well as some documents released under FOIA. Thus, in my view, the two articles complement each other.

Both of these articles are available to the readers of this journal, so I see no need to counter Professor Hershberg's selective quotes, especially since his argument seems to concern interpretation (my reference is to the entire article rather than particular sentences). But it is worth noting that more information will ultimately become available on Operation Northwoods and new articles and books will be written. I look forward to reading them, although I will unquestionably disagree with some of the new interpretations. No one "owns" history, which is why it is so interesting.

REVIEWS

RECENT WORK IN CUBAN STUDIES

CONTRIBUTORS

Reviews

Alfredo A. Fernández. *Adrift: The Cuban Raft People.* **Houston: Arte Público Press, 2000. 263 pp.**

Alfredo Fernández has produced a book that should be required reading for academics, researchers, and the general public interested in the Cuban raft phenomenon, human rights, and/or immigration. Fernández covers all aspects of rafting, from the raft crisis of 1994 through the opening and closing of rafter refugee camps in Guantánamo and Panamá, the sinking of the tugboat *13 de Marzo* by Cuban officials, the shootdown of two Hermanos al Rescate planes in international waters, and the resolution of the Elián González case in 2000. Moreover, he uses the colorful and engaging prose of a prize-winning novelist and scriptwriter.

Fernández's text has the ring of truth, as it presents detailed anecdotes about the actors, political dynamics, and drama of key events. The story is larded with testimony from rafters, showing the range of motivations, experiences, and outcomes of those who set out to sea in fragile crafts. Of all the accounts of the raft exodus, *Adrift* is the most compelling and comprehensive.

Unfortunately, the book lacks an index, bibliography, and footnotes to substantiate the sources of this richly specific account. Rafters who gave testimony are named, as are some analysts of the events, but many are not. We do not know if the author was present at events, or interviewed participants himself, or received the stories from third parties. The work is more an impressive and readable tale than a fully documented historical account. Lack of verifiable sources leaves its credibility open to attack. Nonetheless, as one who helped establish the demography of rafting and gathered oral history on this subject, this reviewer would evaluate the tale as one based in fact. Fernández has clearly investigated the story from many angles.

Still, parts of the story are distorted and contain minor inaccuracies. For example, indignation regarding living conditions during the first months at the U.S. Naval Base leads to simplistic and inaccurate explanations of problems. A heartless and lazy military staff is blamed for having allowed the rafters' latrines to overflow, which presented a degrading public health hazard. In fact, for security and privacy reasons, the rafters themselves were the ones who sealed the latrines using various improvised devices in order to "privatize" their use among family and friends. This meant that the soldiers assigned to latrine duty often could not enter sealed units for several days, resulting in a health hazard. The author shows little patience or empathy with the logistical task or with U.S. officialdom in general.

Of course, the same criticisms could be made of many footnote-laden but inaccurate academic accounts as well. Yet, in an academic work we would have the benefit of a stated hypothesis or research question revealing the researcher's frame of reference, as well as an explicit methodological trail that could be retraced. One wishes that *Adrift* had more academic rigor.

Despite the occasional error, the work is a solid package that covers the rafters' saga with sensitivity and style. It is the most complex appreciation yet written on the subject and deserves to be widely read.

Holly Ackerman
University of Miami

Gustavo Pérez Firmat. *My Own Private Cuba: Essays on Cuban Literature and Culture*. Boulder, Colo.: Society of Spanish and Spanish-American Studies, 1999. 251 pp.

Desde la introducción misma, incluso desde el título, *My Own Private Cuba*, el nuevo libro de ensayos de Gustavo Pérez Firmat no niega su carácter subversivo contra las expectativas creadas por el ensayo dentro de la academia norteamericana a la cual el profesor y ensayista pertenece. La vocación deconstructora que rige el libro festivamente se nota en el formato seguido por los ensayos que establecen un juego de inversión de la metodología tradicional del trabajo investigativo norteamericano. Sabemos que la correcta documentación, el estudio exhaustivo de las fuentes, el dominio de las previas investigaciones sobre el asunto, la calidad de la bibliografía utilizada son elementos que deben formar parte de un "buen" ensayo. Todo esto lo podrá encontrar el lector en las notas, es decir, en la posición marginal. En el texto central se privilegia un lenguaje gozoso que discurre sin atarse a citas o pruebas, sino creando a la vez un tipo de argumentación que discutiremos en sus líneas generales en los párrafos que siguen.

La estructura del libro responde a dos partes. La primera es un conjunto de ensayos que básicamente reproduce con cierta actualización de los recogidos bajo el título *The Cuban Condition* en el año 1989. La segunda, explica el autor, se compone de "essays that anticipated, extend and modify the arguments of that book" (6). La analogía que Firmat establece entre este continuo explorar el tema de la literatura y la cultura cubana (que por supuesto tiene en cuenta sus obras más colindantes con la autobiografía o el testimonio como *Life on the Hyphen* (1994) o *Next Year in Cuba* (1995) con el trabajo del cartógrafo de Borges en "El Hacedor," que termina identificando su nunca acabado mapa con la imagen de su rostro, ilumina aun más para el público el costado personal de estas disquisiciones. Este aspecto íntimo, parte de su identidad, y por lo tanto inevitable, de la ensayística de Firmat actúa como una suerte de lava demoledora de los sólidos y profundos fundamentos teóricos de sus investigaciones, algo que no deja trazo de los mismos, que sin negarlos los transforma, los deglute, en el ya reconocido canibalismo de la literatura cubana.

No puedo dejar de recordar a Michel Foucault y su conceptualización del "autor" cuando leo en Firmat las consecuencias del "magisterio" de Jorge Mañach. Ni puedo evitar a Jacques Derrida y a Mijail Batjin cuando leo los juegos de palabras, a la manera de las "coco-connections" que establece Firmat. Pero sé que no estoy frente al desplazamiento derridiano ni a la heteroglosia que celebra Batjin, sino más cerca, mucho más cerca, de la improvisación, del exaltado juego con el ingenio y el humor que caracterizan al decir cubano desde la decimonónica décima, hasta la oratoria de nuestros líderes de ayer a hoy, de allá y de acá, y que atraviesa con su sexismo desde el teatro vernáculo hasta los chistes de Pepito. Esta práctica del pensamiento preñado de una risa inteligente que borra toda pretensión de conclusividad fue, no lo olvidemos, el primer ejercicio de independencia intelectual de los cubanos en la metrópolis, cuando desde las tablas del bufo se comenzó a abuchear a los españoles. Retomarlo es un ejercicio de continuidad con la búsqueda de un modo independiente de repensar nuestra identidad.

En cuanto a la composición, hay que decir del libro que su estilo no es original, lo cual por supuesto debe ser tomado como un elogio. El autor, en su capacidad para la absorción creativa puede, al referirse a los escritores que discute, recrear sus estilos en una suerte de pastiche de su propia voz de analista con aquellas que trata de explorar, facilitando así al lector el entendimiento de los mecanismo más íntimos de pensamiento que crearon las obras objeto de estudio. Así vemos usar constantemente el choteo a lo Mañach en las aventuras etimológicas de Firmat en busca de una nueva forma de nombrar una concepto, pero sobre todo el contrapunteo a lo Ortiz, cuando trata de comparar procesos históricos culturales.

La contraposición entre lo objetivo y lo subjetivo es parte constitutiva del estilo de Firmat, su búsqueda "privada" de esa "nuestra expresión" que él distingue y celebra en los trabajos seminales de la cultura cubana discutidos en su libro. Sólo sería necesario reparar en el epígrafe de Bola Nieve que abre estas páginas "Yo soy la canción que canto" para saber que Firmat escribe bajo el deseo de lograr aquello que ocurría cuando Bola se sentaba frente al piano: una interpretación, a la vez que una estilización, de eso que ha dado en llamarse "lo cubano."

Madeline Cámara
University of South Florida

Alexander von Humboldt. *The Island of Cuba: A Political Essay.* Translated and edited by Luis Martínez-Fernández. Kingston: Ian Randle Publishers, 2001. 280 pp.

Alexander von Humboldt, whom José de la Luz y Caballero referred to as "the second discoverer of Cuba," was the first and most important of many nineteenth-century traveler writers and scientists to rediscover Cuba. Humboldt visited the island as part of a five-year trip, in which he and the French physician and naturalist Aimé Bonpland visited Venezuela, Colombia, Ecuador, Peru, Chile, Mexico, and the United States.

Arriving in Havana from Cumaná in December 1800, the German scientist and the French naturalist spent three months in Cuba, mingling with the island's leading citizens and scientists and gathering data on the island. Humboldt and Bonpland largely confined their travels to Havana and its environs, venturing only to Batabanó on the southern coast, the Isle of Pines, Cayo Bonito, and the city of Trinidad. Departing Cuba for Cartagena in March 1801, Humboldt and Bonpland returned to Cuba for only a brief stay in the Spring of 1804, visiting the Cerro of Guanabacoa.

For the next two decades Humboldt continued to collect data on Cuba before publishing his findings and observations on the island colony in 1826. His *Political Essay* appeared in French in 1826, in Spanish in 1827, and in English in 1829. Decades later, in 1856, John S. Thrasher, an American expansionist and proponent of the annexation of Cuba, translated and abridged Humboldt's work, adding notes throughout the text, updating statistics, fronting Humboldt's essay with one of his own, and deleting Humboldt's chapter on the Nature of Slavery.

This 2001 edition of Humboldt's *Political Essay* is Thrasher's 1856 translation, with some valuable additions. Although unauthorized and abridged, the 1856 translation is considered far superior to the 1829 effort, which is virtually unreadable. This latest edition includes an excellent introduction by Luis Martínez Fernández; the original chapter on the Nature of Slavery, translated by Shelley L. Frisch; letters from Humboldt and Thrasher that appeared in the *New York Times* concerning the controversial 1856 translation; and a brief essay by Frank Argote-Freyre on the relationship between Humboldt and the Cuban economist and statesman Francisco de Arango y Pareño.

The greatest value of Humboldt's *Political Essay* and Thrasher's Preliminary Essay and extensive notes are as historical documents written for nineteenth-century European and American audiences. A contemporary Cuban, such as Arango y Pareño, could find fault in Humboldt's facts. A modern student of Cuba will find frustrating the lack of specificity in Humboldt's analyses. Is he describing Cuban society as it existed in 1800, when he visited the island, or in 1825 when his data gathering came to a close? A reader may find Humboldt's scientific writing — "veins twelve or fourteen inches thick, filled with fibrous quartz, amethyst, and rich mammilated stalactiform chalcedony" (96) — less than appealing. There is, however, much to savor in this edition.

This 2001 edition of Humboldt's *Political Essay* that includes Thrasher's essay and notes to the 1856 edition, an excellent introduction, the chapter on the nature of slavery that had been missing from the earlier edition, letters from the German scientist and the American expansionist and annexationist published in 1856, and an analysis of the Humboldt and Arango y Pareño dialogue is a good primary reader on nineteenth-century Cuba. This book is appropriate for upper-level undergraduate and graduate courses on Cuba and Cuban-American relations in the nineteenth century.

John James Clune
University of West Florida

Jorge Ibarra. *Prologue to Revolution: Cuba, 1898–1958*. Translated by Marjorie Moore. Boulder, Colo.: Lynne Rienner Publishers, 1998. 229 pp.

Jorge Ibarra Cuesta has approached Cuban history from many different vantage points in a series of articles and books. He has published comparative work on the formation of nations in the nineteenth-century Antilles, and has studied the political history of the dependent Cuban republic and the long-term development of Cuban mentalities as seen in the popular idiom, such as fiction and pictorial art. He is known for his influential writings on the ideology and politics of the antislavery independence movement, sustaining the continuities with the 1959 revolution (*Ideología mambisa*, 1967).

The present volume is a groundbreaking, systematic study of the development of Cuban economic and social structures between the installation of U.S. control in 1898 and the beginning of revolutionary change in 1959. It incorporates the contributions of many scholars to important aspects of the question, contests some, and explores a number of new areas in order to complete the coverage.

Long in the making, the book reflects several factors in the author's personal development: the influence of the revolutionary conjuncture of the 1950s, which marked him as it did the leaders of the 1959 revolution; his early polemics with Marxist historians of an older generation, which led him by 1970 to a careful examination of Lenin's methodology for researching capitalism; the rejection of wishful historiography; and the choice of a structural approach for this economic and social history of the dependent republic, complementary to his work on mentalities. It will challenge students of Cuban history for many years to come.

The text comes mostly from *Cuba, 1898–1958: Estructura y procesos sociales* (Havana, 1995). The English title, *Prologue to Revolution* — the publishers' attempt to draw the attention of a broader audience — leaves room for some misunderstanding about the book's objectives. The book does not aim to encompass social movements, politics, or ideology except as indicators of the evolving state of mind of different social groups. It is more about structure and thus about the potential for organized struggle, but not about its political processes and outcomes. The book makes no inferences about the inevitability of revolution or of socialism — which might have been a temptation in the balmy days of 1980s Cuba when the original text was written. Rather, Ibarra analyzes the weakness and disintegration of Cuban society in its unstable capitalist development, its complex web of dependency that accommodated privileged elements while excluding a steadily growing, proletarianized mass of chronically unemployed, typically young people.

Ibarra researches the pace and manner of capitalist development as practiced by Cubans in the different branches of economic activity. From there, he explores Cuban class structure in its different strata and regions, examining each strata one-by-one from sources. The urban/rural and generational divides are organically tied into the analysis. At the most general level, the fruit of all this analysis is found in some truly remarkable synthetic passages in the final chapters, such as his comparison of the crisis situations of 1928–34 and 1953–57.

Despite the effort to fill gaps in the existing research, there is some unevenness. The chapter on Black Cubans in the period is less developed than others, and the one on women is, frankly, weak. In at least one case, Ibarra lapses into a formulaic judgment, reducing the historic political conservativism of Pinar del Rio tobacco farmers to semifeudal production relations (sharecropping).

This is an important work, but not an easy read for an unspecialized audience. Though an ambitious synthesis, it was written as an innovative and often polemical scholarly essay — a basis for future study — not a general introduction to the subject. It includes some fairly dense theoretical and methodological passages and considerable statistical data and discussion of sources, necessary to sustain the author's points rather than merely to illustrate them. The translation is uneven and occasionally reverses the author's meaning.

The present reviewer would have liked to have seen a systematic discussion of the vast regulatory apparatus of government created during the second half of the period — a major structural factor aimed at countermanding the tendencies of disintegration traced by Jorge Ibarra. But this was, perhaps, too much to include in this volume.

John Dumoulin
Gainesville, Florida

Charley Gerard. *Music from Cuba: Mongo Santamaría, Chocolate Armenteros, and Cuban Musicians in the United States.* Westport, Conn.: Praeger, 2001. 155 pp.

This book is a detailed descriptive account of the musical lives of a number of Cuban musicians — Mongo Santamaría, Jesús Caunedo, Pupi Legarreta, Juan Pablo Torres, Juan Carlos Formell, and Chocolate Armenteros — who migrated and spent a good portion of their lives in the United States. The author utilizes mini biographies of these musicians to support his case for the existence of what he calls "stateside Cuban music."

The more detailed portions of the book are dedicated to the percussionist Mongo Santamaría (whose story takes up three of the eleven chapters) and to the trumpet player Alfredo "Chocolate" Armenteros. The author's narrative style is varied; while some chapters, (e.g., those on Mongo and Chocolate) are more analytical, one chapter (on Caunedo) contains paraphrases of oral interviews, while another (the chapter on Pupi Legarreta) simply presents a transcription of interviews. This variation makes the reading easier, and the direct transcriptions allow the reader a glimpse into the musician's own view of events.

At times the author appears to simplify the early history of the migration of Cuban musicians to the United States by reducing it to a question of racism. While racism may indeed have played a part in the migration of black-skinned musicians to the United States in the 1930s and 1940s, it is not the complete story. Economic factors also played a role. In any event, racism against black musicians cannot explain the migration of numerous white-skinned Cuban musicians to the United States during the same period.

At other times, the author, inexplicably, does not credit the musicians' own accounts of their actions, as, for example, when he expresses his disbelief that the politics of the Cuban revolution had little to do with Chocolate Armenteros's decision to migrate. Since Armenteros left Cuba for New York in 1957, two years before the Revolution succeeded, his statement does not appear so hard to accept.

The author is to be congratulated for his use of a wide variety of sources, including some interviews with Cuban musicians from the Smithsonian Institution's Oral History Program. Yet some statements suggest that further research on Cuban history might have improved the quality of the book. For example, the reader familiar with Cuban history may regard as unnecessarily tentative the author's statement that General Batista "was apparently a mulatto" (14), since Batista's racially mixed background is fairly common knowledge.

One cannot fault the author for his repetition of the statement that "the son was a music of the demimonde, associated with criminals and prostitution" (66), which he carefully attributes to another source. Yet this notion, which of late has crept into scholarly writings in the United States, is one based not on historical facts but on fallacious interpretations that too easily equate the everyday lives of working-class men with crime and those of working-class women with prostitution.

While in this reviewer's view the author may not have completely succeeded in demonstrating the existence of a "stateside Cuban music," he certainly has laid much of the groundwork for that argument. Gerard has written a very useful book that begins to fill a large gap in our knowledge about the lives of Cuban popular musicians in the United States.

Raúl Fernández
University of California, Irvine

Alberto F. Álvarez García and Gerardo González Núñez. *¿Intelectuales vs revolución?: El caso del Centro de Estudios sobre América, CEA*. Montreal: Ediciones Arte D.T., 2001. 212 pp.

Revolutionary Cuba abounds with enigmas, especially in the realm of the State's relation with those intellectuals committed to constructive criticism of the regime. Such criticism occurs and serves to reveal aspects of the inner workings of state policies, but only rarely does evidence emerge about these debates from areas other than those within the principal governing bodies. Since its founding in 1977, the Centro de Estudios sobre América (CEA) has directed its social scientist staff to research and publish on public policy topics pertaining to the Americas. After 1989, the Center turned as well to Cuban topics because of the urgency to right the economy and rethink socialism. As nationalists concerned with the survival of the country's independence amid brutal economic changes, these intellectuals sought to advance ideas and strategies Cuba could embrace to ensure equity to all parts of society during the transition. CEA researchers Alberto F. Álvarez García and Gerardo González Núñez discuss and critique the events of the last decade that led to the State's intervention and subsequent silencing through reorganization and exile of CEA's intellectuals. This account offers insights likely to clarify speculation while also providing valuable knowledge of the State's penetrating role in all aspects of intellectual life. As such, it builds upon the compilation of Maurizio Giuliano, *El caso CEA: Intelectuales e inquisidores en Cuba. ¿Perestroika en la isla?* (Miami: Ediciones Universal, 1998).

Could Cuba meet international expectations for the autonomy of academic institutions? Substantial evidence exists that it could not because of the interconnectedness among the State, the Communist Party of Cuba, and its Central Committee. Pluralism of ideas expressed privately was individualism, but when the State-sponsored research network embraced this pluralism, only distrust and censorial responses emerged. The authors relate with often intriguing detail the State's tactics of increased monitoring to stifle intellectual openings and debate. By the early 1990s it had become evident that reforms would be economic, not political. Part of the CEA's staff argued for democratic politics within socialism as an important reform to incorporate into the overall transition then occurring. The assessment that economic reforms were introducing a type of economic apartheid was not welcome. This response signaled that CEA's incursion into Cuban affairs using the same intellectual prowess and critiquing capacity that it had applied to other countries in the Americas was not acceptable. The implications rippled throughout the CEA and served to warn other State-affiliated researchers.

The authors experienced CEA's reduction in autonomy during the 1990s. Continual reminders that academics could never successfully separate themselves from political objectives were part of a generational difference of expectations and experimental space for socialism. State intervention in the CEA's respected journal, *Cuadernos de Nuestro América,* by the placement of hardline government functionaries on the editorial board, coupled with the appointment of personnel from the armed forces, Ministry of the Interior, and agencies of the Central Committee, were all actions underscoring CEA's transformation into mediocrity and ideological purity.

The example of the CEA's decline adds to the critiques of the failure of authoritarian rule to create and securely maintain an atmosphere favorable for intellectual creativity in the social sciences. Furthermore, a moderate left, concerned as it is internationally with socioeconomic and political inequalities, cannot, as yet, be part of the Cuban public debate or institutional framework. A redefinition of the State and the role of nationalist critics must await a future date.

The authors appear to be doing just that from their posts in Canadian and Puerto Rican academic venues.

Peter T. Johnson
Princeton University

Carlos Lechuga. *Cuba and the Missile Crisis.* **Translated by Mary Todd. Melbourne, Australia: Ocean Press, 2001. 174 pp.**

Robert M. Levine. *Secret Missions to Cuba: Fidel Castro, Bernardo Benes, and Cuban Miami.* **New York: Palgrave, 2001. 323 pp.**

In his book *Cuba and the Missile Crisis*, Carlos Lechuga blames the United States for the crisis and does not present any innovative argument that would contribute to our understanding of this event. The book is basically a political tract, full of the official rhetoric of the Cuban government. According to Lechuga, Nikita Khrushchev came out of his meeting with John Kennedy in Vienna in June 1961 convinced that the Americans were going to invade Cuba. From then onward, Khrushchev repeatedly told Fidel Castro that the Americans were coming. Lechuga affirms that, indeed, the Kennedy administration, after the Bay of Pigs experience, planned to topple the Castro government with an invasion by the U.S. military. Lechuga informs us that, at the end of May 1962, a Soviet delegation traveled to Cuba and offered the Cuban government deployment of nuclear weapons in the island. Castro immediately accepted.

The author says that the two main motivations, for both the Soviet and the Cuban governments, for deploying the missiles in Cuba were to defend Cuba against an attack by the United States and to strengthen the nuclear capabilities of the Soviet military in the face of an American quantitative advantage in nuclear weapons. Yet Lechuga emphasizes that the foremost cause of the missile crisis was growing threats of a military invasion of Cuba by U.S. armed forces. He asserts that an attack by the United States against the island appeared imminent at the time. He argues, "That—nothing else—was the root cause of the dangerous confrontation [the missile crisis]" (4).

Despite the litany that Lechuga presents of real or imputed threats to the Castro government in various American spheres—for example, in the press, in Congress, and in military exercises—he fails to refute a conclusion that various scholars have reached: that the Kennedy administration never intended to use the armed forces of the United States to attack Cuba. Not even after the Americans discovered the Soviet missiles in Cuba was an invasion (advocated by some top officials) of the island a first choice for Kennedy. Had Kennedy wanted to attack Cuba, he would not have discarded and abandoned the Cuban exiles at the Bay of Pigs.

Of the two main reasons for stationing the missiles in Cuba that Lechuga presents, he wants to emphasize the defense of the Castro regime from a possible American invasion. But from the story he tells, one could also conclude that the main motivation for the Soviets was to gain a bargaining chip in their worldwide confrontation with the United States. Lechuga's book does not refute this alternative explanation as the main cause for the deployment of the Soviet missiles. For example, the American missiles in Turkey bothered the Russians. Soviet rulers saw an opportunity to put missiles in Cuba, and apparently they intentionally played on the fears of the Cuban government that the Marines could land on the island. The Soviets got the Americans to remove their missiles from Turkey, and the Americans promised not to do what they did not want to do anyway—invade Cuba. When, on 27 October 1962, Robert Kennedy conveyed the offer to Ambassador Anatoly Dobrynin that the Kennedy administration was willing to trade the missiles in Cuba for a public announcement that the Americans would not invade Cuba and a verbal agreement to remove the missiles from Turkey, Khrushchev immediately accepted the trade.

Despite the superior scholarly quality of Levine's work, in contrast to Lechuga's book, one thing the two books have in common is that they present distorted views, Lechuga's of the Cuba policies of the Kennedy administration and Levine's of groups of activists in Miami who were opposed to the Castro government and of the Cuban American community in that city. Early in the book, Levine does justice to the fact that most Cubans arrived in Miami practically penniless and that through hard work ended up being mostly responsible for the growth and progress of the Miami metropolitan area. Also, Levine has made an important contribution in compiling a lot of details about interactions between the Cuban and American governments during the Carter and Reagan administrations. However, *Secret Missions to Cuba: Fidel Castro, Bernardo Benes, and Cuban Miami* ends up presenting a biased characterization of the Cuban-American community. The book intends to portray the nature of the Cuban-American community from 1959 to 2000. Extending the analysis to recent times makes the constructed image of the exiled community even more illusory.

To produce his portrait of the exiles, Levine uses the story of Cuban American Bernardo Benes who attempted to normalize relations between the Castro and U.S. governments and who advocated engagement with the Cuban regime. Levine equates groups or activists opposed to the Castro dictatorship with being "right-wing" and prone to terrorism, of having a tendency to suppress (usually by violent means) the freedom of speech of those who deviate from certain political views, and even of being anti-Semitic. The author implies that these attributes also apply in a more general sense to the Cuban-American community in Miami.

The facts are that anti-Castro (I would say pro-democracy) groups in the United States, and even in Miami, have never been homogeneous in their political views or in their strategies. This heterogeneity has increased with time. Exiles all along the politico-ideological spectrum want to see a democratic regime in Cuba. To attach the label "right-wing" to all those opposed to the Castro regime is unreasonable. For years now, there have been groups of Cuban exiles very active in the anti-embargo, pro-dialogue movement, and there are some radio programs in Miami that are quite sympathetic to the Castro government. Yet "the anti-Castro militants" are not perpetrating violence against them. For quite some time, the vast majority of pro-democracy groups in the exile community have adopted the position that change in Cuba should be sought by peaceful means. Cuban American support for opposition groups in Cuba has increased with time, and it is very clear that the activists in the island want to bring about a transition by peaceful means. More recently, the

Varela Project, created and promoted by a leading democratic activist in Cuba, Osvaldo Payá, has gained widespread support among Cuban Americans. The project has petitioned the Castro government to hold a referendum on steps toward democratization based on legal statues of the 1976 communist constitution. Although many groups and individuals in Miami do not support the Varela Project, in large part because it is perceived to be a strategy for change within the communist system, disagreements about the project have not led to threats or violence in the community. In one last example that shows how far removed from current reality Levine's book is, the Cuban American National Foundation has officially adopted a position in favor of negotiations with officials in the Castro regime.

Juan J. López
University of Illinois at Chicago

Antoni Kapcia. *Cuba: Island of Dreams*. New York: Berg, 2000. 295 pp.

This book is not an easy review because it is not an easy read. The reasons are evident from the start: an excessively complex conceptual scheme from which the author draws selectively to guide the historical and empirical analysis. Claiming that scholars have been reluctant to deal with the issue of Cuban ideology, and that whenever they did, they "misunderstood" it (5), Kapcia believes that his book fills that gap. To him, Cuban revolutionary ideology is *cubanía rebelde,* which he claims is the line that runs throughout Cuban history and which he argues should not be confused with *cubanidad,* or Cubanness. In order to show the difference, he establishes the conceptual parameters of the discussion of this *cubanía* in an introductory chapter entitled "The Concept of *Cubanía* and the Nature of Myth." As part of what he calls his "methodological concerns" (33), that chapter analyzes the concepts of nationalism (as "imagined communities"), political historical myth, symbols and icons, political totemization, political culture, ritual, gender, and language.

Let it be said, this is an author who knows his theory. Each of these concepts is brilliantly discussed and on those grounds alone the introductory chapter makes a contribution. The problem is that most of these conceptual concerns are subsequently hardly touched upon in a book that is fundamentally intended to elucidate what the author calls "codes" in both prerevolutionary and postrevolutionary Cuban history. His central thesis is that throughout Cuban history there has been "an emerging potential code" struggling to become reality only to be repeatedly frustrated. He calls that code *cubanía rebelde.* His argument that those potential codes are to be found at the "popular-empirical" and not the "intellectual-theoretical" level (17) hardly clarifies how one is to discover what is popular and "potential" in history. The author offers the following as clarification: "It can be deemed 'popular' in two senses. Firstly, it exists at the more 'unconscious' level of understanding and motivation, not so much unthinking as unthought and largely uncodified formally, except through the 'codes.' Secondly, it exists as the collective context in which the second level of ideology — the 'intellectual-theoretical' — takes root, develops and adapts" (17). Without claiming to understand such conceptual twists and turns, this reviewer does understand that the author believes that *cubanía rebelde* was a "code," an "ideological reservoir" (123), which, while "potential" and essentially "implicit" (97), finally became reality with the 1959 revolution. With opportunity, context, and personal direction, *cubanía rebelde* emerged as radical revolution, "its legitimacy unchallenged" (92).

There were three fundamental historical watersheds in the realization of true *cubanía rebelde,* according to the author. First, there was, of course, José Martí — hardly a controversial point. Secondly, there was the 1921–31 period, when the Communist party of Cuba was founded. Marxism (based on Leninist theories of imperialism), says the author, began to exercise a subsequent "unchallenged hegemony" within the evolving dissidence, as an explanation of Cuba's situation (76). Needless to say, there is no unanimity on this point. Nor is there agreement on the role of the third watershed, Fidel Castro's 1953 "History Will Absolve Me" speech. Kapcia calls this speech "quintessentially cubanist" and claims that it "evoked the whole *cubanista* tradition" so as to finally codify "the more coherent ideology of *cubanía*" (95). The problem is that Castro's 1953 discourse, while certainly recalling Martí, had nothing to say, directly or indirectly, about the Marxist-Leninist past or present. It was, and not surprisingly at that, very much a social democratic statement, as one would have expected from Castro, a member of the Ortodoxo party sworn to restore the Constitution of 1940, who was, in addition, an active participant in the Caribbean-wide social democratic currents then sweeping the region. And, wasn't that the line taken during the first months of the revolution? Was it not the line evident in that brilliant publication, *Lunes de Revolucion,* led by Guillermo Cabrera Infante, Carlos Franqui, and Heberto Padilla (among others), all to be purged once the revolution swerved toward Marxism-Leninism? Again, those seeking the author's explanation of this radical redirection of the revolution will find the going tough. By the late 1960s, says the author, "*cubanía revolucionaria* could be said to be explicitly Marxist in inspiration and direction, and thus capable of accepting both interpretations of the hegemonic intellectual ideology, unconsciously gravitating towards the 'inwardly oriented' perspective, but more consciously attracted by the 'outwardly oriented' discourse, which offered protection, security and stability" (140). If by protection, security, and stability the author means the military and economic patronage of the USSR, it eludes me as to how this is ideological, as he defines it, rather than simply geopolitical, as much of the literature has long maintained. If this is so, on what grounds can the author argue that while the Marxist-Leninist discourse fit "Cuban criteria and empirical models," liberal or social democratic ones represented "exogenous models" (137)?

Finally, this reviewer finds it frankly quite inexcusable that having cited Afro-Cubans, both in terms of their historical struggles and their cultural/religious contributions to Cuban "revolutionary dreams" (64–65), he then decides that since the history of black radicalism "remains to be written," it necessarily "falls outside the remit of . . . this study" (34). Alas, what Jorge Domínguez once called "the classic non-topic" of Cuban historiography remains unaltered in this book.

Anthony P. Maingot
Florida International University

Jaime Suchlicki. *Historical Dictionary of Cuba.* **2nd ed. Lanham, Md.: Scarecrow Press, 2001. 880 pp.**

Within reach of my desk sits a worn copy of the enormously useful first edition of Jaime Suchlicki's *Historical Dictionary of Cuba* (1988). Having routinely recurred to this work of reference, I join fellow Cubanists in welcoming the publication of a second, expanded and updated, edition of this work. This new edition, the latest volume in a series of historical dictionaries of the Latin American nations, has 453 more pages and is far more attractive than the previous edition as far as typesetting and page design are concerned. The dictionary consists of more than 2,000 alphabetically arranged entries, a new preface by Suchlicki entitled "Cuba beyond Castro," a historical chronology, a 153-page bibliography, 10 maps, and an index.

The dictionary's entries follow a strict A-to-Z format and range in length from four and a half pages (Fidel Castro's) to a single sentence (Eduardo Abela's, for example: "(1899–1965). Painter from San Antonio de los Baños."). The biographical entries include several hundred individuals, from Indian chieftain Hatuey (?–1511) to the *balserito* Elián González. The majority of the people about whom biographies are written have been chosen because of their importance in politics or international relations. Numerous entries are devoted to Cuba's colonial governors, some of them rather obscure, as well as to some lackluster U.S. officials who served in Cuba in some diplomatic capacity. While a few authors, musicians, and painters are included in the dictionary, the work reflects a strong bias in favor of political figures over those of the cultural, religious, and economic realms. Cubans of the diaspora are also underrepresented. Significantly, for example, there is no entry on Roberto Goizueta, the late, long-time president of the Coca-Cola corporation. As far as balance between pre- and post-1959 historical figures, however, the author appears to have struck a very good balance.

Other entries cover organizations and institutions, from the ABC political organization to the Venceremos Brigades; municipalities from Bahía Honda to Zulueta; Cuban terms such as *caballería, choteo, mulatto,* and *zafra*; and historical and contemporary topics from agriculture and banditry to women and yellow fever.

While overall a reliable and accurate source of reference, the *Historical Dictionary* exhibits a few weaknesses and errors that should be noted. Throughout the book, Suchlicki demonstrates a preference for older toponyms rather than those more recently imposed by the Cuban revolutionary government. As unpopular and absurd as some of the recent place name changes may be, the Isle of Youth is still the official name of what used to be the Isle of Pines. By the way, both pines and youth appear to have fled the island, and we may sometime soon have yet another name for the fabled Treasure Island. Significantly, the *Historical Dictionary* includes a map of Cuba's provinces as they stood until 1976 but not one of the current provincial borders.

Authors are painfully aware, this reviewer included, that there is no such thing as a perfect book; typos and misspelled names of people and places routinely slip by authors, editors, and proofreaders, only to be discovered later by seemingly infallible readers and reviewers. A number of such typos or misspellings appear throughout the dictionary. Among those that caught my eye were Reynaldo (instead of Reinaldo) Arenas; Rafael (instead of Ramón) Barquín López; Gaspar Cisneros Betancourt (instead of Betancourt Cisneros), and Barú (instead of Baní). Many of the Spanish words in the text are not spelled with an orthographic accent when one was required; others include an accent that does not belong.

Despite some of the shortcomings outlined above, the new edition of Suchlicki's *Historical Dictionary of Cuba* will be welcomed by students and researchers interested in Cuban topics. My copy of this new edition will sit near my desk next to the older edition, and I look forward to using them both.

Luis Martínez-Fernández
Rutgers University

Madeline Cámara. *Vocación de Casandra: Poesía femenina cubana subversiva en María Elena Cruz Varela.* **New York: Peter Lang, 2001. 131 pp.**

La escritura femenina, puerta hacia un imaginario más amplio que constata la visión de la mujer y su vivencia personal e histórica, representa un reto para los estudios cubanos, ya que, en muchos casos, se ha suprimido, minimizado, u opacado la contribución de la mujer a la cultura cubana, reto agudizado más con la escisión entre isla y exilio. En épocas de crisis, la coyuntura actual del declive del socialismo y el esperado renacer de la democracia en Cuba, surgen figuras como María Elena Cruz Varela, cuya poesía abarca tanto la conciencia agónica de la nación como el compromiso de la mujer en medio de las circunstancias opresivas que le tocó vivir.

En *Vocación de Casandra: Poesía femenina cubana subversiva en María Elena Cruz Varela*, Madeline Cámara nos ofrece el primer estudio crítico de esta importante poeta disidente en las letras cubanas, y responde, asimismo, al reto de la crítica literaria de valorar la escritura femenina en su amplia dimensión y anchura creativa. A partir de una introducción en la cual la autora expone un modelo teórico derivado del feminismo continental y latinoamericano, el argumento central es que la obra de María Elena Cruz Varela se sitúa dentro de la poesía social escrita por mujeres cubanas desde el siglo XIX a la posrevolución. Esta tradición alternativa responde, desde diferentes vivencias, a la necesidad de articular "la Voz de mujer" (7) como contra-discurso a una tradición poética dominantemente masculina. Tras un recuento de esta tradición en el primer capítulo, que va desde Gertrudis Gómez de Avellaneda hasta la poesía femenina del exilio, la autora se detiene en un extensivo análisis de *Afuera está lloviendo* (1987) y *El ángel agotado* (1991), dos poemarios que conjugan los temas principales de "el amor, el autoconocimiento, y la convocación" (31). A la vez, estos temas aparecen como diferentes "fases del proceso de conformación del discurso femenino subversivo" (31), que consiste en mostrar la voz del Otro y la experiencia colectiva de todas las mujeres (54). Hacia el final del segundo capítulo, se empalma la poesía de María Elena Cruz Varela con sus escritos políticos; notablemente, se reproducen tanto la "Declaración de principios," texto donde la poeta declara su oposición al caudillismo castrista, como la hermosa "Alocución por la dignidad nacional," donde urge a sus conciudadanos a no claudicar (71–74). En base a estos dos documentos y a la poesía anterior, el último capítulo sopesa la contribución de la poeta al discurso agónico de la nación en términos de una "utopía de la resistencia" basada en un código de conducta moral (79).

La autora llega a la conclusión de que "el proyecto utópico de Cruz Varela se mantiene dentro del espacio de la ética individual" (83). En una elocuente y conmovedora entrevista final, María Elena Cruz Varela recuenta la persecución a la que fue sometida y declara que su intención no fue explícitamente política (90). Sus poemarios dan fe de una escritura del exceso, producida una vez que se cierran todas las alternativas y más allá del silencio. La fuerza de las imágenes rebasa, en efecto, cualquier intento de domesticar el lenguaje poético en un molde teórico identificable, lo cual resulta, a ratos, en un desajuste del modelo feminista asumido inicialmente (4, 33, 49).

A pesar de marcar hitos importantes en la vigorosa producción de las poetas cubanas de todos los tiempos, el recorrido por la poesía social femenina omite algunas poetas mayores que han surgido en el exilio. *Vocación de Casandra* cumple una tarea importante en las letras cubanas: iniciar la re-escritura de *Lo cubano en la poesía* desde la barrera del género, y poner el acento en una de las voces poéticas más valientes e importantes del presente siglo.

Adriana Méndez Rodenas
University of Iowa

Pedro Pérez Sarduy and Jean Stubbs, eds. *Afro-Cuban Voices: On Race and Identity in Contemporary Cuba*. Gainesville: University Press of Florida, 2000. 200 pp.

This publication appears as part of a series launched by the University Press of Florida on all aspects of socialist Cuba, edited by John Kirk. It represents an ongoing attempt by the authors to provide information on topics related to race on the island. Their present book consists of interviews with black Cubans of distinct ages, backgrounds, interests, and political convictions, though all are professionals. The interviews themselves were conducted between 1995 and 1997. Stubbs and Pérez Sarduy offer the reader views from those with firsthand experience on the nature of racial problems and how they might best be addressed. The authors describe their publication as falling between disciplines, neither a social science study, literary text, or historical narrative, but drawing from all of these fields.

The preface to *Afro-Cuban Voices* underscores the importance of racial issues in contemporary Cuba. It notes the ongoing lack of information on the subject and recognizes that racial friction has increased in the 1990s. The long introduction consists of an essay on literature related to race in Cuba. This section is impressive, demonstrating the authors' thorough command of secondary literature. It begins by touching upon subjects including the effect of involvement in the Angolan civil war on racial discourse and the effects of the "special period" on job opportunities in the black community. After providing an overview of the book's contents, the introduction continues with a summary of racial attitudes throughout Latin America as they developed in colonial times. It underscores the fact that Afro-Cubans have been commenting on their social circumstances in published sources for well over a century, but that such literature remains largely unknown. The authors comment on the similarities between racial stereotypes in Cuba and Brazil, then analyze specifically Cuban-related studies. The introduction ends with a critique of existing literature on racial matters written on the island, noting that Afro-Cubans themselves generally find it superficial, dogmatic, and not sufficiently focused on the present.

The interviews themselves are divided into three sections, "The Lived Experience of Race," "The Representations of Race," and "Race and Identity." Part I concentrates primarily on older interviewees. Chapter 1 considers the life of retired journalist Reynaldo Peñalver, his early years in poverty, and the tremendous obstacles he overcame to become educated. Chapter 2 recounts episodes in the lives of industrial chemist Elpidio de la Trinidad Molina, his wife Egipcia Pérez, and their son Jorge. Chapter 3 includes interviews with doctors of different class backgrounds and ages, Liliam Cordiés Jackson and Nuria Pérez Sesma. While grateful for what they have been able to accomplish under the revolution, they recognize that few publications exist on racial matters within their country and that no forum for public discussion of race is currently available.

Part II explores racial representations in Cuban fiction and the mass media. Print journalist Marta Rojas is featured in chapter 4 with an account of her involvement in the 1953 Moncada trial as well as more recent professional aspirations. Scriptwriter Eliseo Altunaga appears in chapter 5. He discusses biased depictions of Antonio Maceo in the work of Cuban historians and discrimination against Afro-Cuban religions, among other topics. Chapter 6 focuses on actress Elvira Cervera and her experiences with discrimination in radio broadcasting. This is one of the most critical essays, ending with her decision to create an all-black drama troupe as a reaction to the marginalization of Afro-Cuban dramatists. Chapter 7 considers the career of screen actor Alden Knight. He is also highly critical of the present, mentioning that the black community has no authority within the power structure of the media. This section ends with an interview of the poet Georgina Herrera (chapter 8), who began writing after growing up in poverty in Jovellanos, Matanzas.

Part III contains some of the most widely known interviewees. It begins with filmmaker Gloria Rolando's comments in chapter 9 on how difficult it has been for her to receive approval for projects with Afro-Cuban subject matter in the national film institute (ICAIC). She is followed by Juan Benkomo (chapter 10), a drum maker and *santero* who has suffered persecution as a result of his religious beliefs. Chapter 11 continues with anecdotes from the career of Guillermina Ramos Cruz and the difficulties she has experienced attempting to study African-derived culture in Cuba. Afro-Cuban specialist Rogelio Martínez Furé is cited in chapter 12, critiquing the term "Latin American" as exclusionary and noting the racism frequently implicit in the use of the terms "Cuban" and "Afro-Cuban." He underscores the fact that there is no homogeneous "Cuban culture" and calls for a greater celebration of the fact. The thoughts of author Nancy Morejón (chapter 13) end the book. She reflects on the concept of the African diaspora and its meanings for African Americans throughout the hemisphere. She shares her thoughts on the state of black intellectual development within Cuba and—as in the case of Martínez Furé—comments on the implicit, unconscious racism evident in many forms of national discourse.

More than anything else, *Afro-Cuban Voices* does an excellent job of problematizing the concept of "the Afro-Cuban community" and "the Afro-Cuban perspective," providing the reader with a surprisingly wide spectrum of distinct views and life experiences. It does the international community a service in this sense by offering relatively direct access to a few of the countless voices in Cuba that have no means of making themselves heard. The writing style is clear and easy to read, and the content highly significant. I found the testimonies to be very compelling. For instance, I was amazed to discover how many middle-aged Cubans had grandparents who were born into slavery and had been told firsthand about that period when they were young. The sense of awareness among Afro-Cubans about the extent of suffering in their recent past and the gains they have achieved over the past century is striking. Equally noteworthy are their views on the ways they have benefited from the revolution and the areas in which it has failed to meet expectations. While the interviews provide more basic information than synthetic analysis, it is information that has been sorely lacking. *Afro-Cuban Voices* is an important work for all those interested in contemporary race relations and one I highly recommend.

Robin Moore
Temple University

María de los Reyes Castillo Bueno. *Reyita: The Life of a Black Cuban Woman in the Twentieth Century*. With a new introduction by Elizabeth Dore. Edited by Daisy Rubiera Castillo. Translated by Anne McLean. Durham, N.C.: Duke University Press, 2000. 182 pp.

This testimonial history by María de los Reyes Castillo Bueno (1902–1997), *Reyita*, provides a unique perspective on Cuba's past, interpreting it through the often-disregarded experiences of a black woman. Like the best testimonial literature, Reyita's clear, matter-of-fact narrative, translated from the original published in Cuba in 1996, offers a refreshing break from the traditions in Cuban social scholarship that generalize the experiences of all women and all blacks. She represents another of the voices from below, the most alienated segments of Cuban society. Within Cuban studies, *Reyita* can be viewed as a continuation of the classic tales of Esteban Montejo in *Autobiography of a*

Runaway Slave, but one that now speaks from a female viewpoint and recalls critical moments for the nation, from the final abolition of slavery, through the intense racial politics of the 1910s, to the uncertainties of the Batista dictatorship, and to the initial euphoria of the 1959 Revolution. In Latin American Studies more generally, it is comparable to the Brazilian diaries of Carolina María de Jesus's *Child of the Dark* or the earlier chapters of Rigoberta Menchu's *I, Rigoberta Menchu*, which are less concerned with class violence than they are with ethnic traditions and familial struggles for survival.

Reyita recounts her options and the limitations imposed on her, which were distinctively defined by race, gender, and class, but invariably privileges class over the others. Race determined her family's entry point into Cuban society, their liberation from slavery, and their continuing fight against discrimination. It also created a color consciousness that no one escaped. Gender determined her economic possibilities and the nature of her marriage. Yet, ultimately, Reyita accepts that class was the greatest determinant of one's social value in Cuba at midcentury. When speaking of some of her unofficial foster children, she defends her explicit mention of race. "If I point out that some of those children were white, it's to emphasize that the most fundamental problem in Cuba was not just being black, but being poor" (72).

Stylistically, in its first two chapters *Reyita* follows a chronological arrangement that it later rejects in favor of a more random organization. This potentially could leave the reader unsure of the work's direction. The book does not recount Reyita's life to the end; in fact, the period after 1963 remains unclear. By that time, Reyita had chosen to focus on her responsibilities as a grandmother and made few social critiques. She makes no evaluation of the Revolution beyond an appreciation for the new access to education and employment made available to her children and grandchildren. One of the most surprising statements in this book comes not from the main storyteller's own words, but appears early in the scholarly introduction. There, noted feminist historian Elizabeth Dore declares, "*Reyita* is the story of a woman who did *not* [her emphasis] make history because of the conditions she inherited from the past" (1). The assumption is that to "make history" one must create transformations that reach beyond the personal, and that a simple existence is generally not worthy of historical attention. Despite this clear rejection of the subject's historical agency, this work is of pedagogical value to introductory Cuban or Latin American history courses that want to escape the teleological emphasis on the Revolution and teach the value of an ordinary life making history in the most simple ways. Reyita lived the majority of her life "just as a mother," but if her circumstances did not allow her to "make history," at least she was able to interpret it.

Kym Morrison
Moravian College

Katherine J. Hagedorn. *Divine Utterances: The Performance of Afro-Cuban Santería.* **Washington, D.C.: Smithsonian Institute Press, 2001. 296 pp.**

Communal rituals in African-derived religions of the Americas like Santería and Vodou feature drums and dancing centrally. Over the last few decades such drum and dance forms have become increasingly visible in secular space, raising thorny ethical questions about representation, authenticity, and authority. This is nowhere truer than in Cuba, where the rise of "Santurismo" (a tourist market catering mainly to foreigners who initiate into Santería and other African-derived religions for a fee) draws hundreds of "religious tourists" to the island annually. Katherine Hagedorn provides well-researched and detailed insight into this phenomenon, as well as an important portrayal of Cuba's legendary *Conjunto Folkórico Nacional*, which, manipulated by the Castro government, regularly performs "folkloricized" renditions of originally sacred dance and drum performance for public (i.e., profane) consumption. A CD recording of twenty masterful samplings by two of the Conjunto's leading drummers and their ensembles is included with the text, and is well worth the price of the book in itself.

This book is of interest primarily to ethnomusicologists (like the author), dance ethnographers, anthropologists with interests in performativity and the representation of race, and, of course, anyone interested in Cuba and Afro-Cuban religion. Hagedorn's discussion of the development of the thought and influence of Fernando Ortíz is an especially important contribution to Cuban studies. Secondarily, *Divine Utterances* is of interest to religious studies scholars for its rich descriptions of Santería ritual and ritual paraphernalia. Scholars of religion will, however, be disappointed in Hagedorn's perfunctory engagement of syncretism and her dismissive oversimplification of Cuban Catholicism. To generalize, for example, that all Cubans see the nation's patron saint, La Virgen de la Caridad del Cobre, merely as a mask for the Yoruba-derived water goddess Ochún is an uncritical misrepresentation. This flaw is in part explicable by the author's apparent ignorance of Thomas Tweed's award-winning book on Cuban Marianism, *Our Lady of the Exile*, which does not appear in Hagedorn's bibliography. Scholars of Yoruba-influenced religion around the world will likewise find inadequate Hagedorn's preferred definition of *ashe (ache)* as "ritual performative power" (241), perhaps reflecting other significant gaps in her reading.

Beyond these substantive issues, the book has two major problems. First, whereas Hagedorn apparently intends to be creative by inserting "nonlinear motion into the narrative structure of the book" (12), she only confuses the reader with this weird organization; we are not, for example, told much at all about the *orishas* until page 73, or about the transatlantic slave trade until page 185. And second, readers will unwittingly overdose on Hagedorn's frequent forays into self-reflection (including the entirety of chapter 1). The book's many valuable insights are bogged down by sometimes overwrought descriptions of her dreams, self-doubt, and dubious initiation into the religion (e.g., "We giggled softly as the liquid brown eyes of a child followed us briefly" [45]; and ". . . dreams of a panacea shattered by the insistent rumblings of my lower abdomen" [217]). The reader could well do without so much self-reflection, not to mention the redundant reminders that Hagedorn studied with master *batá* drummer Alberto Villareal.

These criticisms aside, *Divine Utterances* is an important book that simply must be read by anyone with serious interest in Cuban culture. Hagedorn has gone to great lengths to understand the performativity of Santería, and her voice straddles the proverbial insider/outsider fence in a refreshing and valuable way. Where she resists the temptation to write about herself, the narrative becomes quite engaging to read, and on the whole the book is an expert and informative analysis of Santería music and dance in both the sacred and profane realms, and a trenchant commentary on what, if anything, constitutes the boundary between the two.

Terry Rey
Florida International University

Marta Bizcarrondo and Antonio Elorza. *Cuba/España: El dilema autonomista, 1878–1898.* **Madrid: Editorial Colibrí, 2001. 452 pp.**

With the exception of the subject of the Cuban Revolution, no other topic has received better scholarly attention and popular reception than the relationship between Spain and Cuba, before and after independence. Considered an intimate family affair, much deeper in emotions than the relationship with the United States, the link between Spain and Cuba still leaves many stones unturned.

Part of the excellent series published by Colibrí, this is an impeccable volume jointly authored by Marta Bizcarrondo, a history professor at the Universidad Autónoma de Madrid, and Antonio Elorza, professor of political science at the Universidad Complutense, who, along with Elena Hernández Sandoica, recently produced a milestone work, *La Guerra de Cuba (1895–1898)* (Madrid: Alianza, 1998). This new work masterfully traces the evolution and death of the experiment of the Partido Autonomista Liberal and peripheral interests that attempted to maintain the linkage with Spain and develop a home rule in which native personalities governed and managed local institutions, subject to many limitations.

The book is aptly titled "the dilemma," because it describes the anguishing choice between the apparently unstoppable road to independence and the maintenance of strict colonial ties with Spain. From a Cuban point of view, the historical relationship between the two nations is mostly treated in heroic terms that stress the long struggle toward independence. From a Spanish angle, the impact of *el desastre* has dominated traditional and recent scholarship, exemplified by the selective, impressive production of books issued during the centennial commemoration of the defeat of 1898.

What is unusual about this book is that it deals with a special dimension of a unique *desastre*. Ironically, it was not a Spanish failure, but a genuine, native Cuban loss. It has been buried and disdained by both scholarly and ideological extremists. The war of 1898 (Spaniards and Cubans alike refuse to call it the "Spanish-American" War) was not only lost by Spain's colonial authorities, backed by Antonio Cánovas del Castillo's suicidal policy of "hasta el último hombre y la última peseta," it was also resoundingly lost by the Cuban *autonomistas*.

Spanish conservatives and patriotic commentators have considered the *autonomista* experiment as the beginning of the loss of Cuba. This responds to an overall perception of Spain as a centralized state, of which Cuba was an intrinsic part since the loss of the continental colonies in the Americas. In essence, "autonomy" has been a bad policy, whether applied to Catalonia, the Basque Country, or Cuba. In Cuba, it was one more example of a *"tarde y mal"* decolonization process that has been the mark of Spanish colonial administration for centuries.

For Cuban nationalists, *autonomistas* were basically *españolistas*, who lost the struggle to keep Cuba under the Spanish yoke. From a U.S. perception, there was not much difference between the thesis espoused by the autonomous experiment and the rule of the Captain General. After independence, the economic and social interests once defended by *autonomistas* were subsumed under the overall context of the conservative movements. Thus, the bad press they received during the Republic era gained new strength (or silence) with the Revolution.

Part of the explanation for the historical disdain for *autonomismo* expressed from different quarters is the fact that *autonomistas* tried to combine several irreconcilable forces. On the one hand, they pretended to solidly maintain the link with Spain. On the other, their economic and social origins and interests dictated that they seek a link with the United States. At the same time, they adamantly expressed their will to maintain a *personalidad cubana*. This strategy was too ambitious and collapsed in 1898. The book convincingly manages to portray and to explain the simultaneous struggle of convincing Madrid of the goodness of the project while neutralizing the effects of the desertions toward the growing ranks of *independentismo*.

Joaquín Roy
University of Miami

Sherry Johnson. *The Social Transformation of Eighteenth-Century Cuba.*
Gainesville: University Press of Florida, 2001. 267 pp.

Sherry Johnson's new book, based on careful archival research in Cuba, Spain, and the United States, seeks to displace the centrality of sugar from our understanding of Cuban social transformations and political loyalties in the later eighteenth century. She sees the rise of sugar as a contingent and contested process, one that ultimately superseded an earlier vision of colonial society based on a diverse agricultural and commercial economy and active Creole participation in the military and administration.

The starting point of her account is the Spanish Crown's response to the fall of Havana in 1762 to the British. When Spain regained control in 1763, it inaugurated important changes in its imperial defense system with Havana, and its people occupied a central role in the process. In Johnson's view, the development of Havana as a strategic military site had important implications for local society. Cubans of different classes and colors were co-opted by the Spanish military; the *fuero militar* was extremely attractive to many Cubans, as it allowed them special economic prerogatives. Moreover, the influx of Spanish military officials produced increased intermarriage between elite *creoles* and *peninsulares*. Thus, through the military buildup, the Spanish Crown was able to win the loyalty of different strata of colonial society. While Cubans used the military as a source of social mobility and prestige, they also fought valiantly for the Crown in numerous military engagements in the Caribbean.

However, the new pact between colony and metropolis, sealed by arms and by marriage, proved to be short-lived. The fate of the colonial militias was always dependent on the shifting nature of Court politics and changes in ministerial personnel, factors that Johnson reconstructs with great skill. After the death of Charles III and the passing of the Gálvez clan from prominence in the governance of the colonies, Spanish policy was less sensitive to the interests of colonial subjects. The villain of Johnson's account is Luis de las Casas, Captain General of Cuba from 1790 to 1796. Las Casas's abuses were many: he sought to change the *fuero militar*, thus shaking the foundation of Creole loyalty to the crown, and to impress free laborers for public works projects. Moreover, he favored those Creole and peninsular merchants and planters, such as Francisco Arango y Parreño, who advocated Cuba's whole-hearted embrace of slavery and the slave trade. By the end of his tenure, he had alienated practically every segment of colonial society and had set the stage for slavery and sugar's takeoff. The sense of *"Cubanidad"* expressed by *"el pueblo cubano"* in the independence wars of the later nineteenth century thus had its roots deep in the eighteenth century when the metropolis made and then broke a new contract with the colony.

Social Transformation is an important work and deserves to be read widely.

In particular, it moves convincingly from Court politics in Spain to social unrest in the streets of Havana. It thus joins a growing body of work — by scholars such as Manuel Moreno Fraginals, Allan Kuethe, Josep M. Fradera, and Joan Casanovas — that has reconsidered the tensions and points of adhesion between Spain and Cuba from the late eighteenth century to the late nineteenth. This reader was therefore surprised by Johnson's characterization of Cuban historiography as "held hostage to studies of sugar, slavery, colonialism, and dependence" (1). That description does not do justice to a rich and diverse historiographic tradition, one to which Johnson has made a welcome addition.

Christopher Schmidt-Nowara
Fordham University

Efrén Córdova. *El trabajo forzoso en Cuba: Un recorrido amargo de la historia.* **Miami: Ediciones Universal, 2001. 262 pp.**

In this book a prominent scholar of Cuban labor history, Efrén Córdova, examines four periods of Cuban history by looking at the marginalized elements in society (workers) to find the continuity of five hundred years of Cuban history. For Córdova, that continuity is the history of forced labor. Ultimately, the author suggests that workers in post-1959 Cuba are the inheritors of this history. In fact, concludes Córdova, today's workers are more coerced than at any time in Cuban history, including the nearly three hundred years of African slavery.

Córdova examines the history of the *encomienda*, African slavery, coerced labor of Chinese and other migrants during the nineteenth century, and the Cuban Revolution. These labor systems represent forms of institutional and structural violence levied upon workers. Using a judicious selection of both primary and secondary sources, and building from his own two-volume history of Cuban labor, Córdova provides useful overviews of all four periods. For instance, in Part I he addresses the origins of the *encomienda* system, how indigenous workers were employed, the debates and laws attempting to curtail the *encomienda,* and the problems with enforcing those laws. In Part II, the largest section with five chapters, Córdova succinctly examines why slavery arrived and grew in Cuba, the different uses of slavery, and the dilemmas arising from the gradual abolition of slavery in the late 1800s. But in this section Córdova begins to let his political views show. He challenges Marxist historians who examine slavery and its downfall from a purely materialist point of view and who toe the Communist party line that slavery really did not end until 1959 (168). Part III is the pleasant surprise of the book, as Córdova examines various forms of coerced migrant labor, including that of the Irish,

Chinese, and Yucatecan Indians during the nineteenth century. This topic is virtually unknown to most readers and rarely addressed in Cuban histories. While he does not call these forms of labor "forced," he acknowledges that neither were they free. The Chinese case is poignant: they arrived on eight-year contracts, but when those contracts were up, most could not afford return passage and had to either scramble for menial jobs or sign new contracts.

Part IV focuses on Socialist Cuba. According to Córdova, the three previous forms of labor differed from (and were in fact less severe than) the post-1959 system because the current system obligates and coerces *everyone* to work. Córdova locates the present system's origins in Castro's manipulation of patriotic and revolutionary fervor to create a better society shortly after the Revolution came to power. Castro immediately called for voluntary labor and a great national effort. This opened the door for him to later impose measures that forced workers to sacrifice their time for the patriotic and revolutionary good of the country (213). Schools that had work components may have been portrayed by the Revolution as promoting self-sacrifice for the larger good and instilling a service-minded mentality, but for Córdova they were little better than venues for forced child labor. The author carries the same theme of coercion into his examination of overtime, the microbrigades, and other forms of so-called voluntary labor.

Writing from the perspective of a former functionary of the Organización Internacional del Trabajo (OIT) and from the stated positions on freedom to work as laid out in the Universal Declaration of Human Rights, Córdova challenges readers to examine the state of labor and labor-state relations on the island. Near the book's end he asks: "Where does all the money go that is generated by free, forced labor? No one asks" (228). While no one should deny that coerced labor exists in Cuba, Córdova turns a blind eye to workers benefits since 1959. More disturbing is his almost total neglect of female laborers throughout the entire book. This becomes particularly intriguing when one thinks about the stated goals of the 1975 Family Code that "forced" husbands to share household work and child raising with their wives, who were increasingly going to work outside of the home. Yet Córdova neither addresses women's labor issues nor this important law.

While *El trabajo forzoso en Cuba* is a useful overview of important periods in Cuban labor history, ultimately one must see it as more than a history. It is "history" serving a political agenda: to discredit the contemporary state of Cuban labor conditions and state-labor relations, which, according to Córdova, are worse than at any time in the island's history. In fact, the three sections of the book merely foreshadow Part IV. For instance, each section argues that elites sought to maximize labor for their own enrichment and power. Since 1959, "el régimen de Castro se ha caracterizado por su tendencia a extraer el máximo de esfuerzo posible de los trabajadores" (256). Secondly, each era had collaborators who propped up tyranny; since 1959, much to Córdova's surprise, many Cubans have joined with Fidel and their participation is "aparentemente consensual en parte" (213). In the same vein, elites of each era dominated workers by imposing previously unknown work regimens. There are other foreshadowings: urban slaves who feared being sent to the *campo* foreshadow post-1959 urban residents being sent to the countryside in work brigades, and a nineteenth-century Chinese government report on the labor conditions of Chinese workers foreshadows the reports of international labor organizations decrying Cuban labor conditions since the Revolution.

Finally, the book takes a traditional institutional labor-history focus that obscures the social dimensions of labor. In fact, workers as people are strangely anonymous. In over 250 pages of text, no workers are identified by name. In a book that purports to show how workers have been tyrannized, the author's inability to put a human face (or even a name) on workers serves to obliterate them from history. More to the point, the book borders on "victim history." Workers are pawns of elite powers, with little ability to resist and shape their own lives. But, of course, workers did resist and shape their own lives, even if they were highly restricted. Which raises a larger question: Why should we see Cuban labor history as a story of coercion and victimology? Why not one, too, of resistance and agency?

Kirwin Shaffer
Penn State University — Berks

MARIAN GOSLINGA

Recent Work in Cuban Studies 2002

Agriculture and Fishing

Books and Monographs

Asociación Latinoamericana de Integración. *El impacto de ALCA en el sector agropecuario de Chile, Cuba y México.* Montevideo: ALADI, 2002. 106 pp.
Instituto Nacional de Ciencias Agrícolas (Cuba). *Programa y resúmenes.* 13th Congreso Científico, Havana, 2002. Edited by María Mariana Pérez Jorge. Havana: INCA, 2002. 180 pp.
Jiménez Guethón, Reynaldo. "Las cooperativas cañeras en Cuba: Estudio de caso." Master's thesis, Université de Sherbrooke, 2002. 78 pp. (Also available as microfiche)
Mara, William P. *Cubans: The Ultimate Cigars.* New York: Lyons, 2002. 176 pp.

Articles and Papers

"Cashing in on Cuba: Role of Agriculture in Opening Markets to Our Island Neighbor." *Agri Marketing* 40, pt. 9 (2002): 54–58.
Cruz, Raúl, et al. "Regional and Seasonal Prediction of the Caribbean Lobster (Panulirus argus) Commercial Catch in Cuba." *Marine and Freshwater Research* 52, no. 8 (2002): 1633–34.
Gillis, D. M., and Mark Alexander Showell. "Risk and Information Use in Two Competing Fleets: Russian and Cuban Exploitation of Silver Hake (Merluccius bilinearis)." *Canadian Journal of Fisheries and Aquatic Sciences/Journal des Sciences Hallieutiques et Aquatiques* 59, no. 8 (August 2002): 1275–87.
Hägstrom, Jerry. "Chipping Away at the Cuban Trade Embargo." *National Journal* 34, no. 40 (2002): 2908–10. (Discusses Cuban farm products and the embargo)
Kost, William E. "Cuba's Citrus Industry: Growth and Trade Prospects." *Agricultural Outlook* (June/July 2002): 6–7.
Morales, A., et al. "Integrated Management to Control Cylas formicarius of Sweet Potato (Ipomoea baratas [L.]Lam) in Cuba." *Acta Horticultura* 583 (2002): 163–71.
Pérez Talavera, Susana, et al. "Papel de la estación experimental agronómica de Santiago de las Vegas en el fomento del cultivo de trigo en Cuba." *Alimentaria* 39, no. 332 (2002): 67–75.
Ramos-Ledón, Leandro J. "Historical Essay of Cuban Agriculture, Food, and Natural Resources from 1898 to 1958." *Herencia* 8, no. 2 (Fall 2002): 48–57.

Anthropology and Sociology

Books and Monographs

Aber, Shaina C. "Race and Racism in Cuba before and after the Revolution." Honor's paper, Macalester College, 2002. 85 pp.
Beverley, John R. *From Cuba*. Durham, N.C.: Duke University Press, 2002. 246 pp.
Britton, Tamara L. *Cuba*. Edina, Minn.: Abdo, 2002. 40 pp.
Bueno, Salvador, ed. *Cuban Legends*. Translated by Christine Ayorinde. Princeton, N.J.: Markus Wiener Publishers, 2002. 215 pp. (Translation of *Leyendas cubanas*)
Cárdenas Ramírez, Nelson. *Isla que no existe*. Havana: Editorial Letras Cubanas, 2002. 93 pp. (Focuses on Cuban national characteristics)
Castellanos, Jorge. *Pioneros de la etnografía afrocubana: Fernando Ortiz—Rómulo Lachatañeré—Lydia Cabrera*. Miami: Ediciones Universal, 2002. 240 pp.
Castellanos, Jorge, and Isabel Castellanos. *Cultura afrocubana*. 2d ed. Miami: Ediciones Universal, 2002.
Cirules, Enrique. *Mafia in Cuba*. Melbourne, Australia: Ocean Press; London: Global, 2002. 200 pp.
Corbett, Ben. *This Is Cuba: An Outlaw Culture Survives*. Cambridge, Mass.: Westview Press, 2002. 292 pp.
Crooker, Richard A. *Cuba*. Philadelphia: Chelsea House Publishers, 2002. 135 pp.
Di Leo, Octavio. *El descubrimiento de África en Cuba y Brasil, 1889–1969*. Madrid: Editorial Colibrí, 2001. 161 pp.
Díaz Canals, Teresa. *Moral y sociedad: Una intelección de la moral en la primera mitad del siglo XX cubano*. Havana: Publicaciones Acuario [y] Centro Félix Varela, 2002. 143 pp.
Fernández Soneira, Teresa. *Con la estrella y la cruz: Historia de la Federación de las Juventudes de Acción Católica Cubana*. Miami: Ediciones Universal, 2002. 2 vols. 887 pp.
Figueredo, Jorge S. *Cuban Baseball: A Statistical History, 1878–1961*. Jefferson, N.C.: McFarland, 2002.
Fornet, Ambrosio. *La coartada perpetua*. Mexico City: Siglo Veintiuno Editores, 2002. 153 pp.
Fuentes, Norberto. *Narcotráfico y tareas revolucionarias: El concepto cubano*. Miami: Ediciones Universal, 2002. 212 pp. (Discusses the drug trade as well as narcotics control)
Gravette, Andy. *Classic Cuban Cuisine*. London: Fusion Press, 2002. 232 pp. (Reprint of the 1999 edition, which was published under title *Classic Cuban Cookery*)
Gutiérrez Baró, Elsa. *Muy en serio y algo en broma: Diálogo con los adolescentes*. Havana: Editorial Científico-Técnica, 2002. 95 pp.
Hansing, Katrin. "Rasta, Race, and Revolution: The Emergence and Development of the Rastafari Movement in Socialist Cuba." Ph.D. diss., University of Oxford, 2002. 276 pp.
Hernández-Reguant, Ariana. "Radio Taino and the Globalization of the Cuban Culture Industries." Ph.D. diss., University of Chicago, 2002. 2 vols.
Lee, Rensselaer W. *The Cuban Drug Trade*. Basingstoke, U.K.; New York: Palgrave Macmillan, 2002. 304 pp.

López Valdés, Rafael L. *Africanos de Cuba.* San Juan, P.R.: Centro de Estudios Avanzados de Puerto Rico y el Caribe con la colaboración del Instituto de Cultura Puertorriqueña, 2002. 324 pp.
Martínez-Fernández, Luis, ed. *Encyclopedia of Cuba: People, History, Culture.* Phoenix, Ariz.: Oryx, 2002. 1 vol. (Various pagings)
Matos, Luis, ed. *Maisí y sus tradiciones orales.* Havana: Editorial Letras Cubanas, 2002. 63 pp. (Maisí is a Cuban province)
Mendoza, Sylvia. *The Cuban Mama's Kitchen.* London: MQ, 2002. 144 pp.
Otovo, Okezi Tiffani. "Cuba, Puerto Rico, and Brazil: Race, Sexuality, and Nation at the Turn of the Century." Master's thesis, Georgetown University, 2002. 94 pp.
Padura Fuentes, Leonardo. *El viaje más largo.* [New ed.] San Juan, P.R.: Editorial Plaza Mayor, 2002. 294 pp. (Writings on folklore, social life, and customs)
Presswood, William K. "Cuba's New Middle Class." Master's thesis, University of West Georgia, 2002. 58 pp.
Price, Scott L. *Pitching around Fidel: A Journey into the Heart of Cuban Sports.* 1st Ecco paperback ed. New York: Ecco Press, 2002. 279 pp.
Rossiiskii, Mikhail Anatolevich. *Russkoe zarubezh'e na Kube: Stranitsy istorii.* Moscow: Veche, 2002. 221 pp. (Discusses the Russian presence in Cuba at the beginning of the twentieth century)
Santí, Enrico Mario. *Bienes del siglo: Sobre cultura cubana.* Mexico City: Fondo de Cultura Económica, 2002. 434 pp.
Scarpaci, Joseph L., Roberto Segre, and Mario Coyula. *Havana: Two Faces of the Antillean Metropolis.* Rev. ed. Chapel Hill: University of North Carolina Press, 2002. 437 pp.
Sierra Madero, Abel. *La nación sexuada: Relaciones de género y sexo en Cuba, 1830–1855.* Havana: Editorial de Ciencias Sociales, 2002. 108 pp.
Sweig, Julia E. *Inside the Cuban Revolution: Fidel Castro and the Urban Underground.* Cambridge, Mass.: Harvard University Press, 2002. 254 pp.
Unión de Periodistas de Cuba. *¿Libertad de prensa?* Havana: P. de la Torriente Editorial, 2002. 84 pp. (Papers presented at a conference sponsored by the Union)
Vázquez Díaz, René. *El sabor de Cuba.* Photographs by Merja Vázquez Díaz. Barcelona: Tusquets Editores, 2002. 213 pp. (Cookbook with colored photographs)
Vitier, Cintio. *Ese sol del mundo moral.* Havana: Unión de Escritores y Artistas de Cuba, 2002. 223 pp. (Reprint of the 1975 edition)
Wedel, Johan. "Santería Healing in Cuba." Ph.D. diss., Göteborg University, 2002. 179 pp.

Articles and Papers

Aguirre, Benigno E. "Social Control in Cuba." *Latin American Politics and Society* 44, no. 2 (Summer 2002): 67–98.
Altunaga Cantero, Lidia, et al. "Impacto de la evaluación sanitaria de cosméticos en Cuba en el último quinquenio." *Alimentaria* 39, no. 338 (2002): 129–33.
Arroyo, Jossianna. "Travestismos culturales: Tropicalismo y transculturación en Gilberto Freyre y Fernando Ortiz." *Estudios: Revista de Investigaciones Literarias y Culturales* 10, no. 19 (January–July 2002): 11–34.

Becerra de León, Berta. "Las revistas cubanas más importantes en los últimos 50 años" (The Most Important Cuban Magazines in the Last 50 Years). *Herencia* 8, no. 2 (Fall 2002): 74–83.
Behar, Ruth. "While Waiting for the Ferry to Cuba: Afterthoughts about *Adio Kerida*." *Michigan Quarterly Review* 41, pt. 4 (2002): 651–67. (Focuses on Cuba's Sephardic Jewish heritage)
Bermúdez, Silvia. "La Habana para un exiliado gallego: Manuel Curros Enriquez, *La Terra Gallega* y la modernidad nacional transatlántica." *MLN: Modern Language Notes* 117, no. 2 (2002): 331–42.
Branche, Jerome. "'Soul for Sale? Contrapunteo cubano en Madrid." *Estudios: Revista de Investigaciones Literarias y Culturales* 10, no. 19 (January–July 2002): 163–87. (Essay on the Cuban race question and the portrayal of blacks in popular culture)
Brundenius, Claes. "Cuba: The Retreat from Entitlement?" In *Exclusion and Engagement: Social Policy in Latin America*, edited by Christopher Abel and Colin M. Lewis, 336–48. London: Institute of Latin American Studies, University of London, 2002. (Discusses the social inequalities caused by the government's economic reforms)
Burchardt, Hans-Jürgen. "Contours of the Future: The New Social Dynamics in Cuba." *Latin American Perspectives* 29, no. 3 (May 2002): 57–74.
Caballero, Rufo. "Bailarina en la oscuridad: Una teleología de la resistencia en el retorno social y estético del cubano hoy." *Temas* 28 (January–March 2002): 36–43.
Carranza Valdés, Julio. "Culture and Development: Some Considerations for Debate." Translated by Richard Stoller. *Latin American Perspectives* 29, no. 4 (July 2002): 31–46.
Conangla Fontanillas, José. "Panorama del periodismo cubano" (Panorama of Cuban Journalism). *Herencia* 8, no. 2 (Fall 2002): 84–99.
D'Angelo Hernández, Ovidio S. "Cuba y los retos de la complejidad: Subjetividad social y desarrollo." *Temas* 28 (January–March 2002): 90–105.
Damián, Rodolfo. "¿Es la juventud cubana revolucionaria?" *Revista Hispano Cubana* 13 (May–September 2002): 15–16.
Daniels, Anthony. "Dubai, Havana, and Choosing between Evils." *New Criterion* 21, no. 2 (October 2002): 29–34. (Describes and compares visits to bookshops in both cities)
Dawdy, Shannon Lee. "'La comida mambisa': Food, Farming, and Cuban Identity, 1839–1999." *Nieuwe West Indische Gids/New West Indian Guide* 76, no. 1–2 (2002): 47–80.
Díaz, Jesús. "Los suicidios de la burguesía cubana y el dilema del futuro." *Encuentro de la Cultura Cubana* 23 (Winter 2001/2002): 86–88.
Dilla Alfonso, Haroldo, and Philip D. Oxhorn. "The Virtues and Misfortunes of Civil Society in Cuba." Translated by Juan Pereira Marsiaj. *Latin American Perspectives* 29, no. 4 (July 2002): 11–30.
Duno Gottberg, Luis. "La invención de la identidad de la mestiza: Reflexiones sobre la ideología del mestizaje cubano." *Estudios: Revista de Investigacones Literarias y Culturales* 10, no. 19 (January–July 2002): 35–64.
Fernández Cifontes, Flor María, and Mirtha Yordi García. "Estado y seguridad social:

Experiencia cubana." In *Política social y trabajo social,* edited by Nilsa M. Burgos Ortiz, 158–72. San Juan, P.R.: Proyecto Atlantea, Vicepresidencia para Asuntos Académicos e Investigación, Universidad de Puerto Rico, 2002.

Fowler Calzada, Víctor. "Estrategias para cuerpos tensos: Po(lí)(é)tica del cruce interracial." *Temas* 28 (January–March 2002): 107–19.

González, Ricardo. "El mundo era rectangular." *Revista Hispano Cubana* 13 (May–September 2002): 7–10. (Discusses the Cuban periodical *El Mundo*)

Grossman, Lawrence K. "TV Martí Has No Viewers: It's Time to Shut It Down." *Columbia Journalism Review* 40, no. 6 (March/April 2002): 69–70.

Guedes, Antonio. "La sanidad silenciada." *Encuentro de la Cultura Cubana* 24 (Spring 2002): 250–59. (Includes vital statistics)

Gutiérrez, Mariela A. "Réplica de Rómulo Lachatañeré a Fernando Ortiz." *Encuentro de la Cultura Cubana* 24 (Spring 2002): 267–73. (Discusses Lachatañeré's critique of *Los negros brujos* by Ortiz)

Hasson, Liliane. "¿Y en Francia qué?" *Revista Hispano Cubana* 12 (January–March 2002): 95–106. (Discusses French publishers of Cuban books)

Joseph, P. E. "Where Blackness Is Bright: Cuba, Africa, and Black Liberation during the Age of Civil Rights." *New Formations* 45 (2002): 111–24.

Landau, Saul. "The Day the Counterrevolutionaries Had Waited for Arrived: 'Y en eso llegó Fidel.'" *Latin American Perspectives* 29, no. 4 (July 2002):77–79. (About social conflict in Cuba)

Lanon, Philippe. "Cuba libro." *World Press Review* 49, no. 5 (May 2002): 42–44. (About books and booksellers in today's Cuba)

Losada Alvarez, Abel F. "Cuba 1898–1958: Modernización social y económica y descenso de la mortalidad." *Secuencia* 54 (September–December 2002): 39–65.

Lowenfish, Lee. "Full Count: Inside Cuban Baseball." *Journal of Baseball History and Culture* 10, no. 2 (2002): 166–68. (Review article)

Luna Martínez, María Victoria, et al. "Papel del 'Codex Alimentarius' en la nutrición e higiene de los alimentos en Cuba." *Alimentaria* 39, no. 330 (2002): 47–51.

Martínez Bauzá, Pedro. "Cuba: País de campeones" (Cuba: Land of Champions). *Herencia* 8, no. 2 (Fall 2002): 122–27. (About sports in Cuba)

Martínez Heredia, Fernando. "In the Furnace of the Nineties: Identity and Society in Cuba Today." *Boundary 2* 29, no. 3 (Fall 2002): 137–47.

Martínez-Fernández, Luis. "La frontera y la plantación: Reflexiones sobre dos claves para empezar a entender las culturas cubana y caribeña." In *Visitando la isla: Temas de historia de Cuba,* edited by Josef Opatrn'y and Consuelo Naranjo Orovio, 149–59. Münster, Ger.: AHILA; Madrid: Iberoamericana; Frankfurt: Vervuert, 2002.

Menéndez Pryce, César. "Afrocubano . . . Oh! No." *Revista Hispano Cubana* 12 (January–March 2002): 43–46.

Mesa-Lago, Carmelo. "La seguridad social." *Encuentro de la Cultura Cubana* 24 (Spring 2002): 238–49.

——. "La seguridad social: Bajo la Revolución, 1958–2002." *Encuentro de la Cultura Cubana* 25 (Summer 2002): 313–24. (Continues the above)

Muguercia, Magaly. "The Body and Its Politics in Cuba of the Nineties." *Boundary 2* 29, no. 3 (Fall 2002): 175–85. (Also published in Spanish—see below)

———. "El cuerpo y sus escenarios en la Cuba de los 90." *Apuntes*, no. 121 (2002): 124–30. (Also published in English — see above)
O'Brien, Glenn. "The Guayabera." *Gentlemen's Quarterly* 72, no. 7 (July 2002): 43–44. (Discusses the typical Cuban shirt)
Oberg, Larry R. "How Criminal Was Castro?" *Gay and Lesbian Review* 8, no. 6 (December 2001): 9–11. (Discusses Castro's treatment of gays)
Ortiz Hernández, Ernesto. "The Cuban Sociocultural Journal *Vitral*: The Freedom of Light." In *Creating Culture in Defiance: Spaces of Freedom*, edited by Els van der Plas, Malu Halassa, and Marlous Willemsen, 94–105. London: Saqi Books; The Hague: Prince Claus Fund Library, 2002.
Payen, Nikòl. "Lavalas: The Flood after the Flood." *Callaloo* 25, no. 3 (2002): 759–71. (Describes the experiences of a Haitian at Guantanamo Bay, Cuba)
Paz Sánchez, Manuel de. "El bandolerismo en Cuba: Acerca del estado de la cuestión." In *Visitando la isla: Temas de historia de Cuba*, edited by Josef Opatrn'y and Consuelo Naranjo Orovio, 133–48. Münster, Ger.: AHILA; Madrid: Iberoamericana; Frankfurt: Vervuert, 2002.
Pettavino, Paula J., and Geralyn Pye. "Sport in Cuba: Castro's Last Stand." In *Sports in Latin America*, edited by Joseph L. Arbena and David G. LaFrance, 145–62. Wilmington, Del: Scholarly Resources, 2002.
Phaf, Ineke. "Un cortocircuito en el 'relé' postcolonial: Wilfredo Lam, José Lezama Lima y la vanguardia colonial." *Estudios: Revista de Investigaciones Literarias y Culturales* 10, no. 19 (January–July 2002): 187–207.
Pino, Julio César. "Fernando Ortiz y Gilberto Freyre: Racismo, democracia racial y revolución." *Estudios: Revista de Investigaciones Literarias y Culturales* 10, no. 19 (January–July 2002): 73–89.
Power, Kevin. "Cuba: Una historia tras otra." In *Atravesados: Deslizamientos de identidad y género*, 68–89. Madrid: Fundación Telefónica, 2002.
Rodríguez Chávez, Ernest. "Notas sobre la identidad cubana en su relación con la diáspora." *Temas* 28 (January–March 2002): 44–55.
Sociedad de Periodistas Manuel Márquez Sterling. "Encuesta por la República: Cien dirigentes de la sociedad civil responden." *Revista Hispano Cubana* 13 (May–September 2002): 161.
"'Sociedad de Periodistas Manuel Márquez Sterling, Informe anual." *Revista Hispano Cubana* 12 (January–March 2002): 179–80.
Triff, Soren. "La sociedad civil y la perspectiva cultural." *Herencia* 8, no. 2 (Fall 2002): 8–15. ("Para Calixto Masó y Vázquez: in memoriam en el 80 aniversario de la presentación de *El carácter cubano*")
Valero, Arnaldo E. "Nación y transculturación en la etnología y la narrativa cubana." *Revista de Investigaciones Literarias y Culturales* 10, no. 19 (January–July 2002): 55–71.
Valle Rojas, Ramón. "Del color púrpura." *Revista Hispano Cubana* 12 (January–March 2002): 47–54. (Discusses the theme of racism in Rolando Díaz's 1998 videorecording *Si me comprendieras*)
Vásquez, Miguel. "Cultural Integrity in Non-Traditional Societies: Cuba Encounters the Global Market System." *Cultural Dynamics* 14, no. 2 (2002): 185–204.

Vilar, Alberto A. "Las comunicaciones en Cuba." *Herencia* 8, no. 2 (Fall 2002): 100–13.
Welch, Matt. "Foul Ball: How a Communist Dictatorship and a U.S. Embargo Silenced a Cuban Historian." *Reason* 34, pt. 2 (2002): 50–54. (About Cuban baseball historian Severo Nieto)

Architecture and Urban Development

Books and Monographs

Castro Martín, Elvia Rosa, and Concepción Otero, eds. *Arquitectura cubana: Metamorfosis, pensamiento y crítica*. Havana: Artecubano Ediciones [y] Consejo Nacional de las Artes Plásticas, 2002. 115 pp.
Pietropaolo, Vincenzo, and Cecelia Elisabeth Burke Lawless. *Making Home in Havana*. New Brunswick, N.J.: Rutgers University Press, 2002. 115 pp. (Photographs by Pietropaolo; text by Lawless)
Taylor-Foley, Kristin Elaine. "Remembering Havana's Gran Hotel El Trotcha: Preserving the Ruins of an Historic Hotel as a Social Club and Adapting the Site for Multifamily Housing." Master's thesis, University of Washington, 2002. 65 pp.

Articles and Papers

Alepuz, Manuel, and Humberto Valdés-Ríos. "The Urban Transportation in Time of Crisis: The Case of Havana." In *Urban Mobility for All: Proceedings of the Tenth International CODATU Conference, Lomé, Togo, 12–15 November 2002,* 547–51. Lisse and Exton, Pa.: A. A. Balkema, 2002.
Kepecs, Susan. "Saving Old Havana." *Archaeology* 55, no. 2 (March–April 2002): 42–47. (Discusses restoration projects)
Martín, Baltasar. "Arte y arquitectura: Un divorcio a la cubana — ¿Hay futuro para un patrimonio arquitectónico que a duras penas sobrevive el presente?" *Encuentro de la Cultura Cubana* 23 (Winter 2001/2002): 55–61.
Merino Acosta, Luz, et al. "Hacer la ciudad." *Temas* 28 (January–March 2002): 56–77. (Round table on urbanization in Cuba)

The Arts (Performing Arts)

Books and Monographs

Acosta, Leonardo. *Descarga número dos: El jazz en Cuba, 1950–2000*. Havana: Unión de Escritores y Artistas de Cuba, 2002. 214 pp.
Alonso Grau, Alpidio, ed.. *Otros alzan las cabezas: Cancionero de la joven trova santaclareña*. Santa Clara, Cuba: Ediciones Sed de Belleza, 2002. 76 pp. (Chiefly song texts; some with melody line)
Cedeño Pineda, Reinaldo, and Michel Damián Suárez. *Son de la loma: Los dioses de la música cantan en Santiago de Cuba*. Havana: Editora Musical de Cuba, 2002. 272 pp.
Chang Melis, Leiling. *Métissages et résonnances: Essais sur la musique et la littérature cubaines*. Paris: L'Harmattan, 2002. 202 pp.

Delgado, Kevin Miguel. "Iyesa: Afro-Cuban Music and Culture in Contemporary Cuba." Ph.D. diss., University of California at Los Angeles, 2001. 514 pp.

Kirk, John M., and Leonardo Padura Fuentes. *La cultura y la Revolución Cubana: Conversaciones en La Habana.* San Juan, P.R.: Editorial Plaza Mayor, 2002. 342 pp. (Interviews with Cuban artists, writers, and musicians; also published in English under title *Culture and the Cuban Revolution*)

Leymarie, Isabelle. *Cuban Fire: The Story of Salsa and Latin Jazz.* London and New York: Continuum, 2002. 394 pp. (Original French edition has title *Cuban Fire: Musiques populaires d'expression cubaine*)

Lobato Morchón, Ricardo. *El teatro del absurdo en Cuba, 1948–1968.* Madrid: Editorial Verbum, 2002. 333 pp.

Lobo, Eric. *Son de Cuba.* Barcelona: Barataria Ediciones, 2002. 153 pp. (Includes a compact disc)

Montes Huidobro, Matías. *El teatro cubano en el vórtice del compromiso, 1959–1961.* Miami: Ediciones Universal, 2002. 309 pp.

Moore, Robin D. *Música y mestizaje: Revolución artística y cambio social en La Habana, 1920–1940.* Madrid: Editorial Colibrí, 2002. 362 pp. (American edition has title *Nationalizing Blackness*)

Newman, David. "Demystifying the Latin Question: Afro-Cuban and Brazilian Drumming in Small Combo Jazz." B.A. thesis, Polytechnic State University, 2002. 1 vol. (Various pagings)

Rey Alfonso, Francisco. *Grandes momentos del ballet romántico en Cuba.* Havana: Editorial Letras Cubanas, 2002. 282 pp.

Río Prado, Enrique. *La Venus de bronce: Hacia una historia de la zarzuela cubana.* Boulder, Colo.: Society of Spanish and Spanish American Studies, 2002. 413 pp.

Roy, Maya. *Cuban Music: From Son and Rumba to the Buena Vista Social Club and Timba Cubana.* Translated by Denise Asfar and Gabriel Asfar. Princeton, N.J.: Markus Wiener Publishers, 2002. 246 pp. (Translation of *Musiques cubaines*)

Streng, Sarah B. "Self-Reflection of Learning for an Afro-Cuban Dance Class in a Community Setting." Master's thesis, University of California at Los Angeles, 2002. 195 pp.

Thomas, Susan R. "Lo más femenino de los géneros: Gender, Race, and Representation in the Cuban Zarzuela, 1927–1944." Ph.D. diss., Brandeis University, 2002. 334 pp.

Articles and Papers

Aparicio, Frances R. "La Lupe, la India, and Celia: Toward a Feminist Genealogy of Salsa Music." In *Situating Salsa: Global Markets and Local Meanings in Latin Popular Music,* edited by Lise Waxer, 135–60. New York: Routledge, 2002. (Features two Cuban singers and one Puerto Rican singer)

Arrizón, Alicia. "Race-ing Performativity through Transculturation, Taste, and the Mulata Body." *Theatre Research International* 27, no. 2 (2002): 136–52.

Benarós, León. "Brindis de Salas en Buenos Aires: De la fama a la más penosa ruina." *Todo Es Historia* 35, no. 416 (March 2002): 50–51. (About Cuban violinist Claudio José Domingo Brindis de Salas)

Chanan, Michael. "We Are Losing All Our Values: Interview with Tomás Gutiérrez Alea." *Boundary 2* 29, no. 3 (Fall 2002): 47–52. (Gutiérrez Alea is a Cuban filmmaker commenting on the island's film industry)
Díaz Ayala, Cristóbal. "Buscando la melodía: La música popular cubana de 1902 a 1959." *Encuentro de la Cultura Cubana* 24 (Spring 2002): 79–93.
Durbin, Paula. "Review of Ballet Nacional de Cuba Performing Giselle, Choreographed by Alicia Alonso, at the Opera House, John F. Kennedy Center for the Performing Arts, Washington, D.C., Nov. 20–25, 2001." *Dance Magazine* (March 2002): 78–79.
Guillot Carvajal, Mario L. "¿De dónde son los cantantes?" *Revista Hispano Cubana* 12 (January–March 2002): 55–60. (Analyzes recent Cuban popular music)
Hernández, Rafael, et al. "La música popular como espejo social." *Temas* 29 (April–June 2002): 61–80. (Round table)
Loza, Steven Joseph. "Poncho Sánchez, Latin Jazz, and the Cuban 'Son': A Stylistic and Social Analysis." In *Situating Salsa: Global Markets and Local Meanings in Latin Popular Music,* edited by Lise Waxer, 201–15. New York: Routledge, 2002.
Matos, Dennys. "Los nuevos cantautores cubanos." *Revista Hispano Cubana* 12 (January–March 2002): 207–12.
Moore, Robin D. "Echale salsita: El 'son' y la revolución musical en La Habana." *Estudios: Revista de Investigaciones Literarias y Culturales* 10, no. 19 (January–July 2002): 229–44.
———. "La fiebre de la rumba." *Encuentro de la Cultura Cubana* 23 (Winter 2001/2002): 175–94.
———. "Salsa and Socialism: Dance Music in Cuba, 1959–99." In *Situating Salsa: Global Markets and Local Meanings in Latin Popular Music,* edited by Lise Waxer, 51–74. New York: Routledge, 2002.
Neustadt, Robert. "Buena Vista Social Club versus La Charanga Habanera: The Politics of Cuban Rhythm." *Journal of Popular Music Studies* 14, no. 2 (2002): 139–62.
Olavarría, Margot. "Rap and Revolution: Hip-Hop Comes to Cuba." *NACLA Report on the Americas* 35, no. 6 (May–June 2002): 28–32.
Olivares Baró, Carlos. "Ni salsa ni son, baila con Timba: El fenómeno musical cubano más importante de fines de siglo, a pesar de sus escépticos, se abre paso igual que sus hermanos de décadas anteriores." *Encuentro de la Cultura Cubana* 23 (Winter 2001/2002):195–97.
Perna, Vincenzo. "Dancing the Crisis, Singing the Past: Musical Dissonances in Cuba during the 'Período Especial.'" *Journal of Latin American Cultural Studies* 11, no. 2 (August 2002): 213–29.
Sánchez León, Miguel. "Cuba: En torno a los proyectos teatrales de los '90." *Gestos* 17, no. 33 (April 2002): 145–62.
Turnley, David. "Documenting the Rhythms of Cuba." *Nieman Reports* 56, no. 1 (2002): 93–97. (A photographer uses digital video to capture the passion and grittiness of contemporary Cuba)
Vega, Aurelio de la. "Nostalgia que no muere: La música clásica en la República." *Encuentro de la Cultura Cubana* 24 (Spring 2002): 68–78.

The Arts (Visual)

Books and Monographs

Bozzi, Pénélope de, and Ernesto Oroza. *Objets réinventés: La création populaire à Cuba.* Paris: Alternatives, 2002. 125 pp.

Budelman, Shannon Nicole. " 'Especially the Mulato Ones Like to Dance': Cuban Films and Discourses of Ethnic Difference." Honors thesis, Western Washington University, 2002. 35 pp.

Caprile, Luciano, ed. *Wilfredo Lam: Cuba-Italia, un percorso.* Milan, Italy: Cinisello Balsamo, 2002. (Exhibition catalog)

Cien años del paisaje cubano, 1850 a 1959 (One Hundred Years of Cuban Landscape, 1850 to 1950). Coral Gables, Fla.: Cernuda Arte, 2002. 40 pp. (Exhibition catalog)

González, Reynaldo. *Cine cubano: Ese ojo que nos ve.* San Juan, P.R.: Plaza Mayor Editorial, 2002. 211 pp.

Independencia e identidad: En el centenario de la República de Cuba (Independence and Identity: The Hundredth Anniversary of the Cuban Republic). Miami: Cuban Masters Collection (CMC), 2002. 45 pp. (Catalog of paintings)

Kassamali, Sorayya. " 'Memorias del subdesarrollo': Decolonizations of the Spectator — An Analysis of Tomás Gutiérrez Alea's Cuban Revolutionary Film." Honors thesis in Humanities, State University of New York at Binghamton, 2002. 81 pp.

Korda, Alberto. *Cuba par Korda: Photographies.* Edited by Christophe Loviny. Paris: Calmann-Lévy, 2002. 156 pp.

Kunst aus Kuba: Sammlung Ludwig (Art from Cuba: The Ludwig Collection). Bad Breisig, Ger.: Palace Editions, 2002. 239 pp. (Catalog of an exhibition, held 15 April–3 June 2002, at the Ludwig Museum, St. Petersburg; in English, German, and Russian)

Lapique Becali, Zoila. *La memoria en las piedras.* Havana: Ediciones Boloña, 2002. 217 pp. (Discusses the art of lithography in colonial Havana)

Leymarie, Jean, and André Breton, eds. *Agustín Cárdenas: Desire and Grace, May 16–July 13, 2002.* New York: Dominique Haim Chanin Fine Arts Center, 2002. 48 pp. (Exhibition catalog of works by the Cuban sculptor)

Maldonado González, Sonia, ed. *Wilfredo Lam: Mito y convivencia — Centenario, 18 de julio–15 de septiembre, 2002.* Havana: Museo Nacional de Bellas Artes, 2002. 81 pp.

Roldán, Alberto. *La mirada viva.* Miami: Ediciones Universal, 2002. 371 pp. (Discusses the internal structure of the Instituto de Arte e Industria Cinematográfica de Cuba [ICAIC] and the island's film industry)

Salon de Arte Cubano Contemporáneo. *Catálogo.* 3rd Catalog, 2001, Havana. Havana: Centro de Desarrollo de las Artes Visuales, 2002. 73 pp.

Sims, Lowery Stokes. *Wilfredo Lam and the International Avant–Garde, 1923–1982.* Austin: University of Texas Press, 2002. 281 pp.

Uhrhane, Jennifer, Lou Jones, and Peter Kayafas. *Two Views of Cuba: An Exhibition Held January 19–March 17, 2002, DeCordova Museum and Sculpture Park, Lincoln, Massachusetts.* Lincoln, Mass.: The Museum, 2002. 1 vol. (unpaged). (Text by Jennifer Uhrhane; photographs by Lou Jones and Peter Kayafas)

Veigas, José, et al. *Cuban Art of the Twentieth Century.* Los Angeles: California/International Arts Foundation, 2002. 576 pp. (Accompanying CD-ROM contains artists' biographies)

Articles and Papers

Adell, Elena. "*Pon tu pensamiento en mí* y *El elefante y la bicicleta*: El protagonismo del cine dentro de la filmografía cubana." *Torre de Papel* 12, no. 1–2 (Spring–Summer 2002): 63–81. (Discusses the films by Arturo Sotto Díaz and Juan Carlos Tabío)

Alvarez, Lupe. "Un acercamiento cómplice a la obra de Saidel Brito." In *Atravesados: Deslizamientos de identidad y género.* Madrid: Fundación Telefónica, 2002: 30–35.

———. "Contar en Cuba: El relato y la sospecha." In *Atravesados: Deslizamientos de identidad y género,* 26–29. Madrid: Fundación Telefónica, 2002.

Ballester, Juan Pablo. "Soñando en cubano." In *Atravesados: Deslizamientos de identidad y género,* 36–43. Madrid: Fundación Telefónica, 2002.

Birbragher, Francine. "Humberto Castro: Museum of Art, Fort Lauderdale." *Art Nexus* 43 (January–March 2002): 108–9. (Discusses the first individual exhibition of the Cuban painter's work in a U.S. museum)

Blanco de la Cruz, Caridad. "Agustín Bejarano: Fundación Habana Club." *Art Nexus* 45 (July/September 2002): 101–2.

Boyce, David B. "Grimshaw-Gudewicz Gallery at Bristol Community College/Fall River: Maferefún — African Spirituality in Cuban Art." *Art New England* 23, no. 3 (April/May 2002): 33–34.

Castro Flórez, Fernando. "Ropa vieja." In *Atravesados: Deslizamientos de identidad y género,* 44–51. Madrid: Fundación Telefónica, 2002.

Chattopdhyay, Collette. "Raúl Corrales: Courtier Gallery." *Art Nexus* 45 (July/September 2002): 104–5.

Dalton, Trinie. "Los Carpinteros." Translated by Eva Golinger. *Bomb* 78 (Winter 2001/2002): 60–65. (Discusses the trio of Cuban sculptors)

Eligio Fernández, Antonio. "The Island, the Map, the Travelers: Notes on Recent Developments in Cuban Art." Translated by Kenya Dworkin. *Boundary 2* 29, no. 3 (Fall 2002): 77–89.

———. "Tania Bruguera." *Art Nexus* 46 (October–December 2002): 99.

Espinosa, Carlos. "Umberto Peña: De la madurez a la excelencia." *Encuentro de la Cultura Cubana* 25 (Summer 2002): 303–12. (Mostly illustrated; includes the painter's biography as well as a list of his works)

González Alfonso, Ricardo. "El Bobo de Abela en la isla del doctor Castro." *Encuentro de la Cultura Cubana* 24 (Spring 2002): 335–36. (Discusses a well-known local caricature)

González-Mora, Magda. "Market and Seduction in the Contemporary Cuban Art Scene." *Make: The Magazine of Women's Art* 92 (2002): 41–43.

Hernández, Erena. "Carlos Garaicoa: From Ruins to Desire." *Art Nexus* 44 (April–June 2002): 44–49.

———. "Museo Nacional de Bellas Artes." Photographs by Oscar Camaraza. *Art Nexus* 43 (January–March 2002): 68–69.

Herrera Ysla, Nelson. "Wifredo Lam in His Other House: Centro de Arte Contemporáneo Wifredo Lam, Havana, Cuba." *Art Nexus* 45 (July/September 2002): 18–19.
Kupfer, Mónica. "Arturo Montoto: Legacy Fine Art." *Art Nexus* 43 (January–March 2002): 122–23. (Discusses the Cuban painter)
Lauren, Stacey. "University Art Museum/Albany: Passionately Cuban — Nine Artists from Habana." *Art New England* 23, no. 2 (February/March 2002): 43.
Lauro Pino-Escalante, Alberto. "Clara Morera: Musa errante." *Revista Hispano Cubana* 12 (January–March 2002): 227–34. (Provides an analysis of the painter's works as well as biographical details)
León, Dermis P. "Havana, Biennial, Tourism: The Spectacle of Utopia." *Art Journal* 60, no. 4 (Winter 2001): 68–73. (About the Havana Biennial, established in 1984, which is, after the São Paulo Biennial, the most important international art biennial in the Western Hemisphere)
Loy, Ramón. "Los dibujantes en el periodismo cubano en los 50 años de la República" (Illustrators in Cuban Journalism, 1902–1958). *Herencia* 8, no. 2 (Fall 2002): 114–21.
Miles, Christopher. "Los Carpinteros: Your Home Is My Home — The Global Familiarity." *Art Nexus* 45 (July–September 2002): 28–31. (About the trio of Cuban sculptors)
Morejón, Nancy. "Elogio de Manuel Mendive." *Casa de las Américas* 226 (January–March 2002): 146–48. (Mendive is a contemporary Cuban painter)
Mosquera, Gerardo. "La isla infinita: Introducción al nuevo arte cubano." In *Atravesados: Deslizamientos de identidad y género*, 52–61. Madrid: Fundación Telefónica, 2002.
"Una muestra de pintores de la República." *Encuentro de la Cultura Cubana* 24 (Spring 2002): 343–60. (Chiefly illustrated)
Navarrete, William. "El quinquenio dorado de la pintura cubana, 1940–1945." *Encuentro de la Cultura Cubana* 24 (Spring 2002): 337–42.
"Obras." In *Atravesados: Deslizamientos de identidad y género*, 97–171. Madrid: Fundación Telefónica, 2002. (Biographies and works of: Juan Abreu, Pedro Alvarez, Juan Pablo Ballester, Saidel Brito, Raúl Cordero, Douglas Darnis, Inés Garrido, Kcho [Alexis Leyva], Los Carpinteros, Armando Mariño, Ibrahim Miranda, Elsa Mora, Heriberto Mora, Gabinete Ordo Amoria, Sandra Ramos, Lázaro Saavedra, Esterio Segura, and Vincench Barrera)
Paranaguá, Paulo Antonio. "Diálogo y contemporaneidad en el cine de Jesús Díaz." *Encuentro de la Cultura Cubana* 25 (Summer 2002): 28–33. ("Homenaje a Jesús Díaz")
Ponte, Antonio José. "Cine cubano: Nada." *Encuentro de la Cultura Cubana* 23 (Winter 2001/2002): 226–30.
Rodríguez-Mangual, Edna. "Driving a Dead Body through the Nation: Death and Allegory in the Film *Guantanamera*." *Chasqui* 31, no. 4 (May 2002): 50–61.
Roth, Charlene. "Los Carpinteros: Los Angeles County Museum of Art." *Sculpture* 21, no. 5 (June 2002): 64–65. (Discusses Cuban sculptors)
Santana, Andrés Isaac. "Waldo Balart y el exorcismo de la pintura." *Revista Hispano Cubana* 13 (May–September 2002): 217–22.

Shulman, Ken. "Photographing in Cuba: Beyond the Buena Vista." *Graphis* 337 (2002): 14–18.
"Sobre Tomás Sánchez." *Encuentro de la Cultura Cubana* 23 (Winter 2001/2002): 232–40. (Chiefly illustrated)
Strut, Rachel. "Cuba Calling." *Art New England* 23, no. 5 (August/September 2002): 12–14, 67.
Toledo Sande, Luis. "Nuez con Guillén." *Casa de las Américas* 228 (July–September 2002): 136–41. (Discusses the exposition of drawings by René de la Nuez at the Galería Latinoamericana of the Casa de las Américas, held 28 June 2002; all drawings feature themes popularized by Nicolás Guillén)
Webster, Mary Hull. "'Photographic Memory and other Shots in the Dark' at Galería de la Raza." *Artweek* 33, no. 4 (May 2002): 19–20. (Discusses the exhibition by Cuban artist Carolina Ponce de León)
Weinstein, Joel. "Bad Painting and Tired Revolutionaries." *Art Papers* 26, no. 2 (March/April 2002): 14–15.
Zaya, Antonio. "Lecturas fragmentarias, sincréticas, promiscuas y superpuestas: Sobre la diferencia cubana en la plástica de los ochentas." In *Atravesados: Deslizamientos de identidad y género*, 90–95. Madrid: Fundación Telefónica, 2002.

Bibliography and Information Science

Books and Monographs

García-Carranza, Araceli, and Josefina García-Carranza. *Biobibliografía de Lisandro Otero*. Havana: Editorial Letras Cubanas, 2002. 269 pp.
Montalvo, Berta G. *Indice bibliográfico de la "Revista de La Habana," 1930*. Miami: Ediciones Universal, 2002. (Includes a CD with all the articles published in the periodical)
Scott, Rebecca J., et al. *Societies after Slavery: A Select Annotated Bibliography of Printed Sources on Cuba, Brazil, British Colonial Africa, South Africa, and the British West Indies*. Pittsburgh: University of Pittsburgh Press, 2002. 411 pp.

Articles and Papers

Goslinga, Marian. "Recent Work in Cuban Studies." *Cuban Studies* 32 (2001): 199–229. (Comprehensive bibliography, organized by subject, of monographs, articles, papers, databases, etc. published on Cuba during 2002; includes Cubans abroad)
Kempf, Andrea. "Viva Cuba!: Contemporary Fiction." *Library Journal* 127, no. 6 (April 2002): 168.

Biography

Books and Monographs

Alba, Alvaro. *Almas gemelas: Las vidas de Castro y Stalin con sus puntos de convergencia*. Madrid: Libroslibres, 2002. 164 pp.

Alberto, Eliseo. *Informe contra mí mismo*. 2d ed. Madrid: Alfaguara/Santillana, 2002. 357 pp. (Autobiographical treatise by the Cuban author)
Barnet, Miguel. *Cimarrón: Historia de un esclavo*. Madrid: Siruela Ediciones, 2002. 224 pp.
Braun, Paul F. "Passage to War: A Missing Chapter in the Life of a Cuban Legend — José Martí's Journey to Join the Cuban Revolution of 1895." Master's thesis, Valdosta State University, 2002. 126 pp.
Cartaya Cotta, Perla. *El legado del Padre Varela*. 2nd ed. Mexico City: Obra Nacional de la Buena Prensa, 2002. 256 pp.
Connolly, Sean. *Castro*. London: Hodder and Stoughton, 2002. 96 pp.
Contreras, Félix. ed.. *Yo conocí a Benny Moré*. Havana: Unión de Escritores y Artistas de Cuba, 2002. 176 pp. (Moré is a well-known Cuban musician)
Costa, Octavio Ramón. *Caruca (1917–2000)*. Miami: Ediciones Universal, 2002. 176 pp. (Autobiographical treatise by a Cuban historian)
Dathe, Wilfried, and Rosa María González López. *Johann Christoph Gundlach, 1810–1896: Un naturalista en Cuba*. Marburg an der Lahn, Ger.: Basilisken Presse, 2002. 245 pp.
Hagemann, Albrecht. *Fidel Castro*. München, Ger.: Deutscher Taschenbuch Verlag, 2002. 188 pp.
Leante, César. *Volviendo la mirada*. Miami: Ediciones Universal, 2002. 203 pp. (Autobiography of the Cuban politician)
Masetti, Jorge. *In the Pirate's Den: My Life as a Secret Agent for Castro*. San Francisco: Encounter Books, 2002. 164 pp.
Matos, Huber. *Cómo llegó la noche*. Barcelona: Tusquets Editores, 2002. 589 pp. (Autobiographical)
Morales, Larry. *El jefe del Pelotón Suicida*. Havana: Casa Editora Abril, 2002. 236 pp. (Biography of Roberto Rodríguez Fernández)
Oltuski, Enrique. *Vida clandestina: My Life in the Cuban Revolution*. Translated by Thomas and Carol Christensen. San Francisco: Wiley, 2002. 302 pp. (Translation of *Gente del llano*)
Pin Vilar, Juan. *Santiago Feliú: Un hippie en el comunismo*. Madrid: Fundación Autor, 2002. 86 pp. (Biography of and interviews with the Cuban musician)
Rodríguez, José Ignacio. *Vida del presbítero Don Félix Varela*. Miami: Editorial Cubana, 2002. 448 pp.
Sanclemente, Vicenç. *La Habana no es una isla: Crónica de un corresponsal en Cuba*. Barcelona: Jaque Mate Comunicacón, 2002. 319 pp. (Personal reminiscences)
Skierka, Volker. *Fidel*. Barcelona: Martínez Roca Ediciones, 2002. 589 pp. (Originally published in German under the title *Fidel Castro, eine Biographie*)
Suárez León, Carmen. *José Martí et Victor Hugo: Au carrefour des modernités*. Translated by Jacques-François Bonaldi. Paris: Temps des Cerises, 2002. 193 pp. (Translation of *José Martí y Victor Hugo en el fiel de las modernidades*)
Viñalet, Ricardo. *Fernando Ortiz ante las secuelas del 98: Un regeneracionismo transculturado*. Havana: Fundación Fernando Ortiz, 2001. 177 pp.
White, Charles W. *Alejandro García Caturla: A Cuban Composer in the Twentieth Century*. Lanham, Md.: Scarecrow Press, 2002. (Biography of the Afro-Cuban composer)

Articles and Papers

Alcides, Rafael. "Carta." *Encuentro de la Cultura Cubana* 25 (Summer 2002): 93–94. ("Homenaje a Jesús Díaz")

Alonso, Aurelio. "Pensando en Jesús, ausente ya." *Encuentro de la Cultura Cubana* 25 (Summer 2002): 62–64. ("Homenaje a Jesús Díaz")

Anreus, Alejandro. "Las cartas de un enajenado en el trópico." *Encuentro de la Cultura Cubana* 23 (Winter 2001/2002): 51–83.

"Antonio Benítez Rojo: Entrevisto." *Encuentro de la Cultura Cubana* 23 (Winter 2001/2002): 9–15.

Argote-Freyre, Frank. "The Political Afterlife of Eduardo Chibás: Evolution of a Symbol, 1951–1991." *Cuban Studies* 32 (2001): 74–97. (Chibás was a well-known Cuban politician)

Benítez Rojo, Antonio. "Jesús en dos momentos." *Encuentro de la Cultura Cubana* 25 (Summer 2002): 96–97. ("Homenaje a Jesús Díaz")

Böhringerr, Astrid. "Una perspectiva muy personal." *Encuentro de la Cultura Cubana* 25 (Summer 2002): 124. ("Homenaje a Jesús Díaz")

Burgos-Debray, Elizabeth. "La carta que nunca te envié." *Encuentro de la Cultura Cubana* 25 (Summer 2002): 51–61. ("Homenaje a Jesús Díaz")

Castañeda, Jorge. "Una postura políticamente congruente." *Encuentro de la Cultura Cubana* 25 (Summer 2002): 99. ("Homenaje a Jesús Díaz")

Céspedes, Carlos Manuel de. "Breve testimonio de un agradecido amigo de la periferia." *Encuentro de la Cultura Cubana* 25 (Summer 2002): 100–1. ("Homenaje a Jesús Díaz")

Crespo, Paul. "Castro's Connections: Is the Anti-American Dictator Acting as a Nexus for Terror Groups and Rogue States?" *American Legion Magazine* 152, no. 4: 32–36.

Debray, Régis. "Fiel a sí mismo." *Encuentro de la Cultura Cubana* 25 (Summer 2002): 95. ("Homenaje a Jesús Díaz")

"Del epistolario de Dulce María Loynaz." *Casa de las Américas* 228 (July–September 2002): 119–35. (Facsimiles of letters to and from the author)

Dénis, Jean Claude. "Une reine à la Havane." *Danser* 208 (March 2002): 22–24. (Biography of Cuban bailerina Alicia Alonso)

Dezcallar, Rafael. "Un hombre casi renacentista." *Encuentro de la Cultura Cubana* 25 (Summer 2002): 105. ("Homenaje a Jesús Díaz")

Díaz, Amalia. "Alguién especial." *Encuentro de la Cultura Cubana* 25 (Summer 2002): 83–84. ("Homenaje a Jesús Díaz")

Díaz Martínez, Manuel. "Jesús." *Encuentro de la Cultura Cubana* 25 (Summer 2002): 7–9. ("Homenaje a Jesús Díaz")

Díaz Rodríguez, Rolando. "Mi hermano Jesús: Ráfagas de la memoria." *Encuentro de la Cultura Cubana* 25 (Summer 2002): 75–84. ("Homenaje a Jesús Díaz")

Elorza, Antonio. "Fidel Castro, el poder y la máscara." *Letras Libres* 4, no. 47 (November 2002): 48–54.

"En la prensa internacional." *Encuentro de la Cultura Cubana* 25 (Summer 2002): 136–40. (Transcripts of articles about Jesús Díaz accompanied by a portrait)

Espinosa Domínguez, Carlos. "Un dramaturgo de obra breve." *Encuentro de la Cultura Cubana* 25 (Summer 2002): 34–37. ("Homenaje a Jesús Díaz")

Fernández Larrea, Ramón. "Carta a Alberto Yarini." *Encuentro de la Cultura Cubana* 24 (Spring 2002): 125–28.
———. "Carta a Bonifacio Byrne." *Encuentro de la Cultura Cubana* 24 (Spring 2002): 13–16.
———. "Carta a Capablanca." *Encuentro de la Cultura Cubana* 24 (Spring 2002): 148–51.
———. "Carta a Chan Li Pó." *Encuentro de la Cultura Cubana* 24 (Spring 2002): 235–37.
———. "Carta a Dámaso Pérez Prado." *Encuentro de la Cultura Cubana* 24 (Spring 2002): 313–15.
———. "Carta a Kid Chocolate." *Encuentro de la Cultura Cubana* 24 (Spring 2002): 279–82.
———."Carta a Ramón Fonst." *Encuentro de la Cultura Cubana* 24 (Spring 2002): 50–52.
———. "Carta Sindo Garay." *Encuentro de la Cultura Cubana* 24 (Spring 2002): 262–65.
———. "Carta al Andarín Félix Carvajal." *Encuentro de la Cultura Cubana* 24 (Spring 2002): 94–96.
———. "Carta al Caballero de París." *Encuentro de la Cultura Cubana* 24 (Spring 2002): 331–34.
———. "La importancia de llamarse Ernesto: A los 30 años de la muerte de Ernest Miller Hemingway." *Revista Hispano Cubana* 12 (January–March 2002): 77–81.
Fornet, Ambrosio. "Jesús en la memoria." *Encuentro de la Cultura Cubana* 25 (Summer 2002): 42–50. ("Homenaje a Jesús Díaz")
Fuente, Alejandro de la. "Manuel Moreno Fraginals (1920–2001)." *Hispanic American Historical Review* 82, no. 1 (February 2002): 121–24.
Goldenberg, Jorge. "El lugar imposible." *Encuentro de la Cultura Cubana* 25 (Summer 2002): 111–12. ("Homenaje a Jesús Díaz")
González, Felipe. "Lo que retengo." *Encuentro de la Cultura Cubana* 25 (Summer 2002): 91–92. ("Homenaje a Jesús Díaz")
González, Gilda. "Jesús González de Armas (1934–2002)." *Art Nexus* 46 (October–December 2002): 56. (The artist's obituary)
González Alfonso, Ricardo. "De la esperanza al paredón." *Encuentro de la Cultura Cubana* 24 (Spring 2002): 306–12. (Personal reminiscences during the Revolution)
González Echevarría, Roberto. "Los días de Jesús." *Encuentro de la Cultura Cubana* 25 (Summer 2002): 91–92. ("Homenaje a Jesús Díaz")
González Freire, Natividad. *Descubriendo a Fidel Castro.* Madrid: Editorial Pliegos, 2002. 368 pp. (Autobiography of the actress currently living in exile)
Guelbenzu, José María. "El amigo habanero." *Encuentro de la Cultura Cubana* 25 (Summer 2002): 115–16. ("Homenaje a Jesús Díaz")
Guerrero, Gustavo. "Jesús Díaz: Ilusión y desilusión." *Encuentro de la Cultura Cubana* 25 (Summer 2002): 10–18. ("Homenaje a Jesús Díaz")
Lauro, Alberto. "Responso y diatriba: A Jesus Díaz in memoriam" [poema]. *Encuentro de la Cultura Cubana* 25 (Summer 2002): 113–14. ("Homenaje a Jesús Díaz")
Lázaro, Felipe. "Juan Manuel Salvat: Decano de los editores cubanos." *Revista Hispano Cubana* 13 (May–September 2002): 29–32.

Lorenzo Fuentes, José. "A la mayor brevedad posible." *Encuentro de la Cultura Cubana* 25 (Summer 2002): 125–26. ("Homenaje a Jesús Díaz")

Manet, Eduardo. "Jesús Díaz y Le Flore." *Encuentro de la Cultura Cubana* 25 (Summer 2002): 127–28. ("Homenaje a Jesús Díaz")

Marinas, José Miguel. "Fábula del bazar americano: Martí y la cultura del consumo." *Temas* 29 (April–June 2002): 21–35.

Monsiváis, Carlos. "Jesús Díaz, el memorioso." *Encuentro de la Cultura Cubana* 25 (Summer 2002): 102–3. ("Homenaje a Jesús Díaz")

Nordlinger, Jay. "'I Can't Just Do Nothing.'" *National Review* 54, no. 4 (March 2002): 26–28. (Biography of Maritza Lugo Fernández, one of Cuba's most famous political prisoners)

Nuez, Iván de la. "El intelectual, el corazón y la piel." *Encuentro de la Cultura Cubana* 25 (Summer 2002): 39–41. ("Homenaje a Jesús Díaz")

O'Donnell, Rosie. "Viva Gloria." *Rosie* 129, no. 6 (April 2002): 70–77. (About Cuban American singer Gloria Estefan)

Ocasio, Rafael. "Gays and the Cuban Revolution: The Case of Reinaldo Arenas." *Latin American Perspectives* 29, no. 2 (March 2002): 78–98.

Ordoqui, Joaquín. "Jesús Díaz: La intensidad de lo cotidiano." *Encuentro de la Cultura Cubana* 25 (Summer 2002): 19–23. ("Homenaje a Jesús Díaz")

Ortega, Julio. "Concurrencia de Jesús Díaz." *Encuentro de la Cultura Cubana* 25 (Summer 2002): 24–27 ("Homenaje a Jesús Díaz")

Pomar, Jorge A. "Jesús: El cubano perfectible." *Encuentro de la Cultura Cubana* 25 (Summer 2002): 69–73. ("Homenaje a Jesús Díaz")

Prieto Benavent, José Luis. "Mercedes de Santa Cruz y Montalvo, Condesa de Merlin: 'Une femme du monde.'" *Revista Hispano Cubana* 13 (May–September 2002): 83–96.

Quintana, Nicolás. "Jesús en contacto directo." *Encuentro de la Cultura Cubana* 25 (Summer 2002): 121–23. ("Homenaje a Jesús Díaz")

——. "Yo estaba allí." *Encuentro de la Cultura Cubana* 24 (Spring 2002): 35–43.

Quintero, Tania. "Mis 15 años." *Encuentro de la Cultura Cubana* 24 (Spring 2002): 260–61. (Tania Quintero is a Cuban journalist residing in Havana)

Rivero, Miguel. "Correspondencia personal." *Encuentro de la Cultura Cubana* 25 (Summer 2002): 85–90. ("Homenaje a Jesús Díaz")

Rivero, Raúl. "Cenizas y caimanes." *Encuentro de la Cultura Cubana* 25 (Summer 2002): 117–18. ("Homenaje a Jesús Díaz")

——. "El hombre que se fué por el agua." *Revista Hispano Cubana* 13 (May–September 2002): 19–20. (Biographical data on Cuban journalist Plácido Hernández Fuentes)

Rodríguez Abad, Angel. "Trocadero en Alcalá: Recuerdo de José Lezama Lima en el vigésimo quinto aniversario de su muerte." *Revista Hispano Cubana* 12 (January–March 2002): 235–38.

Rodríguez Rivera, Guillermo. "Carta." *Encuentro de la Cultura Cubana* 25 (Summer 2002): 109. ("Homenaje a Jesús Díaz")

Roffé, Reina. "Entrevista con Antonio Benítez Rojo." *Cuadernos Hispanoamericanos* 627 (September 2002): 125–36.

Ropp, Steven Masami, and Romy Chávez de Ropp. "An Interview with Francisco

Miyasaka, President of the Japanese Cuban Association." *Amerasia Journal* 28, no. 2 (2002): 129–47.
Schmidt-Nowara, Christopher. "Manuel Moreno Fraginals: An Appreciation." *Hispanic American Historical Review* 82, no. 1 (February 2002): 124–27.
Serrano, Pío E. "Homenaje a Salvat: Un homenaje merecido." *Revista Hispano Cubana* 13 (May–September 2002): 27–28. (About Cuban American bookdealer Juan Manuel Salvat)
Simmen, Andreas. "Tras la muerte de Jesús Díaz." *Encuentro de la Cultura Cubana* 25 (Summer 2002): 65–68. ("Homenaje a Jesús Díaz")
Stavans, Ilán. "Crónica de una amistad." *Encuentro de la Cultura Cubana* 23 (Winter 2001/2002): 22–27. (Discusses the author's friendship with Antonio Benítez Rojo)
Sublette, Ned. "Bebo Valdés: Interview." *Bomb* 78 (Winter 2001/2002): 78–80. (Cuban pianist Bebo Valdés talks about his decision to leave Cuba.)
Suñén, Luis. "El círculo cerrado." *Encuentro de la Cultura Cubana* 25 (Summer 2002): 119. ("Homenaje a Jesús Díaz")
Tutino, Saverio. "La autonomía moral." *Encuentro de la Cultura Cubana* 25 (Summer 2002): 104. ("Homenaje a Jesús Díaz")
Varela, Elvira. "Desde Galicia." *Encuentro de la Cultura Cubana* 25 (Summer 2002): 131–35. ("Homenaje a Jesús Díaz")
Vega, Aurelio de la. "Gladiador infatigable." *Encuentro de la Cultura Cubana* 25 (Summer 2002): 129–30. ("Homenaje a Jesús Díaz")

Cubans Abroad

Books and Monographs

Antón, Alex, and Roger E. Hernández. *Cubans in America: A Vibrant History of a People in Exile.* New York: Kensington Books, 2002. 286 pp.
Boswell, Thomas D. *A Demographic Profile of Cuban Americans.* Edited by Guarione M. Díaz. Miami: Cuban American Policy Center, Cuban American National Council, 2002. 45 pp.
Burke, Nancy Jean. *Pre-paid Phone Cards, "Cosas," and Photos of Saints: Transnational Santería Practices in a Southwest City.* Albuquerque: Latin American Institute, University of New Mexico, 2002. 42 pp. (Focuses on Albuquerque)
Con honor, valentía y orgullo: Alegatos presentados en las vistas de sentencia por los cinco patriotas cubanos injustamente condenados por un tribunal federal de la ciudad de Miami. 3rd ed. Havana: Oficina de Publicaciones del Consejo de Estado, 2002. 97 pp. (Illustrated bookmark with biographies in pocket)
Eli, Lisa G. "Altars, Ancestors, and Divinities: Feminine Spirituality in *Dreaming in Cuban* and *Esperanza's Box of Saints.*" Master's thesis, Rollins College, 2002. 110 pp. (Analyzes the works by Cristina García and María Amparo Escandón)
Fernández, Gastón A. *The Mariel Exodus Twenty Years Later: A Study on the Politics of Stigma and a Research Bibliography.* Miami: Ediciones Universal, 2002. 207 pp.
Greenbaum, Susan D. *More than Black: Afro-Cubans in Tampa.* Gainesville: University Press of Florida, 2002. 383 pp.
Hahn, Laura M. *The Cuban Americans.* Broomall, Pa.: n.p., 2002. 64 pp.

Hernández Nordelo, Gerardo, et al. *Miami Five: Guilty of Defending Cuba—Defence Statements from the Dock.* Merseyside, U.K.: Merseyside Cuba Solidarity, 2002. 53 pp.
Hernández-Miyares, Julio E., Gastón Fernández-Torriente, and Leonardo Fernández-Marcané, eds. *Cuba, exilio y cultura: Memoria del congreso del milenio.* Miami: Ediciones Universal, 2002. 272 pp. (At head of title reads: Asociación de Educadorers Cubano-Americanos, Herencia Cultural Cubana)
Levine, Robert M. *Secret Missions to Cuba: Fidel Castro, Bernardo Benes, and Cuban Miami.* Basingstoke, U.K.: Palgrave Macmillan, 2002. 320 pp.
Medina, Pablo. *Exiled Memories: A Cuban Childhood.* 1st paperback ed. New York: Persea Books, 2002. 135 pp.
Menard, Valerie. *¡Celebremos!: Las fiestas de México, Cuba, y Puerto Rico y su vigencia en los Estados Unidos.* New York: Random House, 2002. 203 pp.
Murrieta Rodríguez, Fabio, ed. *Creación y exilio: Memorias del I Encuentro Internacional con Cuba en la Distancia.* Madrid: Editorial Hispano Cubano, 2002. 363 pp.
Paluch, Jennifer A. "Distance from Miami as a Measurement of Differences in the Cuban American Community: A Demographic and Political Study." Master's thesis, San Diego State University, 2002. 104 pp.
Paris, Margaret L. *Embracing America: A Cuban Exile Comes of Age.* Gainesville: University of Florida Press, 2002. 226 pp.
Peña, Susana. "Visibility and Silence: Cuban American Gay Male Culture in Miami." Ph.D. diss., University of California at Santa Barbara, 2002. 28 pp.
Rasco, José Ignacio. *Huellas de mi cubanía.* Miami: Ediciones Universal, 2002. 366 pp. (A collection of the author's newspaper articles)
Sonneborn, Liz. *The Cuban Americans.* San Diego: Lucent Books, 2002. 112 pp.
Tucker, Phillip Thomas. *Cubans in the Confederacy: José Agustín Quintero, Ambrosio José González, and Loreta Janeta Velázquez.* 2001; reprint, Jefferson, N.C.: McFarland, 2002. 176 pp.
Tweed, Thomas A. *Our Lady of the Exile: Diasporic Religion at a Cuban Catholic Shrine in Miami.* Oxford: Oxford University Press, 2002. 240 pp.
Valdés, Zoé (text), and Robert Van der Hilst (photographs). *Intérieurs cubains: Cuba–Miami miroir en abyme.* Paris: Institut Néerlandais, 2002. 63 pp.
West, Todd MacEgan. "The Effects of Human Capital, Social Capital, and the Ethnic Enclave Economy on the Earnings of Immigrants: The Case of the Mariel Cuban Emigrés." Master's thesis, Georgia Southern University, 2002. 35 pp.

Articles and Papers

Aguirre, Benigno E., and Eduardo Bonilla Silva. "Does Race Matter among Cuban Immigrants?: An Analysis of the Racial Characteristics of Recent Cuban Immigrants." *Journal of Latin American Studies* 34, no. 2 (May 2002): 311–24.
Aguirre, Benigno E., and Rogelio Sáenz. "Testing the Effects of Collectively Expected Durations of Migration: The Naturalization of Mexicans and Cubans." *International Migration Review (IMR)* 36, no. 1 (Spring 2002): 103–24.
Bonnin, Rodolfo, and Chris Brown. "The Cuban Diaspora: A Comparative Analysis of

the Search for Meaning among Recent Cuban Exiles and Cuban Americans." *Hispanic Journal of Behavioral Sciences* 24, no. 4 (2002): 465–78.

Brandon, Peter David. "The Living Arrangements of Children in Immigrant Families in the United States." *Journal of Latin American Studies* 34, no. 2 (May 2002): 365–95. (Includes data on Cuban children)

Buscaglia-Salgado, José F. "Leaving Us for Nowhere: The Cuban Pursuit of 'the American Dream.'" *CR: The New Centennial Review* 2, no. 2 (Summer 2002): 285–98.

Caminero-Santangelo, Marta. "Margarita Engle, Cuban American Conservatism, and the Construction of (Left) U.S. Latino/a Ethnicity." *LIT: Literature Interpretation Theory* 13, no. 4 (2002): 249–67.

Eckstein, Susan, and Lorena Barberia. "Grounding Immigrant Generations in History: Cuban Americans and Their Transnational Ties." *International Migration Review (IMR)* 36, no. 3 (2002): 799–838.

Erkut, Sumru, and Allison J. Tracy. "Predicting Adolescent Self-Esteem from Participation in School Sports among Latino Subgroups." *Hispanic Journal of Behavioral Sciences* 24, no. 4 (2002): 407–49.

Greenhill, Kelly M. "Engineered Migration and the Use of Refugees as Political Weapons: A Case Study of the 1944 Cuban Balseros Crisis." *International Migration (MIR)* 40, no. 4 (2002): 39–74.

Highton, Benjamin, and Arthur L. Burns. "New Perspectives on Latino Voter Turnout in the United States." *American Politics Research* 30, no. 3 (2002): 285–306.

Hill, Kevin A., Darío V. Moreno, and Lourdes Cue. "Racial and Partisan Voting in a Tr-Ethnic City: The 1996 Dade County Mayoral Election." *Journal of Planning Literature* 16, no. 3 (2002): 397–477.

Hilst, Robert van der (photographs), and José Manuel Prieto González (text). "Siete islas en Miami." *Letras Libres* 4, no. 47 (November 2002): 56–63. (Mostly illustrated with colored photographs)

Murrieta, Fabio. "Congreso Creación y Exilio 'Con Cuba en la Distancia.'" *Revista Hispano Cubana* 13 (May–September 2002): 21–24. (About the organization of the conference; includes the opening remarks, "Palabras de apertura," by Guillermo Cortázar, pp. 25–26, and the closing remarks, "Palabras de clausura," by Manuel Díaz Martínez, pp. 63–64)

Nuez, Iván de la. "El destierro de Calibán: Diáspora de la cultura cubana de los noventa en Europa." In *Atravesados: Deslizamientos de identidad y género*, 62–67. Madrid: Fundación Telefónica, 2002.

Ögelman, Nedim, Jeanette Moray, and Philip Martin. "Immigrant Cohesion and Political Access in Influencing Foreign Policy." *SAIS Review* 22, no. 2 (2002): 145–65. (Covers Cuban immigrants to the United States)

Oppenheimer, Andrés. "¿Revolución en Miami?" *Letras Libres* 4, no. 47 (November 2002): 38–40.

Parloff, Roger. "Deep Freezing Terror's Assets: The Long-Term Needs of Wise Foreign Policy Should Trump the Temporary Catharsis of Paying Terror Victims Huge Awards out of Blocked Assets (Blocked Cuban Assets)." *American Lawyer* 24, no. 6 (June 2002): 122–24.

Pellón, Gustavo. "Painful Ghosts: Cuban Reflections on the Confederate Flag." *Callaloo* 24, no. 1 (Winter 2001): 140–51.

Rodríguez, Tomás. "Oppositional Culture and Academic Performance among Children of Immigrants in the USA." *Race, Ethnicity, and Education* 5, no. 2 (2002): 199–215. (Includes data on Cubans)
Rothe, Eugenio M., et al. "Posttraumatic Stress Disorder among Cuban Children and Adolescents after Release from a Refugee Camp." *Psychiatric Services* 53, no. 8 (2002): 970–77.
——. "Posttraumatic Stress Symptoms in Cuban Adolescent Refugees during Camp Confinement." *Adolescent Psychiatry* 26 (2002): 97–124.
Ruiz, Gloria P. "Cultural Factors in the Prevention of AIDS among Cuban American Women." *Cuban Studies* 32 (2001): 120–44.
Tweed, Thomas A. "On Moving Across: Translocative Religion and the Interpreter's Position." *Journal of the American Academy of Religion* 70, no. 2 (June 2002): 733–78. (Drawn from work with Cuban exiles)

Demography, Medicine, and Public Health

Books and Monographs

Durán García, Rosa Margarita. "Risk Factors for Dengue Infection during the 1997 Cuban Epidemic." Ph.D. diss., Johns Hopkins University, 2002. 164 pp.
Guerrero, Natividad, and Olga Cecilia García. *SIDA desde los afectos: Una invitación a la reflexión*. Havana: Casa Editora Abril, 2002. 217 pp.
Johnson, Kelly. "Living with HIV/AIDS in Cuba: A Sequel to Quarantine." Honors paper, Macalester College, 2002. 147 pp.
Lemus Lago, Elia Rosa, Gonzalo Estévez Torres, and Juan Carlos Velázquez Acosta. *Campaña por la esperanza: La lucha contra el dengue*. Havana: Editora Política, 2002. 287 pp.
Ubieta Gómez, Enrique. *La utopía rearmada: Historias de un viaje al Nuevo Mundo*. Havana: Casa Editora Abril, 2002. 327 pp. (History of Cuban medical missions to Haiti and Central America)

Articles and Papers

Baker, Stephen R. "Radiology in Cuba Shows a Different Path to Success." *Diagnostic Imaging* 24, no. 11 (2002): 31–34.
Collinson, S. R., and T. H. Turner. "Not Just Salsa and Cigars: Mental Health Care in Cuba." *Psychiatric Bulletin* 26, pt. 5 (2002): 185–88.
Cruz-Bustillo, Diana, et al. "Preliminary Results of the Molecular Diagnosis of Familial Adenomatous Polyposis in Cuban Families." *International Journal of Colorectal Disease* 17, no. 5 (2002): 344–48.
Cuevas, M. T. "High HIV-1 Genetic Diversity in Cuba." *AIDS* 16, pt. 12 (2002): 1643–54.
Debesa, F., et al. "Spontaneous Reporting of Adverse Drug Reactions in Cuba: Integrating Continuous Education, Training, and Research in a Network Approach." *British Journal of Clinical Pharmacology* 54, pt. 3 (2002): 335–36.
Dickinson, F. O., and A. E. Pérez. "Bacterial Meningitis in Elderly Cuba, 1998–2000." *Geriátrika* 18, pt. 6 (2002): 41–47.

Erkens, K., et al. "Histoplasmosis in a Group of Bat Researchers Returning from Cuba." *Deutsche Medizinische Wochenschrift* 127, no. 1 (2002): 21–26.
Guedes, Antonio. "La sanidad silenciada." *Encuentro de la Cultura Cubana* 24 (Spring 2002): 250–59. (Includes vital statistics)
Gutiérrez, J., et al. "High Blood Pressure and Decreased Heart Rate Variability in the Cuban Epidemic Neuropathy." *Journal of Neurology, Neurosurgery and Psychiatry* 73, no. 1 (July 2002): 71–73.
Hsieh Ying-Hen, et al. "Estimating the Number of Cubans Infected Sexually by Human Immunodeficiency Virus Using Contact Tracing Data." *International Journal of Epidemiology* 31, no. 3 (2002): 679–84.
Krasevec, J. M., et al. "Maternal and Infant Essential Fatty Acid Status in Havana, Cuba." *American Journal of Clinical Nutrition* 76, no. 4 (2002): 834–45.
Otero-Ojeda, Angel A. "Third Cuban Glossary of Psychiatry (GC-3): Key Features and Contributions." *Psychopathology* 35, no. 2–3 (2002): 181–85.
Prilleltensky, Isaac, et al. "Applied Ethics in Mental Health in Cuba: Part II, Power Differentials, Dilemmas, Resources, and Limitations." *Ethics and Behavior* 12, no. 3 (2002): 243–60.
Romamo, Michael. "A Gift from Fidel." *Modern Healthcare* 32, no. 27 (July 2002): 32–33. (Discusses free medical education in Cuba)
Rossiter, Amy, Richard Walsh-Bowers, and Isaac Prilleltensky. "Ethics as a Located Story: A Comparison of North American and Cuban Clinical Ethics." *Theory and Psychology* 12, no. 4 (2002): 533–56.
Sánchez Valdés, Laura, et al. "Applied Ethics in Mental Health in Cuba: Part I, Guiding Concepts and Values." *Ethics and Behavior* 12, no. 3 (2002): 223–43.
Sankaranarayanan, R., et al. "Visual Inspection in Oral Cancer Screening in Cuba: A Case-Control Study." *Oral Oncology* 38, no. 2 (2002): 131–37.
Saucier Lundy, Karen, and Sharyn Janes. "Nursing and Health Care in Socialist Cuba: What Can We Learn from Each Other?" *Applied Nursing Research* 15, no. 2 (2002): 712–13.
Wakai, S. "Mobilisation of Cuban Doctors in Developing Countries." *The Lancet* 9326 (6 July 2002): 92–93.
Whitney, W. T. "Stop Abusing Cuban Children—and Their Doctors." *Monthly Review* 54, no. 5 (2002): 48–53.

Description and Travel

Books and Monographs

Aeberhard, Danny, ed. *Cuba*. 3d ed. Singapore and Maspeth, N.Y.: APA Publications, 2002. 381 pp. (Insight Guide)
Attilini, Daniela. *L'isola sospesa.* Rome: Prospettiva, 2002. 83 pp.
Belleville, Bill. *Deep Cuba: The Inside Story of an American Oceanographic Expedition*. Athens: University of Georgia Press, 2002. 273 pp.
Brân, Zoë. *Enduring Cuba*. Melbourne, Vic. and London: Lonely Planet, 2002. 255 pp.
Bremer, Frederika. *Cartas desde Cuba*. Translated by Matilde Goulard de Westberg.

Havana: Fundación Fernando Ortiz, 2002. 196 pp. (Translation of *Hemmen i den Nya verleden*)
Cameron, Sarah. *Cuba Handbook: The Travel Guide.* 3d ed. Bath, U.K.: Footprint, 2002. 449 pp.
———. *Havana.* Bath, U.K.: Footprint, 2002. 256 pp.
Cepero, Eloy Guillermo, and Antonio Magaz García. *Cuba 1902–1962: Un viaje a través de deber postales — Memorias de un Pedro Pan.* Hialeah, Fla.: E. G. Cepero, 2002. 224 pp. (Chiefly illustrated)
Coghill, Liz, ed. *Routard Cuba.* London: Hachette, 2002. 380 pp.
Croppi, Gabriele. *Cuba Last Minute.* Milan: Comedit, 2002. 1 vol. (Unpaged)
Cortanze, Gérard de. *Hemingway en Cuba.* Photographs by Jean-Bernard Naudin. Barcelona: Océano, 2002. 167 pp. (Translation of *Hemingway à Cuba*)
Cuba. 1st American ed. New York: Dorling Kindersley, 2002. 328 pp. (Eyewitness travel guide)
Cuba: Framing Time. Santa Barbara, Calif.: Brooks Institute of Photography, 2002. 139 pp.
Ellis, Kirsten, and Joe Yogerst. *Traveler's Cuba Companion.* 2nd ed. Old Saybrook, Conn.: Globe Pequot Press, 2002. 349 pp.
Fagiuoli, Martino, ed. *Cuba: La isla grande.* Translated by Kevin Maciel. Vercelli, Italy: White Star; San Diego, Calif: Thunder Bay Press, 2002. 290 pp.
Ferguson, Ted. *Blue Cuban Nights.* Chichester, U.K.: Summersdale, 2002. 320 pp.
Glinn, Burt. *Havana: The Revolutionary Movement.* Stockport, U.K.: Dewi Lewis, 2002. 128 pp. (Mostly photographs with excerpts from the writings of Che Guevara, José Martí, and Nancy Morejón)
Gloaguen, Philippe, ed. *Cuba 2003.* Paris: Hachette, 2002. 459 pp.
Jenkins, Gareth, ed. *Havana in My Heart: Seventy-five Years of Cuban Photography.* 1st U.S. ed. Chicago: Chicago Review Press, 2002. 192 pp. (British edition has subtitle *A Celebration of Cuban Photography*)
———. *La Habana de mi corazón: Una fiesta de la fotografía cubana.* Translated by Santiago Pujol. Chicago.: Chicago Review Press, 2002. 192 pp. (Translation of *Havana in My Heart*)
Jenkins, John, ed. *Travellers' Tales of Old Cuba: From Treasure Island to Mafia Den.* Melbourne, Australia: Ocean Press; London: Global Press, 2002. 160 pp.
Kidder, Laura M. *Cuba: The Guide for all Budgets.* 2d ed., completely updated with many maps and travel tips. New York: Fodor's Travel Publications, 2002. 215 pp.
Ledbetter, Ernest Wright, Louis A. Pérez, and Ambrosio Fornet. *Cuba: Picturing Change.* Albuquerque: University of New Mexico Press, 2002. 207 pp. (Photographs by Ledbetter; essays by Pérez and Fornet)
Lightfoot, Claudia. *Havana: A Cultural and Literary Companion.* New York: Interlink Books, 2002. 273 pp.
Monk, Moisés P. *Cuba le ofrece: Guía turística.* Photographs by Julio Larramendi. Havana: Editorial SI-MAR, 2002. 216 pp.
Moore, Andrew. *Inside Havana.* San Francisco: Chronicle Books, 2002. 132 pp. (Photographs)
Pietropaolo, Vincenzo (photographs), and Cecelia Elisabeth Burke Lawless (text). *Making Home in Havana.* New Brunswick, N.J.: Rutgers University Press, 2002. 115 pp.

Rosemond de Beauvallon, Jean Baptiste. *La isla de Cuba*. Edited and translated by Olga Portuondo Zúñiga. Santiago de Cuba: Editorial Oriente, 2002. 293 pp. (Annotated edition of *L'île de Cuba*, the author's description of his 1841 visit to Cuba)

The Rough Guide to Cuba. 2nd ed. London: Rough Guides, 2002. 624 pp.

Runge, Jonathan. *Rum and Reggae's Cuba: Havana and Beyond*. Prides Crossing, Mass.: Rum and Reggae Guidebooks, 2002. 67 pp.

Sanclemente, Vicenç. *La Habana no es una isla: Crónica de un corresponsal en Cuba*. Barcelona: Jaque Mata Comunicación, 2002. 319 pp.

Schlecht, Neil, and Eliot Greenspan. *Cuba*. New York: Hungry Minds; Chichester, U.K.: Wiley, 2002. 288 pp.

Silvestri-Levy, Alessandra. *Les années Cuba*. La Tour d'Aigues, France: Aube, 2002. 93 pp. (Photographs)

Smith, Wally, and Barbara Smith. *Bicycling Cuba: Fifty Days of Detailed Ride Routes from Havana to Pinar del Río and El Oriente*. Woodstock, Vt.: Backcountry Guides, 2002.

Tattlin, Isadora. *Cuba Diaries: An American Housewife in Havana*. Chapel Hill, N.C.: Alonquin Books of Chapel Hill, 2002. 308 pp.

Torrent, Ferran. *Living la Habana*. Photographs by Joan Llenas.Valencia, Spain: Editorial Ingenting, 2002. 157 pp.

Articles and Papers

Fowler, Victor. "A Traveler's Album: Variations on 'Cubanidad.'" *Boundary 2* 29, no. 3 (Fall 2002): 105–19.

Gott, Richard. "Sweet Revolution." Photographs by Lucy Davies. *New Statesman* 131 (April 2002): 43–44.

Hamilton, Kendra. "A Passion for Cuba." *Black Issues in Higher Education* 19, no. 13 (15 August 2002): 26–28. (University of Connecticut professor explores his African roots in Cuba)

Kayafas, Peter. "An American in Cuba: Photographs." *Doubletake* 8, no. 1 (Winter 2002): 12–13. (Photographs of street scenes in Cuba)

La Fountain-Stokes, Lawrence Martin. "De un pájaro las dos alas: Travel Notes of a Queer Puerto Rican in Havana." *GLQ* 8, no. 1/2 (2002): 7–33. (Alleges that since 1990, Havana has become one of the world's prime locations for sexual tourism)

Shulman, Ken. "Photographing in Cuba: Beyond the Buena Vista." *Graphis* 337 (2002): 14–18.

Documents

Books ands Monographs

U.S. Congress. House. Committee on International Relations. Subcommittee on International Operations and Human Rights. *An Assessment of Cuba Broadcasting: The Voice of Freedom — Hearing before the Subcommittee on International Operations and Human Rights of the Committee on International Relations*, 107th Cong., 2nd sess., 6 June 2002. 82 pp.

———. Senate. Committee on Appropriations. Subcommittee on Treasury and Gen-

Recent Work in Cuban Studies : 253

eral Documents. *Restrictions on Travel to Cuba: Hearing before a Subcommittee of the Committee on Appropriations,* 107th Cong., 2nd sess., 11 February 2002. 74 pp.

———. Committee on Foreign Relations. Subcommittee on Western Hemisphere, Peace Corps, and Narcotic Affairs. *Bridges to the Cuban People Act of 2001, S. 1017: Hearing before the Subcommittee on Western Hemisphere, Peace Corps, and Narcotics Affairs of the Committee on Foreign Relations,* 107th Cong., 2nd sess., 19 June 2002. 61 pp.

———. *Cuba's Pursuit of Biological Weapons: Fact or Fiction?—Hearing before the Subcommittee on Western Hemisphere, Peace Corps, and Narcotic Affairs of the Committee on Foreign Relations,* 107th Cong., 2nd sess., 5 June 2002. 45 pp.

U.S. President (George H.W. Bush). "Continuation of the National Emergency with Respect to Cuba: Message from the President of the United States Transmitting Notification that the Emergency Declared with Respect to the Government of Cuba's Destruction of Two Unarmed U.S.-Registered Civilian Aircraft in International Airspace North of Cuba on February 24, 1996, Is to Continue in Effect beyond March 1, 2002, Pursuant to 50 U.S.C. 1622 (d)." 3 pp.

Articles and Papers

Inter-American Commission on Human Rights (IACHR). "Decision on Request for Precautionary Measures: Detainees at Guantanamo Bay, Cuba." *International Legal Materials* 41, no. 3 (2002): 532–36.

Gómez Manzano, René, and Félix Bonne Carcassés, eds. "Iniciativa por la Patria de Todos." *Revista Hispano Cubana* 13 (May–September 2002): 149–56. (Documents mostly on human rights)

"Our Heritage in Documents: Forty Years Ago, the Cuban Missile Crisis." *Journal of the National Archives* 34, no. 3 (2002): 218–24.

"El Proyecto Varela." *Encuentro de la Cultura Cubana,* no. 25 (Summer 2002): 275–82.

United Nations Commission on Human Rights. "Resolución sobre Cuba aprobada en la Comisión de Derechos Humanos de la ONU, reunida en Ginebra en abril de 2002." *Revista Hispano Cubana* 13 (May–September 2002): 147–48.

U.S. President (George H.W. Bush). "An Initiative for a New Cuba: The Chance Rests with Mr. Castro." *Vital Speeches of the Day* 68, no. 16 (2002): 492–94.

———. "Remarks Announcing the Initiative for a New Cuba." *Weekly Compilation of Presidential Documents* 38, no. 21 (27 May 2002): 852–55.

———. "Remarks on the 100th Anniversary of Cuban Independence in Miami, Florida." *Weekly Compilation of Presidential Documents* 38, no. 21 (27 May 2002): 854–59.

Economics, Industry, and Planning

Books and Monographs

Brown, Katja Schroer. "Opportunities and Challenges for U.S. Business in Post-Castro Cuba." Honors thesis, University of Texas at Arlington, 2002. 21 pp.

Brundenius, Claes. *Tourism as an Engine of Growth: Reflections on Cuba's New Development Strategy.* Copenhagen: Centre for Development Research, 2002. 21 pp.

Buell, Raymond Leslie, et al. *Problemas de la nueva Cuba.* Miami: Editorial Cubana, 2002. 574 pp. (Facsimile reprint of the 1935 edition)
Calvo Ospina, Hernando. *Bacardi: The Hidden War.* London; Sterling, Va.: Pluto Press, 2002. 127 pp. (Discusses Cuba's rum industry)
Castro, Fidel. *De Seattle al 11 de septiembre.* Tafalla, Spain: Txalaparta, 2002. 323 pp.
Falcoff, Mark. *Cuba: The Morning After: Normalization and Its Discontents.* Washington, D.C.: American Enterprise Institute Press, 2002.
Fernandez, Susan J. *Encumbered Cuba: Capital Markets and Revolt, 1878–1895.* Gainesville: University Press of Florida, 2002. 203 pp.
Howard, Christopher. *Living and Investing in the "New" Cuba: A Guide to Inexpensive Living and Making Money in the Caribbean's Most Beautiful Tropical Paradise.* Miami: Costa Rica Books, 2002. 214 pp.
Marqués Dolz, María Antonia. *Las industrias menores: Empresarios y empresas en Cuba (1880–1920).* Havana: Editora Política, 2002. 318 pp.
Mesa-Lago, Carmelo, et al. *Buscando un modelo económico en América Latina: Mercado, socialista o mixta? – Chile, Cuba y Costa Rica.* Translated by Malena Barro. Caracas: Nueva Sociedad; Miami: Florida International University, 2002. 681 pp. (Translation of *Market, Socialist, and Mixed Economies: Comparative Policy and Performance – Chile, Cuba, and Costa Rica*)
Miranda Parrondo, Mauricio de, ed. *Alternativas de política económica y social en América Latina y el Caribe: Cuatro casos de estiudio – Colombia, Costa Rica, Cuba y México.* Bogotá: Centro Editorial Javeriano, 2002. 415 pp.
Monreal González, Pedro M., ed. *Development Prospects in Cuba: An Agenda in the Making.* London: Institute of Latin American Studies, School of Advanced Study, University of London, 2002. 244 pp.
Ortiz, Fernando. *Contrapunteo cubano del tabaco y el azúcar: Advertencia de sus contrastes agrarios, económicos, históricos y sociales.* Edited by Enrico Mario Santí. Madrid: Música Mundana Maqueda, 2002. 805 pp. (New edition of a work published in 1940)
Pelverts, Karl. *Cuban Economic Sanctions: The Time Has Come to Lift Them and Move Forward.* Carlisle Barracks, Pa.: U.S. Army War College, 2002. 24 pp.
Spadoni, Paolo. "Impact of the Helms–Burton Law on Foreign Investment in Cuba: An Analysis." Master's thesis, University of Florida, 2002. 132 pp.

Articles and Papers

Brundenius, Claes. "Whither the Cuban Economy after Recovery?: The Reform Process, Upgrading Strategies, and the Question of Transition." *Journal of Latin American Studies* 34, no. 2 (May 2002): 365–95. (Includes statistics)
Bustamante, Alberto S. "Economic Statistics and Facts about Cuba, 1952–1958." *Herencia* 8, no. 2 (Fall 2002): 24–25.
Clancy, Michael. "The Globalization of Sex Tourism and Cuba: A Commodity Chains Approach." *Studies in Comparative International Development* 36, no. 4 (2002): 63–89.
Cole, Ken. "Cuba: The Process of Socialist Development." *Latin American Perspectives* 29, no. 3 (May 2002): 40–56.

Collazo Pérez, Enrique. "Presencia económica de los asturianos en Cuba." *Revista Hispano Cubana* 12 (January–March 2002): 129–42.
Cruz, Consuelo, and Anna Seleny. "Reform and Counter Reform: The Path to Market in Hungary and Cuba." *Comparative Politics* 34, no. 2 (January 2002): 211–33.
"Cuba's Banking Sector Has Gone through a Spectacular Period of Growth, despite a Hostile U.S." *Banker* 152, no. 916 (2002): 63–68.
Díaz-Marzo, Ramón. "Pan con tortilla." *Revista Hispano Cubana* 13 (May–September 2002): 13–14.
Dilla Alfonso, Haroldo. "Municipios, crisis y reforma económica en Cuba." *Encuentro de la Cultura Cubana* 23 (Winter 2001/2002): 199–206.
Espina Prieto, Mayra. "Reajuste, pobreza y desarrollo: La experiencia cubana." In *Política social y trabajo social,* edited by Nilsa M. Burgos Ortiz, 42–70. San Juan, P.R.: Proyecto Atlantea, Vicepresidencia para Asuntos Académicos e Investigación, Universidad de Puerto Rico, 2002.
Espinosa Chepe, Oscar. "Consignas y más consignas." *Revista Hispano Cubana* 12 (May–September 2002): 17–18. (Discusses Cuba's sugar production)
———. "Cuba y el Area de Libre Comercio de las Américas." *Revista Hispano Cubana* 12 (January–March 2002): 21–24.
———. "Para salir de la crisis." *Encuentro de la Cultura Cubana* 23 (Winter 2001/2002): 156–64.
Espinosa Martínez, Eugenio. "Etica y economía: Valores y estrategia cubana de desarrollo en los '90." *Impulso* 13, no. 31 (May–August 2002): 71–94.
Garrigues, C. "Is the Cuban Rum Battle Over?" *European Intellectual Property Review* 24, pt. 3 (2002): 147–48.
González Gutiérrez, Alfredo. "Un viaje a Granada: Julián Alienes y la economía cubana." *Temas* 29 (April–June 2002): 82–96. (Discusses Aliens's works on the Cuban economy)
González Núñez, Gerardo. "¿Se encuentra Cuba en transición?: Premisa y condicionantes de la fase actual." In *El Caribe en la era de globalización: Retos, transiciones y reajustes,* edited by Gerardo González Núñez and Emilio Pantojas García, 135–72. Mayagüez, P.R.: Centro de Investigaciones Sociales [y] Publicaciones Puertorriqueños, 2002.
González Rubí, Rafael. "Cuba: ¿Un camino proprio a la hora de la globalización?" *Comercio Exterior* 51, no. 11 (November 2001): 985–91.
Hamilton, Douglas. "Whither Cuban Socialism?: The Changing Political Economy of the Cuban Revolution." *Latin American Perspectives* 29, no. 3 (May 2002): 18–39.
Lauzurique, Arnaldo R., and Marta Beatriz Roque Cabello. "La cara oculta de un movimiento." *Encuentro de la Cultura Cubana* 24 (Spring 2002): 274–77. (Analyzes the economic aspects of the twenty-sixth of July movement based on *La tesis económica del movimiento 26 de julio* by Felipe Pazos and Regino Eladio Botí y Barreiro, written in 1957 and published in 1959 in Mexico)
Leogrande, William Mack, and Julie M. Thomas. "Cuba's Quest for Economic Independence." *Journal of Latin American Studies* 34, no. 2 (May 2002): 325–63. (Includes statistics)
Monreal González, Pedro M. "Development as an Unfinished Affair: Cuba after the

'Great Adjustment' of the 1990's." *Latin American Perspectives* 29, no. 3 (May 2002): 75–90.
Nadler, P. S. "Cuba: The Light That Failed." *Secured Lender* 58, pt. 6 (2002): 102–3.
Ritter, Archibald R. M., and Nicolas Rowe. "Cuba: From 'Dollarization' to 'Euroization' or 'Peso Reconsolidation?'" *Latin American Politics and Society* 44, no. 2 (Summer 2002): 99–125.
Roca Antúnez, Vladimiro. "Informe desde La Habana." *Letras Libres* 4, no. 47 (November 2002): 30–33. (Discusses the serious socioeconomic situation in today's Cuba; the author is president of the Comité Gestor of the Partido Socialdemócrata Cubano)
Roque, Martha Beatriz. "La transición a la democracia en Cuba: Algunas consideraciones." *Encuentro de la Cultura Cubana* 23 (Winter 2001/2002): 142–55.
Salazar-Carrillo, Jorge. "Cien años de economía cubana" (One Hundred Years of Cuban Economy). *Herencia* 8, no. 2 (Fall 2002): 16–23.
"The Steel Industry of Three Countries of Latin America and the Caribbean: Cuba, Costa Rica, and Ecuador." *Acero Latinoamericano* 473 (2002): 36–42.

Education

Books and Monographs

Ortiz, María Dolores. *En mitad de cien caminos.* Havana: Editorial "Félix Varela," 2002. 214 pp. (A history of Cuban education)
Sáez, José L. *Breve historia del Colegio de Belén.* Miami: Belén Jesuit Preparatory Scool, 2002. (Only vol. 1, covering 1854–1961 has been published)

Articles and Papers

Cuba, Severo, et al. "¿Hemos aprendido?" *Debate (Peru)* 23, no. 115 (June–July 2002): 22–32. (About students and learning in Cuba)
Fernández Soneira, Teresa. "La educación en Cuba durante la República" (Education in Cuba during the Republic). *Herencia* 8, no. 2 (Fall 2002): 36–47.
Hamilton, Stuart. "Librarians or Dissidents?: Critics and Supporters of the Independent Libraries in Cuba Project." *Progressive Librarian* 19/20 (Spring 2002): 3–46.
Harris, Violet J., and Rosalinda B. Barrera. "Images of Literacy and Literature in Cuba." *New Advocate* 15, no. 1 (Winter 2002): 68–70. (Photographs highlighting literacy, education, and literature in Havana, Cuba)
Henderson, Mae. "Cuba's Intellectual Blockade: U.S. Embargo or Cuban Censorship?" *Black Issues in Higher Education* 18, no. 19 (November 2001): 36–37.
Martínez Figueras, Carlos E. "La enseñanza marítima en Cuba" (Maritime Education in Cuba). *Herencia* 8, no. 2 (Fall 2002): 60–73.
Miller, Susan A. "Early Childhood Education in Cuba." *Childhood Education* 78, no. 6 (September 2002): 359–63.
Olson, Beatriz. "Mass Health Education on Sex and Sexuality and Its Impact on Cuba: An Interview-Based Medical Report on the Development, Evolution, and Current Status of This Educational Program in Cuba, with Emphasis on Women's Health." *Journal of Women's Health* 11, no. 9 (2002): 767–71.

"Preschool Education in Cuba." *Childhood Education* 78, no. 6 (September 2002): 363–67.
Proveyer Cervantes, Clotilde. "Las políticas sociales en la esfera educacional: La experiencia cubana." In *Política social y trabajo social,* edited by Nilsa M. Burgos Ortiz, 173–82. San Juan, P.R.: Proyecto Atlantea, Vicepresidencia para Asuntos Académicos e Investigación, Universidad de Puerto Rico, 2002.

Flora and Fauna

Books and Monographs

Claro, Rodolfo, ed. *Ecology of the Marine Fishes of Cuba.* Washington, D.C.: Smithsonian Institution, 2002. 224 pp.
Cueto, Emilio. *Illustrating Cuba's Flora and Fauna.* Miami: Historical Museum of Southern Florida, 2002. 112 pp. (Includes a CD-ROM with the title *Exhibit of Cuba's Flora and Fauna at the Historical Museum of Southern Florida, Sept. 6, 2002–Jan. 19, 2003*)
Díaz, Carlos Jesús. *Límites socioculturales de la educación ambiental: Acercamiento desde la experiencia caribeña.* Mexico City: Siglo Veintiuno Editores, 2002. 189 pp.
Kaczmarek, Lukasz, and Lukasz Michalczyk. *Echiniscus barbarae: A New Species of Tardigrade from Cuba Island (Tardigrada: Heterotardigrada, Echiniscidae, "Arctomys" Group).* Auckland, N.Z.: Magnolia Press, 2002. 4 pp.
Liberman, Louisa M. "Shell Form in Urocoptid Land Snails from Cuba." Undergraduate honors paper, Mount Holyoke College, 2002. 58 pp.

Articles and Papers

Aira, María Jesús, Teresa Irene Rojas, and Victoria Jato. "Fungi Associated with Three Houses in Havana (Cuba)." *Grana* 41, no. 2 (2002): 114–18.
Alberts, Allison C., et al. "Temporary Alteration of Local Social Structure in a Threatened Population of Cuban Iguanas (Cyclura nubila)." *Behavioral Ecology and Sociobiology* 51, no. 4 (2002): 324–36.
Anderberg, Zhang. "Phylogenetic Relationships of Cyrillaceae and Clethraceae (Ericales) with Special Emphasis on the Genus Purdiaea Planch." *Organisms Diversity and Evolution* 2, no. 2 (2002): 127–37.
Benchley, Peter. "Cuba Reefs: A Last Caribbean Refuge." *National Geographic* 201, no. 2 (February 2002): 44–68.
Caiuff, M.G., and G.S. Serrano. "Cuban Novelties in the Genus Alsophila (Cyatheaceae)." *Wildenowia* 32, pt. 2 (2002): 303–10.
Cuesta-Rubio, O., et al. "Polysoprenylated Benzophenones in Cuban Propolis: Biological Activity of Nemorosone." *Zeitschrift für Naturforschung/Journal of Biosciences* 57. no. 3 (2002): 372–85.
De Silva, D., and J. Hemingway. "Structural Organization of the Estalpha3 Gene in a Colombian Strain of Culex quinquefasciatus Differs from that in Cuba." *Medical and Veterinary Entomology* 16, no. 1 (2002): 99–105.
Dominguez, M., et al. "Molecular Characterization of Tobacco Leaf Rugose Virus, a

New B Egomovirus Infecting Tobacco in Cuba." *Plant Disease* 86, no. 9 (2002): 1050–51.
Fa, J. E., et al. "Biodiversity of Sierra del Cristal, Cuba: First Insights." *Oryx* 36, pt. 4 (2002): 389–95.
Hedges, S. Blair, and Orlando H. Garrido. "A New Snake of the Genus Tropidophis (Tropidophiidae) from Eastern Cuba." *Journal of Herpetology* 36, no. 2 (June 2002): 157–61.
Hnizdo, J., and O. Hes. "A Case of Renal Neoplasia in a Cuban Sand Boa (Tropidophis melanurus). *Veterinárstvi* 52, pt. 8 (2002): 355–59.
Kornicker, L. S., and J. Yager. "Description of Spelaeoecia saturno: A New Species from an Anchialine Cave in Cuba (Crustacea: Ostracoda: Mydocopa: Halocyprididae)." *Proceedings of the Biological Society of Washington* 115, pt. 1 (2002): 153–70.
Llauger, R., et al. "Detection and Molecular Characterization of Phytoplasma Associated with Lethal Yellowing Disease of Coconut Palms in Cuba." *Journal of Phytopathology* 150, no. 7 (2002): 390–96.
Machado Rodríguez, Sonia, and Pedro P. Herrera Oliver. "Pollen Morphology of Arecaceae from Cuba." *Grana* 41, no. 3 (2002): 149–57.
Martínez Callís, Cándida R., Lázara Sotolongo Molina, and Pedro Herrera. "A Survey of People's Knowledge about Pollen in Havana City, Cuba." *Grana* 41, no. 3 (2002): 199–200.
Núñez Selles, A. J., et al. "Isolation and Quantitative Analysis of Phenolic Antioxidants, Free Sugars, and Polyols from Mango (Mangifera Indica L.) Stem Bark Aqueous Decoction Used in Cuba as a Nutritional Supplement." *Journal of Agricultural and Food Chemistry* 50, no. 4 (2002): 762–67.
Pino, J. A., et al. "Chemical Composition of Cajuput Oil (Melaleuca leucadendra L.) from Cuba." *Journal of Essential Oil Research (JEOR)* 14, no. 1 (2002): 12–14.
———. "Essential Oil of Plinia Ribrinervia Urb. from Cuba." *Journal of Essential Oil Research (JEOR)* 14, no. 5 (2002): 372.
———. "Study of Essential Oils of Eucalyptus Resinifera." *Flavour and Fragrance Journal* 17, pt. 1 (2002): 1–4.
Pino, J. A., A. Bello, and A. Urquiola. "The Leaf Oil of Piper Ossanum Trel. from Cuba." *Journal of Essential Oil Research (JEOR)* 14, no. 5 (2002): 375.
———. "Leaf Oil of Eugenia Rocana Britt, et Wils. from Cuba." *Journal of Essential Oil Research (JEOR)*: 412–14.
———. "The Leaf Oil of Pimenta Adenociada (Urb.) Burret from Cuba." *Journal of Essential Oil Research (JEOR)* 14, no. 6 (2002): 400–2.
Pino, J. A., J. Aguero, and V. Fuentes. "Essential Oil of Salvia Officinalis L. ssp. altissima Grown in Cuba." *Journal of Essential Oil Research (JEOR)* 14, no. 5 (2002): 373–75.
Pino, J. A., R. Marbot, and A. Rosado. "Volatile Constituents of Star Apple (Chrysophyllum sainito L.) from Cuba." *Flavour and Fragrance Journal* 17, pt. 5 (2002): 401–3.
Quiñones, M., et al. "First Report of Tomato Yellow Leaf Curl Virus Infecting Pepper Plants in Cuba." *Plant Disease* 86, no. 1 (2002): 73–74.

Regalado, Ledis, and Carlos Sánchez. "Spore Morphology as a Taxonomic Tool in the Delimitation of Three Asplenium L. Species Complexes (Aspleniaceae: Pteridophya) in Cuba." *Grana* 41, no. 2 (2002): 107–13.
Rodríguez, María M., et al. "Cross-Resistance to Pyrethroid and Organophosphorus Insecticides Induced by Selection with Temephos in Aedes Aegypti (Diptera: Culicidae) from Cuba." *Journal of Medical Entomology* 39, no. 5 (2002): 882–88.
Ruiz-García, M., et al. "Coat Gene Profiles of Several Cat Populations in Cuba, Costa Rica, Colombia, Paraguay, Chile, and Argentina, and Possible Genetic Origins of These Cat Populations." *Russian Journal of Genetics* 38, no. 2 (2002): 165–80.
Santana Romero, J. L., et al. "Radioisotope Method for Characterization of Vegetable Tannins, Extracted from Waste of Forestry Production in Cuba." *Journal of Radioanalytical and Nuclear Chemistry* 253, no. 1 (2002): 101–16.

Foreign Relations

Books and Monographs

Bardach, Ann Louise. *Cuba Confidential: Love and Vengeance in Miami and Havana.* New York: Random House, 2002. 417 pp.
Basdeo, Sahadeo, and Heather N. Nicol. *Canada, the United States, and Cuba.* Boulder, Colo.: Lynne Riener, 2002. 170 pp.
Benemelis, Juan F. *Las guerras secretas de Fidel Castro.* Madrid: San Martín, 2002. 439 pp.
Blight, James G., and Philip Brenner. *Sad and Luminous Days: Cuba's Secret Struggle with the Superpowers after the Missile Crisis.* Lanham, Md.: Rowman and Littlefield, 2002. 324 pp.
Brandt, Jason K. "Effects of Humanitarian Aid: A Cuban Case Study." Master's thesis, Naval Postgraduate School, Springfield, Va., 2002. 79 pp.
Breuer, Ralf. *Deutschland, Kuba: Die bilateralen Beziehungen im Spannungsfeld internationaler Politik.* Hamburg, Ger.: Institut für Iberoamerika-Kunde, 2002. 93 pp.
Camacho Navarro, Enrique, ed. *Siete vistas de Cuba: Interpretaciones de su independencia.* Mexico City: Centro Coordinador y Difusor de Estudios Latinoamericanos, Universidad Nacional Autónoma de México, 2002. 205 pp. (Focuses on Mexico–Cuba relations)
Cary, Ryan Charles. "The Big Con: The Failure of CIA Propaganda Strategy and Tactics in 1954 Guatemala and 1961 Cuba." Master's thesis, Kent State University, 2002. 128 pp.
Comité Salvadoreño de Solaridad con Cuba. *En las entrañas del monstruo.* San Salvador: El Comité, 2002. 94 pp. (Essays by Gerardo Hernández Nordelo, Ramón Labañino Salazar, René González Schwerert, Fernando González Llort, and Antonio Guerrero Rodríguez on U.S.-Cuba relations)
Erisman, H. Michael. *Cuba's Foreign Relations in a Post-Soviet World.* Gainesville: University Press of Florida, 2002. 270 pp.
Fonte Zarabozo, Luisa Irene. *La nación cubana y Estados Unidos: Un estudio del discurso periodístico, 1906–1921.* Mexico City: Centro de Estudios Lingüísticos y

Literarios, El Colegio de México [y] Unidad Iztapalapa, Universidad Autónoma Metropolitana, 2002. 276 pp. (Includes 139 newspaper articles from the *Diario de la Marina* and *La Lucha*; also available as a computer file)

Giscard, John C. "U.S.–Cuba Relations: Revisiting the Sanctions Policy." Master's thesis, Naval Postgraduate School, Springfield, Va., 2002. 82 pp.

Gleijeses, Piero. *Conflicting Missions: Havana, Washington, and Africa, 1959–1976*. Chapel Hill: University of North Carolina Press, 2002. 552 pp.

Lorenz, Marita, and Wilfried Huismann. *Mi querido Fidel: Mi vida, mi amor, mi traición*. Translated by Sibylle Hunzinger. Barcelona: Salvat Editores, 2002. 303 pp. (Translation of *Lieber Fidel*)

Machado y Ortega, Luis. *La Enmienda Platt: La isla de Corcho*. Facsimile edition. Miami: Editorial Cubana, 2002. 150, 32 pp. (Reprint of two works published in 1922 and 1936, respectively)

Morley, Morris Hyman, and Christopher McGillion. *Unfinished Business: America and Cuba after the Cold War, 1989–2001*. Cambridge: Cambridge University Press, 2002. 253 pp.

Pérez, Lisandro, and Grisel Sangroniz, eds. *Cuba and U.S. Nonprofits: Resource Guide and Directory*. Miami: Cuban Research Institute, Florida International University, 2002. 82 pp.

Pérez Castellón, Ninoska. *Moral vs. crimen*. Miami: Fondo de Estudios Cubanos, 2002. 21 pp. (About the shooting down by the government of Cuban Brothers to the Rescue aircraft in the Florida Straits)

Richardson, James R. *United States–Cuba Relations: Does the War on Terrorism Change Our Stance?* Carlisle Barracks, Pa.: U.S. Army War College, 2002. 22 pp. (Also available on public STINET at http://stinet.dtic.mil/)

Roberts, Randy Howard. "Illusion of Independence: U.S. Foreign Policy in Cuba after the Platt Amendment, 1934–1958." Master's thesis, New Mexico State University, 2002. 162 pp.

Rojas, Rafael. *Cuba mexicana: Historia de una anexión imposible*. Mexico City: Secretaría de Relaciones Exteriores, 2001. 478 pp.

Rose, Michael S. *Cuba after Castro: What Policy Best Serves U.S. National Interests?* Carlisle Barracks, Pa.: U.S. Army War College, 2002. 22 pp. (Also available on public STINET: http://stinet.dtic.mil/)

Shahi, Laura A. "Conceptual Convergences: A Study of Public Diplomacy and Public Relations in U.S. and Cuban Relations throughout the Bay of Pigs and Elián González Issues." Master's thesis, University of Florida, 2002. 112 pp.

Valdés-Dapena, Jacinto. *La CIA contra Cuba: La actividad subversiva de la CIA y la contrarrevolución*. Havana: Editorial Capitán San Luis, 2002. 270 pp.

White, Christopher M. "Weaving the Mexi-Cuban Blanket: The Development and Maintenance of Mexican–Cuban Relations." Master's thesis, University of Kansas, 2002. 129 pp.

Articles and Papers

"1975: Angola, Cuba and the CIA." *West Africa* 4321 (15 April 2002): 22–23.

Aguilar Rivera, José Antonio. "El zorro y la tortuga." *Encuentro de la Cultura Cubana*

25 (Summer 2002): 298–300. (Article about Cuba's relations with Mexico; previously published in *El Universal*)
Alarcón, Ricardo. "Carter Visit Was Historic: Bush Initiative Laughable—and What about Anti-Cuban Terrorists?" *New Perspectives Quarterly (NPQ)* 19, pt. 3 (2002): 52–53.
Alarcón Quesada, Ricardo. "Respuesta del pueblo." *Casa de las Américas* 228 (July–September 2002): 5–10. (Paper edited by Casa de las Américas, presented at the "Sesión Extraordinaria de la Asamblea Nacional del Poder Popular de Cuba," which took place 24–26 June in Havana, on the theme of foreign relations with the United States; the author is president of the Asamblea)
Botifoll, Luis J. "La República de Cuba y la Enmienda Platt" (The Republic of Cuba and the Platt Amendment). *Herencia* 8, no. 2 (Fall 2002): 4–8.
Brenner, Philip, Patrick J. Haney, and Walter Vanderbush. "The Confluence of Domestic and International Interests: U.S. Policy toward Cuba, 1998–2001." *International Studies Perspectives* 3, no. 2 (2002): 192–208.
Brittain, V. "Cuba in Africa." *New Left Review* 17 (2002): 166–72.
Castro, Fidel. "Junto a todo un pueblo." *Casa de las Américas* 226 (July–September 2002): 32–37. (Paper edited by Casa de las Américas, presented at the "Sesión Extraordinaria de la Asamblea Nacional del Poder Popular de Cuba," which took place 24–26 June in Havana, on the theme of foreign relations with the United States)
Castro Mariño, Soraya M. "U.S.–Cuban Relations during the Clinton Administration." *Latin American Perspectives* 29, no. 4 (July 2002): 47–76.
Doder, D. "The Push for Normalized U.S.–Cuban Relations Grows." *American Prospect* 13, pt. 18 (2002): 26–28.
Domínguez Michael, Christopher. "Castro y los huérfanos de la Revolución Mexicana." *Encuentro de la Cultura Cubana* 25 (Summer 2002): 295–97.
Dumoulin, John. "Diálogo norteamericano–cubano a partir de 1898." In *La Guerra de Cuba desde el Río de la Plata: Actas/Cuartas Jornadas de Historia, Buenos Aires, 14–16 Abril, 1998*, 35–62. Buenos Aires: Ediciones CEPAI, 2002.
Dur, Philip F., and Christopher Gilcrease. "U.S. Diplomacy and the Downfall of a Cuban Dictator: Machado in 1933." *Journal of Latin American Studies* 34, no. 2 (May 2002): 255–82.
Erikson, Daniel P. "The New Cuba Divide." *National Interest* 67 (Spring 2002): 65–71. (Discusses the unexpected alliance of farmers, northern liberals, and Western conservatives challenging the U.S. political status quo on Cuba)
Fernández, José Ramón. "Que no vuelva el oprobio." *Casa de las Améicas* 226 (July–September 2002): 24–26. (Paper edited by Casa de las Américas, presented at the "Sesión Extraordinaria de la Asamblea Nacional del Poder Popular de Cuba," which took place 24–26 June in Havana, on the theme of foreign relations with the United States; the author is Cuba's Minister of Education)
Hernández, Rafael. "Frozen Relations: Washington and Cuba after the Cold War." Translated by NACLA. *NACLA Report on the Americas* 35, no. 4 (January–February 2002): 21–28.
La Rae-Pérez, Cassandra. "Economic Sanctions as a Use of Force: Re-evaluating the Legality of Sanctions from an Effects-Based Perspective." *Boston University International Law Journal* 20, no. 1 (Spring 2002): 161–88.

Pérez, Louis A., Jr. "Fear and Loathing of Fidel Castro: Sources of U.S. Policy toward Cuba." *Journal of Latin American Studies* 34, no. 2 (May 2002): 227–54.
Pérez Roque, Felipe. "Hacia el futuro." *Casa de las Américas* 228 (July–September 2002): 19–23. (Paper edited by Casa de las Américas, presented at the "Sesión Extraordinaria de la Asamblea Nacional del Poder Popular de Cuba," which took place 24–26 June in Havana, on the theme of foreign relations with the United States)
Power, Kevin. "Cuba: Una historia tras otra." In *Atravesados: Deslizamientos de identidad y género,* 68–89. Madrid: Fundación Telefónica, 2002.
Prieto, Abel. "Rambo y Bush." *Casa de las Américas* 228 (July–September 2002): 5–10. (Paper edited by Casa de las Américas, presented at the "Sesión Extraordinaria de la Asamblea Nacional del Poder Popular de Cuba," which took place 24–26 June in Havana, on the theme of foreign relations with the United States)
Salanueva, Olga L. "Razones por una humanidad." *Casa de las Américas* 228 (July–September 2002): 10–12. (Paper presented at the "Sesión Extraordinaria de la Asamblea Nacional del Poder Popular de Cuba," which took place 24–26 June in Havana, on the theme of foreign relations with the United States; the author is the wife of one of the five "patriotas cubanos injustamente prisioneros en cárceles del imperio.")
Schoultz, Lars. "Blessings of Liberty: The United States and the Promotion of Democracy in Cuba." *Journal of Latin American Studies* 34, no. 2 (May 2002): 397–425.
Silva-Herzog Márquez, Jesús. "El castrismo mexicano." *Encuentro de la Cultura Cubana* 25 (Summer 2002): 301–2. (Previously published in *Reforma*)
———. "Zócalo: Republicanizar la diplomacia." *Letras Libres* 4, no. 47 (November 2002): 70. (About relations between Cuba and Mexico)

Geology

Articles and Papers

Alva-Valdivia, L., et al. "Palaeomagnetism of the Guaniquanico Cordillera, Western Cuba: A Pilot Study." *Cretaceous Research* 22, no. 6 (2002): 705–18.
García-Casco, A., et al. "Oscillatory Zoning Ineclogitic Garnet and Amphibole, Northern Serpentinite Melange, Cuba: A Record of Tectonic Instability during Subduction?" *Journal of Metamorphic Geology* 20, no. 6 (2002): 581–98.
Gasparini, Z., N. Bardet, and M. Iturralde-Vinent. "A New Cryptoclidid Plesiosaur from the Oxfordian (Late Jurassic) of Cuba." *Geobios* 35, no. 2 (2002): 201–11.
Grimalt, J. O., et al. "Organic Geochemistry of the Oils from the Southern Geological Province of Cuba." *Applied Geochemistry* 17, no. 1 (2002): 1–10.
Kiyokawa, S., et al. "Cretaceous–Tertiary Boundary Sequence in the Cacarajicara Formation, Western Cuba: An Impact-Related, High-Energy Gravity-Flow Deposit." *Special Papers of the Geological Society of America* 356 (2002): 125–44.
Moreno, Bladimir, Margaret Grandison, and Kuvvet Atakan. "Crustal Velocity Model along the Southern Cuban Margin: Implications for the Tectonic Regime at an Active Plate Boundary." *Geophysical Journal International* 151, no. 2 (2002): 632–45.

"New Structures Identified Off Cuba." *Offshore* 62, no. 9 (2002): 44–48. (The petroleum potential of the Cuban deepwater is being reevaluated based on seismic surveys)
Rodríguez, R., and J. Herrera. "Field Evaluation of Partially Acidulated Phosphate Rocks in a Ferralsol from Cuba." *Nutrient Cycling in Agroecosystems* 63, no. 1 (2002): 21–26.
Tada, R., et al. "Complex Tsunami Waves Suggested by the Cretaceous–Tertiary Boundary Deposit at the Moncada Section, Western Cuba." *Special Papers of the Geological Society of America* 356 (2002): 109–24.

History and Historiography

Books and Monographs

Arnalte, Arturo. *Los últimos esclavos de Cuba: Los niños cautivos de la goleta "Batans."* Madrid: Alianza Editorial, 2001. 198 pp.
Burton, Gera. "Ambivalence in the Colonized Subject: The Counter-Discourse of Richard Robert Madden and Francisco Manzano." Ph.D. diss., University of Missouri—Columbia, 2002. 224 pp.
Cairo Ballester, Ana. *Veinte de mayo: ¿Fecha gloriosa?* Havana: Editorial de Ciencias Sociales, 2002. 197 pp.
Dreke, Víctor. *From the Escambray to the Congo: In the Whirlwind of the Cuban Revolution.* Edited by Mary-Alice Waters. New York: Pathfinder Press, 2002. 182 pp.
Faria, Miguel A. *Cuba in Revolution: Escape from a Lost Paradise.* Macon, Ga.: Hacienda Publications, 2002. 452 pp.
Fernández Santalices, Manuel. *Cronología histórica de Cuba, 1492–2000.* Miami: Ediciones Universal, 2001. 183 pp.
Guerra, Ramiro. *The Territorial Expansion of the United States: At the Expense of Spain and the Hispanic-American Countries.* Edited and translated by Fernando E. Pérez Peña. Lanham, Md.: University Press of America, 2002. (Translation of *Expansión territorial*; includes a section on the "Cuban Question")
Hudson, Rex A., ed. *Cuba: A Country Study.* 4th ed. Washington: Federal Research Division, Library of Congress, 2002. 454 pp.
Krause-Fuchs, Monika. *Monika y la Revolución: Una mirada singular sobre la historia reciente de Cuba.* Gran Canaria, Spain: Centro de la Cultura Popular Canaria, 2002. 288 pp.
Martínez-Fernández, Luis, et al., eds. *Encyclopedia of Cuba: People, History, Culture.* 2 vols. Phoenix, Ariz.: Oryx, 2002. 576 pp.
May, Robert E. *The Southern Dream of a Caribbean Empire, 1854–1861.* 2nd paperback ed, with a new preface. Gainesville: University of Florida Press, 2002. 304 pp. (Features a section on the "Cuban Question")
McGillivray, Gillian. "Blazing Cane: Sugar Communities, Power, and Politics in Cuba, 1868–1948." Ph.D. diss., Georgetown University, 2002. 370 pp.
Milán, Manuela. *Recuento de la historia de Cuba.* Miami: n.p., 2002. 2 vols. (Vol. 1: 1492–1902; vol. 2.: 1902–2002)

Murray, David R. *Odious Commerce: Britain, Spain, and the Abolition of the Cuban Slave Trade.* 1980; reprint, Cambridge, U.K.: Cambridge University Press, 2002. 437 pp.

Navarrete, William, and Javier de Castro Mori, eds. *Centenario de la República Cubana, 1902–2002.* Miami.: Ediciones Universal, 2002. 542 pp. (Contributions by Marifeli Pérez-Stable and others)

Nieto, Clara. *Masters of War: Cuba, the United States, and Latin America.* Translated by Chris Brandt. New York: Seven Stories; London: Turnaround, 2002. 640 pp.

Núñez Vega, Jorge. *La república ambigua: Soberanía, caudillismo y ciudadanía en la construcción de la I República cubana.* Barcelona: Institut de Ciències Polítiques i Socials, 2002. 41 pp.

Opatrn'y, Josef. *Kuba.* Prague: Libri, 2002. 100 pp.

Pérez-Cisneros, Enrique. *El reformismo español en Cuba.* Madrid: Editorial Verbum, 2002. 171 pp.

Perinat Maceres, Santiago. *Las guerras mambisas.* Barcelona: Carena Editorial, 2002. 405 pp. (About Cuba during the 1868–98 period)

Saco, José Antonio. *Obras.* Edited by Eduardo Torres-Cuevas. Havana: Imagen Contemporánea [and] Casa de Altos Estudios de Fernando Ortiz, 2002. (Only vol. 1 has been published)

Schornick, Andrew. "Reporting a Revolution: American Magazine Coverage of the Cuban Revolution, 1956–1959." Master's thesis, Wayne State University, 2002. 186 pp.

Scott, Rebecca J. *La emancipación de los esclavos en Cuba: La transición al trabajo libre, 1860–1899.* Havana: Editorial Caminos, 2002. 378 pp. (Translation of *Slave Emancipation in Cuba*)

Suchlicki, Jaime. *Cuba: From Columbus to Castro and Beyond.* 5th ed. Washington: Brassey's, 2002. 285 pp.

Thomas, Hugh. *Cuba: The Pursuit of Freedom.* Rev. and abridged ed. London: Pan, 2002. 1151 pp. (Reprint of the 2001 rev. ed.)

Torres-Cuevas, Eduardo, and Oscar Loyola Vega. *Historia de Cuba, 1492–1898: Formación y liberación de la nación.* Havana: Editorial Pueblo y Educación, 2001. (Only vol. 1 has been published)

Twigg, Alan. *Cuba: A Concise History for Travellers.* Toronto: Penguin Books, 2002. 198 pp.

Articles and Papers

Aguilar León, Luis. "Cuba: Nacimiento de la República." *Revista Hispano Cubana* 13 (May–September 2002): 65–70.

Alvarez Bravo, Armando. "Martí, la Plaza de la Libertad y el centenario de la instauración de la República de Cuba." *Herencia* 8, no. 2 (Fall 2002): 128.

Bronfman, Alejandra Marina. "'En plena libertad y democracia': Negros Brutos and the Social Question, 1904–1919." *Hispanic American Historical Review* 82, no. 3 (2002): 549–87.

Cantón Navarro, José. "La República Cubana de 1902: Logros y frustración." *Casa de las Américas* 226 (January–March 2002): 19–30.

Cavendish, Richard. "General Batista Returns to Power in Cuba: March 10, 1952." *History Today* 52, no. 3 (March 2002): 56–57.
Díaz Martínez, Manuel. "Ah, la República." *Encuentro de la Cultura Cubana* 24 (Spring 2002): 143–47.
Dopico, Ana María. "Picturing Havana: History, Vision, and the Scramble for Cuba." *Nepantla: Views from the South* 3, no. 3 (2002): 451–93.
Erisman, H. Michael. "The Cuban Revolution's Evolving Identity." *Latin American Politics and Society* 44, no. 1 (Spring 2002): 145–53.
Franqui, Carlos. "La ruina y la esperanza." *Letras Libres* 4, no. 47 (November 2002): 36–37. (Summarizes recent Cuban history with a positive outlook for the future)
Guillot Carvajal, Mario L. "Réquiem por Coppelia." *Revista Hispano Cubana* 13 (May–September 2002): 103–9. (Coppelia is a brand of Cuban ice cream)
Hassan, Sarah D. "'Origins' of Postmodern Cuba." *CR: The New Centennial Review* 2, no. 2 (Summer 2002): 1–17.
Horowitz, Irving Louis. "One Hundred Years of Ambiguity." *National Interest* 67 (2002): 58–65. (Discusses the historical ambiguity of Cuban independence and nationalism)
Iglesias, Marial. "Pedestales vacíos." *Encuentro de la Cultura Cubana* 24 (Spring 2002): 17–34.
Jennings, Evelyn Powell. "State Enslavement in Colonial Havana, 1763–1790." In *Slavery without Sugar: Diversity in Caribbean Economy and Society since the Seventeenth Century,* edited by Verene A. Shepherd, 152–82. Gainesville: University Press of Florida, 2002.
Kapcia, Antoni. "Explaining Cuba." *Revista Europea de Estudios Latinoamericanos y del Caribe / European Review of Latin American and Caribbean Studies* 73 (October 2002): 127–32. (Review article)
———. "The Siege of the Hotel Nacional, Cuba, 1933: A Reassessment." *Journal of Latin American Studies* 34, no. 2 (May 2002): 283–309.
Knight, Franklin W. "The Free Colored Population in Cuba during the Nineteenth Century." In *Slavery without Sugar: Diversity in Caribbean Economy and Society since the Seventeenth Century,* edited by Verene A. Shepherd, 224–47. Gainesville: University Press of Florida, 2002.
Menéndez, Jorge, and Stephen D. Gingerich. "Story of the Sierra." *CR: The New Centennial Review* 2, no. 2 (Summer 2002): 118–27.
Montero, Oscar. "Casal y Maceo en la Habana elegante." *Casa de las Américas* 225 (October–December 2001): 57–70. (Discusses the historical meeting, in 1890, between Julián del Casal and Antonio Maceo)
Naranjo Orovio, Consuelo, and Josef Opatrn'y, eds. "Estudios cubanos a fines del milenio." In *Visitando la isla: Temas de historia de Cuba,* edited by Josef Opatrn'y and Consuelo Naranjo Orovio, 9–26. Münster, Ger.: AHILA; Madrid: Iberoamericana; Frankfurt: Vervuert, 2002.
Ortega, Ana Lucía. "Las mentiras de Baracoa." *Revista Hispano Cubana* 12 (January–March 2002): 61–63.
Pérez-Stable, Marifeli. "La transición pacífica que no tuvo lugar: 1954–1956." *Encuentro de la Cultura Cubana* 24 (Spring 2002): 283–305.
Piqueras Arenas, José Antonio. "Relaciones coloniales, intercambios económicos y

grupos de poder." In *Visitando la isla: Temas de historia de Cuba,* edited by Josef Opatrn'y and Consuelo Naranjo Orovio, 77–101. Münster, Ger.: AHILA; Madrid: Iberoamericana; Frankfurt: Vervuert, 2002.

Roca Antúnez, Vladimiro. "Reflexiones para el centenario de la República." *Revista Hispano Cubana* 13 (July–September 2002): 97–99.

Rojas, Rafael. "Otro gallo cantaría: Ensayo sobre el primer republicanismo cubano." *Encuentro de la Cultura Cubana* 24 (Spring 2002): 97–111.

Roldán de Montaud, Inés. "Los partidos políticos cubanos de la época colonial en la historiografía reciente." In *Visitando la isla: Temas de historia de Cuba,* edited by Josef Opatrn'y and Consuelo Naranjo Orovio, 27–76. Münster, Ger.: AHILA; Madrid: Iberoamericana; Frankfurt: Vervuert, 2002.

Santamaría García, Antonio. "Los márgenes de la especialización: La economía cubana, 1790–1880—Crecimiento agregado y diversificación." In *Visitando la isla: Temas de historia de Cuba,* edited by Josef Opatrn'y and Consuelo Naranjo Orovio, 103–31. Münster, Ger.: AHILA; Madrid: Iberoamericana; Frankfurt: Vervuert, 2002.

Santí, Enrico Mario. "Sobre la Primera República." *Encuentro de la Cultura Cubana* 24 (Spring 2002): 44–49.

Scott, Rebecca J., and Michael Zeuske. "Property in Writing, Property on the Ground: Pigs, Horses, Land, and Citizenship in the Aftermath of Slavery—Cuba, 1880–1909." *Comparative Studies in Society and History* 44, no. 4 (2002): 669–99.

Toledo Sande, Luis. "Cuba, República(s)." *Casa de las Américas* 226 (January–March 2002): 31–39. (About the Republics established 20 May 1902 and 31 December 1958)

Tone, John Lawrence. "How the Mosquito (Man) Liberated Cuba." *History and Technology* 18, no. 4 (2002): 277–308.

Zeuske, Michael. "Lux veritatis, vita memoriae, magistra vitae: Dieciseis vidas y la historia de Cuba." In *Visitando la isla: Temas de historia de Cuba,* edited by Josef Opatrn'y and Consuelo Naranjo Orovio, 161–90. Münster, Ger.: AHILA; Madrid: Iberoamericana; Frankfurt: Vervuert, 2002).

History (Missile Crisis)

Books and Monographs

Blight, James G., Bruce J. Allyn, and David A. Welch. *Cuba on the Brink: Castro, the Missile Crisis, and the Soviet Collapse.* Rev. and expanded ed. Lanham, Md.: Rowman and Littlefield, 2002. 537 pp.

Chrisp, Peter. *The Cuban Missile Crisis.* Milwaukee: World Almanac Libraty, 2002. 64 pp.

Diez Acosta, Tomás. *October 1962: The "Missile" Crisis as Seen from Cuba.* Translated by Ornán Batista Peña. New York: Pathfinder Press, 2002. 333 pp.

Fleming, Fergus. *The Cuban Missile Crisis: To the Brink of World War III.* 2001; reprint, Oxford, U.K.: Heinemann, 2002. 32 pp.

Freedman, Lawrence. *Kennedy's Wars: Berlin, Cuba, Laos, and Vietnam.* 2000; reprint, Oxford, U.K: Oxford University Press, 2002. 528 pp.

Harris, Nathaniel. *The Cuban Missile Crisis.* London: Hodder Wayland, 2002. 32 pp.

Huchthausen, Peter A. *October Fury.* Hoboken, N.J.: Wiley, 2002. 281 pp.
May, Ernest R., and Philip Zelikow, eds. *The Kennedy Tapes: Inside the White House during the Missile Crisis.* Concise ed. New York: Norton, 2002. 514 pp.
Medina, Loreta M., ed. *The Cuban Missile Crisis.* San Diego, Calif.: Greenhaven Press, 2002. 123 pp.
Mozgovoi, Aleksandr Fedorovich. *Kubinskaia samba kvarteta "Fokstrotov."* Moscow: Voennyi Parad, 2002. 117 pp.

Articles and Papers

"The Cuban Missile Crisis Revisited." *Arms Control Today* 32, pt. 9 (2002): 3–4.
Frankel, Max. "Learning from the Missile Crisis." *Smithsonian* 33, no. 7 (October 2002): 52–64.
Jeffreys-Jones, Rhodri. "Man of the People?: JFK and the Cuban Missile Crisis." *Reviews in American History* 30, no. 3 (2002): 486–91.
Krushchev, Sergei. "How My Father and President Kennedy Saved the World: The Cuban Missile Crisis as Seen from the Kremlin." *American Heritage* (October 2002): 66–76.
Lawrence, Mark, ed. "The Kennedy Tapes." *Presidential Studies Quarterly* 32, no. 4 (2002): 810–14.
McKeown, Timothy J. "Plans and Routines, Bureaucratic Bargaining, and the Cuban Missile Crisis." *Journal of Politics* 63, no. 4 (2001): 1163–90.
Miller, Nicola. "The Real Gap in the Cuban Missile Crisis: The Post–Cold War Historiography and the Continued Omission of Cuba." In *War and Cold War in American Foreign Policy, 1942–62,* edited by Dale Carter and Robin Clifton, 211–39. Basingstoke, U.K.; New York: Palgrave, 2002.
Nelson, Anna Karsten. "Operation Northwoods and the Covert War against Cuba, 1961–1963." *Cuban Studies* 32 (2001): 145–54.
White, Mark J. "New Scholarship on the Cuban Missile Crisis." *Diplomatic History* 26, no. 1 (2002): 147–53.
Worsthorne, Peregrine. "Kennedy's Finest Hour: The Excitement of Washington during the Cuban Missile Crisis." *Spectator* (19 October 2002): 22–24.

History (Spanish American War)

Books and Monographs

Acosta Matos, Eliades. *Los colores secretos del Imperio.* Havana: Mercie Ediciones, 2002. 327 pp.
Alonso Romero, María Paz. *Cuba en la España liberal, 1837–1898: Génesis y desarrollo del régimen autonómico.* Madrid: Centro de Estudios Constitucionales, 2002. 223 pp.
Comellas, José Luis. *Del 98 a la semana trágica, 1898–1909: Crisis de conciencia y renovación política.* Madrid: Biblioteca Nueva, 2002. 302 pp.
Crutchfield, James Andrew. *Spanish–American War.* Amawalk, N.Y.: Golden Owl Publishing, 2002. (Consists of 1 portfolio with 22 pieces and a 19-page study guide)

Green, Carl R. *The Spanish American War.* Berkeley Heights, N.J.: MyReportLinks.com Books, 2002. 48 pp.
McNeese, Tim. *Remember the Maine: The Spanish–American War Begins.* Greensboro, N.C.: Morgan Reynolds, 2002. 112 pp.

Articles and Papers

Clementi, Hebe. "1898: Desde Estados Unidos." In *La Guerra de Cuba desde el Río de la Plata: Actas/Cuartas Jornadas de Historia, Buenos Aires, 14–16 Abril, 1998,* 25–53. Buenos Aires: Ediciones CEPAI, 2002.
Dumoulin, John. "Diálogos norteamericanos–cubanos a partir de 1898." In *La Guerra de Cuba desde el Río de la Plata: Actas/Cuartas Jornadas de Historia, Buenos Aires, 14–16 Abril, 1998,* 35–62. Buenos Aires: Ediciones CEPAI, 2002.
Gould, Lewis. "The Reluctant Imperialist." *The New Leader* 85, no. 5 (September/October 2001): 19–21. (Discusses the decision by the United States to go to war with Spain in 1898)
Lértora Mendoza, Celina Ana. "La guerra de Cuba y los silencios." In *La Guerra de Cuba desde el Río de la Plata: Actas/Cuartas Jornadas de Historia, Buenos Aires, 14–16 Abril, 1998,* 75–82. Buenos Aires: Ediciones CEPAI, 2002.
Pelosi, Hebe Carmen. "Las representaciones de la guerra hispano–norteamericana del 98 en la prensa periódica argentina." In *La Guerra de Cuba desde el Río de la Plata: Actas/Cuartas Jornadas de Historia, Buenos Aires, 14–16 Abril, 1998,* 83–96. Buenos Aires: Ediciones CEPAI, 2002.
Riquelme de Lobos, Norma Dolores. "La 'vuelta' a la hispanidad: Una mirada argentina a la guerra de Cuba." In *La Guerra de Cuba desde el Río de la Plata: Actas/Cuartas Jornadas de Historia, Buenos Aires, 14–16 Abril, 1998,* 97–110. Buenos Aires: Ediciones CEPAI, 2002.
Szarazgat, Alex. "La independencia retaceada." In *La Guerra de Cuba desde el Río de la Plata: Actas/Cuartas Jornadas de Historia, Buenos Aires, 14–16 Abril, 1998,* 111–18. Buenos Aires: Ediciones CEPAI, 2002.

Ideology and Philosophy

Books and Monographs

Gott, Richard. *Karl Krause and the Ideological Origins of the Cuban Revolution.* London: Institute of Latin American Studies, University of London, 2002. 16 pp.
Ichikawa Morin, Emilio. *Contra el sacrificio: Del camarada al buen vecino.* Miami: Ediciones Universal, 2002. 163 pp.
Martí, José. *Así pensaba Martí.* Edited by Delfín Leyva Avila. Arecibo, P.R.: Impresos Isla, 2002. 142 pp.
Monal, Isabel, and Olivia Miranda Francisco, eds. *Pensamiento cubano, siglo XIX.* 2 vols. Havana: Editorial de Ciencias Sociales, 2002.

Articles and Papers

Aguilar, Luis E. "La hora de la unanimidad." *Encuentro de la Cultura Cubana* 24 (Spring 2002): 328–29.

Blanco, Juan Antonio. "Una obligación ética." *Encuentro de la Cultura Cubana* 25 (Summer 2002): 283–93. (An ideological interpretation of the government's Proyecto Varela)
Cordoví Núñez, Yoel. "Intelectualidad y regeneración en Cuba, 1880–1902." *Cuadernos Americanos* 95 (2002): 187–215.
Cruz Varela, María Elena. "11 de septiembre de 2001: Comienza el fin de una era." *Revista Hispano Cubana* 12 (January–March 2002): 33–39.
Hernández, Pablo J. "Una observación sobre el mundo al advenimiento de la República de Cuba (1902)." *Encuentro de la Cultura Cubana* 24 (Spring 2002): 7–12.
Hernández, Rafael. "Looking at Cuba: Notes toward a Discussion." Translated by Dick Cluster. *Boundary 2* 29, no. 3 (Fall 2002): 123–26. (Translation of *Mirar a Cuba*)
Mateo Palmer, Margarita. "Signs after the Last Shipwreck." *Boundary 2* 29, no. 3 (Fall 2002): 149–57.
Navarro, Desiderio. "In Medias Res Publicas: On Intellectuals and Social Criticism in the Cuban Public Sphere." Translated by Alessandro Fornazzari and Desiderio Navarro. *Boundary 2* 29, no. 3 (Fall 2002): 187–203.
Ortega, Gregorio. "La república que se fué a pique." *Encuentro de la Cultura Cubana* 24 (Spring 2002): 112–17.
Ortega, Luis. "Los raíces del castrismo." *Encuentro de la Cultura Cubana* 24 (Spring 2002): 317–27.
Rodríguez, Silvio. "Por la patria socialista perfectible." *Casa de las Américas* 228 (July–September 2002): 15–19. (Paper edited by Casa de las Américas, presented at the "Sesión Extraordinaria de la Asamblea Nacional del Poder Popular de Cuba," which took place 24–26 June in Havana)
Vitier, Cintio. "Resistance and Freedom." *Boundary 2* 29, no. 3 (Fall 2002): 247–52.

Labor

Books and Monographs

Alexander, Robert Jackson. *A History of Organized Labor in Cuba*. Westport, Conn.: Praeger, 2002. 287 pp.
Fu, May Chuan. "Rethinking Chinese Workers in Cuban History: Race and Labor in the Transition from Slavery to Freedom, 1847–1899." Master's thesis, University of California at San Diego, 2002. 96 pp.
Piqueras, José Antonio, ed. *Azúcar y esclavitud en el final del trabajo forzado: Homenaje a M. Moreno Fraginals*. Madrid: Fondo de Cultura Económica, 2002. 395 pp.
Workers' Rights in Cuba: Report of the United States Delegation to the 2002 Exchange between U.S. and Cuban Labor and Employment Lawyers, Neutrals, and Trade Unions. Sponsored by the National Lawyers Guild Labor and Employment Committee and the U.S. Health Care Trade Union Committee. New York: National Lawyers Guild, 2002. 32 pp.

Articles and Papers

Córdova, Efrén. "El movimiento obrero" (The Labor Movement). *Herencia* 8, no. 2 (Fall 2002): 26–35.

———. "Política laboral y legislación del trabajo." *Encuentro de la Cultura Cubana* 24 (Spring 2002): 212–22.

Language and Literature

Books and Monographs

Aleza Izquierdo, Milagros, ed. *Estudios lingüísticos cubanos: Homenaje a Leandro Caballero Díaz.* Valencia, Spain: Universitat de València, 2002. 169 pp.

Alvarez, José B. *Contestatory Cuban Short Story of the Revolution.* Lanham, Md.: University Press of America, 2002. 140 pp.

Bardach, Ann Louise, ed. *Cuba.* Berkeley, Calif.: Whereabouts Press, 2002. 234 pp. (Collection of Cuban short stories translated into English)

Barquet, Jesús J., ed. *Teatro y Revolución Cubana: Subversión y utopía en "Los siete contra Tebas" de Antón Arrufat (Theatre and the Cuban Revolution: Subversion and Utopia in "Seven Against Thebes" by Antón Arrufat).* Lewiston, N.Y.: Edwin Mellen Press, 2002. 162 pp.

Barquet, Jesús J., et al. *Poesía cubana del siglo XX: Antología.* Mexico City: Fondo de Cultura Económica, 2002. 556 pp.

Bobes León, Marilyn, ed. *Cuentistas cubanas de hoy.* Mexico City: Océano, 2002. 150 pp.

Bordao, Rafael. *La sátira, la ironía y el carnival literario en "Leporosorio (trilogía poética)" de Reinaldo Arenas.* Lewiston, N.Y.: E. Mellen Press, 2002. 175 pp.

Cacheiro Varela, Maximino. *Diccionario de símbolos y personajes en "Paradiso" y "Oppiano Licario" de José Lezama Lima.* Vigo, Spain: Universidad de Vigo, 2001. 235 pp.

Cámara, Madeline. *La letra rebelde: Estudio de escritoras cubanas.* Miami.: Ediciones Universal, 2002. 155 pp.

Casanova-Marengo, Ilia. *El intersticio de la colonia: Ruptura y mediación en la narrativa antiesclavista cubana.* Madrid: Iberoamericana; Frankfurt-am-Main: Vervuert, 2002. 126 pp.

Castellanos, Jorge. *Invención poética de la nación cubana.* Miami: Ediciones Universal, 2002. 233 pp.

Caulfield, Carlota, ed. *Voces viajeras: Poetisas cubanas de hoy.* Madrid: Ediciones Torremozas, 2002. 111 pp.

Cuentos sin visado: Antología cubano–mexicana. Havana: Unión de Escritores y Artistas de Cuba, 2002. 182 pp.

Deblois, Marie-Josée. "Littérature et politiques culturelles sous Castro: Liberté d'expression, histoire et représentation littéraire dans le roman cubain depuis 1959." Master's thesis, Université de Laval, 2002. 137 pp.

Del Monte, Domingo. *Centón epistolario.* Edited by Sophie Andioc-Torres. 2 vols. Havana: Imagen Contemporánea, 2002. (The author's collected letters, 1822–1835)

Díaz Martínez, Manuel, ed. *Poemas cubanos del siglo XX: Antología.* Madrid: Hiperión, 2002. 276 pp.

Fornet, Jorge, and Carlos Espinosa Domínguez, eds. *Cuento cubano del siglo XX: Antología*. Mexico City: Fondo de Cultura Económica, 2002. 392 pp.
González Díaz, Juan, and Larry Javier González, eds. *De Cuba te cuento*. San Juan, P.R.: Editorial Plaza Mayor, 2002. 302 pp. (Collected short stories)
González López, Waldo. *Viajera intacta del sueño: Antología de la décima cubana*. Havana: Editorial José Martí, 2002. 146 pp.
Hernández Pérez, Jorge Angel. *Ensayos raros y de uso*. Santa Clara, Cuba: Ediciones Sed de Belleza, 2002. 103 pp. (Review of twentieth-century Cuban poetry)
Hernández Rodríguez, Rafael, and Rafael Rojas, eds. *Ensayo cubano del siglo XX: Antología*. Mexico City: Fondo de Cultura Económica, 2002. 738 pp.
Hernández-Ojeda, María. "La palabra frente a la represión: La condición transatlántica de Nivaria Tejera y su trayectoría narrativa en Canarias, Cuba y Francia." Ph.D. diss., University of Florida, 2002. 163 pp.
Lezama Lima, José, ed. *Antología de la poesía cubana*. 4 vols. Madrid: Editorial Verbum, 2002. (First three volumes originally published in 1965; vol. 4, first published in 2002, edited by Angel Esteban and Alvaro Salvador)
Lobato Morchón, Ricardo. *El teatro del absurdo en Cuba, 1948–1968*. Madrid: Editorial Verbum, 2002. 333 pp.
Méndez Rodenas, Adriana. *Cuba en su imagen: Historia e identidad en la literatura cubana*. Madrid: Editorial Verbum, 2002. 228 pp.
Moore, Anita K. "Perspectives of Anti-Imperialism before and after the Cuban Revolution in the Poetry of Nicolás Guillén." Master's thesis, University of Nebraska—Lincoln, 2002. 81 pp.
Morales, Fátima M. "De esclavo a cimarrón: Mito y héroe en dos novelas cubanas: 'Francisco' de Anselmo Suárez y Romero y 'Los guerrilleros negros' de César Leante." Master's thesis, Universidad de Puerto Rico, 2002. 132 pp.
Padura Fuentes, Leonardo. *Un camino de medio siglo: Alejo Carpentier y la narrativa de lo real maravilloso*. Mexico City: Fondo de Cultura Económica, 2002. 392 pp. (First published in 1994)
Pérez, Olga Marta, Thelma Jiménez, and Andrés Blanco Díaz., eds. *Mujeres como islas: Antología de narradoras cubanas, dominicanas y puertorriqueñas*. Santo Domingo: Ediciones Ferilibro; Havana: Unión de Escritores y Artistas de Cuba, 2002. 202 pp.
Quintero-Herencia, Juan Carlos. *Fulguración del espacio: Letras e imaginario institucional de la Revolución Cubana (1960–1971)*. Rosario, Argentina: B. Viterbo Editora, 2002. 574 pp. (Based on the author's doctoral dissertation, Princeton University, 1995)
Ramos, Patricia, and Osvaldo Cleger. *Amor y conocimiento en Cintio Vitier: Aproximaciones a su obra crítica*. Havana: Editora Abril, 2002. 58 pp.
Rexach, Rosario. *Nuevos estudios sobre Martí*. Miami: Ediciones Universal, 2002. 172 pp. (Discusses Martí's literary works)
Sánchez, Francis. *Antología de la décima cósmica de Ciego de Avila, Cuba*. Mexico City: Frente de Afirmación Hispanista, 2002. 70 pp.
Sefami, Jacobo, ed. *La voracidad grafómana: José Kozer*. Mexico City: Universidad Nacional Autónoma de México, 2002. (Includes a long interview with the poet as well as eighteen articles, reviews and commentaries about Koser's work)

Shoaf, Kristin E. *La evolución ideológica del teatro de José Triana: Una contextualización de la identidad nacional cubana.* Lanham, Md.: University Press of America, 2002. 90 pp.

Souza, Jorge, ed. *Heridos por la luz: Muestra de poesía cubana contemporánea.* Guadalajara, Mex.: Centro Universitario de Ciencias Sociales y Humanidades, Universidad de Guadalajara, 2002. 367 pp.

Strausfeld, Michi. *Nuevos narradores cubanos.* Madrid: Siruela Ediciones, 2002. 346 pp. (Reprint of the 2000 edition)

Vitier, Cintio. *Lo cubano en la poesía.* Ed. definitiva. Havana: Editorial Letras Cubanas, 2002. 406 pp. (Reprint of the 1998 edition)

Articles and Papers

Abudu, Gabriel A. "African Oral Arts in Excilia Saldaña's 'Kele Kele.'" *Afro-Hispanic Review* 21, no. 1–2 (Spring–Fall 2002): 134–43.

Almanza, Rafael. "La teología de la poesía en Cuba: Cuatro autores del siglo XX." *Encuentro de la Cultura Cubana* 24 (Spring 2002): 118–24.

Alonso Gallo, Laura P. "Un largo archipiélago de otras in*cuba*ciones: La condición cubana del exilio en la obra de Gustavo Pérez Firmat." *Revista Hispano Cubana* 13 (May–September 2002): 51–62.

Añel, Armando. "Censura y autocensura en la literatura cubana de los noventa: Una observación y algunos apuntes." *Revista Hispano Cubana* 13 (May–September 2002): 71–78.

Araújo, Nara. "Erizar y divertir: La poética de Ena Lucía Portela." *Cuban Studies* 32 (2001): 55–73.

Arencibia, Lourdes. "En busca de un tiempo de fábulas." *Temas* 28 (January–March 2002): 120–33. (Discussion of Reinaldo Arenas)

Barquet, Jesús J., and Kathleen West, eds. "The Island Odyssey, 2002: Contemporary Cuban Poets." *Puerto de Sol* 37, no. 1 (Spring 2002): 1–120.

Barrio-Vilar, Laura. "Narrating the Slave Self in the Americas: Issues of Authority, Voice, and Identity in Cuban Narratives of Slavery." *Journal of Caribbean Studies* 17, nos. 1 and 2 (Summer and Fall 2002): 33–50.

Birkenmaier, Anke. "Más allá del realismo sucio: *El Rey de La Habana* de Pedro Juan Gutiérrez." *Cuban Studies* 32 (2001): 37–54.

Caulfield, Carlota. "Cuban Literature and Culture: Critical Junctures." *Latin American Research Review* 37, no. 3 (Summer 2002): 231–48. (Review essay)

Díaz, Fidel. "Pero los dientes no hincan en la luz." *Temas* 29 (April–June 2002): 111–18. (Analyzes Antonio José Ponte's *El abrigo de aire*, published in *Encuentro de la Cultura Cubana* 16–17 [Spring–Summer 2000])

Draper, Susana. "Voluntad de intelectual: Juan Francisco Manzano entre las redes de un humanismo sin derechos." *Chasqui* 31, no. 1 (May 2002): 3–17.

Ellis, Keith. "National Ties and Metonymic Imagery: The Epistle as Used by Nicolás Guillén." *The Modern Language Review* 97, pt. 3 (July 2002): 592–601.

Enkvist, Inger. "Juan Goytisolo, Cuba y el mundo conceptual del 68." *Revista Hispano Cubana* 12 (January–March 2002): 65–76.

Espinosa Mendoza, Norge. "Sobre *Lo cubano en la poesía*." *Encuentro de la Cultura Cubana* 24 (Spring 2002): 140–42. (Reviews the 1957 edition of the work by Cintio Vitier)

Febles, Jorge. "La ineludible voz tácita del otro en *El negrero: Vida novelada de Pedro Blanco Fernández de Trava*." *Hispania* 84, no. 4 (December 2001): 758–66. (Discusses the novel on the slave trade by Lino Novás Calvo)

Fondevila, Orlando. "José Martí, poeta total: Cuba, su mayor poema." *Revista Hispano Cubana* 13 (May–September 2002): 33–40.

Fornet, Ambrosio. "The Cuban Literary Diaspora and Its Contexts: A Glossary." *Boundary 2* 29, no. 3 (Fall 2002): 91–103.

Fowler-Calzada, Víctor. "Casey's Nineteenth Century and the Ciclón Project." Translated by Jacqueline E. Loss. *CR: The New Centennial Review* 2, no. 2 (Summer 2002): 187–200.

García Chichester, Ana. "Virgilio Piñera and the Formulation of a National Literature." *CR: The New Centennial Review* 2, no. 2 (Summer 2002): 231–51.

García Verdecia, Manuel. "*Paradiso*: La imagen y el caos." *Temas* 28 (January–March 2002): 79–89. (Analyzes the poem by José Lezama Lima)

González Alvarez, José Manuel. "Virgilio Piñera y *Orígenes*: La voz de un disidente." *Studi di Letteratura Ispano-Americano* 34–35 (2002): 101–6.

González Echevarría, Roberto. "*Mujer en traje de batalla*." *Encuentro de la Cultura Cubana* 23 (Winter 2001/2002): 207–18. (Critique of the novel by Antonio Benítez Rojo)

Harris, V. J., and R. B. Barrera. "Images of Literacy and Literature in Cuba." *New Advocate* 15, pt. 1 (2002): 68–70.

Iñigo Madrigal, Luis. "Lo oral y Nicolás Guillén." *Casa de las Américas* 226 (January–March 2002): 122–28.

Lazo, Rodrigo. "Filibustering Cuba: *Cecilia Valdés* and a Memory of Nation in the Americas." *American Literature* 74, no. 1 (March 2002): 1–30. (Discusses the ways in which Cuban culture and politics are portrayed in Cirilo Villaverde's *Cecilia Valdés o La loma del angel*)

Lee, Debbie. "Regino Pedroso and *El ciruelo de Yuan Pei Fu: Poemas chinos*." *Amerasia Journal* 28, no. 2 (2002): 93–105. (Part of a special issue on Asians in the Americas)

———. "Regino Pedroso and *Nosotros*: Decolonization and Reconstruction of Self." *Palara* 6 (Fall 2002): 72–83.

López, César. "Presencia y ausencia de una revista de poesía." *Encuentro de la Cultura Cubana* 23 (Winter 2001/2002): 46–50.

López Cruz, Humberto. "Las microficciones dentro de la narrativa de Roberto G. Fernández." *Cuban Studies* 32 (2001): 1–12.

López Sacha, Francisco. "De *Motivos de son* a *Concierto barroco*: La integración del negro en la cultura anericana." *Casa de las Américas* 226 (January–March 2002): 129–33. (Analyzes the role of blacks in the works of Nicolás Guillén and Alejo Carpentier)

Luis, William. "Exhuming *Lunes de Revolución*." *CR: The New Centennial Review* 2, no. 2 (Summer 2002): 253–83. (About the most widely read literary supplement in the history of Cuban and Latin American literature)

Machover, Jacobo. "Detrás de los barrotes, la poesía." *Revista Hispano Cubana* 13 (May–September 2002): 163–68.

Olivares, Jorge. "A Twice-Told Tail: Reinaldo Arenas's *El Cometa Halley.*" *PMLA* 117, no. 5 (October 2002): 1188–1206.

Pérez Firmat, Gustavo. "Bilingual Blues, Bilingual Bliss: El caso Casey." *MLN: Modern Language Notes* 117, no. 2 (March 2002): 432–48. (Argues that Cuban writer Calvert Casey uses English and Spanish for different purposes)

Piñera, Virgilio, and Stephen D. Gingerich. "Cuba and Literature." *CR: The New Centennial Review* 2, no. 2 (2002): 89–100.

Repilado, Ricardo. "El tapiz de Angeles." *Casa de las Américas* 228 (July–September 2002): 51–66. (Analyzes the novel *Otro golpe de dados*, by Pablo Armando Fernández, published in 1993 by Editorial Letras Cubanas in Havana)

Rojas, Rafael. "El campo roturado: Políticas intelectuales de la narrativa cubana de fin de siglo." *Revista Hispano Cubana* 13 (May–September 2002): 41–50.

———. "Cintio Vitier: Poesía y poder." *Letras Libres* 4, no. 47 (November 2002): 74–79.

———. "*Orígenes* and the Poetics of History." Translated by Luis R. Aguilar Moreno. *CR: The New Centennial Review* 2, no. 2 (Summer 2002): 151–85.

Salgado, César A. "The Novels of *Orígenes.*" *CR: The New Centennial Review* 2, no. 2 (Summer 2002): 201–30.

Sampedro, Benita. "Afro-Cuban Literature: Critical Juncture." *Research in African Literatures* 33, no. 4 (2002): 224–26. (Review essay)

Sapphire. "Nancy Morejón." Translated by Jason Weiss. *Bomb* 78 (Winter 2001/2002): 72–75. (An African American woman novelist and poet interviews the most internationally successful and widely translated Cuban woman poet of the postrevolutionary period)

"Selected articles from *Orígenes* (1944–56) and *Ciclón* (1955–59)." Translated by Stephen D. Gingerich. *CR: The New Centennial Review* 2, no. 2 (Summer 2002): 19–150. (Articles by José Lezama Lima, Julián Orbón, and Cintio Vitier, reprinted from *Orígenes,* and by Virgilio Piñera, Calvert Casey, Guillermo Cabrera Infante, Jorge Menéndez, and Pablo Armando Fernández, reprinted from *Ciclón*)

Serafín, Silvana. "María Elena Llana, una scrittice a Cuba." *Studi di Letteratura Ispano-Americana* 34–35 (2002): 107–18.

Serrano, Pío E. "La poesía de María Elena Cruz Varela." *Revista Hispano Cubana* 12 (January–March 2002): 83–88.

Stone, Marta Elena. "Articulating Risk: Spirituality and Bilingualism in the Poetry of Armando Fernández." *Cuban Studies* 32 (2001): 13–36.

Updike, John. "Sobre 'El mar de las lentejas.'" *Encuentro de la Cultura Cubana* 23 (Winter 2001/2002): 28–31. (Discusses the work by Antonio Benítez Rojo)

Valdés, Armando. "La escritura de la isla: Notas sobre la narrativa cubana." *Revista Hispano Cubana* 13 (May–September 2002): 125–34.

Valero, Arnaldo E. "Nación y transculturación en la etnología y la narrativa cubana." *Estudios: Revista de Investigaciones Literarias y Culturales* 10, no. 19 (January–July 2002): 55–71.

Vallejo, Catharina. "Women Writers and Modernism: Strategies of Expression in the Cuban Poet Nieves Xenes." *Revista Canadiense de Estudios Hispánicos* 26, no. 3 (2002): 511–27.
Walcott, Derek. "Cabrera Infante: El gran exiliado." Translated by Adriana Santoveña. *Letras Libres* 4, no. 47 (November 2002): 22–28.

Law and Human Rights

Books and Monographs

Amnesty International. *Cuba: Questions and Answers on the Work of Amnesty International.* London: Amnesty International, International Secretariat, 2002. 4 pp.
———. *Memorandum to the U.S. Government on the Rights of People in U.S. Custody in Afghanistan and Guantánamo Bay.* London: Amnesty International Secretariat, 2002. 61 pp.
Carbonell Cortina, Néstor, ed. *Grandes debates de la Constitución cubana de 1940.* Miami: Ediciones Universal, 2001. 365 pp.
Linares Estrella, Angel. *Un problema de la parte general del derecho penal económico: El actuar en nombre de otro — Un análisis del derecho penal español y cubano.* Granada: Editorial Comares, 2002. 409 pp.
Walton, Clifford Stevens. *The Civil Law in Spain and the Spanish Civil Code in Force, Annotated and with References to the Civil Codes of Mexico, Central, and South America.* Union, N.J.: Lawbook Exchange, 2002. (Reprint of the 1900 edition)

Articles and Papers

Basdeo, Sahadeo, and Ian Hesketh. "Canada, Cuba, and Constructive Engagement into the New Millenium: Political Dissidents and Human Rights." In *Caribbean Survival and the Global Challenge,* edited by Ramesh Ramsaran, 187–211. Kingston: Ian Randle; Boulder, Colo.: L. Rienner, 2002.
Bernal, Beatriz. "Estudio histórico-jurídico de la Constitución de 1901." *Encuentro de la Cultura Cubana* 24 (Spring 2002): 154–70.
Céspedes, Carlos Manuel de. "Aproximación a la Constitución de 1940." *Encuentro de la Cultura Cubana* 24 (Spring 2002): 171–89.
De la Cuesta, Leonel Antonio. "Cuatro décadas de historia constitucional cubana, 1959–1999." *Cuban Studies* 32 (2001): 98–119.
De la Torre, Rogelio A. "El derecho civil." *Encuentro de la Cultura Cubana* 24 (Spring 2002): 190–99.
Gómez González, Orlando Tadeo. "Evolución del derecho penal." *Encuentro de la Cultura Cubana* 24 (Spring 2002): 200–11.
González Alfonso, Ricardo. "La carta de Carter." *Revista Hispano Cubana* 13 (May–September 2002): 157–60. (Features a roundtable with former President Jimmy Carter and Cuban officials on human rights and other issues)
Guerra, Irene. "Habla el disidente cubano Elizardo Sánchez." *Revista Hispano Cubana* 12 (January–March 2002): 161–70. (Interview with the Cuban human rights activist)
Mesa-Lago, Carmelo. "Cuba en el 'Indice de Desarrollo Humano' en los 90: Caída,

rebote milagroso y exclusión." *Encuentro de la Cultura Cubana* 23 (Winter 2001/ 2002): 89–104.

Yip Aramillo, Josefa, et al. "Regulaciones sanitarias para cosméticos en la República de Cuba." *Alimentaria* 39, no. 332 (2002): 133–37.

Literature (Individual Authors — Cubans and Cubans Abroad)
Books and Monographs

Abreu Felippe, José. *Sabanalamar.* Miami: Ediciones Universal, 2002. 287 pp. (A novel)

Albertini, José A. *El entierro del enterrador.* Miami: Ediciones Universal, 2002. 253 pp. (A novel)

Alvarez, Ileana. *Oscura cicatriz.* Ciego de Avila, Cuba: Ediciones Avila, 2002. 78 pp. (Poetry)

Alvarez Alvarez, Luis. *Difícil de descifrar.* Havana: Editorial Letras Cubanas, 2002. 56 pp. (Poetry)

Aragón, Uva de. *Memoria del silencio.* Miami: Ediciones Universal, 2002. 256 pp. (A novel)

Bernardo, José Raúl. *The Wise Women of Havana.* New York: Rayo, 2002. 323 pp. (A novel simultaneously published in Spanish as *Las sabias mujeres de La Habana*)

Boti y Barreiro, Regino Eladio. *El mar y la montaña.* Havana: Unión de Escritores y Artistas de Cuba, 2002. 154 pp. (Poetry first published in 1921)

Campo, Rafael. *Landscape with Human Figure.* Durham, N.C.: Duke University Press, 2002. 88 pp. (Poetry)

Castillo, Sandra M. *My Father Sings to My Embarrassment.* Buffalo, N.Y.: White Pine Press, 2002. 93 pp. (Poetry)

Consuegra, Pedro. *Sonetario máximo.* Marseilles, France: P. Consuegra, 2002. 293 pp.

Cueto Roig, Juan. *Ex-cuetos.* Miami: Ediciones Universal, 2002. 157 pp. (Short stories)

Díaz Canto, Lourdes. *Prohibido pasar la senda.* Edited by Michel Martín. Cienfuegos, Cuba: Ediciones Mecenas, 2002. 100 pp. (Poetry)

Garcia, Cristina. *Las hermanas Agüero.* Translated by Alan West. Waterville, Me.: Thorndike Press, 2002. (Translation of the novel *The Agüero Sisters*)

García Marruz, Fina. *Antología poética.* Mexico City: Fondo de Cultura Económica, 2002. 327 pp. (Reprint of the 1997 edition)

Garcia-Aguilera, Carolina. *Aguas sangrientas.* Miami: Planeta Publishing, 2002. 311 pp. (Translation of the novel *Bloody Waters*)

———. *Bitter Sugar: A Lupe Solano Mystery.* New York: Avon Books, 2002. 315 pp. (Reprint of the 2001 edition)

———. *One Hot Summer: A Novel.* New York: Rayo, 2002. 276 pp. (Focuses on Cuban-American women in Miami)

Gonzalez, Edward. *Ernesto's Ghost: A Novel.* New Brunswick, N.J.: Transaction Publishers, 2002. 341 pp.

González-Llorente, José Miguel. *La odisea del Obalunko: Relato de una invasión pacífica a la isla.* Miami: Ediciones Universal, 2002. 488 pp. (A novel)

Guillén, Nicolás. *Donde nacen las aguas: Antología.* Mexico City: Fondo de Cultura Económica, 2002. 573 pp. (Poetry)
Haug Morales, Susana. *Claroscuro.* Havana: Editora Abril, 2002. 49 pp. (A short story)
Iturralde, Iraída. *La isla rota.* Madrid: Verbum Editorial, 2002. 47 pp. (Poetry)
Jiménez, Onilda A. *Vuelta al génesis.* Miami: Ediciones Universal, 2002. 167 pp. (A novel)
Jorge, Andrés. *Voyeurs.* Mexico City: Alfaguara, 2002. 290 pp. (A novel)
Kozer, José. *Anima.* Mexico City: Fondo de Cultura Económica, 2002. 161 pp. (Poetry)
Ladaga, Leopoldo Elio. *Jessica: Historia de un aborto.* Miami: Ediciones Universal, 2002. 154 pp. (A novel)
Leyva Portal, Waldo. *La distancia y el tiempo.* Havana: Unión de Escritores y Artistas de Cuba, 2002. 222 pp. (Poetry)
Lezama Lima, José. *Poesía y prosa: Antología.* Edited by Iván González Cruz. Madrid: Editorial Verbum, 2002. 365 pp.
Lorenzo, Ismael. *Matías Pérez entre los locos.* n.p.: Ediciones El Gato Tuerto, 2002. 131 pp. (A novel)
Manzano Díaz, Roberto. *El racimo y la estrella.* Havana: Unión de Escritores y Artistas de Cuba, 2002. 93 pp. (Poetry)
Martí Fuentes, Adolfo. *Sonetos fieles.* Havana: Unión de Escritores y Artistas de Cuba, 2002. 117 pp.
Matas, Julio. *El rapto de La Habana: Ocho obras dramáticas.* Bloomington, Ind.: First Books Library, 2002. 264 pp.
Mitjans Cabrera, Julio Hilario. *Alejándose del resto.* Havana: Casa Editora Abril, 2002. 31 pp. (Poetry)
Montenegro, Nivia. *Mi música en otra parte.* Madrid: Editorial Verbum, 2001. 80 pp. (Poetry)
Morejón, Nancy. *Cuerda veloz: Antología poética, 1962–1992.* Havana: Editorial Letras Cubanas, 2002. 192 pp.
Núñez Miró, Isidoro. *Humos de poeta.* Havana: Unión de Escritores y Artistas de Cuba, 2002. 147 pp.
Obejas, Achy. *Days of Awe.* 1st trade paperback ed. New York: Ballantine Books, 2002. 370 pp. (A novel about Cuban-American women and families; first published in 2001)
Padura Fuentes, Leonardo. *L'automne à Cuba: Roman.* Translated by Mara Hernández and René Solí. Paris: Editions Métaillé, 2002. 232 pp. (Translation of *Paisaje de otoño*)
Pérez-Boitel, Luis Manuel. *Aún nos pertenece el otoño.* Havana: Casa de las Américas, 2002. 96 pp. (Poetry)
———. *La oración del inquilino.* Santa Clara, Cuba: Ediciones Sed de Belleza, 2002. 47 pp. (Poetry)
Ponte, Antonio José. *Contrabando de sombras.* Barcelona: Mondadori, 2002. 358 pp. (A novel)
———. *Tales from the Cuban Empire.* Translated by Cola Franzen. San Francisco: City Light Books, 2002. 90 pp. (Translation of *Cuentos de todas partes del imperio*)
Prats, Delfín. *El esplendor y el caos.* Havana: Unión de Artistas y Escritores de Cuba, 2002. 61 pp. (Poetry)

San Francisco, Julio. *Todo mi corazón y otros agravantes: Poemas escritos en La Habana y Madrid.* Miami: Ediciones Universal, 2002. 95 pp.
Sánchez Rodríguez, Francisco. *Reserva federal: Relatos.* Ciego de Avila, Cuba: Ediciones Avila, 2002. 96 pp.
Silverio-Latour, Juan. *Historias en poesías.* Miami: Ediciones Universal, 2002. 109 pp.
Suarez, Virgil. *Guide to the Blue Tongue: Poems.* Urbana: University of Illinois Press, 2002. 88 pp.
———. *Infinite Refuge.* Houston: Arte Público Press, 2002. 130 pp. (Autobiographical)
———. *Latin Jazz.* Baton Rouge: Louisiana State University Press, 2002. 290 pp. (A novel)
Tejera, Nivaria. *Espero la noche para soñarte, Revolución.* Miami: Ediciones Universal, 2002. 176 pp. (A novel condemning the present regime)
Valdés, Zoé. *Les mystères de la Havane.* Translated by Julie Amiot and Carmen Val Julián. Paris: Calmann-Lévy, 2002. 249 pp. (Translation of the novel *Los misterios de La Habana*)
———. *El pie de mi padre.* Barcelona: Editorial Planeta, 2002. 225 pp. (A novel)
Valle Ojeda, Amir. *Muchacha azul bajo la lluvia.* Havana: Editorial Letras Cubanas, 2002. 131 pp. (A novel)
———. *Las puertas de la noche.* San Juan, P.R.: Editorial Plaza Mayor, 2002. 198 pp. (A novel)
Vázquez Díaz, René. *La isla del Cundeamor.* Havana: Editorial Letras Cubanas, 2002. 348 pp. (A novel first published in 1995)
Veciana-Suarez, Ana. *Flight to Freedom.* New York: Orena Books, 2002. 197 pp. (A novel)
Vitier, Cintio. *Antología poética.* Mexico City: Fondo de Cultura Económica, 2002. 522 pp. (Reprint of the 1997 edition)

Articles and Papers

Aguado, Ladisleo. "Abril de whisky y viernes en las rocas." *Encuentro de la Cultura Cubana* 23 (Winter 2001/2002): 219–25. (Poetry)
Alberto, Eliseo. "Epílogo." *Encuentro de la Cultura Cubana* 25 (Summer 2002): 157–72. ("Fragmentos del epílogo de la nueva edición de [su] *Informe contra mí mismo*")
Alcides, Rafael. "La princesa dormida." *Encuentro de la Cultura Cubana* 24 (Spring 2002): 129–39. (A short story)
Arencibia, Lourdes. "La fiesta del cazador." *Encuentro de la Cultura Cubana* 25 (Summer 2002): 152–53. (A short story)
Barnet, Miguel. "Three Poems." *Boundary 2* 29, no. 3 (Fall 2002): 31–33.
Benítez Rojo, Antonio. "Lafcadio Hearn, mi tía Gloria y lo sobrenatural." *Encuentro de la Cultura Cubana* 23 (Winter 2001/2002): 5–8. ("Homenaje a Anonio Benítez Rojo")
Díaz Espí, Pablo. "Los perros." *Encuentro de la Cultura Cubana* 25 (Summer 2002): 143–50. (A short story)
Diego, Josefina de. "El viejito del cementerio." *Encuentro de la Cultura Cubana* 25 (Summer 2002): 151. (A short story)

Fleites, Alex. "De Sargadelos." *Encuentro de la Cultura Cubana* 23 (Winter 2001/ 2002): 207–18. (A short story)
Fuertes, José Guillermo. "El mar y el poder." *Revista Hispano Cubana* 12 (January– March 2002): 143–56. (A short story)
García Marruz, Fina. "[Poesías.]" *Casa de las Américas* 226 (January–March 2002): 66–68. (Cruz de palomas—Sarcófago de los esposos—Sabores—Italia—Como un romano—Me acuerdo de Darío—"La pietá" de Miguel Angel)
———. "To the Statue of Liberty." *Boundary 2* 29, no. 3 (Fall 2002): 121–22. (A poem)
García Monreal, Emilio. "Presentación del olvido y otros poemas." *Encuentro de la Cultura Cubana* 23 (Winter 2001/2002): 65–68.
Gil, Lourdes. "Poesía." *Encuentro de la Cultura Cubana* 25 (Summer 2002): 173–80. (Fata Morgana—El secreto de Onegin—Regina María—El extravío—Finisterre)
Kozer, José. "Anima—Pascua." *Casa de las Américas* 228 (July–September 2002): 80–83. (Selections from the poems)
Martín, Baltasar. "Clon de oveja negra: ¿Infiel Castrol II? (Cuento de ciencia-ficción)." *Revista Hispano Cubana* 13 (July–September 2002): 135–41.
Méndez Alpízar, L. Santiago. "Cuatro poemas del libro inédito *Flash-Back*." *Revista Hispano Cubana* 13 (July–September 2002): 144–45.
Morales, Adrián. "Separados por el agua." *Revista Hispano Cubana* 13 (July– September 2002): 143. (A short story)
Morejón, Nancy. *Three Poems*. Translated by Dawn Duke. *Boundary 2* 29, no. 3 (Fall 2002): 159–62.
Pérez, Omar. "Four Poems." Translated by Kristin Dykstra. *Boundary 2* 29, no. 3 (Fall 2002): 211–13. (From his 1996 collection *Algo de lo sagrado*)
Ponte, Antonio José. "El abrigo de aire." *Temas* 29 (April–June 2002): 118–23. (Excerpt from the original short story published in 2001 with Mónica Bernabé and Marcela Zanin by Viterbio Editora; Rosario, Argentina)
———. "The Supervised Party." *Boundary 2* 29, no. 3 (Fall 2002) 215–24. (A short story about Havana)
Prats Sariol, José. "Grilled Shrimp Pasta." *Boundary 2* 29, no. 3 (Fall 2002): 235–46. (A short story)
Rivero, Raúl. "Chango's Little White Horse." *Boundary 2* 29, no. 3 (Fall 2002): 225– 27. (A short story)
Rodríguez, Reina María. "Two Prose Poems." Translated by Kristin Dykstra and Nancy Gates Madsen. *Boundary 2* 29, no. 3 (Fall 2002): 229–33.
Rodríguez Rivera, Guillermo. "Una isla en palabras." *Encuentro de la Cultura Cubana* 23 (Winter 2001/2002): 62–64.
Suarez, Virgil. "Hilario: El carretero del barrio." *Manoa* 14, no. 1 (2002): 62–64. (A short story)
———. "My Paternal Grandmother's Instructions before We Left Cuba." *Prairie Schooner* 76, no. 1 (Spring 2002): 28–29. (A poem)
Victoria, Carlos. "Cuentos de una isla que se repite." *Encuentro de la Cultura Cubana* 23 (Winter 2001/2002): 19–21.
Vidal, Guillermo. "Las polluelas." *Encuentro de la Cultura Cubana* 25 (Summer 2002): 154–55. (A short story)

Literature about Cuba

Books and Monographs

Bandera, María del Carmen de la. *Cuba linda y perdida.* 7th ed. Miami: Ediciones Universal, 2002. 256 pp. (A novel by a Spanish author)

Bussières, Paul. *Olimpia de La Havane: Roman.* Paris: R. Laffont, 2002. 343 pp.

Camín, Alfonso. *Carey y nuevos poemas.* Mexico City: n.p., 2002. (Reprint of the 1945 edition)

Coffey, Tom. *Miami Twilight.* New York: Pocket Books, 2002. 292 pp.

Coleman, Lynn A. *One Man's Honor.* Urichsville, Ohio: Heartsong Presents, 2002. 169 pp.

Crowley, John. *The Translator.* New York: W. Morrow, 2002. 295 pp. (A novel about the Cuban missile crisis)

Edwards, John. *Crucible of Empire.* n.p.: First Books, 2002. 301 pp. (A novel about the Spanish–American War)

Eringer, Robert. *Spookaroonie.* Mt. Pleasant, S.C.: Corinthian Books, 2002. 196 pp.

Figueredo, D. H. *The Road to Santiago.* New York: Lee and Low Books, 2002. (A novel based on a true incident in the life of the author)

Franz Rosell, Joel. *Mi tesoro te espera en Cuba.* Buenos Aires: Editorial Sudamericana, 2002. 148 pp. (A novel)

Greene, Graham. *Nuestro hombre en La Habana.* Translated by Ana Golder. Madrid: Alianza Editorial, 2002. (Translation of the novel *Our Man in Havana*)

Hijuelos, Oscar. *A Simple Habana Melody (from when the World Was Good).* New York: HarperCollins Publishers, 2002. 342 pp. (A novel about a Cuban composer returning to Havana)

Jordan, Pat. *A.k.a. Sheila Doyle.* 1st Carroll and Graf ed. New York: Carroll and Graf, 2002. 330 pp. (A suspense novel)

Kelleher, Michael. *Cuba.* New Haven, Conn.: Phylum Press, 2002. (A poem)

Latour, José. *The Fool.* London: HarperCollins, 2002. 256 pp. (A novel)

———. *Havana Best Friends.* London: HarperCollins, 2002. 378 pp. (A novel)

———. *Outcast.* New York: Perennial, 2002. 295 pp. (A novel)

Lemon, Brendan. *Last Night.* Los Angeles: Alyson, 2002. 237 pp. (The author recounts the events that led him from Manhattan to a Cuban jail on the eve of his execution)

Leonard, Elmore. *Cuba libre.* Paperback ed. New York: HarperTorch, 2002. 405 pp.

Pereda, David. *Havana Confidential.* Baltimore, Md.: America House, 2002. 171 pp. (A novel)

Lostal, S. L. *Traficantes de libertad: La saga del vapor Virginius.* n.p., 2002. 284 pp. (Novel by a Spanish author)

Muldoon, Thomas. *An Execution of Honor.* New York: Leisure Books, 2002. 395 pp.

Pickens, Lucy Petaway Holcombe. *The Free Flag of Cuba: The Lost Novel of Lucy Holcombe Pickens.* Edited by Orville Vernon Burton and Georganne B. Burton. Baton Rouge: Louisiana State University Press, 2002. 212 pp.

Truman, Margaret. *Murder in Havana.* New York: Fawcett Books, 2002. 373 pp. (A mystery novel)

Williams, Lee. *Author of Destiny: Also Known as the Ochoa Case.* Livingston, Ala.: Livingston Press at the University of West Alabama, 2002. 231 pp. (A novel)

Wispelaere, Paul de. *Cuba en andere reisverhalen (Cuba and other Travel Tales).* Amsterdam: Adams, 2002. 174 pp.

Articles and Papers

Ott, Bill. "Cuba in Crime Fiction." *American Libraries* 33, no. 5 (May 2002): 86. (Annotated bibliography of crime fiction set in Cuba)

Politics, Government, and Armed Forces

Books and Monographs

Buch, Luis, and Reinaldo Suárez Suárez. *Otros pasos del gobierno revolucionario cubano: El fin de la luna de miel.* Havana: Editorial de Ciencias Sociales, 2002. 320 pp.
Chaffee, Wilber A., and Gary Prevost, eds. *Cuba: A Different America.* rev. ed. Lanham, Md.: Rowman and Littlefield, 2002. 206 pp.
Cuba. Consejo de Estado. *Cuba's Answer to Bush: A Yes for Socialism.* Havana: Editora Política, 2002. 107 pp.
Delgado Díaz, Carlos Jesús. *Límites socioculturales de la educación ambiental: Acercamiento desde la experiencia caribeña.* Mexico City: Siglo Veintiuno, 2002. 189 pp. (Treatise on political ecology)
Dolgoff, Sam. *Kub'ansk 'a revoluce: Kritick'y pohled.* Prague: Anarchistick'a knihovna FSA, 2002. 220 pp.
Hernández Rodríguez, Rafael. *Mirar a Cuba: Ensayos sobre cultura y sociedad civil.* Mexico City: Fondo de Cultura Económica, 2002. 194 pp.
López, Juan José. *Democracy Delayed: The Case of Castro's Cuba.* Baltimore, Md.: Johns Hopkins University Press, 2002. 232 pp. (Also available as an electronic book)
Montaner, Carlos Alberto. *Cuba: Un siglo de doloroso aprendizaje.* Miami: Brickell Communications Group, 2002. 206 pp.
Mercier, David. "Cuba dans le temps mondial, 1989–2000: Ou, L'histoire d'un sens contre la mondialisation?" Ottawa: National Library of Canada, 2002. 3 microfiche. (Master's thesis, Université de Ottawa, 2000)
Muller, Alberto. *El Proyecto Varela: Vaclav Havel propone a Oswaldo Payá para el Premio Nobel de la Paz.* Miami: Ediciones Universal, 2002. 111 pp.
Roman, Peter. *People's Power: Cuba's Experience with Representative Government.* Boulder, Colo.: Westview Press, 2002. 284 pp.
Simeón, Roberto. *El proceso político cubano y su relación con el exterior.* Llerena, Spain: Muñoz Moya Editores Extremeños, 2002. 229 pp.

Articles and Papers

Anderson, Bruce. "Cuban Heel: Decades of Instability Will Follow Castro's Departure." *The Spectator* (26 January 2002): 14–16.
Azicri, Max, and Jorge I. Dominguez. "Cuba Today and Tomorrow: Reinventing Socialism." *Annals of the American Academy of Political and Social Science* 579 (2002): 277.

Blanco, Juan Antonio. "Una obligación ética." *Encuentro de la Cultura Cubana* 25 (Summer 2002): 283–93. (About the Proyecto Varela)
Bobes, Velia Cecilia. "Democracia, ciudadanía y sistema político." *Encuentro de la Cultura Cubana* 24 (Spring 2002): 223–33.
Bray, Donald W., and Marjorie Woodford Bray. "The Cuban Revolution and World Change." *Latin American Perspectives* 29, no. 3 (2002): 3–17.
Burchardt, Hans-Jürgen. "Kuba nach Castro: Die neue Ungleichheit und das sich formierende neopopulistische Bündnis." *Internationale Politik und Gesellschaft/ International Politics and Society* 3 (2002): 67–89.
Díaz, Jesús. "Por una segunda República Cubana." *Letras Libres* 4, no. 47 (November 2002): 18–19.
Dilla Alfonso, Haroldo. "Cuba: The Changing Scenarios of Governability." *Boundary 2* 29, no. 3 (Fall 2002): 55–75.
Montaner, Carlos Alberto. "Castro o el dictador inmóvil." *Letras Libres* 4, no. 47 (November 2002): 12–14. (Analyzes Cuba's choices after Castro)
Mora, Frank O. "A Comparative Study of Civil–Military Relations in Cuba and China: The Effects of Bingshang." *Armed Forces and Society* 28, no. 2 (Winter 2002): 183–209.
———. "Cuba: Between Retrenchment and Change." *Problems of Post-Communism* 6 (November/December 2001): 3–63.
Mujal-León, Eusebio, and Joshua W. Busby. "¿Mucho ruido y pocas nueces?: El cambio de régimen político en Cuba." *Encuentro de la Cultura Cubana* 23 (Winter 2001/ 2002): 105–24.
Núñez Vega, Jorge. "La fuga de Ariel: Crisis republicano y síndrome autocrático en Cuba." *Encuentro de la Cultura Cubana* 24 (Spring 2002): 53–67.
Provost, Gary. "Cuba." In *Politics of Latin America: The Power Game,* edited by Harry E. Vanden and Gary Provost, 325–55. New York: Oxford University Press, 2002.
Sabatini, Christopher. "Las políticas posmodernas y sus partidos." *Encuentro de la Cultura Cubana* 23 (Winter 2001/2002): 74–83.
Sims, H. "Public Administration in Cuba." *Public Administration and Development* 22, pt. 3 (2002): 2891.
Suchlicki, Jaime. "La Cuba de Castro: Más continuidad que cambio." *Encuentro de la Cultura Cubana* 23 (Winter 2001/2002): 125–41.
Tugend, Alina. "Cuba: Waiting for Fidel's Finale." *Columbia Journalism Review* 41, no. 2 (July/August 2002): 13–14.

Religion

Books and Monographs

De la Torre, Miguel A. *The Quest for the Cuban Christ: A Historical Search.* Gainesville: University Press of Florida, 2002. 202 pp.
Feraudy Espino, Heriberto. *Irna: Un encuentro con la santería, el espiritismo y el Palo Monte.* Santo Domingo: Editora Manatí, 2002. 182 pp. (First published in 1999)
Mason, Michael Atwood. *Living Santería: Rituals and Experiences in an Afro-Cuban Religion.* Washington, D.C.: Smithsonian Institution Press, 2002. 165 pp.

Palmié, Stephan. *Wizards and Scientists: Explorations in Afro-Cuban Modernity and Tradition.* Durham, N.C.: Duke University Press, 2002. 399 pp.

Portuondo Zúñiga, Olga. *La Virgen de la Caridad del Cobre: Símbolo de cubanía.* Madrid: Agualarga, 2002. 258 pp.

Ramírez Calzadilla, Jorge J., and Alessandra Ciattini. *Religione, politica e cultura a Cuba.* Rome: Bnulzonio, 2002. 312 pp.

Rodés-González, Francisco Antonio. "La orientación pastoral en cuestiones éticas en el contexto cubano actual." Thesis (D. Min.), Columbia Technological Seminary, 2002. 45 pp.

Stevens-Arroyo, Anthony M., ed. *Papal Overtures in a Cuban Key: The Pope's Visit and Civic Space for Cuban Religion.* Scranton, Pa.: University of Scranton Press, 2002. 174 pp.

Articles and Papers

Bejarano, Margalit. "Sephardic Jews in Cuba." *Judaism* 51, no. 1 (Winter 2002): 96–109.

Dianteill, Erwan. "Deterritorialization and Reterritorialization of the Orisha Religion in Africa and the New World: Nigeria, Cuba, and the United States." *International Journal of Urban and Regional Research* 26, no. 1 (2002): 121–38.

Ishemo, Shubi L. "From Africa to Cuba: An Historical Analysis of the 'Sociedad Secreta Abakua.'" *Review of African Political Economy* 92 (2002): 253–73.

Quigley, Thomas E. "The Church and Cuba's International Ties." *America* 186, no. 12 (April 2002): 15–17.

Science and Technology

Books and Monographs

Castro Diaz-Balart, Fidel, ed. *Cuba: Amanecer del tercer milenio — Ciencia, sociología y tecnología.* Madrid: Editorial Debate, 2002. 414 pp.

Articles and Papers

Aitsiselmi, Amina. "Despite U.S. Embargo, Cuban Biotech Booms." *NACLA Report on the Americas* 35, no. 5 (March–April 2002): 38–39.

Alonso-Hernández, C., et al. "137Cs and 210Po Dose Assessment from Marine Food in Cienfuegos Bay (Cuba)." *Journal of Environmental Radioactivity* 61, no. 2 (2002): 203–11.

Hernández-Triana, M., et al. "Total Energy Expenditure by the Doubly Labeled Water Method in Rural Preschool Children in Cuba." *Food and Nutrition Bulletin* 23, no. 3 (2002): 76–82.

"Kinetic Study of a Grinding System in a Cuban Cement Factory." *Materiales de Construcción* 266 (2002): 203–11.

Lage, Agustín. "Ciencia, paz y justicia." *Casa de las Américas* 228 (July–September 2002): 27–31. (Paper edited by Casa de las Américas, presented at the "Sesión Extraordinaria de la Asamblea Nacional del Poder Popular de Cuba," which took place 24–26 June in Havana)

McCormick, Carroll. "Cuban Control: Cuba's Air Traffic Controllers Will Soon Be Using a Powerful New Air Traffic Management System." *Airports International* 35, no. 4 (May 2002): 34–37.

Women

Books and Monographs

Holgado Fernández, Isabel. *No es fácil: Mujeres cubanas y la crisis revolucionaria.* 2nd ed. Barcelona: Icaria, 2002. 358 pp.

Kampwirth, Karen. *Women and Guerrilla Movements: Nicaragua, El Salvador, Chiapas, Cuba.* University Park: Pennsylvania State University Press, 2002. 194 pp.

Articles and Papers

Jenninsen, Therese, and Colleen Lundy. "Women in Cuba and the Move to a Private Market Economy." *Women's Studies International Forum* 24, no. 2 (March–April 2001): 181–98.

Martínez-Fernández, Luis. "The 'Male City' of Havana: The Coexisting Logics of Colonialism, Slavery, and Patriarchy in Nineteenth-Century Cuba." In *Women and the Colonial Gaze,* edited by Tamara L. Hunt and Micheline R. Lessard, 104–16. New York: New York University Press, 2002.

Rose-Green-Williams, Claudette. "Re-Writing the History of the Afro-Cuban Woman: Nancy Morejón's 'Mujer negra.'" *Afro-Hispanic Review* 21, no. 1–2 (Spring–Fall 2002): 154–60.

Suárez, Margarita M. W. "Across the Kitchen Table: Cuban Women Pastors and Theology." In *Gender, Ethnicity, and Theology,* edited by Rosemary Radford Ruether, 173–96. Minneapolis, Minn.: Fortress Press, 2002.

Thruplaew, Noy, and Jan Strout. "Cuba: Crossing Borders and Building a Movement." *Peace and Freedom* 62, no. 3 (Summer 2002): 22–24. (About the women's movement in Cuba)

Wilson, Suzanne. "Por amor al juego: Cuban Women Athletes." *Sports Illustrated Women* 3, no. 7 (November 2001): 90–93.

Internet Resources, Computer Files, Electronic Books, and Microform

¡Bienvenido! Agencia Cubana de Noticias (AIN). (Web site)
Created by the Cuban News Agency in 2002, this web site provides headlines of national and international news relating to Cuba. It also has links to separate sections for information about history, economy, culture, health, ecology, health, women, sports, etc. In addition, there are links to Fidel Castro's speeches as well as to data on elections.
http://www.ain.cubaweb.cu/

Blanton, Tom. *The Real Thirteen Days: The Cuban Missile Crisis, 1962.* Edited by Michael Evans. Washington, D.C.: National Security Archive, 2001. (Computer file; mode of access: Internet)

Cuba Climbing Home. n.p., 2002. (Web site)
http://www.cubaclimbing.com/
Cubafacts.com (Web site)
Created in 2002, this site features information on Cuba's society, history, government, economy, and human rights situation. Also contains current news and reference data.
http://www.cubafacts.com/
The Cuban Missile Crisis and Television. New York: Museum of Television and Radio, 2002. (Videocassette)
Presents a collection of archival news footage covering events leading up to the Cuban missile crisis followed by a panel discussion.
Cubasource: A Web Resource of FOCAL's Research Forum on Cuba. (Web site)
Website provided by the Canadian Foundation for the Americas featuring information available on Cuba on the Web. In English and Spanish. Features 2002 documents (in PDF format) online
http://www.cubasource.org/
González Núñez, Gerardo. *Cuba's Relations with the Caribbean: Trends and Prospects.* Ottawa: FOCAL, 2002. (Title from title screen)
http://www.focal.ca/images/pdf/cuba__caribbean.pdf
Ritter, Archibald R.M. *Cuba's Economic Performance and the Challenges Ahead.* Ottawa: FOCAL, 2002. (Title from title screen)
http://www.cubasource.org/pdf/aritter.pdf
Dockx, Cristina. "Migration of the North American Monarch Danaus Plexippus to Cuba." Ph.D. diss., University of Florida, 2002. (Web site; mode of access: Internet)
http://purl.fcla.edu/fcla/etd/UFE1001134
Forum for the Study of Cuba (University of Wolverhampton). (Web site)
2002 site featuring research on Cuban politics, history, culture, and economy. Also lists upcoming conferences on Cuban studies, recent events, news, an online international directory of academic research on Cuba, and details of the Hennessy Collection archive of Cuban newspapers, journals, and books, held at the University.
http://asp2.wlv.ac.uk/hlss/research/Cuba/
Havana Home Page. (Web site)
Home page of the U.S. Interests Section in Havana, Cuba. Provides U.S. government statements, policy, as well as links to related sites. Includes the latest Amnesty International Annual Report on Cuba in English and/or Spanish.
http://usembassy.state.gov/havana/
Instituto Cubano del Arte e Industria Cinematográficos. *La vida es silbar* (videorecording). Coproduced by Wanda Distribución de Filmes; produced by Rafael Rey; writers: Humberto Jiménez, Fernando Pérez, and Eduardo del Llano; directed by Fernando Pérez. New York: New Yorker Video, 2002. 1 videodisc (106 min.).
(In Spanish with English subtitles; originally produced as a motion picture in 1998)
Lester, Robert E., editor and project coordinator. *Confidential U.S. State Department Central Files: Cuba, 1960–January 1963: Internal Affairs* (Microform). Bethesda, Md.: University Publications of America, 2002. (Microfilm reels accompanied by a

printed guide, by Blair Hydrick, entitled *A Guide to the Microfilm Edition of Confidential U.S. State Department Central Files: Cuba, 1960–January 1963*)

MD Travel Health: Cuba—Vaccinations, Safety, and Other Medical Advice. n.p., 2002. (Web site)
http://www.mdtravelhealth.com/destinations/mamerica%5Fcarib/cuba.html

U.S.–Cuba Trade and Economic Council, Inc. (Web site)
A private, not-for-profit membership-based corporation, created in 1994 and located in New York to provide the U.S. business community with information on matters relating to U.S.–Cuba commercial, economic, and poltical relations.
http://www.cubatrade.org/

Contributors

MAYRA E. BEERS is a doctoral candidate at Florida International University, where she was the recipient of an Andrew P. Mellon Fellowship from the Latin American and Caribbean Center from 1997 to 1999. She also received a James Scobie Award for Dissertation Research from the Conference on Latin American History, a Cuban Research Institute award for research in Cuba (funded by the Ford Foundation), and the Colonial Dames of America Scholarship in 1994.

SHERRY JOHNSON is Associate Professor of History at Florida International University in Miami, and is Book Review Co-Editor for *Cuban Studies/Estudios Cubanos*. She is the author of *The Social Transformation of Eighteenth-Century Cuba* (2001), and her current project, *Mercantilism Meets Mother Nature: El Niño's Atlantic World Repercussions in the Age of Revolution*, is nearing completion.

MARISA S. MONTES is pursuing her Master's degree in Latin American and Caribbean Studies, with a concentration in international relations, at Florida International University. She is currently working at FIU's Cuban Research Institute as a teaching and research assistant.

OBÁ ORIATÉ MIGUEL W. RAMOS, ILARÍ OBÁ was ordained into the Lukumí priesthood as a young child, over thirty years ago, following in the steps of family members who have practiced the religion for at least five generations. Currently, he is an adjunct professor in sociology and anthropology at Florida International University and is one of the most respected Obá Oriaté in the United States. He has conducted research on Lukumí (Yoruba) religion and on this ethnic group's influence in the Americas for over thirty years. Recently, he curated an exhibition on Lukumí arts at the Historical Museum of Southern Florida (Miami) and installed a Lukumí altar for Shangó, his tutelary *orisha*, which is part of the AAltars of the World@ exhibition, a major German exposition currently touring in Europe.

KIRWIN (KIRK) SHAFFER is Assistant Professor of Latin American Studies at Penn State University—Berks/Lehigh Valley. He has taught courses in Cuban culture, Caribbean popular culture, Latin American film and literature, and Latin American history. His published work and current research center on examining anarchism in Cuba and the larger interactions between popular and political culture. His articles have appeared in *Studies in Latin American Popular Culture* and *Cuban Studies*. He has completed a manuscript on anarchist cultural politics and experiments in Cuba from 1898 to 1925 that is under editorial consideration. His next line of research will focus on Cuban and Puerto Rican labor radicals who moved between the islands and the United States from the 1890s to the 1930s.

Contributors

K. LYNN STONER is associate professor of history at Arizona State University. She has published a monograph, *From the House to the Streets: The Cuban Woman's Movement for Legal Reform, 1898–1940*. She has made her research sources available to other scholars in the *Stoner Collection*, a microfilm collection of journals and papers of Cuban women's organizations during the Early Republic. In 2000, in conjunction with the Cuban History Institute in Havana, she coedited, with Luis H. Serrano, *Cuban and Cuban American Women: An Annotated Interdisciplinary Bibliography*.

TIFFANY THOMAS-WOODARD is a doctoral candidate in history at the University of New Mexico. She has been awarded a Fulbright-Hays fellowship to complete her dissertation, titled "Between Bomba and Zanja: Prostitution, Race, and National Identity in Cuba, 1880–1930."